T0371728

The Psychology of Marketing

Cross-Cultural Perspectives

GERHARD RAAB
Ludwigshafen University of Applied Sciences, Germany

G. JASON GODDARD
Wachovia Bank, A Wells Fargo Company, USA

RIAD A. AJAMI
Wright State University, USA

ALEXANDER UNGER
Ludwigshafen University of Applied Sciences, Germany

Routledge
Taylor & Francis Group

LONDON AND NEW YORK

First published in paperback 2024

First published 2010 by Gower Publishing

Published 2016 by Routledge
4 Park Square, Milton Park, Abingdon, Oxon OX14 4RN

and by Routledge
605 Third Avenue, New York, NY 10158

Routledge is an imprint of the Taylor & Francis Group, an informa business

© 2010, 2016, 2024 Gerhard Raab, G. Jason Goddard, Riad A. Ajami and Alexander Unger

Publisher's Note
The publisher has gone to great lengths to ensure the quality of this reprint but points out that some imperfections in the original copies may be apparent.

Gower Applied Business Research
Our programme provides leaders, practitioners, scholars and researchers with thought provoking, cutting edge books that combine conceptual insights, interdisciplinary rigour and practical relevance in key areas of business and management.

British Library Cataloguing in Publication Data
The psychology of marketing : cross-cultural perspectives.
   1. Marketing—Psychological aspects. 2. Consumer behavior. 3. Consumer behavior—Cross-cultural studies.
   I. Raab, Gerhard.
   658.8'0019—dc22

Library of Congress Cataloging-in-Publication Data
The psychology of marketing : cross-cultural perspectives / by Gerhard Raab ... [et al.].
   p. cm.
   Includes index.
   ISBN 978-0-566-08903-9 (hardback : alk. paper)
  1. Marketing—Psychological aspects. 2. Consumer behavior—Psychological aspects. 3. Consumer's preferences—Cross-cultural studies. I. Raab, Gerhard.

   HF5415.P734 2010
   658.8001'9—dc22

        2010010152

ISBN: 978-0-566-08903-9 (hbk)
ISBN: 978-1-03-283824-3 (pbk)
ISBN: 978-1-315-55379-5 (ebk)

DOI: 10.4324/9781315553795

Contents

List of Figures

List of Tables

About the Authors

Riad A. Ajami

Riad A. Ajami is currently Professor of International Business and Global Strategy and Director, Center for Global Business Education and Research at Wright State University. Previously, Dr Ajami held the position of Professor of International Business (with Tenure) and Director International Business Program at the Fisher College of Business at The Ohio State University. Prior to joining Wright State Dr Ajami was the Charles A. Hayes Distinguished Professor of International Business and Director, Center for Global Business Education and Research, at the University of North Carolina, Greensboro. Dr Ajami also served as the Benjamin Forman Distinguished Professor of International Business, and Director, Center for International Business and Economic Growth at the Rochester Institute of Technology. Dr Ajami is the editor-in-chief for the *Journal of Asia-Pacific Business*. Dr Ajami has had visiting professorships at The University of California, Berkley; University of Pennsylvania, The Wharton School; and the Harvard Center for International Affairs at Harvard University; Dr M. Lee Pearce Distinguished Professor of International Business and Economic Cooperation, School of International Studies at the University of Miami; Hautes Etudes Commercials—HEC (Grande Ecole of Management), France; American University, Beirut; and the University of Istanbul, Turkey, among others. Professor Ajami serves on the editorial boards of several journals, including *The Journal of Transnational Management*, among many others. He is a frequent contributor to books on international business and has co-authored, *The Global Enterprise: Entrepreneurship and Value Creation*, and *International Business: Theory and Practice*. His expertise has been sought by U.S. and international media, including ABC Nightline, PBS News Hour, NBC News, CNN and National Public Radio.

G. Jason Goddard

G. Jason Goddard is currently Vice President at Wachovia Bank (a Wells Fargo Company), where he has been a commercial lender for over 15 years. Mr Goddard is currently real estate risk adviser for income producing investment real estate loans in the business and community banking segments, and works in Winston-Salem. He obtained his MBA from the Bryan School at the University of North Carolina at Greensboro. Mr Goddard is currently instructor at Wake Forest University and at the Bryan School, UNC-Greensboro, and is the Assistant Editor of the *Journal of Asia-Pacific Business*, where he has authored numerous articles. Mr Goddard teaches the investment real estate course at Wake Forest University each spring and fall semester. Mr Goddard also teaches the subject annually at the RMA-ECU Commercial Real Estate Lending School at East Carolina University in Greenville, NC. He has also taught an undergraduate course in international business at UNCG, and has taught the subject in the MBA program at the Bryan School. Mr Goddard has twice led a group of MBA students on the study abroad program in Paris, France, and teaches annually in Ludwigshafen Germany at the University of Applied Sciences. Mr Goddard also teaches Customer Relationship Management, an elective in the UNCG MBA program. Mr Goddard is co-author of *International Business: Theory and Practice, Second Edition*, which was issued by M.E. Sharpe Publishers in September 2006. His second co-authored book, *Customer Relationship Management: A Global Perspective*, was issued by Gower Publishing in May 2008.

Gerhard Raab

Prof. Dr Gerhard Raab, Master of business administration and Master of psychology; pursued studies in business administration and economic psychology at the universities of Mainz and Hagen. After studying, Dr Raab worked as a research associate and was promoted to Doctor of Economics at the University of Hohenheim. He subsequently was appointed strategy adviser and project leader on the management board of the DG Bank—Deutsche Genossenschaftsbank AG (German Mutual Savings Bank) in Frankfurt am Main, from 1992–1997. Since 1997 he has been Professor of marketing and management at the Ludwigshafen University of Applied Sciences, Germany. He is also the Executive Director of the Transatlantic Institute at Ludwigshafen University of Applied Sciences. Dr Raab has authored or co-authored many books and articles on customer relationship management, customer behavior, market psychology and neuromarketing. Since 2001, Dr Raab has been the Guest Professor for Customer Relationship Management at the University of North Carolina at Greensboro, and from 2010 he has been head of the research center of Neuroeconomics and Market Psychology at the Ludwigshafen University of Applied Sciences.

Alexander Unger

Alexander Unger is research assistant at the Transatlantic Institute, Ludwigshafen University of Applied Sciences, Germany. Dr Unger has authored and co-authored numerous publications in German concerning the subject of the psychology of marketing.

Preface

The following textbook is oriented toward all students interested in gaining an overview of those psychological theories that may be considered relevant within market psychology. Each theory is presented in its key propositions. Subsequently possible applications are given. At the beginning there is an introductory chapter dealing with market psychology and its theoretical, scientific classification. Then we start in with an examination of cognition-oriented theories. Cognitions are all elements of thought that a person can experience of himself or of his environment: opinions, insights, hopes, expectations, memory contents. All of these cognitive theories have something in common: they show how people deal with information (that is, with possible new cognitions) and how they change in the process of doing so. People do not experience the world the way it really is, but do so rather in a distorted manner. They proceed according to existing assumptions, look for comparisons that correspond with their worldviews, adapt information to their expectations, experience many items of information as constricting of freedom and as threatening, explain the world, process information more or less intensively, and make use of prefabricated concepts in information processing. For all of these statements there is a cognitive theory, or several cognitive theories, dealt with in Chapters 2 to 9.

The next section (Chapters 10 to 13) deals with a person's development, with the ensuing personality, capacity to learn, perception, and cognition, and the resultant memory contents and structures.

This is followed by emotion and motivation theories (Chapters 14 and 15), which in many ways can be seen as complementary to cognitive theories. It is said that in psychology there is a cognitive school on the one hand, and an emotional/motivational school on the other hand. We do not subscribe to this. We tend more to see overlaps and supplementations.

The theories of "power, control, and exchange" are particularly relevant for a market psychology. These are the topics of Chapters 16 to 18. Power is any potential a person or authority has to influence the behavior of other people. In markets, influence is exercised over the behavior of other market participants to a significant degree. On the other hand everyone seeks to have control over him or herself; they seek to avoid external influence. The relevance of exchange theories in turn arises directly out of the essence of markets. Markets are oriented toward exchange. Thus markets can be explained via power structures.

Chapter 19 is of particular interest for prospective managers. Everyone who is trusted with marketing or other leadership tasks in the management of all manner of organizations will attempt to exercise influence over others. In this regard they have developed assumptions concerning the possibilities of exercising influence. They also have hypotheses regarding the psychology of the people to be influenced. However, these are largely lay hypotheses. In the psychological sense these managers engage in a lay search for insight into the psychology of the other market participants. They are "amateur psychologists". It is exactly this that is the subject matter of lay psychology. Here, so to speak, the mirror is held up to management.

Chapter 20 provides a valuable link with biological psychology, and ends the chapter portion of the text on a particularly medically-oriented note. This fascinating chapter provides the reader with the biological basis of much of what the majority of the book has described in a more business-oriented context.

Finally, the last section consists of short case studies which help to elucidate primary theories and ideas described in the body of the text. The authors will present case studies to help the reader more fully to understand the concepts explored in this book. These cases will be from varying cultural viewpoints, aiding the theme of the sub-title "cross-cultural perspectives".

We feel that the best target audience for this book would be higher level undergraduate and masters level courses in Marketing Psychology, Consumer Behavior, Industrial Psychology, and other such courses. We feel that the book would be broadly targeted to doctoral candidates in the field of marketing and psychology, as well as to marketing executives and managers in both large and small organizations.

The authors would like to thank Marion Werner for researching various sources of literature, Regina Kalteis for editorial work, and Georg Emunds and Karin Zettler for many stylistic improvements. Edward Clarke and Leila Goddard provided additional valuable insights after reviewing portions of the manuscript. Finally, the authors thank Susan Resko for the cover art design, which can now be enjoyed by a wide audience.

Gerhard Raab, G. Jason Goddard, Riad A. Ajami and Alexander Unger

1 *Market Psychology in the Context of Systematics*

> *Many psychologists working today in an applied field are keenly aware of the need for close cooperation between theoretical and applied psychology. This can be accomplished in psychology, as it has been accomplished in physics, if the theorist does not look toward applied problems with high eyebrow aversion or with a fear of social problems, and if the applied psychologist realizes that there is nothing so practical as a good theory"*
>
> *(Lewin, 1944)*

The Subject of Market Psychology

As a science, market psychology explains and predicts human behavior with regard to markets. We can speak of a market whenever something of worth to someone is being exchanged for something else.

The most popular market is the goods market, within which goods of a material or immaterial kind are exchanged for money. In these markets the striving toward financial profit is a definitive determinant of supplier behavior. Buyers are looking for utility (buyers of productive goods) or for satisfaction of desires or needs (buyers of consumable goods). Regular exchange also occurs in cases where striving for profit is not the essential goal. If a governmental department starts a communications campaign against drink driving, then it is offering something (safety, health), and receives as a return the curtailing of alcohol consumption. That is an example of non-profit marketing and at the same time of social marketing. The situation of parties working against each other for votes in an election is also a market, in that trust in the election platform is being exchanged for votes. Another example of a market is the financial market, including the stock market. All of these examples are indisputably relevant within any discipline that calls itself "market psychology".

Wiswede's (1995, pp. 14–18) treatment of economic psychology is considerably more extensive. This subject includes, according to Wiswede (1995, p. 17) "special economic psychology" topics like work and organizational psychology, especially with regard to the related discipline of management psychology. For Wiswede savings behavior, perception and reaction in relation to inflation, also belong to economic psychology. Certainly it is self evident that in these areas exchange processes can also be postulated: In the area of management behavior a particular type of work performance is exchanged for incentives (of a material or immaterial kind); the same goes for human resources management or for organizational psychology.

Saving means nothing more than momentary renunciation of consumption in exchange for a reward (interest). If it in fact has to do with reaction to price changes, reaction to inflation is included within the scope of the goods market described initially. Taxation is also nothing other than a fee in return for service. It lacks the element of free will however. Seen in that light, the element of taxation certainly does not belong within market psychology.

To us it seems a bit arbitrary, starting from the point of view of a field of market psychology on the one hand, and from a field of work and organization psychology on the other hand, to exclude certain exchange processes from the field of market psychology, and then, aside from market psychology, to assign these elements within an overarching field of economic psychology. Kieser and Kubicek (1992, p. 10) clearly perceive the possibility of understanding customers or clients of organizations as also being members of those organizations, so that these members then influence the organization's decisions. As an outgrowth of this viewpoint Irle comes to a conclusion whereby consumer psychology is understood as "a special offshoot of organization psychology". According to Wiswede economic psychology can be presented as in Figure 1.1 below:

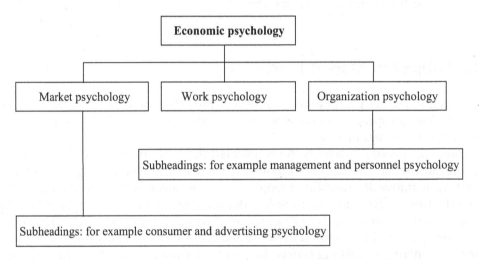

Figure 1.1   Subheadings of economic psychology (from Wiswede, 1995, p. 17)

Since we are starting from a comprehensive market concept, we can also proceed according to a comprehensive market psychology that can be divided at will into many different subheadings. Which subheadings result from this and how they are ordered depend, among other things, on the individual researcher. The meaning of whatever classification is chosen will prove itself, as a hypothesis, during the course of the research process.

In market psychology we have that science which explains behavior within all markets: consumer psychology, work psychology, organization psychology, management psychology, communication psychology, media psychology, and the psychology of decision making, are all special disciplines which certainly can overlap. Where there is a market for health products and for behavioral advice relevant to health, even parts of health psychology can be considered to be aspects of market psychology.

Market Psychology as an Applied Science

We can differentiate between three levels of research: The level of fundamental research, that of applied research, and the level of evaluation of scientific findings in practice.

Fundamental research is theory oriented. It seeks insights in order to advance itself. It is a continuous, never-ending search for ever-better explanations for all manner of phenomena. It would be misguided to measure fundamental research on the basis of its future "utility" (however that may be understood). On the way to discovering new insights it can never be said to what use they will be put. Having said that, practitioners seeking insight need an arsenal of proven theoretical findings, just as practitioners of applied research do. In general it is not economical to begin by searching for new solutions to problems with the advent of every problem. The worth of scientific insight lies in already available, generically valid theoretical statements, which can be applied to any number of problem areas, or which simply further the process of gathering insights. Examples of fundamental research areas are: psychology, social psychology, sociology, pure economics, biology, chemistry, and physics. All of these areas have one procedure in common: Insights are sought on the basis of specific theoretical concepts. The field of application could then be anything.

Applied research on the other hand is oriented toward problem areas of human existence that need to be explained. Some examples are: pedagogy, interaction psychology, market psychology, marketing, medicine, and research into well-being. The problem area is given, and then solutions can be sought and brought to bear on the existing problem from any number of fundamental research areas. Admittedly there then arises the danger of arbitrariness. Since the arsenal of theoretical statements from the area of fundamental research has become extremely large, the possibility can certainly be seen of arbitrarily construing a theory within the applied science, and then to convincingly support this theory via equally arbitrarily selected areas of fundamental research. From the point of view of scientific theory however, this is entirely unproblematic. Through the inductive transfer of theoretical and completely proven scientific pronouncements, no new insight is culled concerning new areas. Obtainment of scientific insight is only possible through the empirical testing of theories. The construction of theories in applied science, through the creative use of proven theories from fundamental science research, is to be seen as a phase of hypothesis formulation. There is no "restraint to method" here at all. Here, but truly only here, can we follow Feyerabend's plea against restraint to method (Feyerabend, 1993). Otherwise we are proceeding according to a strict, scientific, deductive approach, which amounts to formulating provable hypotheses, rather than exposing their flaws toward the end of testing them for truth content. The deduction phase follows: a critical examination according to empirical method. It does not make any difference how systematic or arbitrary, plausible or implausible the constructed hypotheses are; if they prove themselves now we can keep them, and if they fail the test we can go back to the drawing board, check over the reasons for their flaws, correct them, bring them back into play, and test them again. Or we reject them for the time being (just as there is no conclusive proof as to the final verity of a hypothesis, it is similarly the case as to the definitive failure of a hypothesis). The analysis of market events is an example of applied science. When we speak of market psychology, it is thereby being indicated that we want to elucidate market events by using psychological theories.

From the beginning it is being stated that problem areas of human existence should be explained. Closely related with that, and what for later evaluation in practice is of great significance, is the prognosis.

EXPLANATION

Whoever wants to learn from mistakes has to be able to explain things, and therefore must possess well-founded suppositions as to why an effect or set of facts has been arrived at, or why not.

1. In order arrive at an explanation an exact description of a problem is necessary, of its actual condition (for example, declining market share).
2. Then we look for theories (of a scientific kind, or resulting from experience), which perhaps can lend themselves to our problem (for example, "When our relative quality—in comparison to the competition—declines, we lose market share").
3. Finally we check whether the suppositions of applicability of the theory at hand agree with our problem and its context (we come to the conclusion that the competitor has improved their quality, which entails a relative depreciation of our quality).
4. Having found a theory with valid suppositions of applicability, and thus having arrived at a possible explanation, it is normally advisable to look for alternative explanations (the competitor may simultaneously have expanded his product line and improved his market communication).

PROGNOSIS

The prognosis is an explanation "in advance"

1. We come up with a general plan (for example, improvement of quality) in connection with a particular goal.
2. If we want to predict the outcome of the plan, to possess well-founded suppositions as to whether we can attain our goal, then we need a theory with regard to the impact our plan will have (see above). Normally we will have come up with the above plan according to a known theory.
3. We can count on increasing market share unless further factors unknown to us come into play (future condition).

A second area of application for scientific insight is that of empirical examination; every empirical study is to be seen as an example of applied research (Irle, 1983, p. 25). This can be of use in the examination of a theory, of an explanation and/or prognosis of a problematic circumstance, and also in the development of new theories.

A particular quantity of elements coming into a relatively high (more than accidental) level of agreement with a theory is still not quite a satisfactory scientific explanation of why a particular resultant set of factors has been arrived at; this approach merely displays a meaningful character (Irle, 1983, p. 18). It is at least advisable to systematically rule out the possible relevance of other influences, which may be responsible for the designated factors rather than the theory currently being focused on.

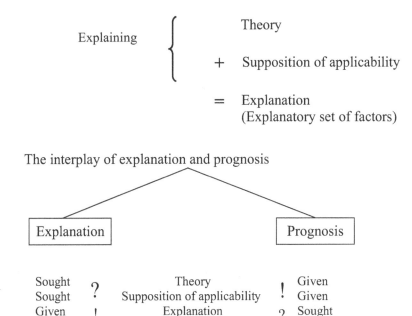

Figure 1.2   The interplay of explanation and prognosis (see Raffée, 1995, p. 34)

Experimental or field experimental research is also scientifically relevant. In practice plausible models can occasionally suffice.

The evaluation of scientific insight in practice, the ultimate use of scientific research results, is usually brought out by applied science.

Market psychology is to a large degree oriented toward consumer markets and in that regard is almost exclusively focused on the behavior of consumers. Consumer psychology is as little reducible to buyer behavior as political psychology is to voter behavior (Irle, 1983, p. 12). It is certainly not just about an explanation and prognosis of buyer behavior. Behavior on the side of the provider is just as interesting, especially that of managers, who are responsible for the formation of programs designed to influence buyers. What hypotheses are they acting on? What assumptions concerning wishes and possibilities of influence do they hold? What information do they utilize and how do they come to decisions? The individuals engaged in practical marketing are by no means "scientists", even if they like to see themselves as such. Market researchers, media researchers, working within practical marketing, are work professionals, not scientists. They evaluate scientific insights. Theirs is not a never-ending process of seeking after insights, but instead is oriented toward efficient goal attainment. As much as scientifically verified propositions influence their decisions, so does practical experience, including when such experience has not first been systematically checked. This is quite unscientific, but can however prove itself to be an adequate approach for solving practical problems that fall outside of scientific parameters. There is no reason to neglect practical experience or even to see it as inferior in value in comparison with scientific insights. Practical experience can prove very efficient; it is only that it has yet to be systematically checked. It is true though that some in the marketing field are inclined to noticeably augment their practical experiences with the addition of pseudo-scientific jargon, or to justify them with equally pseudo-scientific explanations. This is a malapropism of practical experience. The interplay of the three levels of insight is illustrated in Figure 1.3.

In the following we will deal with a selection of theories that essentially have proven themselves not only within fundamental research but also within applied research, which we consider to be up to the task of elucidating market phenomena. In keeping with our broad concept of market psychology's scope, the theoretical presentation will be supplemented with examples from many different subtopics of market psychology.

Theoretical Foundations

There is little doubt in economics concerning the idea that economies can be understood to be a goal oriented handling of limited resources, wherein decisions must be arrived at as to how to employ those limited resources. In the end economies facilitate the satisfaction of needs. Needs are subjectively experienced states of deficiency, existing in relation to the desire for satisfaction. In connection with buying, power needs become demands.

Contrary to the viewpoints of many economic schools, needs are not a given. They result from the interplay of supply and demand on the one hand and on the other hand

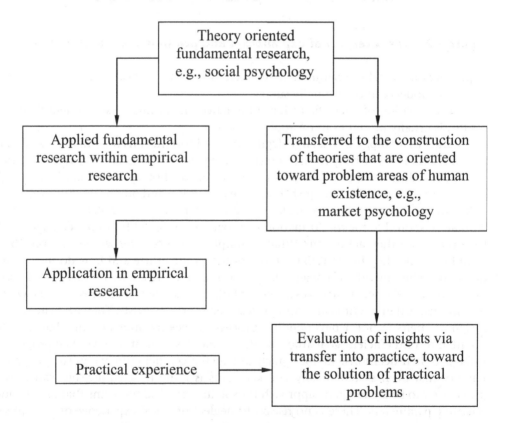

Figure 1.3   The interplay of fundamental research, applied research, and the solution of practical problems seen as evaluation of insights

from constantly shifting nets of social relationships, which likewise are not independent from product offers. "Attitudes, value orientation, convictions, and behavioral modes are to a large extent anchored in social relationships and social patterns" (Albert, 1998, p. 214). In their variability or stability they are dependent on the social milieus they are bound up with.

Furthermore we are not starting from the premise that consumers behave "rationally" according to some clearly structured order of preferences. We are also assuming that this order of preferences, in turn, is not independent of product offers and equally influenced by social milieus. It is not clear how intrinsic of a role social groupings or marketing measures from the provider's side play in activating or triggering consumer needs. Galbraith was one of the first economists to discuss a "revised sequence of marketing" where companies in fact synthesize demand for consumers, as opposed to the consumers necessarily being sovereign in terms of the generation of their own purchasing desires (Galbraith, 1967).

And we are not taking for granted the idea that human needs are "by nature" unlimited. This assumption has been disproved within anthropology. Some of the peoples of North America for example did not conduct themselves (at least until their "discovery") according to an ever-increasing level of need. "The endlessness of goods oriented needs is not a law; it is produced rather than being inherent within human nature" (Scherhorn, 1992, p. 27). "It has already been pointed out often that in the modern economy one part of an organization produces a need, which is necessary as an outlet for another part of the organization's products" (Albert, 1972, p. 64). Another proponent of this view is Marx (1953, p. 14), whose thesis certainly does not completely pertain to production triggering consumption of essential needs, yet does adequately describe the non-independence of needs from supply. Albert (1998, p. 218) perceives the cause of pure economics' shortsightedness in its theoretical isolation; that is to say in its not taking advantage of psychological, especially social psychological theories: "The ad hoc assumption of the existence of an ordering of individual needs, which can be placed in direct, explicit connection with the collection of all possible quantitative combinations of consumer goods is … an artifact of economical thought, whose function is primarily to be seen in the theoretical isolation of pure economics."

The market behavior of consumers is a special case of "individual behavior(s) in a social context" (Albert, 1998, p. 212). Social psychological theories are therefore indispensable in its explanation.

The satisfaction of needs often takes place according to relatively stable patterns of consumer behavior. This does not, however, necessarily have anything to do with a stable or clear order of preferences. Duesenberry (1949, p. 24) proceeds from the assumption that consumer habits are formed according to a learning process. Through trial and error consumers come to experience consumer behavior of varying success. Consumer behavior is successful when it leads to a subjectively evaluated experience of need satisfaction. Patterns of consumption become habituated accordingly.

From these initial statements it is clear that the subject of the market as a social science has to stand in clear opposition to pure economics as a formal science, because for the latter it is currently all too typical that demand is taken as an independent factor, the development of which is associated with any form of real science (see Albert, 1972, p. 29). While pure economics proceeds according to a conception of the market as a completed entity, all of the projects of marketing are aligned with the reality of an unfinished market or market in process, whereby, especially in the area of consumer goods, it is forever being attempted to limit the comparison between offers via increasing differentiation of products and through product diversity. This, together with the considerable information overload, means that we have to assume that all economic decisions have been made on the basis of incomplete, unclear, and presumably incorrect information. This naturally has ramifications for all levels of human existence.

Our decision for the market as a social science subject is also based in scientific theory. The furthering of insight comes from recognizing our mistakes. We recognize mistakes through formulating assumptions (hypotheses) and then checking them for reality content (through experiment or simply observation of what is there). If our hypotheses hold up then we can maintain them for the time being, and if not we have to put them aside temporarily. In both cases a temporary decision is arrived at, because the proof of a hypothesis' applicability may later reveal itself to have been an error, just as its rejection may also have been an error. The consequences of this are therefore that:

- All of our conclusions are no more or less than a structure made up of our proven hypotheses. There is never any certainty. We can act as if propositions exist which are absolutely in true agreement with reality, but we can never be sure if our propositions are completely true, even if they have often proven themselves.
- We have to formulate our assumptions such that they can be proven in reality, and also such that they can be shown up as faulty. Assumptions that are too divorced from reality cannot be checked, and so they also cannot yield any insight.

The practice of seeking scientific insight consists of the perpetual process of drawing up, checking, and improving upon hypotheses. Subsequently these are tested in artificial worlds (in studios or laboratories) or in the natural world (in the field). If the hypothetical assumption does not prove itself, then it is false, whereas if the assumption proves itself, the hypothesis is considered to be verified for the time being. A final verification is out of the question; we can never be sure whether an error was made in the formulation of the hypothesis, during the test procedure, or in the analysis. Even when hypotheses seem to prove themselves again and again, this is not evidence of their truth. The above-described possibilities of failure could be a matter of inherent systematic nature, repeating themselves for that reason.

Science is the search for truth, that is, for propositions which increasingly agree with reality. We can never be sure of our propositions. The search for certainty is meaningless, because certainty is impossible.

The abandonment of the assumption that a proposition can once and for all be proven as to its level of truth or as to how much it is in error, is one of the essential results of Popper's and Albert's scientific doctrine of critical rationalism. Two more ideas are connected with this:

1. Induction is not a means of obtaining new insight. Inductive reasoning can only help in the formulation of hypotheses, but cannot lead to new insight (see Popper, 1979, Introduction, pp. xxx–xxxiii). What remains is the process of deduction, the setting-up and attempt at testing, which, according to the given case, may lead to showing the falsehood of the proposition, but which however may never lead to a final verification (Popper, 1979, pp. 6–9).

2. The demand for value free science. This is based on value judgments never being testable as to their truth content. A proposition like: "XYZ's painting is of artistic worth" or "You should ..." can never be empirically tested. We can merely make statements as to what consequences the adherence or non-adherence to certain normative propositions will have. That would be a scientifically testable hypothesis. Whether we want these consequences or not is again a normative proposition concerning human experience. The demand for value free science is however only in connection with actual scientific propositions. The choice of scientific schemes is only normatively possible. The proposition that science should serve the cause of obtaining insight (!) is also normative. Basis value judgments are inevitable constituents of every human field of practice, just as in science. Value judgments can also be the subject matter of scientific analysis: the origin of particular value judgments can be sought, their functions can be studied (do they serve to bolster the power of certain social groups perhaps?), as can the consequences of maintaining them or not.

Value judgments have three aspects:

1. Value judgments at the basis level of science, which are inevitable. These have to do with goals, the tasks of science, and with the problem of choice.
2. Value judgments as the object of scientific work.
3. Value judgments in the area of propositions; these are not compatible with a science oriented toward obtaining insights. It is only here that the demand for science's freedom from value judgments applies.

The propositions of market psychology are value free (if they are in accordance with the concept of science being dealt with here). The choice of hypotheses and subtopics proceeds normatively. Are the hypotheses being examined those which, in the sense of marketing concepts, can more efficiently influence consumers, or are the hypotheses being examined those which can serve to clarify market mechanisms, or to emancipate consumers?

It should be mentioned here that certain structurally similar problems preside over rationally oriented practice.

a) Rational practice necessitates goals; these goals are not subject to conclusive justification, as they are always normative in essence.
b) The choice of instruments for achieving goals can only proceed solely according to value free considerations. It is admittedly a possibility that certain instruments of use in the efficient attainment of goals should not be utilized for normative reasons (for example, moral reasons).
c) The considerations mentioned in b) are however transparent, and as such make the value free rational discussion approachable or manageable.

We have presented here, in extremely abbreviated form, the scientific standpoint of critical rationalism as professed by Albert and Popper (Albert, 1960, 2000; Popper, 1979, 1982, 1989). A market subject, as social science, contains testable propositions because it proceeds according to truly existent patterns of behavior (as hypotheses). Market psychology is an empirical science that in every respect can be justified according to a conception of science like that of critical rationalism.

At this juncture market psychological propositions can be ordered within a system of categories of propositions. First of all, we can differentiate between so called sciential (conducive to science) and non-sciential propositions. Sciential propositions are those propositions that can be tested by virtue of it being possible that their truth content is in error. The proposition "tomorrow it is going to rain" is testable; propositions that have the meaning of life as their subject matter are not. Value judgments (normative propositions) are also not testable as to their truth content. Science cannot say to anyone what he or she should do, only what he or she is able to do, and perhaps also say what the consequences will be. Sciential propositions can be either empirically or logically tested. Admittedly neither a successful empirical nor logical test of a proposition will assure any certainty in the truth of a proposition. Both possibilities of testing can only be instruments for the critique of propositions, but can never lead to their ultimate substantiation. Empirical propositions can display a descriptive or explanatory character. Explanations can be of a "deterministic" ("Always and everywhere when ..., then follows condition y"), "stochastic" ("Always and everywhere when ..., then follows condition y with x percent probability"), or of a "tendential" ("always and everywhere when ..., then condition y tends to follow") kind. Most market psychology propositions are more of the tendential variety. Market psychological propositions are a) empirical, b) descriptive or explanatory, c) deterministic, stochastic or tendential and they are not d) normative (see Figure 1.4).

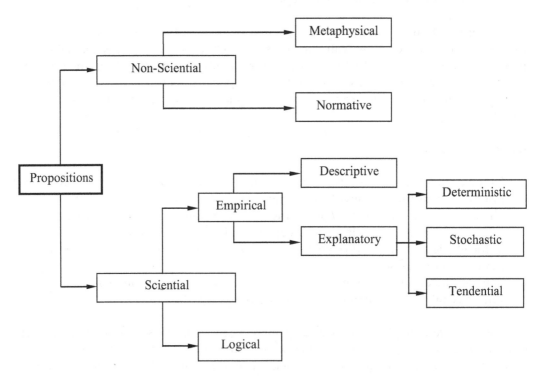

Figure 1.4   Structure of possible propositions (see Raffée, 1995, p. 23)

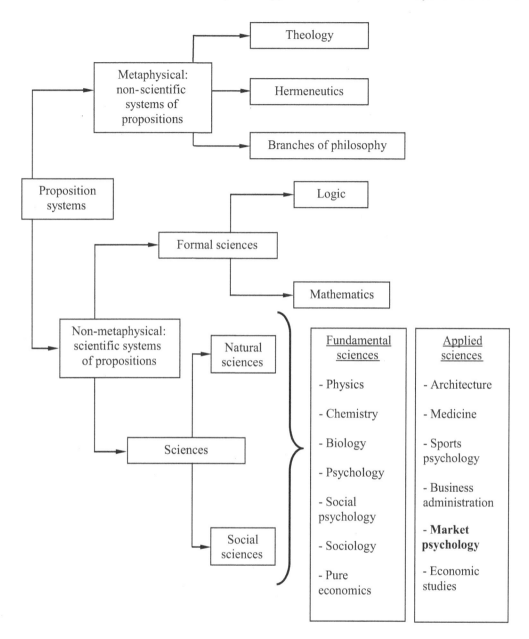

Figure 1.5   Market psychology within a framework of scientific systems of propositions (see Raffée, 1995, pp. 23 and 37)

Analogously, we now want to classify market psychology within a framework of sciences: There are systems of propositions that are metaphysical in nature and those that are non-metaphysical in nature. Metaphysical propositions are not testable with regard to their truth content, and are therefore not understood as being science, if science is understood as serving the attainment of insight. Non-metaphysical systems of propositions, or sciences, can be formal sciences or reality sciences, reality sciences being natural and social sciences. Social sciences and natural sciences can again be divided into two kinds, that of fundamental research and applied research. Market Psychology is an applied social science.

Attentive readers may have noticed that in Figure 1.5 hermeneutics is classified under non-scientific propositions, which may be a cause for wonder considering the recent popularity of this mode of thinking, with Hans-Georg Gadamer possibly being its chief proponent. In accordance with Albert's argument (1991, pp. 156–188, 1994 and 2000) it simply seems appropriate. In keeping with this, psychological approaches heavily influenced by hermeneutical thinking will not be taken into consideration.

The preceding discussion helps put the subject of market psychology in its theoretical perspective. In the chapters that follow, we will discuss various important theories of market psychology, as well as present case studies that will elucidate these concepts for the reader.

QUESTIONS FOR DISCUSSION

1.   Define market psychology as an applied science.
2.   Elaborate on the interplay of explanation and prognosis.
3.   Why is the search for certainty meaningless?
4.   Differentiate between deterministic, stochastic, tendential, empirical, and descriptive propositions.

Bibliography

Albert, H.: Der kritische rationalismus Karl Raimund Poppers. *Archiv für Rechts- und Sozialphilosophie*: 1960, 391–415. (The critical rationalism of Karl Raimund Popper. *Archive for Rights and Social Philosophy*).

—— *Ökonomische Ideologie und Politische Theorie* (2nd edn). Göttingen: 1972. (*Economical Ideology and Political Theory*).

—— *Traktat Über Kritische Vernunft* (5th edn) Tübingen: 1991. (*Treatise on Critical Reason*).

—— *Kritik der Reinen Hermeneutik*. Tübingen: 1994. (*Criticism of Pure Hermeneutics*).

—— *Marktsoziologie und Entscheidungslogik*. Tübingen: 1998. (*Market Sociology and Decision Logic*).

—— *Kritischer Rationalismus*. Tübingen: 2000. (*Critical Rationalism*).

Duesenberry, J.S.: *Income, Saving, and the Theory of Consumer Behaviour*. Cambridge: 1949.

Feyerabend, P.: *Wider den Methodenzwang* (4th edn) Frankfurt am Main: 1993. (*Against the Method Compulsion*).

Galbraith, J.K.: *The New Industrial State*. Boston: 1967.

Irle, M.: Forschungsprogramme in der marktpsychologie. In Irle, M. (ed.): *Marktpsychologie, 1. Halbband: Marktpsychologie als Sozialwissenschaft*. Göttingen, Toronto, Zürich: 1983, 1–44. (Research programs in market psychology. In *Market Psychology, Volume 1: Market Psychology as a Social Science*).

Kieser, A. and Kubicek, H.: *Organisation* (3rd edn). Berlin, New York: 1992.

Lewin, K.: *Constructs in Psychology and Psychological Ecology*. University of Iowa Studies in Child Welfare, 1944, vol. 20, 23–27.

Marx, K.: *Kritik der Politischen Ökonomie*. Berlin: 1953. (*Criticism of Political Economy*).

Popper, K.R.: *Die Beiden Grundprobleme der Erkenntnistheorie.* Tübingen: 1979. (*Basic Problems of Insight Theory*).

—— *Logik der Forschung* (7th edn) Tübingen: 1982. (*Logic of Research*).

—— *Conjectures and Refutations—The Growth of Scientific Knowledge* (5th edn) London: 1989.

Raffée, H.: *Grundprobleme der Betriebswirtschaftslehre* (2nd edn) Göttingen: 1995. (*Basic Problems of the Business Management Scholar*).

Scherhorn, G.: Die funktionsfähigkeit von konsumgütermärkten. In Irle, M. (ed.): *Marktpsychologie, 1. Halbband: Marktpsychologie als Sozialwissenschaft.* Göttingen, Toronto, Zürich: 1983, 45–150. (The utility of consumer good markets. In *Market Psychology, Volume 1: Market Psychology as a Social Science*).

Scherhorn, G.: Kritik des zusatznutzens. *Thexis*: 1992, 9, 2, 24–28. (Criticism of added value).

Wiswede, G.: *Einführung in die Wirtschaftspsychologie* (2nd edn) München, Basel: 1995. (*Introduction to Economic Psychology*).

Cognition Theories

2 *Theories of Perception and Social Judgment Formation as Starting Points*

Hypotheses, Presumptions, and Related Psychological Constructs

Hypotheses are all those postulates or assumptions that a person holds true concerning herself and her environment. If we accept the proposition that human beings cannot know anything with certainty, that rather all of our combined knowledge is nothing other than a system of more or less well founded assumptions, then we can also say that hypotheses are integrally involved with the entirety of our collected knowledge.

Our combined assumed knowledge continuously influences our perception. People cannot perceive in an unbiased manner. In the act of perceiving it, everything is influenced by what the person engaged in the act of perception, through his already existent knowledge, is prepared to believe.

Hypotheses influence perception.

Of course it is certainly not the case that a person learns nothing during the course of perception, or that their knowledge is not altered after a perception. So we can also say:

Perception leads to the formation of hypotheses.

From this it is clear that perception and knowledge (when the concept "knowledge" is used in the following, "assumed knowledge" in the sense of hypotheses is meant) stand in a constantly alternating relationship to each other. The one without the other is unthinkable. Any perception can be understood to be a constant process consisting of the arrangement and formulation of hypotheses.

Presumptions are very closely related to hypotheses; a clear division between them is hardly ever apparent. The presumption construct is often related to, in the sense of being a synonym of, the attitude construct (constructs here are thought constructions, thought formations). We want to differentiate between these two constructions in accordance with Irle (1967, pp. 195–197). Presumptions are understood to constitute an expectation within perception. This factor leads to our having the tendency to confirm our expectations through what is perceived. We believe the perception that we expected we would perceive. As long as the perceived does not diverge too much from expectation, things proceed smoothly, but at the point where perception and expectation strongly diverge, things get complicated. This idea is the focus of "The Theory of Cognitive Dissonance" (see Chapter 4).

The proposition that presumptions express expectations is the basis of Fishbein's theory (1966, and for more recent elaborations, see Assael, 1992, p. 208; Unger, 1997, p. 83). A presumption about a product expresses expectations with regard to the probability that a product will demonstrate certain qualities, multiplied by the subjectively experienced significance of each quality.

Formally expressed this yields:

$$E_{ij} = \sum_{k=1}^{n} B_{ijk} \times a_{ijk}$$

Where:

E_{ij}: A person (i)'s presumption with regard to brand j.

B_{ijk}: A person (i)'s subjective, felt probability that a certain brand will display a certain quality.

a_{ijk}: The subjective significance the existence of quality k holds for person i with regard to product j.

So it hinges on the presumption with regard to the existence of a quality.

In practical market research the assumed characteristic or assessment of a quality is often looked into, rather than the assumed probability of a quality's existence. The following example comes from Fischbein and Ajzen (1980, p. 154): The focus is on color televisions, and among other things, on the assumed "naturalness of colors". The significance of this quality is measured on a 7 point scale from 0 to 6 and the characteristic on a 7 point scale from –3 to +3. The following questions were asked:

1.   In the assessment of a color television the naturalness of the colors is

completely unimportant   :__:__:__:__:__:__:__: extremely important
                                 0 1 2 3 4 5 6

1.   With regard to the naturalness of colors, a Sony® television is

unsatisfactory   :__:__:__:__:__:__:__: very satisfying
                                 -3 -2 -3 0 +1 +2 +3

(The numerical indicators are not contained in the actual questionnaire, but are just used later on in the assessment.)

The total value might be expressed as it is below (for the original see Fishbein and Ajzen, 1980, p. 154):

Evaluative criterion	=	Satisfaction with Sony® vis-à-vis criterion	=	Importance of criterion	=	Satisfaction importance
Natural colors		+2		6		12
Price		-3		3		-9
Reliability		+1		2		2
Appearance		+1		1		1
Overall satisfaction:						+6

The total value (overall satisfaction) obtained in this way is a relatively good approximation of preferred purchase (what the consumer would prefer to purchase), in comparison with the competition's products. Because Fishbein and Ajzen's subjects (1980, pp. 67 and 68) tend to exaggerate the characteristics of perceived features when focusing on features considered important, this method of measurement leads to results that are more extreme than the reality of the situation suggests. In light of this it is advisable to measure the above-defined presumption on the basis of the assumed existence of a feature. So, instead of asking "How economical is a Skoda® TDI (diesel tuning system)?" the question asked is "How convinced are you that a Skoda® TDI is economical?" Both can be measured according to the scales presented above.

According to this model, presumptions are therefore the expectations of consumers with regard to the existence of features. The actual buyer behavior is brought into focus in relation to the degree the consumer is persuaded by or satisfied with a brand or product, and in relation to social norms.

The relationship of factors presented in Figure 2.1 is known as the Theory of Reasoned Action (Wells and Prensky, 1996, p. 324).

A different model will be used to measure the presumption, on the basis of the assumed characteristics of various features, in comparison to ideal characteristics.

This so-called ideal point model has the following structure (Ginter, 1974; Trommsdorff, 1975):

$$E_{ij} = \sum_{k=1}^{n} \left| B_{ijk} - I_{ik} \right|$$

It reads:

E_{ij}:   Presumption of person i with regard to product or brand j.

B_{ijk}:   Characteristic as perceived by person i of feature k of product or brand j.

I_{ik}:   The ideal characteristic as assessed by person i of feature k, in this object class.

$\left| B_{ijk} - I_{ik} \right|$: Person i's expressed value with regard to feature k of product or brand j.

In this case the assessments of the characteristics of features are directly asked for, and are then set against the characteristic that is considered to be ideal. The presumption that stands out the most (in contrast to the above model) is deemed to have the least value in a comparison with the competition. Weighting factors are not necessary, because in the case of features that are considered most important, the divergence of characteristics from the ideal is already exaggerated in relation to what is actually found to be the case. Weighting factors would simply intensify this effect.

It should not be difficult to derive similar presumption constructs for completely different areas of economic life:

Organizations as employers display certain features with varying likelihood and (degree of) significance, just as management does from the point of view of employees, and employees do from the point of view of management. Securities on the stock market can be similarly judged: the profitability of a company, current stock price, expectations of growth and so on all factor in to the assessment of investors.

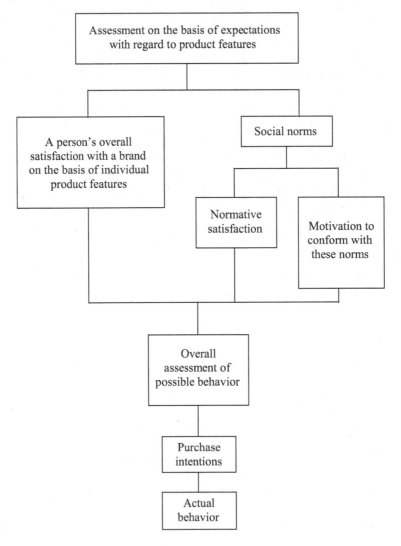

Figure 2.1   From expectation to behavior patterns (Assael, 1992, p. 213, see also Wells and Prensky, 1996, p. 324)

Attitudes consist of tendencies that influence judgments with regard to stimulus complexes, and they also consist of behavioral dispositions (with relation to the perceived object). Attitudes are represented by a system made up of three components:

- A detecting/noticing, or the cognitive component.
- An assessing, or the evaluative component.
- A triggering, or the conative component.

The detecting, cognitive component is related to presumptions, and the other two obviously depart from the presumption concept. Figure 2.2 shows the structure of the attitude concept.

We can understand the "assessing/evaluative" component as the cognitive-emotional basis of behavior. The "detecting/perceiving" component clearly corresponds with a cognitive basis of behavior (for example, in the sense of "social perception"). The behavioral disposition is closely related to the motivational basis of human behavior.

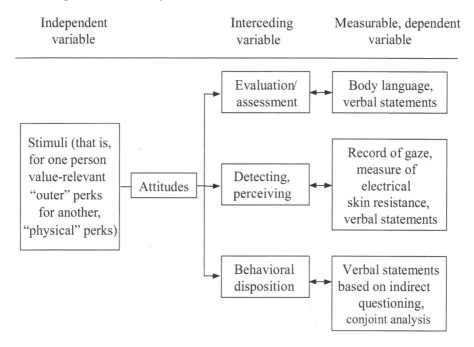

Figure 2.2   Schematic presentation of attitudes, from Rosenberg and Hovland (1980, p. 3); regarding the procedure of gaze recording, measurement of skin's electrical resistance, and conjoint analysis, see *Literatur zur Marktforschung (Literature for Market Research)* (Unger, 1997, pp. 104–114 and 250–290; Unger and Fuchs, 1999, pp. 509–574)

We can conclude the introduction to these concepts by presenting three notions that are closely related to presumptions and attitudes: Image, value, and prejudice.

Image is understood to be the presumptions of many people with regard to a particular object. Certain people are surveyed to get their opinion (and thereby their expectations) with regard to a particular object. The total structure of the survey's results describes the image of the object as far as the surveyed persons are concerned. Opinions are nothing other than expectation-qualified mindsets. When we hold any kind of opinion regarding something, then we are expecting something from the relevant object. Person X is of the opinion that a brand Y vehicle is especially safe, economical, etc. Those are expectations with regard to a brand Y vehicle. When an image of an object is spoken of, we have to make it clear that *that* image is not the *only* image. Thus a) the only image that can result is one that is inspired by the survey that has prompted its formation (which is a general problem of theoretical science in every measurement) and b) the measured image is only in connection with that section of the population that makes up the surveyed sample.

Values   are presumptions that are particularly central for a person. Every person draws upon a large number of presumptions. Some of these presumptions are related to each other and others are not. The presumption with regard to "a healthy life" might have a close relationship to the nourishment presumption and to the presumptions that have to do with the quality of the living space. The holiday presumption might also be relevant, though not to the same extent as the former presumptions, and the presumptions with regard to what is on TV this evening, presumably, have no connection with "a healthy life". At this point we can easily imagine how many presumptions display a very strong, influential connection to many other presumptions, whereas to others they do not. Values are the central, more significant presumptions that influence many other presumptions. They are particularly resistant to change because of the many ramifications such change entails, in the form of the simultaneous altering of many other presumptions. It is easier for people to change those presumptions whose change would lead to less wide-ranging consequences. The late 1980s' concept of increasing value transformation basically expresses the idea that central presumptions are changing to a greater extent now than in previous decades. The increased integration of global markets is also helping to increase the extent of change of values in a market context.

Prejudices   are those presumptions that are maintained even in the face of clearly contradictory perceptions. They are extremely resistant to change. In this sense they are not different from values. However, prejudices do not necessarily pertain to central presumptions. They could also have to do with more peripheral aspects not all that significant for the person.

At this point the important elements of cognitive systems have been presented. In the following we want to present two closely related fundamental theories that serve to elucidate social perception and social judgment formation. The concept "social" here denotes that both phenomena are influenced by the relationships of people with each other. Social behavior is (also) a behavior that is influenced by the behaving person's relationships to other people.

The Hypothesis Theory of Social Perception

Needs, motives, values and wishes influence perception. This assumption is the basis of the so-called "directive state" concept, the empirical foundation of which is certainly still weak (see Lilli and Frey, 1993, p. 51). Nevertheless, this assumption does account for the fact that whatever corresponds to a person's needs, motives or wishes, is preferentially perceived. In the light of information overload (which leads to only a fraction of all available signals being perceived, and to even less of that getting processed), this is of great importance for marketing communication in practically all developed societies. Values might have a similar effect; certainly one must also assume that whatever opposes existent values, in the extreme, will be preferentially perceived. The "directive state" concept fundamentally disposes of the assumption that there is a pure, unbiased state of perception. There is no passive or exclusively reactive information receiver. Every human perception begins with a hypothesis. Hypotheses are a person's assumptions regarding himself and his environment. Perception is a product of existing assumptions about reality (that is, of hypotheses) and of the actually existent, perceivable reality.

The hypothesis theory of social perception (traceable back to Allport, 1955; Bruner, 1951 and 1957; Postman, 1951) is a further development of the "directive state" concept, which can basically be broken down into three central statements (Lilli and Frey, 1993, p. 56):

- The stronger the hypothesis is, the greater the likelihood that it will arouse support, that is, a person believes a confirmation of his hypothesis.
- The stronger a hypothesis is, the less persuasive, supporting information (or signals), which could lead to its confirmation (from the psychological point of view of the affected person), is necessary. For example, someone who very strongly believes something needs very little supporting evidence in order to then proceed with (an even) greater conviction in what they believe.
- The stronger a hypothesis is, the more contradictory information is needed to achieve an effect, such that the person in question is then ready to relinquish his assumption. Whoever very strongly believes something requires a lot of opposing information in order to let go of their assumption.

The theory does not say that existent hypotheses always lead to perceiving reality in accordance with these hypotheses. In the presence of extremely contradictory information people will be prepared to discard existing hypotheses. However, in the case of a strong hypothesis, much less information is necessary to confirm it and much more to discredit it. Out of this comes the statement (Irle, 1975, p. 85):

Hypotheses produce perception, and perceptions produce hypotheses.

The degree to which hypotheses influence perception, or the degree to which hypotheses are changed by perceptions, obviously depends to a large extent on the hypothesis strength. This is determined according to the following factors (see Irle, 1975, pp. 86–88):

- Frequency of past confirmation,

For example, the more frequently a particular course of action has led to success, the more the person in question may form the conviction/hypothesis that they have done the right thing and that they are personally responsible for their success.

- Number of available alternative hypotheses.

The fewer available alternative hypotheses there are for solving a problem, the more sure the person is that these few alternatives are the solution to the problem.

- Strong emotional support.

The more a person wants to perceive a certain thing, the more likely they are to perceive it. Whoever is negatively disposed toward a person, might well be motivated to perceive this person in a negative light.

- The connection of a hypothesis to other hypotheses.

We can proceed under the assumption that a person operates according to an extremely complex system of hypotheses. Between some of these hypotheses there are connections, and between others there are none. Some hypotheses have a great many connections to other hypotheses, while others remain isolated. The alteration of a hypothesis that has many ties with other hypotheses is very difficult for a person, because this frequently also entails changing these other hypotheses. From this we can derive the statement that, the more connections a hypothesis has, the stronger it is, and the more resistant it is to change.

Theory of Social Judgment Formation

The approach that forms the basis of the hypothesis theory of social perception is similar to the approach that forms the basis of the theory of social judgment formation. It is assumed in this regard that existing presumptions as to a given set of factors influence perceptions. This theory can also be traced back to Sherif and Hovland (1961) and Sherif, Sherif and Nebergall (1965) as the social judgment theory, also known as the assimilation-contrast theory.

In order to understand this theory we have to make clear that presumptions can be presented on a scale, which starts at one extreme point, traverses a neutral area, and then reaches an opposing extreme point. The following example can serve to illustrate:

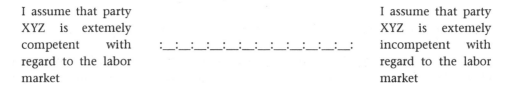

| I assume that party XYZ is extemely competent with regard to the labor market | :__:__:__:__:__:__:__:__:__:__:__: | I assume that party XYZ is extemely incompetent with regard to the labor market |

The viewpoint of the receivers of communications can be presented on such scales, as well as the viewpoint of the perceived (sources of) communications themselves. The thesis is that the receivers of communications do not perceive and judge objectively but rather in dependence upon their own viewpoint.

The theory of social judgment formation consists of the following core statements:

- In a domain that bears very close resemblance to one's own presumptions, the messages of that domain will be perceived as being identical to one's own presumptions. They will be assimilated (assimilation domain).
- In the case of a domain that appears relatively near, the messages of that domain will be perceived as a bit divergent, but still will be perceived as being closer to one's

own presumptions than is the case in reality. These messages will be accepted, and can also end up influencing the person. The person changes her presumption in the direction of the communication. This area is known as the acceptance domain.

• Then we come across a further domain, whose communications are neither accepted nor rejected. In other words it is a neutral domain, in which the viewpoints of other communications are more or less objectively perceived.

• Still further away from the viewpoint of the perceiving person is the rejection or contrast domain. In accordance with one's own viewpoint, the messages perceived here will be experienced as being farther removed from one's point of view than is the case in reality. They will be "contrasted", and will be rejected. A change of presumption in the direction of the communication is not to be expected here. Rather, a boomerang effect is likely in the case of extreme divergence of viewpoints (which will be perceived as even more extreme then is objectively the case), whereby a shift of presumption away from the communication's viewpoint takes place. The person alters his presumption in the opposite direction.

The fact that communications from the rejection (or contrast) domain of increasing divergence, which diverge from the original presumption of the perceiving person, are perceived as being even more removed from the person's point of view than they really are, is known as the contrast effect. The assimilation effect denotes what happens when communications from the domain of increasing acceptance (or assimilation), are increasingly seen as being even more similar, and in the case of extreme similarity, the communication is judged as being completely identical to one's own standpoint.

People are often confronted with communications with the aim of influencing them. The effect the attempted influence will have depends on how the viewpoint of the communication is perceived by the person.

Communications from the assimilation domain do not lead to an influential effect because they are perceived as being identical to one's own presumptions. Communications from the acceptance domain are aimed at an effect that increases in significance, the greater the perceived divergence is from the presumption of the person to be influenced. Communications from the neutral domain do not lead to an effect. Communications from the contrast domain can lead to a boomerang effect, which increases in significance the further away the influencing communication is perceived to be from the viewpoint of the communication recipient (the person to be influenced).

In order for the communicator to foresee the effect of influences, information is needed regarding the extent of the acceptance and rejection domains. The extent or degree of these domains is influenced by two factors:

1. As a rule, the more extreme a viewpoint is, the narrower the acceptance domain is, and the wider the rejection domain is.
2. The more personally relevant (synonyms are "I-participation" or "involvement") the particular subject of opinion is, the narrower the acceptance domain is, and the wider the rejection domain is. There is often a close relationship between these two aspects. In the cases of extreme viewpoints there usually is also a high degree of personal relevance. In light of this we can state that in general: The greater the personal relevance, the narrower the acceptance domain. "The extent of the acceptance

domain's scope is a negative function of the magnitude of I-participation" (Irle, 1975, p. 291).

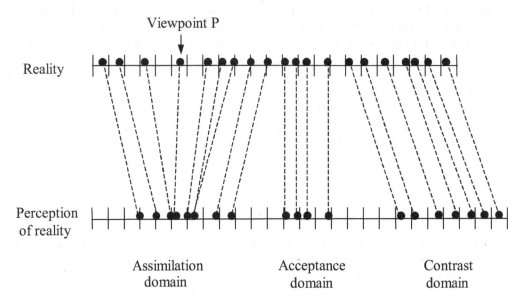

Figure 2.3   Social judgment formation in the assimilation, acceptance, and contrast domains

The variable of "I-participation"/"I-involvement" is of particular significance within the implementation of the theory of social judgment formation. Involvement is dependent on two variables: significance value and utility value. Significance value simply means the significance a value holds for a person. Utility value indicates the degree of utility a given subject has with regard to the realization of a value. Every person has a range of values organized according to their varying significance. Utility, as a qualifying attribute of objects (for example, products), denotes the extent to which this product can further a person's goals. Both factors taken together determine the involvement with regard to a given product. Out of this has come the widespread practice in marketing of differentiating products according to the categories of "high involvement" and "low involvement" (in marketing often quite imprecisely indicated by "high interest" or "low interest"). Let's assume that prestige is very important to a person (high significance value). Let's assume further that the wearing of certain types of brand name clothing is seen by this person as being very useful in terms of enhancing prestige (high utility value). The type of clothing in question is then shown to evoke high product involvement. It is clear from this that it actually is not about a dichotomizing differentiation, but rather is about the more or less pronounced involvement with various products, which products moreover can vary in how pronounced their levels of involvement are, in accordance with various dimensions of quality, making it an important approach for market segmentation. We can assume that the involvement with regard to mineral water is not that pronounced in most people. There is however a market segment of people who are extremely involved with the sodium content of mineral water.

Applications

The hypothesis theory of social perception explains, for example, areas of behavior in the context of personnel management. Managers who have very particular expectations of a person's behavior, tend to see their expectations confirmed with regard to their perception of performance. If, within the context of personnel assessment, managers are asked about behavior, willingness to perform, competence, or personality characteristics, the answers we receive, to a greater or lesser extent, are influenced by the expectations of those managers. The fact that there is no such thing as impartial perception is often not known or too little considered by managers, or by teachers within schools, vocational training, and universities.

In marketing, the hypothesis theory plays a big role in the context of product perception. For example, a lot of consumers assume that caffeine-free coffee is a less "aromatic" taste experience. This hypothesis may lead to the taste of a particular brand of decaffeinated coffee being underplayed in favor of focusing on it as "advisable for health reasons". As part of a TV advertising campaign featuring athletic, dynamic individuals, one of these people, wondering why the person across from her has ordered a particular brand of decaffeinated coffee, at the same time as not noticing that she herself is drinking the same brand, says "Now that's how coffee should taste ...." To a large extent this campaign has set itself the task of altering expectations with regard to the product, and of encouraging the formation of biases with regard to the user of the product. The latter is meant to increase social acceptance of the product.

There are product lines wherein the consumers or the majority of consumers are practically unable to differentiate between competing brands: Beer, mineral water, cigarettes, coffee, brandy. In blind tests (product tests where the subject has no knowledge of which brands they are sampling) the subjects perceived no difference or significantly less difference between brands than in tests when the brands were known by the subjects (see Moser, 1990, p. 68). Perception of brand leads to a hypothesis that then influences perception of taste.

The assimilation-contrast theory has an application for every incidence of influence. For example, it is virtually unthinkable in elections that one could wrest voters from (let's say) the right wing camp, and then make them into voters for the left wing parties. For them, communications from the left wing camp issue from the rejection domain, and are either ignored or lead to boomerang effects. In elections the objective is to motivate supporters to vote ("This time we really have a chance, but only with your help ..."), or to dampen the motivation of the other camp's voters, or to make them unsure and thus dissuade them from voting.

If it so happens that within social marketing our desire is to create biases, we will find ourselves stuck with a similar problem. We cannot expect to turn around an entrenched positive or negative presumption during the course of one communications campaign. Extreme presumptions, which as a rule indicate high involvement, stubbornly resist attempts at persuasion. In social marketing we often have to accept that presumptions can only be changed in small steps. If we were to confront extreme presumptions with extreme presumptions to the contrary, we would likely have to reckon with the boomerang effect.

The assimilation-contrast theory can also clarify why it is difficult to have an effect within the consumer goods sector. In the case of high involvement products the acceptance domain is relatively narrow and the rejection domain relatively broad.

It is very likely that communications for products other than the currently preferred product are coming out of the rejection domain. It is easier to have an effect with regard to low involvement products, which may indicate that the acceptance domain is bigger and the rejection domain smaller. There are other explanations for this phenomenon within the consumer goods sector (especially the "Cognitive Response" theory, Chapter 7). With low involvement information reception takes place more casually or haphazardly, whereby images tend to be registered more than textual communications, and the effect is relayed via emotional, image oriented, colorful presentations, rather than via the quality and structure of arguments. With "high involvement" products, the extent to which target groups are involved in advertising messages should certainly be taken into account. Low involvement with regard to advertising is definitely an issue with products having highly pronounced involvement. This has the consequence that advertising, emotionally regarded as low involvement, creates market sympathy, which leads to the person more thoroughly informing herself about the product and the corresponding arguments for it, via other information sources.

Laczniak and Muehling (1993) have done research into the factors of belief strength and belief certainty in connection with high or low involvement. This has shown that the belief strength with regard to particular product characteristics, or the capacity to satisfy certain needs, does not depend on involvement, but rather is arguably dependent on belief certainty. Consumers are more certain of their convictions in the case of high involvement products than they are with low involvement products. The explanation that Laczniak and Muehling (1993, p. 314) give for this effect is not entirely convincing: "This may be the case since more involved receivers' as evaluations are likely to be based on more criteria and a more meaningful analysis than those of less involved persons". We can more accurately assume that advertisements for high involvement products are observed more briefly, observation being more focused on images, pictures emphasized over text, and where the emotional aspects of image elements tend to attract more attention. Presumably more subtle cognitive processes are responsible for the observed effect, which could be explored within the context of cognitive constituency theory. This is akin to Edward Hall's High-Context and Low-Context cultural theory, where some cultures require more context than do other cultures during communication processes (Ajami, Cool, Goddard et al., 2006). People are less willing to endure insecurity with regard to important things than with unimportant things. The more important the given set of factors is experienced to be, the more pronounced the inner psychological tension engendered by uncertainty will be.

Presumptions and attitudes play a central role in the elucidation of consumer goods purchasing behavior. Marketing communications create product and/or brand expectations. We purchase a consumer good essentially on the basis of expectations, which become more ingrained with repeat purchases than is the case after one purchase as a result of advertising or other influences. Even after the umpteenth purchase we know nothing about the product we are buying, merely holding expectations with regard to it. Attaining this effect is the task of the whole marketing mix, including pricing policy. Prices create certain performance expectations as well. Often price is an indicator of quality.

A core task of marketing is positioning. To position a brand means creating expectations about a definite product feature which are in synch with the same expectations with regard to competing brands. We would like to illustrate this with a simple example: KFZ brand would like to assess purchase expectations according to what extent they are experienced as sportive, promoting of prestige, economical, and reliable. In terms of marketing the tasks are a) to find out which buyer segments are holding what ideal notions and b) how can their brand be made to stand out and seem advantageous in comparison to the competition, within a given market segment. In many areas of the consumer goods market, the distinctive positioning of a product is a result of the technical exchangeability of a product, established via communication of this distinctiveness. When products are interchangeable as far as their particulars are concerned, then what is needed is distinctive emotional communication that concentrates on unusual presentation and on attractive images. (see Kroeber-Riel and Esch, 2000, p. 47; and many examples are given in Kroeber-Riel, 1993).

This chapter helps to clarify why people have the perceptions that they do and how this knowledge can be used when trying to change the opinions of others. Changing opinions, regardless of how deep-seated they may be is no easy task. This is especially true in an age of customized products and saturated marketing mediums. Twenty-four-hour news channels cater to the belief that if you properly segment your audience, you can be successful even if the opinions expressed by the personalities on the channel are relatively one-sided. How things change when we move into the area of social comparison is the subject of our next chapter.

QUESTIONS FOR DISCUSSION

1. What is the theory of social perception, and how is it useful for marketers?
2. What is the theory of social judgment, and how can it be utilized in a successful marketing effort?
3. What is the boomerang effect, and how can it be avoided?
4. What is the assimilation-contrast theory, and how is it useful in a marketing context?

Bibliography

Ajami, R., Cool, K., Goddard, G.J., and Khambata, D.: *International Business: Theory and Practice* (2nd edn). Armonk, NY: 2006.

Ajzen, I. and Fishbein, M. (eds): *Understanding Attitudes and Predicting Social Behavior*. Englewood Cliffs: 1980.

Allport, F.H.: *Theories of Perception and the Concept of Structure*. New York: 1955.

Assael, H.: *Consumer Behavior and Marketing Action* (4th edn). Boston: 1992.

Blake, R.R. and Ramsey, G.B. (eds): *Perception, an Approach to Personality*. New York: 1951.

Bruner, J.S.: Personality dynamics and the process of perceiving. In Blake, R.R. and Ramsey, G.B. (eds): *Perception, an Approach to Personality*. New York: 1951, 121–147.

—— On perceptual readiness. *Psychological Review*, 1957, 64, 123–152.

Feldman, S. (ed.): *Cognitive Consistency*. New York: 1966.

Fishbein, M.: The relationship between beliefs, attitudes, and behavior. In: Feldman, S. (ed.), *Cognitive Consistency*. New York: 1966, 199–223.

Fishbein, M. and Ajzen, I.: Predicting and understanding consumer behavior: Attitude-behavior correspondence. In: Ajzen, I. and Fishbein, M. (eds): *Understanding Attitudes and Predicting Social Behavior*. Englewood Cliffs: 1980, 48–172.

Frey, D. and Irle, M. (eds): *Theorien der Sozialpsychologie, Band I: Kognitive Theorien* (2nd edn). Bern: 1993. (*Theories of Social Psychology*, vol, I: *Cognitive Theories*).

Ginter, J.L.: An experimental investigation of attitude change and choice of a new brand. *Journal of Marketing Research*: 1974, 11, 30–40.

Hovland, C.I. and Rosenberg, M.J. (eds): *Attitude Organization and Change*. Westport: 1980.

Irle, M.: Entstehung und Änderung von Sozialen Einstellungen (Attitüden). In: Merz, F. (ed.): *Bericht über den 25. Kongreß der Deutschen Gesellschaft für Psychologie*. Münster, 1966. Göttingen: 1967, 194–221. (Origin and change of social attitudes. In *Report on the 25th Congress of the German Company for Psychology*).

—— *Lehrbuch der Sozialpsychologie*. Göttingen, Toronto, Zürich: 1975. (*Textbook of Social Psychology*).

Kroeber-Riel, W.: *Bildkommunikation*. München: 1993. (*Picture Communication*).

—— and Esch, F.R.: *Strategie und Technik der Werbung* (5th edn) Stuttgart, Berlin, Köln: 2000. (*Strategy and Technology of Advertising*).

Laczniak, R.N. and Muehling, D.D.: Toward a better understanding of the role of advertising message involvement in ad processing. *Psychology & Marketing*: 1993, 10, 301–319.

Lilli, W. and Frey, D.: Die hypothesentheorie der sozialen wahrnehmung. In: Frey, D. and Irle, M. (eds): *Theorien der Sozialpsychologie, Band I: Kognitive Theorien* (2nd edn). Bern, Göttingen, Toronto, Seattle: 1993, 49–78. (The hypothesis theory of the social perception. In *Theories of Social Psychology, vol. I: Cognitive Theories*).

Merz, F. (ed.): *Bericht über den 25. Kongreß der Deutschen Gesellschaft für Psychologie*. Münster, 1966. Göttingen: 1967. (*Report on the 25th Congress of the German Company for Psychology*).

Moser, K.: *Werbepsychologie*. München: 1990. (*Advertising Psychology*).

Postman, L.: Toward a general theory of cognition. In: Rohrer, J.H. and Sherif, M. (eds): *Social Psychology at the Crossroads*. New York: 1951, 242–272.

Rohrer, J.H. and Sherif, M. (eds): *Social Psychology at the Crossroads*. New York: 1951.

Rosenberg, M.J. and Hovland, C.I.: Cognitive, affective, and behavioral components of attitudes. In: Hovland, C.I. and Rosenberg, M.J. (eds): *Attitude Organization and Change*. Westport: 1980, 1–14.

Sherif, M. and Hovland, C.I.: *Social Judgement*. New Haven: 1961.

Sherif, C.W., Sherif, M. and Nebergall, R.: *Attitude and Attitude Change. The Social Judgement-Involvement Approach*. Philadelphia: 1965.

Trommsdorff, V.: *Die Messung von Produktimages für das Marketing. Grundlagen und Operationalisierung*. Köln: 1975. (*The Measurement of Product Images for Marketing. Basis and Operationalization*).

Unger, F.: *Marktforschung* (2nd edn). Heidelberg: 1997. (*Market Research*).

Unger, F. and Fuchs, W.: *Management der Marktkommunikation* (2nd edn). Heidelberg: 1999. (*Management of Market Communication*).

von Cranach, M., Irle, M. and Vetter, M.: Zur Analyse des bumerang-effektes, größe und richtung der änderung sozialer einstellungen als funktion ihrer verankerung in wertsystemen. *Psychologische Forschung*, 1965, 28, 535–561. (The analysis of the boomerang effect, size and direction of the change of social attitudes as a function of its anchorage in value systems).

Wells, W.D. and Prensky, D.: *Consumer Behavior*. New York, Chichester, Brisbane: 1996.

3 *The Theory of Social Comparisons*

Theory

As isolated entities, people are very insecure in their assessment of their own performance, abilities or convictions. How do we know whether our ability to run 100 m in 24.5 seconds is pretty good or not so great? How do students know whether the assessment of their psychology examination is an indication of acceptable performance or not? One could say that people make these decisions according to their own goals. Goals are in turn the expression of an individual "degree of aspiration" or level of standard. Then there is the question of where the degree of aspiration comes from. When do people assess what individual degree of aspiration is appropriate? People's need to assess abilities, performance and convictions, and the related degree of aspiration that originates from this, is the subject of Festinger's (1954) theory of social comparisons, a theory that, despite its age, has not lost its relevance (see Frey, Dauenheimer, Parge et al., 1993). The theory describes what mechanisms underlie these social comparisons.

People are motivated to assess their own abilities and judgments, and they compare themselves with other people. This motivation comes from the real necessity of being able to react to other people in accordance with everyday situations. Out of this comes the need to "acquire subjective certainty concerning the accuracy of one's own assessments of opinions and abilities, and to avoid incorrect information and cognitions. This need engenders the motivation to check one's own assessments according to criteria that is as trustworthy as possible." (Frey, Dauenheimer, Parge et al., 1993, p. 87). People collect information about themselves in that they compare their own merits, opinions, presumptions and degree of aspiration with those of others. People believe themselves to be in the right when they establish that many others think the same way. Festinger (1954) assumes further that people are especially likely to accept a social comparison if objective criteria (that is, intersubjectively comprehensible standards) are not present. This assumption is no longer considered to be correct. Particularly in the comparison of the attractiveness and significance of role models or "role group models", the preference may be to make the comparison according to so-called objective criteria (Miller, 1977). In comparing opinions people attempt to develop "correct" opinions, whereas the comparison of abilities, in Festinger's opinion, serves the motivation to improve one's own performance.

A key question is who utilizes whose merits and degrees of aspiration as a standard of comparison. According to Festinger (1954), the people who are taken up as standards for comparison are those who are seen as relevant, where this relevance is a function of affinities within particular parameters: age, work experience, gender, birth circumstances, degree of performance, etc. The greater the perceived affinity to the relevant parameters, the more likely it is that the person or group of people will serve as a standard of comparison. That applies equally to comparison of both performance and of opinion. Initially, the affinity with regard to performance comparison is reduced to the performance itself. Subsequently, people compare their own performance with that of others, who display a similar level or degree of performance. Later studies have shown (Goethals and Darley, 1977) that more characteristics of those who are available as standards of comparison will be taken into account, in order to determine who is relevant in terms of being a standard of comparison, naturally all this being from the subjective point of view of the given person. A simple example can illustrate this: It appears that many people assume gender to be a relevant characteristic. Zanna, Goethals and Hill (1975) have shown that people use other people of the same sex as standards of comparison.

One's own positive or negative self assessment depends on whether one falls short of or exceeds the standards of the people being compared. Either satisfaction or dissatisfaction results from this. Satisfaction results from either a concurrence of one's own merits or convictions with those of the standard of comparison, or when one's own merits have exceeded those of the standard of comparison. According to Festinger (1942) exceeding one's own or another's degree of aspiration leads to an increase, whereas falling short leads to a reduction of one's own degree of aspiration. Extreme divergences lead to looking for other people as standards of comparison, or to a change of the criteria of comparison.

Possible reactions following a perceived divergence of opinion depend on whether the given person considers himself to be in a minority or in a majority position. If the person thinks he is in a majority position he will attempt via communication to change the divergent opinion of the other person. If he perceives himself to be in a minority position then a change in the direction of the majority position is more likely. Both (communication with "the divergent ones", or change of opinion in the direction of the majority position) will take place with more intensity, the more attractive the group (in which the comparison takes place) and/or the more relevant the subject of opinion is perceived to be (these and other statements are found in Irle, 1993, pp. 42–46).

GROUP COMPARISONS

Comparisons take place within groups (intra group comparisons) and between groups (inter group comparisons). "Role model groups" are groups relevant in the context of the comparison. Role models or role model groups are all the more important, and the comparison with other people is all the more attempted, the less people have the opportunity to include other social criteria, so called "objective" criteria. In that case social comparisons provide standards for one's own behavior, opinions, presumptions or values. The selection of role model groups also takes place on the basis of similarly normative conceptions, presumptions, capabilities or purchasing power. Role model groups, like individual role models, are attractive via perceived affinity. Attractive role model groups may display a desirable degree of experience, believability, power, or status. Affinity does not mean that members of role model groups display a general level of affinity. The decisive point is the affinity with regard to relevant, graded parameters of comparison.

There are also negative role model groups. These are groups who have declined or spurned the observed standards. They establish norms just as the attractive, positive role model groups do, but in the opposite direction. It is also conceivable that a person finds himself to be a member of a group that acts as a negative role model, in other words a case where the group he is a member of becomes the target of negative judgment. Normally the person will attempt to get out of the group. This is not always possible; we can think for example of young consumers who consciously desire to diverge from their family norms in terms of their stance as consumers. Displaying divergent consumer behavior can here resolve the conflict produced by undesirable membership to a group. Young consumers very often consciously depart from the consumer behavior of their parents.

We can systematize these statements according to whether a person is a member of a group or not, whether the person accepts the membership or not, or if the person would be a willing member or not. Membership groups can be described according to the following features: Contact intensity (we are differentiating between secondary groups with less contact intensity and primary groups with high contact intensity), and the significance of membership for the given person. We are further differentiating between formal and informal groups. This is brought out in Figure 3.1, in accordance with Assael (1992, p. 404).

Symbolical groups are groups the person will never become a member of or aspire to become a member of, which however can be a source of role models in a certain respect. Especially relevant here are leading figures in sport, culture, and entertainment.

A further classification is that of "comparative" and "normative" role model groups (Kelley, 1952). Comparative groups merely serve the end of personal comparison, whereas, due to the results of comparisons, normative groups can also change a person's value system and thus have a more pronounced effect on the person's behavioral patterns.

RESULTS OF PERCEIVED DISCREPANCIES OF OPINION AND PERFORMANCE

People can attempt to adapt their opinions to the majority, or can attempt to adjust their performance to that of those people who are standards of comparison (role models). They can also change their role models, change parameters of comparison, avoid the comparison, or can devalue the role models, or deem them to be irrelevant. In this regard they will choose the strategy that is cognitively experienced by them as being the easiest.

In work groups, "dissenters" can be closed out of the group, at least emotionally, or the dissenters can themselves leave the group. An exclusion from the group is more likely to happen, the greater the discrepancy is from the group standard, the more unattractive the person in question is for the group, and the more the person threatens the group identity (Frey, Dauenheimer, Parge et al., 1993, p. 115). The group can feel threatened by a "downward moving" divergence in level of performance, in that its reputation within the organization is slipping and its group goals are not being attained. In the case of an "upward moving" divergence in level of performance the group can experience a threat in terms of its group climate. A divergent person will try harder to adapt to the group standards, the more attractive group membership is for them, the more difficult available alternatives are, and the more easily they can adapt themselves to the group standards without threatening their feelings of self-worth.

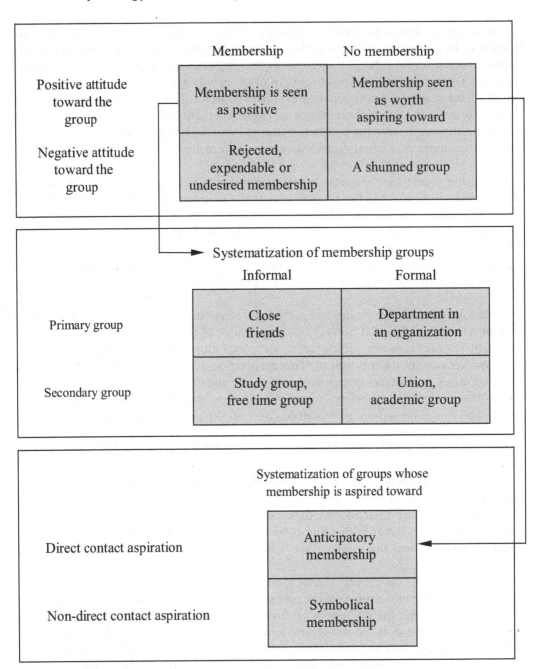

Figure 3.1   Systematization of role model groups (Assael, 1992, p. 404)

Whether the dissenter will try to undermine the group standard, or whether he will attempt to fulfill the group standard, depends on the subjectively assessed chances of success of the possible alternatives.

Applications

PERSONNEL POLICY

Performance comparisons

An activity leads to success insofar as it is assessed according to a measurable level of performance or target. In professional life, such goals can be explicitly formulated and presented within the context of performance incentive systems. If this is not the case, then employees will themselves strive toward such goals. Performance levels can be established in the form of goals that are worth striving for, which originate from comparative processes in relation to role models. These kinds of comparative processes certainly are only relevant when they take place between people whose individual levels of performance are not experienced to be too divergent. The significance of informal, social comparison has already been emphasized by Kosiol (1966, p. 99): "The significance of these informal relationships between people for an organization's formative processes, resides in the fact that the activity of a particular person who has been assigned a task, is not only influenced by the directions that apply to those instances he is responsible for, but is also influenced by the behavioral norms set by the informal groups to which he belongs. A behavioral rule along these lines might involve the daily work quota for example. In this case the extent of work efficiency will be determined by the group opinion, rather than by mental and physical capacity. Furthermore, there is the espoused view that in the majority of executed tasks, the commitment to group norms is stronger than the commitment to the instructions of superiors."

This means that people orient themselves toward co-workers with a similar standard of performance. Inefficient employees do not orient themselves toward topnotch performers, but rather, in the best case, toward slightly harder working co-workers, or in the worst case, they look around for even more inefficient co-workers, next to whom they can maintain their subjectively experienced self-worth. Performance competition certainly does not automatically lead to individual employees feeling motivated to increase performance. In any case, we can count on information being passed around concerning who has to do what and who does not. It can be in the interest of management to try and influence such normative tendencies by linking "official" targets with bonuses (as is often the case in sales).

Social comparisons play a particularly essential role in the commission systems often found in sales; these confute the professional assumption that the commission system features the advantage of a performance incentive with an "unlimited upper limit", thereby favorably distinguishing itself from the bonus idea, which sets up an upper performance limit in the form of performance goals. These (comparisons) result from the human need to assess one's own performance. Furthermore, people derive satisfaction from their own successful action (Scherhorn, 1992, p. 27). Performance assessment and perception presuppose goals—which will be established via social comparisons if they are not otherwise explicitly given. Certainly in sales, where there is a lot of insecurity as to how much is to be done, the individual is driven to find release from this insecurity. This release comes from implied (social) performance comparisons. The goals that originate from such comparisons may be at least as binding as "officially" given goals. From the management's point of view, the performance limits arising in this way have the disadvantage that they are the consequence of social mechanisms that are not always predictable, which only occasionally correspond with the strategic goals. For strategic marketing purposes it therefore seems effective to provide explicit goals.

Work groups also present pertinent practical examples of the theory of social performance processes. We can think of sales teams within the area of sales, where many sales forces are active within a particular shared sales area. Similar work groups are found in production. The pressure is relatively high to conform to judgments, or with the consensus regarding level of performance, in groups where membership and acceptance is considered significant by the individual member. High group cohesion leads to minimization of performance decisions within the group. The level of performance is determined by the performance goals of the majority of group members, or by those members who act as standards of comparison for the others. If people's position on something becomes unanimous as result of a high pressure to conform, this does not mean that their viewpoint has actually changed; what is definitely conceivable, and what has been experimentally demonstrated, is that only the outward viewpoint has adapted to the dominant group consensus, not the real viewpoint. This has been shown by Upmeyer (1971) with the help of the "signal discovery theory" (see for examples of this theory Zimbardo and Gerrig, 1999, pp. 105, 106).

In sales, performance competition between sales groups is organized. In this context management often overestimates the effect the groups with the highest level of performance will have. Groups with a weak level of performance will compare themselves, in the best case, with groups that are not too far above them in terms of performance, but never with the groups displaying the highest level of performance. This also applies when the same kind of competition is encouraged between individuals within sales.

It is not very effective to put forward the best groups or individuals as examples for all the other people, because it necessitates a confession that they have not met performance standards, leading to an increased threat to their self-esteem. A resulting countermeasure may be to view the top performers as irrelevant. Particularities within the given sales area, structures with regard to the customer, tight competition, etc., will be cited as the causes for an obvious performance deficit. This kind of justification is especially common among those who are performance oriented, whose self-esteem may be more strongly threatened by perceived performance deficits, than is the case with less performance oriented people. The attempt to actually attain a high level of performance in the future is connected with the insight that in the past mistakes were made, with all the concomitant negative results for self-esteem. It is psychologically easier to deem the comparison as not being relevant, but this entails inhibiting the "role model function". Along these lines, to motivate someone to increase performance level means to present the person with a role model of performance that is not too divergent from his own level of performance.

Another way is revealed by the theory of convergence and divergence in groups (Irle, 1993, pp. 42–45). According to this an attempt can be made to make it really clear that the role models relevant to the majority are already displaying the desired performance behavior, or that they have already attained particular performance goals. This way it is more difficult for those who are not performing as well to avoid the comparison.

To conclude, employees in sales or production establish behavioral norms through processes of comparison. These norms serve to establish performance standards. In this way employees reduce any insecurity with regard to performance results.

Income comparisons

If we are using levels of performance as examples of application, than it is only a short stretch to bring in levels of income. It is not the objective level of income as a behaviorally relevant absolute measure, but rather it is the subjectively perceived level of income held by role models, that are focused on by the theory of social comparisons. Work experience, age, training, and perceived level of performance, are all factored into the income comparison. We can assume that people will be happy with their income situation when they share their level of income with people who also are similarly endowed with these qualities.

If a person is faced with other people who receive a higher level of income on the basis of the above qualities, this can lead not only to dissatisfaction, but also to the given person feeling threatened in his self-esteem. Since threat to self-esteem is always experienced as uncomfortable, the person is then likely to change the level of standard, by perhaps using different people as standards of comparison, or possibly by "adapting the level of standard to a lower level". These strategies are meant to process "inequities" or "injustices" to a limited extent.

CONSUMER AND MARKET COMMUNICATION

Individual consumers are insecure in many respects. Matters of taste, quantity, value, quality, and factual matters of consuming are causes of individual insecurity. What are "nice" products? What emphasis on consuming is appropriate? What is the "right" amount from a quantitative point of view as far as consumption is concerned? What standards of measurement and what products in general are appropriate? The answers to these questions often lead to comparisons with other people, groups, or classes of consumption.

Groups play a big role in this context. Groups can be families, circles of friends, and formal social groups like clubs or work groups. Individuals are members of various groups, and they compare themselves with the members of various groups, including groups that they are not members of (role model groups). A role model group is any group that serves as a standard of comparison toward the formation of specific or general values, presumptions, or patterns of behavior.

The influence of role model groups is particularly significant with regard to consumption when these groups are outwardly visible and when they are of particular relevance for a person's assessment. For example this applies to luxury goods, fashion products, car accessories, cosmetic products and also to pleasure/indulgence products. There are also products within consumption that instill a lot of insecurity in individuals, where insecurity can be alleviated by comparison with the consumption of other people. In such cases the task of marketing communication might be to facilitate those kinds of comparisons.

Examples of this are products in connection with the continence of the elderly, or socially unacceptable products like alcohol-free beer or caffeine-free coffee. Breaking in products that can be used with regard to the continence of the elderly might involve, among other things, presenting them as being things that are just taken for granted among a certain age group. A particular brand of caffeine-free coffee is touted by having an attractive, relatively young pair drink coffee. Expectations can be changed in this way (see Chapter 2

"Applications" pp. 27–29). Just as important is the presentation of relatively young, athletic people drinking a particular coffee. Alcohol-free beer is also in need of being socially accepted. The German market leader's advertisement for the alcohol-free beer Clausthaler® rests more on the statement that Clausthaler® "has everything that a beer needs", thereby putting more emphasis on the product characteristics. The TV is presented more as a situation comedy.

Within marketing communication the attempt can be made to consider role structures that may exist in groups to which people wish to belong. Roles are the expectations that people believe are oriented toward them from the direction of their social environment. People attempt to come to terms with these expectations. They are the roles that a person takes on within society. One can try to work particular products into the context of these expectations. People are then meant to assume that their relevant social environment expects from them the consumption of particular products. Along these lines products should of course be placed within certain consumption milieus.

There is furthermore the possibility within market communication of picking up on hints from role model groups. The advertisements with stars from sports and show business take advantage of symbolical role model groups.

If it is desired that products be "something really special" then it can be advantageous to present them in the context of symbolical role model groups. The expectation is encouraged that by consuming a certain product one is "symbolically" a member. An important factor for the success of this kind of approach is the question of who do people identify with in the symbolical role model groups, or in other words the question of which individuals, from within the target group, can be taken advantage of as leading figures of that group. In this context "product placement" plays a big role, that is, the placement of brand name products within films, television, videos, etc.

Market communication can lead to the creation of expectations with regard to behavior within groups, to the promotion of products within selected consumption milieus, to the point where they are taken for granted, and can deliver directions with regard to social acceptance, reward, and punishment within groups. Furthermore the significance of standardized behavior can be emphasized.

If the task is to encourage a change in behavior, it is possible to do this via the application of theoretical group statements (Irle, 1993, pp. 42–45) to create the impression that the majority of role models are already displaying the (from a marketing perspective) desired behavior. Moreover it has to be suggested that the given behavior is of great significance.

THE IMPLEMENTATION OF PEOPLE WITHIN MARKET COMMUNICATION

People qualify as attractive when they display a passable level of affinity with regard to the parameters of assessment relevant to a particular context.

In market communication people play the role of communicators or as formative elements within advertising. Here people can be implemented either as leading figures of the target group or as "idealized" people. If people are meant to present or represent the target group, then naturally they ought to have an adequate level of affinity. People who are to be implemented as representatives of a target group, who may be positioned somewhat "above" as leading figures of the target group, must still however be assessed as alike or attainable.

The implementation of sports and entertainment stars is an interesting case. As a rule these people strongly differ from the target group in terms of their consumption behavior. And reference to people in this group is hardly appropriate, in that normally, the income and consumption level is too divergent from the target group. That having been said, the selection of stars proceeds, despite existing differences, and on the basis of very particular personality characteristics, according to the extent to which they display an adequate level of affinity to the target group. The success of advertising with tennis stars like Boris Becker and Steffi Graf can presumably be traced back to both stars having been assessed as "approachable" by a large proportion of the people. A comparable sports star does not appear to have been successful in this sense: Formula One racing car driver Michael Schumacher still seems to have popularity problems. Whenever it has to do with sympathetic identification with people, and this applies particularly to everyday products of little importance, then affinity with regard to particular parameters of personality is of great significance. If communicating product competence is more the goal, then this is less important.

According to these stated principles the implementation of optically pleasing ("beautiful") people within the cosmetic and fashion fields is certainly a thoroughly hot topic of discussion. Using people who differ a little less radically from the target group than is currently the case might be worth considering.

CONCLUDING COMMENTS

In general, it is noteworthy that attempts to change opinions or behavior patterns can be arranged, in the application of the theory of social comparison processes, such that they turn out to be the most cognitively effective strategy for adapting opinions or behavior patterns with regard to the people who are to be influenced. The relevance of role models or role model groups can be presented as having a particularly high level of social acceptance, making a devaluation of the particular role model or role model group, an avoidance of the comparison, or a divergence into other parameters of comparison, especially difficult. Since the choice of behavioral strategies depends on perceived discrepancies as far as subjectively experienced probabilities of success are concerned, there arises the possibility of communicating these probabilities of success within the context of marketing and personnel policy measures.

Broadly speaking it can be assumed that people have the tendency to react favorably to the behavioral strategy that allows them to preserve or increase their feeling of self-worth (see Stahlberg, Osnabrügge and Frey, 1993). It makes sense to take this into consideration in the context of marketing and personnel concepts.

Furthermore people seek information that they can adopt in order to structure and predict their environment, which thereby allows them to assess themselves as sufficiently competent (see Osnabrügge, Stahlberg and Frey, 1993; White, 1959). In market communication, statements given by accepted personalities from public life can make fitting contributions toward satisfying these criteria.

QUESTIONS FOR DISCUSSION

1. Elaborate on the theory of social comparisons.
2. How can the theory of social comparisons be utilized in performance assessment?
3. How can the theory of social comparisons be utilized in consumer and market communication?
4. Provide specific examples of how your organization or university has utilized the theory of social comparisons for success.

Bibliography

Assael, H.: *Consumer Behavior and Marketing Action* (4th edn). Boston: 1992.

Festinger, L.: Wish, expectation, and group standards as factors influencing level of aspiration. *Journal of Abnormal and Social Psychology*, 1942, 37, 184–200.

Festinger, L.: A theory of social comparison processes. *Human Relations*, 1954, 7, 117–140.

Frey, D., Dauenheimer, D., Parge, O. and Haisch, J.: Die theorie sozialer vergleichsprozesse. In: Frey, D. and Irle, M. (eds): *Theorien der Sozialpsychologie, Band I: Kognitive Theorien* (2nd edn). Bern: 1993, 81–121. (The theory of social comparison processes. In *Theories of Social Psychology, vol. I: Cognitive Theories*).

—— *Theorien der Sozialpsychologie, Band I: Kognitive Theorien* (2nd. edn). Bern: 1993. (*Theories of Social Psychology, vol. I, Cognitive Theories*).

—— *Theorien der Sozialpsychologie, Band II: Gruppen- und Lern-theorien* (2nd edn). Bern, Göttingen, Toronto, Seattle: 1993. (*Theories of Social Psychology, vol. II: Group Theories and Trained Theories*).

Goethals, G.R. and Darley, J.M.: Social comparison theory: An attributional approach. In: Suls, J.M. and Miller, R.L. (eds): *Social Comparison Processes: Theoretical and Empirical Perspectives*. Washington: 1977, 259–278.

Irle, M.: Konvergenz und divergenz in gruppen. In Frey, D. and Irle, M. (eds): *Theorien der Sozialpsychologie, Band II: Gruppen- und Lerntheorien* (2nd edn). Bern, Göttingen, Toronto, Seattle: 1993, 39–64. (Convergence and divergence in groups. In: *Theories of Social Psychology, vol. II: Group Theories and Trained Theories*).

Kelley, H.H.: Two functions of reference groups. In: Swanson, G.E., Newcomb, T.M. and Hartley, E.L. (eds): *Readings in Social Psychology* (2nd edn). New York: 1952, 410–414.

Kosiol, E.: *Die Unternehmung als Wirtschaftliches Aktionszentrum*. Reinbek bei Hamburg: 1966. (*The Enterprise as an Economic Action Center*).

Miller, R.L.: Preference for social vs. non-social comparison as a means of self-evaluation. *Journal of Personality*, 1977, 45, 343–355.

Osnabrügge, G.; Stahlberg, D. and Frey, D.: Die theorie der kognitiven kontrolle. In: Frey, D. and Irle, M. (eds): *Theorien der Sozialpsychologien, III: Motivations- und Informationsverarbeitungstheorien* (2nd edn). Bern, Göttingen, Toronto, Seattle: 1993, 127–172. (The theory of cognitive inspection. In *Theories of Social Psychology, vol. III: Motivation Theories and Information Processing Theories*).

Scherhorn, G.: Kritik des zusatznutzens. *Thexis*, 1992, 9, 2, 24–28. (Criticism of added value).

Stahlberg; D., Osnabrügge, G. and Frey, D.: Die theorie des selbstwertschutzes und der selbstwertkontrolle. In: Frey, D. and Irle, M. (eds): *Theorien der Sozialpsychologien, III: Motivations- und Informationsverarbeitungstheorien* (2nd edn). Bern, Göttingen, Toronto, Seattle: 1993, 79–124.

(The theory of self-esteem protection and self-esteem control. In *Theories of Social Psychology, vol. III: Motivation Theories and Information Processing Theories*).

Suls, J.M. and Miller, R.L. (eds): *Social Comparison Processes: Theoretical and Empirical Perspectives*. Washington: 1977.

Swanson, G.E., Newcomb, T.M. and Hartley, E.L. (eds): *Readings in Social Psychology*. (2nd edn). New York: 1952.

Upmeyer, A.: Social perception and signal detectability theory: Group influence on discrimination and usage of scale. *Psychologische Forschung*, 1971, 34, 283–294.

White, R.W.: Motivation reconsidered. The concept of competence. *Psychological Review*, 1959, 66, 297–333.

Zanna, M., Goethals, G. and Hill, J: Evaluating a sex-related ability: Social comparison with similar others and standard setters. *Journal of Experimental Social Psychology*, 1975, 11, 86–93.

Zimbardo, P.G. and Gerrig, R.J.: *Psychology and Life* (15th edn). New York, Reading, Menlo Park: 1999.

4 *The Theory of Cognitive Dissonance*

Theory

FESTINGER'S APPROACH (1957)

The theory of cognitive dissonance is a consistency theory, where consistency theories are understood to be a class of theories that elucidate human aspirations. Humans experience not only various kinds of tension as unpleasant, but also the need to resolve this tension. The theory of cognitive dissonance is a "cognitive consistency theory" which in this case has to do with the dissonance between cognitions and the need to establish cognitive consonance or consistency. This theory originates with Festinger (1957) for whom cognition was the starting point of dissonance theory; he gave the following definition of cognition: "By the term cognition ... I mean any knowledge, opinion, or belief about the environment, about oneself, or about one's behavior" (ibid., p. 3). Cognitions are all wishes and assumptions, awareness of knowledge items, memories, what is perceived of one's own behavior, and the perceived consequences of one's behavioral modes, as well as the assumptions with regard to other people and their behavioral modes, and the experienced or "felt" relationships with other people. A person's cognitive system is all of their cognitions taken together as an aggregate. This means that between these many cognitions there are more or less varied and intense relationships. For example, a close relationship might arise between striving toward health and the taking of different types of medicine, whereas, there is no cognitive relationship between preferences with regard to different wines and the currently experienced air temperature in Moscow. Felt cognitive dissonance leads to activities oriented toward reducing dissonance, just as humans experience the need to reduce hunger.

Cognitive dissonance always arises whenever a person feels that there is an opposition between two perceived cognitions, which is to say that dissonance arises when psychologically, based on the assumptions of a cognition, the opposite then follows based on the assumptions of another cognition. An experienced relevant relationship between the cognitions involved, not present between all cognitions, is a prerequisite for the perception of cognitive dissonance, as the above example shows. Perhaps the most well known example for the arising of cognitive dissonance is that of the smoker who receives information that smoking has negative consequences for health, will at the same time be haunted by a desire for health.

Cognitive dissonance in the context of actions

Festinger's theory of cognitive dissonance (1957) is focused on the arising of cognitive dissonance after actions and on the subsequent information gathering and processing behavior that, toward the end of reducing it, characterizes this dissonance. According to Festinger (1957) a person faced with a decision, for instance when action is called for in a conflict (having to choose between alternatives), will thereafter be in state of cognitive dissonance (having to justify the chosen alternative). All decisions (and the actions coming from them, for example, the buying of a product, the signing of a contract), alongside their intended desired effects, also have undesirable consequences. The statement that in actuality all decisions and actions also have negative aspects may not make sense at first. These negative consequences however stand in opposition to the decision and corresponding action. The perception of them triggers cognitive dissonance.

Why in reality all decisions and their subsequent actions in addition to their positive consequences also have negative consequences, will be explained in the following. Let's assume that a person has to choose between two alternatives. Both alternatives may have advantages and disadvantages. The specific disadvantages and the lost specific advantages of the rejected alternative are the disadvantages of the chosen alternative. Let's assume that an alternative has all the advantages that another has and/or one less disadvantage, and additionally it has some specific advantages that stand out. Where are the undesired consequences then? There will at least be a decreased range of options than there was before. Other possible decisions can no longer be casually made; one would have to at least go back on the previous decision. This substantiates the statement that all decisions also have undesirable consequences. So far we have only been thinking of the expected consequences of actions. In addition there are unexpected consequences. As long as these consequences are not desired, in encountering them the apprehension of cognitive dissonance can be factored in. In the phase directly following an action, people obviously experience the negative consequences of the action especially intensely, assessing their importance more highly. At the same time the desired aspects may even be devalued for a short time. Shortly after the action (as the execution of a preceding decision) people experience regret with regard to their decision (post-decision regret, Festinger, 1964, p. 99). The perceived negative aspects of a decision stand in opposition to the choice that was made, thereby triggering cognitive dissonance. People will become aware of this dissonance shortly after making a decision or taking an action and will tend to regret the decision or action. "As a rule the regret phase arises for only a short time before being reconciled by the dissonance reduction phase"; however, it can also lead to revision of the action (Möntmann, 1978, pp. 310 and 100; Festinger and Walster, 1964, pp. 105–111; Walster, 1964). In the regret phase the original action is re-examined, which basically entails that the search for and processing of information will be organized toward the end of justifying the original action.

Cognitive dissonance is the apprehension of cognitions that stand in opposition to an action, that is, it is the apprehension of cognitions dissonant to the action and the resultant unpleasant state of tension. This leads to the person engaging in actions meant to reduce dissonance or to eliminate it altogether if possible. Cognitive dissonance affects both perceptual and information processing behavior. The greater the dissonance is experienced to be, the greater the motivation will be to dispose of it, and presumably the greater will be the tendency to selectively perceive information and to process it with the aim of reducing dissonance.

In general people who are experiencing cognitive dissonance have the following options for reducing or avoiding cognitive dissonance. In examining these we are assuming a system of cognitions between which either consonant or dissonant relationships can arise.

In general people have the following options toward the aim of reducing dissonance after actions:

- **Elimination**   The cognitions that activate dissonance are eliminated. In the first order this can take place through shunning whatever information stands in opposition to the chosen action. Or it can proceed via the devaluation of the competence and believability of the information's source. Dissonance triggering information can also be evaluated as irrelevant by the given person.
- **Addition**   The addition of consonant information occurs particularly with regard to searching for information with the intent of supporting the actions just taken through revaluation of the source of the information with an eye toward believability, competence, and relevance.
- **Substitution**   The addition of consonant information is often combined with the elimination of dissonant information; dissonant cognitions are substituted with consonant cognitions.
- **Change of goal**   When information is perceived as dissonant the original goals may be reinterpreted and reassessed. A person coming to the belated conclusion that the new car is not quite as sporty as he would have liked, changes his opinion to the effect of: "Actually I've always wanted to drive a comfortable, safe car like this one." Change of goal can be considered to be a form of substitution of cognitions (a goal is substituted for another one).
- **Denying the action**   In retrospect the dissonance triggering action can be denied; one was influenced by others and so one is actually not at all responsible for the action. The denial of an action or of responsibility for an action can be understood as a form of elimination of cognitions.
- **Revising of the action**   Finally it is possible to revise the action. The revising of an action can also be presented as a form of elimination or substitution of cognitions.
- **Combination**   These various possibilities are often combined.

To summarize: Addition, subtraction (elimination), and substitution of cognitions are techniques for reducing cognitive dissonance (see Frey and Gaska, 1993, p. 277).

An exemplary study on this topic was undertaken by Ehrlich, Guttmann, Schönbach et al., (1957). They found that after buying a car, the purchasers of this car brand preferred advertisements featuring that brand. This observation alone is not quite enough in order to substantiate the dissonance effect, since other explanations are available for the effect: Just the fact of owning a car of a particular brand can account for increased attentiveness with regard to advertisements for that brand. However, on the basis of many empirical studies it can be said that after taking actions people seek information that supports those actions, and avoid information that opposes the action. The studies undertaken by Mills are especially interesting (1965a and 1965b). Here we see that the interest for an advertisement for the chosen brand as opposed to the rejected brand is particularly pronounced when both brands are especially similar to each other. The interest for the chosen brand can be interpreted to be the dissonance avoidance effect.

Assume that a person finds a certain type of the "BMW® 3 Class" to be very similar to a particular type of "Mercedes® C Class". After that person has decided for the BMW, advertisements for that type of car as opposed to the Mercedes® advertisements will clearly be preferred, whereas the person's interest for Fiat® Punto advertisements will not be influenced because that type of car had nothing to do with the decision.

On the other hand Mills was not able to thoroughly prove that in all experiments advertisements for the rejected alternative were selectively avoided. Supportive information was preferred, but unsupportive information was not clearly avoided. The dissonance avoidance effect was also not always confirmed in other studies (Feather, 1962; Brock, 1965). Here the problem is that actually in many of the studies dissonance reduction effects were displayed, but not consistently. On the basis of theoretical considerations and on the basis of the empirical results that had been gathered so far Festinger (1957, p. 130) assumed that with increasing cognitive dissonance, initially supportive information is sought and opposing information avoided. In the case of very intense cognitive dissonance both effects will quickly decrease and reverse as much as possible into tolerable information regarding the opposing object. In the end, opposing information will be even sought and supportive information avoided, because theoretically a revising of the action will have taken place as the most intense form of cognitive dissonance reduction.

Festinger (1964, p. 82) has shown that given certain conditions, dissonant information may even be preferred over consonant information. Frey (1979 and 1981a), as well as Frey and Benning (1984), render these conditions more precisely.

a) The question of what kind of information depends on how difficult it is to disprove the information. (Frey and Benning, 1984):
   – Consonant information that is perhaps difficult to disprove, will be preferred over consonant information that is presumed to be easy to disprove. The consonant information that is difficult to disprove is more useful in terms of the stability of the cognitive system.
   – Dissonant information that is perhaps easy to disprove will be preferred over dissonant information that is perceived to be difficult to disprove. The possible disproving of dissonant information also leads to a stabilization of the cognitive system, whereas dissonant information that is difficult to disprove threatens the stability of the system. It could trigger cognitive dissonance that is not easily reduced.
   – Consonant information that is presumably difficult to disprove will be preferred over dissonant information that is considered to be as difficult to disprove. This effect can simply be equated with people's striving to avoid cognitive dissonance and attain cognitive consonance.
   – Dissonant information that is considered easily disproved will be preferentially attended to over consonant information that is also deemed easily disproved. The anticipated disproving of dissonant information makes this information basically unthreatening to the given person's cognitive equilibrium, whereas the anticipated disproving of consonant information represents a potential threat to the stability of the cognitive system.

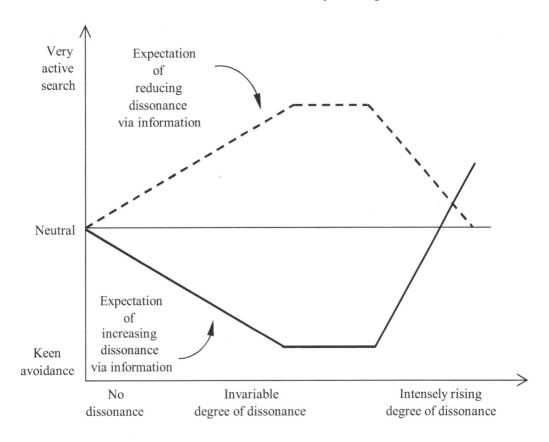

Figure 4.1   Extent of cognitive dissonance and selective search for information after decisions (Festinger, 1957, p. 130)

b) According to Frey (1979) dissonant information is preferred under the following conditions:
    –   If a person already feels that he has enough consonant information, dissonant information will be seen as extra information that will not appear to be oriented toward threatening his cognitive system. The system will be experienced as being stable enough as result of already having lots of information known to be consonant (see also Frey, 1981b, pp. 166–177).
    –   If a person finds himself already to be in an extremely intense state of cognitive dissonance, the person will be thinking of revising the decision. The revised version of the decision will then be able to process or lessen the effect of further dissonant information. Information that is dissonant with regard to the original decision is at the same time consonant with the revised decision. This approach corresponds with the situation in Figure 4.1 to the right of the intersection of both curves. A situation where a revision of the decision is considered possible is a prerequisite for this effect. If a revision does not seem to be possible, then even in the face of increasing dissonance, consonant information will continue to be searched for in order to alleviate the dissonance. The aspect being discussed here can without qualification be equated to striving for consonance.

Frey et al. (1982) have associated the theory of selective search for information with the theory of cognitive dissonance toward the end of modifying the fundamentals of Festinger's (1957) theory with regard to the following conditions.

- Given intense enough trust in consonant information people feel safe enough to process dissonant information.
- If it is anticipated that dissonant information will be disproved, then this information is sympathetic to the goal of consonance.
- If there is a high degree of perceived utility for it, then the gathering of information will be assessed more highly than the dissonance thereby triggered, an assumption here being that the dissonant information is possessed with a high degree of believability.
- In the case of extreme cognitive dissonance and of possible action revision, dissonant information will be consonant with the action revision, and may trigger the latter.

The mechanisms detailed above are compatible with the original consistency assumptions. They serve a person's striving for cognitive equilibrium. Essentially all of these cases have to do with two mechanisms of information gathering and processing:

1. Preference for information that is oriented toward reducing cognitive dissonance, toward bringing the given cognitive system into equilibrium, or toward maintaining it in a state of equilibrium.
2. Avoidance of information that is assessed as being oriented toward bringing the cognitive system out of equilibrium or toward intensifying an already existent disequilibrium.

Cognitive dissonance due to forced compliance

Occasionally situations arise where a person agrees to a viewpoint that does not actually reflect his or her true views, due more or less to social pressure. On the one hand the person experiences self cognitions (opinions, perceptions) and on the other hand observes his own behavior, which he sees is in opposition to his opinions or perceptions. Both types of cognition clearly stand in a dissonant relation to each other. How people cognitively react in this situation is the subject matter of the forced compliance paradigm (Festinger, 1957, p. 84). A person can be made to engage in a dissonant public stating of opinion via threat of punishment or by being offered rewards.

The felt dissonance intensity depends first of all on the importance of the given opinion, and secondly on the extent of the reward or punishment. These interrelationships are illustrated in Figure 4.2.

In the left hand area of the three curves there is as yet no expression of self-contradictory opinion; the reward or possible punishment is not high enough to trigger it. As a result of a reward being offered or of the fact that a punishment may have to be endured, cognitive dissonance arises, which can be reduced by insisting all the more strongly on one's opinion, the extent of this more intense expression increasing proportionately to the increase in the extent of the offered reward or threatened punishment. The situation "turns on its head" the moment the person displays the given self-contradictory behavior

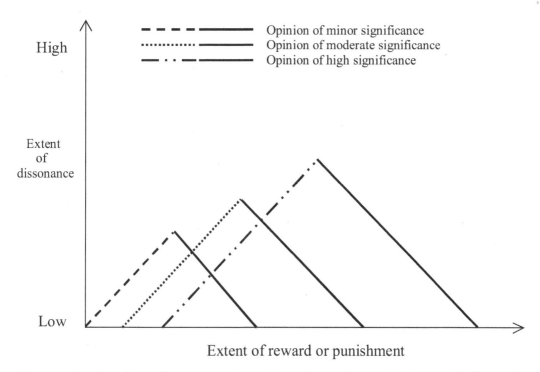

Figure 4.2   Cognitive dissonance due to forced compliance (Festinger, 1957, p. 93)

(that is, which contradicts the person's opinion or idea of what is correct or advantageous). Now the person does not have to contend with justifying the consequences of avoiding the self-contradictory behavior, but instead has to justify the self-contradictory behavior that she is now displaying. If the reward is very high, or the threatened punishment very intense, then the person, by considering the radical consequences, can easily justify her self-contradictory behavior. The person may take on a contract that goes against their own opinion, but the financial reward is high. If the financial reward is high enough, the person will have very little pressure to justify themselves. They will find themselves on the right side of the curve.

Seen from the right, the curve proceeds to the point of highest dissonance, which has been triggered by the decrease in reward or threat of punishment. The person has displayed the self-contradictory behavior, but in return has received an ever lower reward or has avoided an increasingly minor punishment, whereby in both cases it is enough to trigger the self-contradictory behavior. Viewed from the right, finding themselves just before the peak point in the situation of highest cognitive dissonance, the person has to justify to themself the self-contradictory behavior they have displayed, with regard to having received a relatively low reward or having avoided a relatively minor punishment. This can now be reduced insofar as the person's opinion begins to match his outwardly expressed behavior. As dissonance increases, so does conformance of outwardly expressed behavior to the person's actual opinion (viewed from the right). In contrast, as viewed from the left, the person's insistence on their own opinion increases along with their rejection of the pressure to display behavior which contradicts this opinion.

The three curves shift to the right as the significance of the opinion increases because this increasing significance entails that the extent of the reward or threat of punishment must also increase in order to trigger behavior which contracts the opinion. Also according to Festinger's approach the experienced cognitive dissonance is more intense, pointing to the fact that the peak point of more significant opinions is higher and therefore so is the possible extent of experienced cognitive dissonance.

Cognitive dissonance and the search for social support

People are more likely to believe themselves to be in the right, the more other people there are of like mind. Perceiving that another person holds a differing opinion can trigger cognitive dissonance, therefore people seek social support for their opinions (Festinger, 1957, p. 177). However, Festinger holds that there is also an additional range of objective factors: "To the extent that objective, nonsocial, cognitive elements exist which are consonant with a given opinion, belief, or knowledge, the expression of disagreement will produce a lesser magnitude of dissonance" (Festinger, 1957, p. 179). According to Irle's (1975, 1978) subsequent reformulation this thesis cannot be maintained. Dissonance intensity and the question of which cognitions it involves, do not have anything to do with the question of so-called objective or social factors.

The intensity of cognitive dissonance that arises depends on how relevant the given opinion is for the respective people or groups. The extent of cognitive dissonance is determined by the consensus of opinions of these people with regard to the perceived competence, attractiveness, and by the experienced significance (of the opinion in question). If a divergent opinion is held by experts (competence), or by good friends (attractiveness), then the experienced dissonance is relatively high. Whether or not a high degree of dissonance is encountered within a group depends on group cohesion and on the importance of the opinion for that group.

Cognitive dissonance can be reduced by adapting one's opinion to that of others, or by attempting to persuade the other people to conform to one's own opinion. The divergent opinion held by others can also be devalued, or the subject matter of the opinion can be devalued as far as its relevance or importance is concerned. The subject matter of the opinion will be devalued when those holding it cannot be won over and yet display a high degree of attractiveness. In the case of both a high degree of opinion significance and of attractiveness on the part of those who hold the opinion, as a reaction to experienced cognitive dissonance an adaptation to the divergent opinion is likely. Furthermore, in this context dissonance will be reduced or avoided by choosing to communicate with people who share one's opinion. And finally there will also be the above described selective gathering of information (avoidance of dissonant and search for consonant information).

The communication within groups can also be explained according to the striving for social support. A person is more likely to communicate with other group members (who express divergent opinions), the more he expects them to be able to adapt to the group opinion, the more important the person is as a member of the group, the greater the divergence of opinion is, the more important the given opinion is for the group, and the more important the group or group cohesion is for its members (Irle, 1993).

We can establish that in general people look for social support of their opinions and that the tendency is to attempt to win over those who hold divergent opinions. One can also attempt to win over people for whom the given opinion subject matter is in no way relevant, in which case it will be relatively easy to obtain agreement (Festinger, 1957, p. 191).

The factor of seeking social support by way of reducing cognitive dissonance is also used by Festinger (1957, pp. 196–204) to elucidate mass behavior. An assumption here is that there be a mass of people who share the same psychic situation and all experience the same cognitive dissonance: Rumors, mass hysteria, mass proselytism, simultaneous faulty perception on behalf of many people which is pointed out as being such, and also the fear of many people in a region with regard to imminent catastrophe, when there is no objectively substantiated reason for it (ibid., p. 238).

IRLE'S REFORMULATION (1975, 1978)

Festinger's approach is expressly oriented toward the phases that follow actions. According to Irle's (1975, pp. 310–346 and 1978, pp. 98–303) reformulation of the theory however, actions are included as a sufficient condition, but are by no means viewed as a necessary condition for the occurrence of cognitive dissonance. Irle does not fundamentally distinguish between actions and cognitive decisions.

Similar to the hypothesis theory of social perception, in Irle's reformulated theory of cognitive dissonance, reality is thought to be perceived according to (already) existent assumptions, value systems, experiences, or basically according to existent cognitions of any kind. We can also consider these to be hypotheses held by the person. People's perception, taken as a whole, can be understood to be an ongoing process of establishing, verifying, and altering of hypotheses, which is certainly analogous to the process of seeking scientific insight.

All people operate according to subjective hypotheses that explain the relationships between two cognitions on the one hand, and on the other hand the individual cognitions are also subjective hypotheses. a) A relationship between two hypotheses might be: "If someone tries hard he will achieve his goal". A hypothesized relationship between striving and achieving success has been established. b) A single subjective hypothesis (as a cognition) might read: "All swans are white". This person will therefore experience cognitive dissonance if he has to experience a case where he or someone else tries hard and then does not achieve success, or if the person sees a black swan for the first time. The following mechanisms are conceivable as means for reducing cognitive dissonance (while not claiming it as a complete list ...):

a) Downplaying the stress
    – Retrospectively formulating a new goal.
    – Assuming that "actually" the goal was not desired in the first place.
    – Postulating disruptive factors that in this case explain the relationship between striving and achieving of the goal.
    – The silliest possible statement is adopted, namely that of "the exception confirms the rule".
b) The person assumes that there has been an error in perception
    – He decides that this animal cannot be a swan, since swans are white of course.

Any of people's perceptual behaviors can be understood to be an instance of subjective hypothesis testing. The statement that everything people perceive represents an instance of hypothesis verification corresponds with science's critical rationalism mindset. This certainly does not mean that people themselves experience their perceptual behavior as an instance of hypothesis testing, which consequently leads to merely operating according to assumed knowledge. In reality private citizens, scientists, politicians, and managers conduct themselves according to affirmed items of knowledge on the basis of their perceptions. That this approach may not be logically and empirically consistent with reality is a practically irrefutable meta-statement, which however is not understood by the majority of people.

For Irle cognitive dissonance takes place when a person encounters two cognitions which are logically inconsistent, but between which there is a connection. This felt connection is a third cognition necessary for the arising of cognitive dissonance. The psychological inconsistency of cognitions that are seen to be in connection with each other (but which however need not stand in a logical relationship to each other) can result from facts or values. Cognitive dissonance arises whenever a person apprehends an item of information which, and on the basis of their hypotheses, "the person cannot or may not localize within himself" (Irle, 1978, p. 300).

This can be expressed formally in the following way: People have formed the hypothesis that if set of conditions X (as the first cognition) is encountered, then another set of conditions Y will also be encountered (as the second cognition) and therefore a third cognition will be adhered to with regard to the relationship between X and Y. This is labeled as cognition Z. Students might adhere to cognition X: "I will be well prepared for the examination", and then (as consequence X) "I will therefore do well in the examination" (cognition Y). The assumed relationship between effort and result is cognition Z. Professors might adhere to the following X cognition: "I teach courses well" and then (as a consequence of X) "therefore good students will pass the examinations" (cognition Y). The hypothesized relationship Z is that good examination results of good students are a consequence of "brilliantly taught" courses. These cognitive mini systems are consonant with others, like where students assume that they will not do well if they are not well prepared (formally: NON-X is consonant with NON-Y). The hypothesized relationship Z is that of poor preparation being the cause of doing poorly in examinations (formal again NON-X is consonant with NON-Y). The hypothesized relationship Z arises from the assumption that "bad" students are the cause of poor examination performance, where "bad" is understood in the sense of motivation and capacity.

Irle's (1975, p. 312) exact proposition reads: "Whenever any two X and Y cognitions that are encountered in the same space and time can be explained by person P's hypothesis, there exists a relationship of cognitive consonance. Whenever any two cognitions X and NON-Y (or NON-X and Y) that are encountered in the same space and time contradict a given person's hypothesis ..., cognitive dissonance arises".

Thus far the theory of cognitive dissonance according to Irle has been viewed as an expansion of Festinger's theory. It does not just have to do with explaining information gathering and processing after decisions. A person who makes a decision continuously finds himself simultaneously in a before and after decision phase. In order to make this clearer we will examine a simple decision process.

Figure 4.3   Consonant cognitive systems in the theory of cognitive dissonance according to Irle (1975, 1978)

Figure 4.4   Dissonant cognitive systems in the theory of cognitive dissonance according to Irle (1975, 1978)

The formulation of a problem is a first decision, and the decision of what information should be gathered is a further decision. Also underlying the decision is the choice with regard to formulating alternatives. The assessment of alternatives assumes that the assessment criteria have been decided in advance. It is certainly undeniable that the choice of alternatives also entails other decisions: When should the decision be taken, what is being decided about (the choice of alternatives, whether further information should be gathered, whether the problem should be scrutinized again, who should undertake the implementation)? The same goes for the phase of realization. The testing phase also includes detailed decisions: When should the testing take place, according to what standards of measurement, how often, with what methods? Every individual element of the decision-making process presents its own decision-making process, which again càn be divided into a never ending process of further decision-making processes. Festinger only focuses on the phase after the choice of alternatives. Irle demonstrates that we always find ourselves both before and after decisions at the same time, in other words continuously occupied with processing, avoiding, or reducing cognitive dissonance. In this way the reformulated theory of cognitive dissonance has become a very comprehensive theory of information processing.

Along with his expansion of the theory of cognitive dissonance's applicability, Irle's approach involves at the samé time a fine tuning of propositions. Theses with regard to dissonance intensity and resistance to change are established.

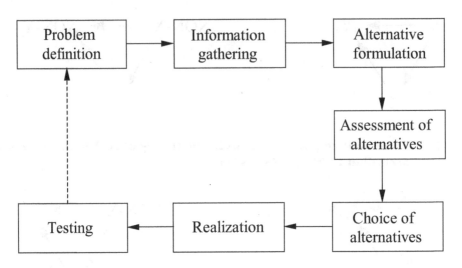

Figure 4.5   Decision process

- Dissonance intensity.

As Festinger has already demonstrated, dissonance intensity determines the intensity of the attempt to eliminate or at least reduce the dissonance.

According to Festinger (1957, p. 8) dissonance intensity depends on two factors:

a) The significance of the given decision; the more important the decision is, the more intense is the subsequent dissonance.

b) The relative attractiveness of the rejected alternative; the more attractive the characteristics of this option are, the greater the dissonance. It can also be assumed that the dissonance is greater, the more (possibly unavoidable) deficiencies the chosen alternative displays (which likewise increases the attractiveness of the rejected alternative).

Dissonance intensity according to Irle (1975, p. 13; 1978, p. 300) and Frey et al. (1982, p. 309) is determined by subjective certainty which the given person has with regard to the truth of his or her hypothesis concerning the relationship between X and Y (and the non-occurrence of X with NON-Y or NON-X with Y). The experienced intensity of dissonance is a function of experienced hypothesis certainty. The more intense the dissonance is experienced to be, the stronger the motivation toward dissonance reduction.

Subjective certainty depends on the frequency with which a hypothesis has been confirmed in the past. The more often a person has found a hypothesis to be confirmed, and the more seldom it has been refuted, the more certain he is that the hypothesis is correct.

Subjective certainty is also triggered by observing other people. The more there are other people who hold this hypothesis, the more likely it is that this hypothesis will be believed.

Furthermore, we can speculate as to how much the subjectively experienced importance of a cognitive system's consonance (X, Y and hypothesized relationship Z) influences the intensity of experienced dissonance and therefore also the motivation to reduce dissonance.

- Change resistance.

In the reformulated theory of cognitive dissonance it is assumed that the people involved in dissonance reduction proceed according to a principle of cognitive efficiency. According to this theory, a cognition (X, NON-Y, or Z) will be changed, where change will bring the least amount of additional disturbance within the cognitive system. The problem is again that the involved cognitions (X, Y, or Z) can all be connected with other cognitions. Therefore if one of the involved cognitions is altered, then it will become dissonant in relation to other cognitions.

Like in the following example: A person has the following cognitions: "I understand something about cars" (cognition X) which is connected (cognition Z) to "the PKW-model I'm going to buy is going to be good" (cognition Y).

The person now has to find out that the auto they have bought has a whole list of problems.

They could change cognition X, but that would perhaps mean placing their entire self concept in question, and they would furthermore suffer a loss of face in their circle of friends (at least they may fear that), because they have often presented themselves as an expert on cars. The fact that they have chosen the particular car (Z) can hardly be denied. Perhaps when objectively considered another person has had, to a negligible extent, some influence. Whether the person discards cognition Z, by ascribing the blame to the other person, may depend on the particular relationship shared by these people. The person can certainly reinterpret the quality characteristics of the car in retrospect (where this is oriented toward alleviating the perceived deficiencies in their subjective view). Perhaps the idea will be embraced that it is a production error, just as there is a 1:1,000 chance with any brand that one will have bad luck, and then the garage can be praised for the manner in which it again and again eliminates the problems.

A cognition is all the more resistant to change, the more relationships to other cognitions it has for the given person (Irle, 1975, p. 316; 1978, p. 302; Frey et al., 1982, p. 305). In other words the change is caught up with the rest of the cognitive system, involving a highly networked cognition representing more significant complexity than a less networked cognition. A highly networked cognition is for example the commitment to a belief or to an ideology that may play a central role in a person's life, toward which actions, commitments, and desires of all kinds are oriented. By contrast dissonance from the purchase of cheap quality goods can possibly be relatively easily reduced through the devaluation of product characteristics (accepting a mistaken purchase). These kinds of cognitions do not play as significant a role in a person's life as do the above indicated kinds. Next time, another brand's product will be purchased. The same way of proceeding is not as easily engaged in with regard to products of high value, because going back on the action is connected with greater expenditure.

"If a cognitive unit is in a state of cognitive dissonance then, independent from the intensity of cognitive dissonance, and toward the end of reducing cognitive dissonance, that cognition will be changed, the changing of which will require the least expenditure of psychic effort" (Irle, 1975, p. 316). A cognition will be changed if the cognitive dissonance that has arisen is greater than the resistance to changing the given cognition.

If this is the case with regard to more than one cognition within the cognitive unit (X, Y—or NON-X, NON-Y—and Z) then that cognition will be changed which most easily satisfies the dictates of this relation.

In this context the construct "commitment" is introduced. What is meant by it is the fact that cognitions will be more resistant to change, the more the given person feels that they are bound to these cognitions. The measure of how bound a person is to a given matter is what is meant by commitment. It will be helpful here to mention the concept of the "zone of tolerance" developed by Liljander and Strandvik (1995). The zone of tolerance is the accepted level of variation in performance levels that are tolerated. The zone of tolerance is increased by the presence of bonds. Bonds are things that increase the probability of continuing a relationship, and can be for legal, geographical, cultural, economic, or psychological reasons. For example, if a person has come out in public for a particular brand it will be significantly more difficult for them to let go of their opinion, even in the case of intensely felt cognitive dissonance, especially if consumption is not taking place in an exclusively private, non-public sphere.

Let's assume that after thorough but not conclusive examinations, a doctor inwardly settles on a diagnosis. Will they engage in subsequent examinations in an unbiased manner? They have tentatively let a colleague that they are friends with know what they suspect, and subsequently they also tells several other colleagues. We have now become aware of several cumulative levels of commitments. How will later, in-depth results that contradict the original diagnosis be assessed?

THE BALANCE THEORY ACCORDING TO HEIDER (1958)

In conclusion we will examine Heider's balance theory (1958, 1977, 1988), which seems relevant here although it is not necessarily considered to fit within the confines of the theory of cognitive dissonance.

Why do people develop mutual sympathy, feel affection toward, share similar preferences, in musical, fashion and in other directions? Why do we begin liking a given brand when an amiable star publicly displays preference for it, even when this is "only" experienced through the medium of an advertisement, or via sponsoring? Why, conversely, is it difficult to like a product that is also liked by a person we are not attracted to? In the language of dissonance theory people undergo cognitive dissonance when they apprehend that objects that they do not like are highly valued by others, or on the other hand when others do not like objects that they themselves highly value. The situation becomes more intense when the possible relationships between people are included. It will appear more serious if P establishes that another person that P really likes does not share their views about whatever object, than if that other person is someone they dislike. From the possible relationships between two people and an object, eight model relationships can be derived, of which four are without tension, being according to Heider in a balanced state, and where four are in a state of unbalanced tension, again according to Heider. It can easily be seen that something that is a matter of opinion can also serve as an object between two people.

We can easily imagine a state in which P1 apprehends that another person P2 likes the same object (O). Equally straightforward is a situation where a person likes an object, and apprehends that another person (P2) does not like the object, but where this person is disliked by P1, perhaps as a consequence of that person not liking the object,

Balanced states

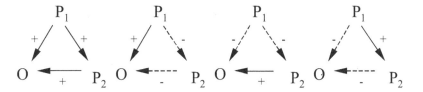

Unbalanced states

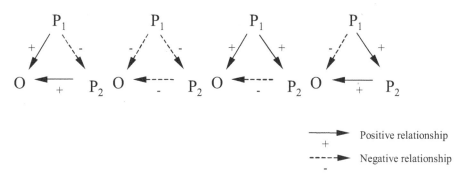

Figure 4.6   Balanced and unbalanced situations according to Heider (1958, 1977, 1988)

and toward the end of reducing cognitive dissonance. The third situation is one where P1 dislikes P2 as well as disliking the object, the subject of opinion, and at the same time apprehends that P2 likes the object. The fourth situation involves two people, P1 and P2 in a positive relationship, who both dislike an object. In general all balanced states can be viewed as consequences of dissonance reduction after experiencing the following unbalanced states.

A situation is unbalanced when P1 finds out that a disliked person P2 shares one of his preferences: The same music is liked, membership in the same club is shared, etc. Equally unbalanced is a situation where someone we are very fond of, really likes something we have rejected, or conversely, when a person we are very fond of rejects an object we really like. The last unbalanced state is one where we apprehend that a person we dislike shares with us aversion for an object.

In general, whenever we perceive difference of opinion with people who we like, an unbalanced state arises, likewise when we perceive that we share the same opinion with people we have rejected. An unproblematic situation is one where we share the same opinion with people we like or one where we have a difference of opinion with people we dislike.

Final remarks concerning the theory

The theory of cognitive dissonance is considered to be one the most significant of social psychological theories (Aronson, 1992), which has spurred a very large quantity of empirical studies and which has undergone a great many reformulations, of which we have only been able to examine a few. It is true though, that Joule and Beauvois (1998) have come up with a radical perspective: They believe that they can reject all (!) reformulations and can go back to Festinger's (1957) original version. In doing this they also reject Heider's (1958, 1977 and 1988) theory and Irle's (1978) reformulation, as well as all of Frey's (among others, 1979, 1981a and 1981b) empirical studies having to do with selective (and thereby relevant to dissonance theory) information gathering.

Aronson (1994, p. 194) identifies behavior "that is directed toward dissonance reduction as irrational". It is maladjusted in that it hinders a person from "experiencing important things or from finding an actual solution to a problem". Basically many cognitive theories within social psychology explain how people ignore, adapt, distort, or just in general irrationally process information. That is true of cognitive emotion theory, of attribution theory, the theory of social perception, the theory of social comparison, etc. That does not mean that human behavior proceeds on a fundamentally irrational basis, but it does mean that a large portion of it does.

Applications

MARKETING

The significance of the theory of cognitive dissonance for marketing has already been shown in the accentuation of post purchase advertising, or in general in the customer's information processing in the post purchase phase (see Raffée, Sauter and Silberer, 1973, pp. 75–79). It is not just about winning over new customers via advertising; it also has to do with strengthening the trust people have in the characteristics of products they have already bought. We can assume that people will tend to close out advertisement of certain brands and that they will tend to avoid the advertisements of other brands (see Frey, 1981, p. 284). The focus is not just on advertising as an instrument of marketing communication. Cognitive dissonance can play a role in all areas of marketing communication.

A further important area of application is social marketing. In this connection Frey (1981a, p. 285) points out examples of communication measures in the area of health marketing. A lot of information having to do with looking into cancer or other ailments gets caught up with avoidance mechanisms on the part of the target groups. Unsavory information about threats to health may be devalued or deemed by a person to be irrelevant. This kind of information can be presented in such a way as to make avoidance seem impossible. Avoidance mechanisms can be removed in that the utility and believability of dissonant information can be so presented as to make avoidance more difficult than observing it. In any case, as plausible as it may be, we cannot assume that useful information will automatically be meaningfully processed.

"The foot in the door" technique is relevant in the context of charity marketing, which can also be explained through cognitive dissonance. If one wants to spur people on to make a donation, success will come more readily if those people have already been persuaded to do some small favor like for example wearing a pin or signing a petition (see Aronson, 1994, p. 201). Whoever has already taken a small first step will experience dissonance when they avoid taking a bigger step. As an initial effort therefore, systematic charity marketing needs to get the target group to perform some easily done task. Additionally, many charity groups are now sending letters requesting donations to people which include free address labels, or even a free nickel to induce a response by the recipient.

PERSONNEL MANAGEMENT

Apart from sales marketing, another area of application for dissonance theory is personnel management. Dissonance theory is relevant in personnel decisions and in the subsequent performance assessments. During job interviews a first impression may lead to performance relevant characteristics being correspondingly perceived. Frey and Irle (1993, p. 306) show that the choice of questions is configured such that consonant results are sought. A comparable situation is that of oral exams in universities and in other areas of education.

In personnel politics there are consequences as far as the perception of performance of other people is concerned. This perception might for example be influenced to the extent that management has or has not already established a "diagnosis" with regard to a person's performance capacity. On the other hand employees might perceive and assess management behavior on the basis of already established diagnoses. Furthermore managers should be aware of the fact that all personnel political decision mechanisms proceed according to the theory of cognitive dissonance. Why is it that managers again and again feel themselves confirmed in their assumptions with regard to the performance motivation of individual employees? Every perception that contradicts their assumption is an instance where cognitive dissonance is experienced. This dissonance can easily be reduced by reinterpreting the perception ... In everyday life, the proposition "the exception proves the rule" is an often heard excuse for the irrational treatment of information that goes against one's own assumptions. In reality this is nothing more than an almost typical mechanism for the reduction of cognitive dissonance.

Sets of conditions relevant to dissonance theory are also found in other areas related to personnel management: Let's assume that as a test it is decided (and approved) that a university (or college within a university) will itself select a part of its new students using its own selection procedures or tests, the other part being selected according to the usual comparison of final marks before entering university. Subsequently it is in fact established that the students who have been selected by the university itself achieve better marks. If students who have been selected do well then this represents a sought for state of consonance for the professors, whereas if these selected students do badly, that would represent a state of dissonance: The universities' approach has perhaps not proved itself, or the professors' choice was in error, etc. This dissonance can be avoided right from the beginning if the students achieve good results. As an outgrowth of this the professors, on the basis of their expectations, will regard these students with positive expectations. These expectations influence the professors' behavior and moreover also influence the behavior of the students. People tend to behave in the way they believe they are expected to behave. Both the slightly different behavior of the professors (which can be completely understood as a search for dissonance avoidance) and the consequent performance oriented behavior on behalf of the students, lead to desired (consonant) states.

The total field of people's performance perception on higher, the same, or lower hierarchical levels can be explained according to the theory of cognitive dissonance: People perceive performance on the basis of given hypotheses, hypotheses which have a tendency of becoming self-fulfilling prophesy.

The fact that managers have to make uncomfortable decisions due to apparent pressing circumstances, for example layoffs or avoidance of employees' desires for raises or advancement, is a factor that can be explained via the forced compliance paradigm. Over time such managers adapt their inner attitudes to suit the given decisions and begin to believe in the corresponding pressing circumstances. They often lose sight of the fact they are themselves employees. It cannot go unrecognized "that status and changes of role, like for example promotion into a management position due to change of tasks and new expectations with regard to the person holding a position, often leads to self-contradictory behavior. If for example a person earlier criticized the decisions of superiors, saw the personnel assessment system as unfair, and was lackadaisical with regard to company goals, now they might see the necessity to make decisions that affect themselves, like the decision to execute personnel assessments, or to take up company goals over those of subordinates." (Frey and Irle, 1993, p. 307). Furthermore managers often view their management style as being much more employee oriented and decentralized than it is in reality, and conversely the "managed" may perceive management style as much less employee oriented and decentralized than it actually is. In this way the theory of cognitive dissonance can also explain inner organizational socialization processes.

It is also supposed that employees assess pay and performance level from a dissonance point of view. An income that is too high will create stress if performance level is perceived to be too low, and by no means automatically leads to an increase in performance, not even leading to the intent to increase performance. An income that is too low leads to performance that is appropriate for that level of income, thereby attaining consonance, that is, reducing dissonance.

Another relevant field of human behavior in this context is that of management decisions (not just in commercial oriented organizations). We continuously have to make decisions, are continuously oriented toward perceiving and processing information in a consistent fashion. That goes for personnel decisions, purchase decisions, strategy decisions and for many other areas.

An example of a purchase decision may serve to illustrate: A person P1 is a purchaser in a company and has been buying product X for years. Salesman P2 has been trying for years to sell Product Y to P1. The longer this state is maintained, the more unlikely it becomes that P2 will have success, no matter so plausible and thorough P2's arguments may be: Y is more economical and superior in quality. Of course P1 has to own up (if only to himself) that he has been conducting himself incompetently for a long period of time. All pro-Y arguments trigger cognitive dissonance in P1, which becomes all the more intense, the longer he maintains his stance. Since the motivation to reduce cognitive dissonance correspondingly increases, it is more and more to be expected that P1 will reduce cognitive dissonance by devaluing the information being received from P2. This is relatively easy to do, because P2 will be experienced as the salesman who is just seeking his own advantage.

P2 has to restructure the situation such that P1 can alter his behavior without having to suffer cognitive dissonance. P2 could for example make the following argument: "We know that you have been buying product X for years and that of course you have your reasons for doing that, but at this point we've improved the quality, have redone advertisements in publications and on TV, and as an introduction into the new improvements, there is a special discount. Apart from that we're also offering a higher participation in your advertising costs." Now P1 can change his purchasing behavior without having to own up that for years that he has been buying the "wrong" product. He is much more likely to avail himself of the new opportunity (as long as it's profitable!).

We can see from this example that suppliers have to engage in a decision-making process as soon as possible, ideally the moment the problem is seen. If a decision for the competitor has already been made, or if purchasing activities are already taking place, then it is more and more difficult to alter the decision. Furthermore after a purchase decision the customer's personal responsibility for the purchase decision can become highlighted, so that later it is all the more difficult to acknowledge an incorrect decision, and also the greater the motivation will be for the customer to justify his purchase decision. This also naturally shows that changing personnel is always a risk for the supplier, in that it makes it easier for customers to go back on decisions.

COGNITIVE DISSONANCE AND THE SEARCH FOR INSIGHT

In the area of scientific work there is also a comprehensive field of application for the theory of cognitive dissonance. The variety and quantity of scientific publications is now enormous and is based on selective information gathering. Just like other people, scientists tend to view information preferentially, favoring information that supports their hypotheses and theories. In empirical research too, scientists are more likely to highly assess results that confirm their hypotheses than results that tend to refute them. People (including non-scientists) tend in general to exaggerate the diagnostic value of "hypothesis-friendly" information and to underestimate hypothesis contradicting information (empirical evidence for this is delivered by Pitz et al., 1967). In the area of science we can protect ourselves from these effects (although never with certainty) by testing strictly against our own hypotheses. As long as no success is had in refuting our hypotheses, we can maintain our original hypotheses. This methodology, as known within critical rationalism, can be translated into the area of management as critically rational management (see Krasser, 1995). People outside of the scientific domain can also experience their knowledge as hypotheses, thereby seeking insight, in that they can try to work against their hypotheses, rather than continuously trying to confirm them. Our world is so complex that finding confirmation for even the most unlikely assumption can be completely successful (perhaps only apparently). Rational people accept that advancement of insight is possible through recognizing our errors. This proposition is known as consequential fallibility and applies to both science and practice equally (see Albert, 1978).

A whole range of other theories from within the field of social psychology elucidate conditions that can be completely explained by dissonance theory. As an example we can mention attribution theory: Why do people attribute their own success more to personality characteristics, and their lack of success more to outer circumstances? Why do they conduct themselves with regard to other people in exactly the opposite way?

Success is then explained by outer circumstances, and lack of success via personality characteristics, like for example inadequate motivation. One's own lack of success stands in a dissonant relationship to self-image. Whoever operates according to a somewhat success oriented self-image, can in the case of lack of success downplay the problem through perception of external circumstances. Attribution theories are partly a special case of dissonance theory.

In the following chapter, the theory of psychological reactance will be explained. This has to do with reactions toward perceived constriction of freedom, for example through communication. This theory has a close relationship to the theory of cognitive dissonance. Is not the perception of constriction to freedom dissonant to the striving for areas of freedom? Is it not also possible to understand the striving against threats to freedom as a process of reducing cognitive dissonance?

QUESTIONS FOR DISCUSSION

1. Explain the theory of cognitive dissonance, how it occurs, and how it can be avoided.
2. Provide an example of Heider's Balance Theory as it relates to your organization or university.
3. Discuss Irle's reformulation and take a position on whether you feel that the theory is valid.
4. Do we live in an age of consonance? Take a position and cite examples from business, popular media, and your personal experiences.

Bibliography

Aronson, E.: *The Social Animal*. San Francisco: 1992.

Aronson, E.: *Sozialpsychologie—Menschliches Verhalten und gesellschaftlicher Einfluß*. Heidelberg, Berlin, Oxford: 1994. (*Social Psychology—Human Behavior and Social Influence*).

Albert, H.: *Traktat über rationale Praxis*. Tübingen: 1978. (*Treatise on Rational Practice*).

Brock, T.C.: Commitment to exposure as a determinant of information receptivity. *Journal of Personality and Social Psychology*, 1965, 2, 10–19.

Eckensberger, L.H. (ed.): *Bericht über den 31. Kongreß der Deutschen Gesellschaft für Psychologie in Mannheim 1978*, vol. 1, Göttingen, Toronto, Zürich: 1979. (*Report on the 31st Congress of the German Company for Psychology in Mannheim 1978*).

Ehrlich, D., Guttmann, I., Schönbach, P. and Mills, J.: Postdecision exposure to relevant information, *Journal of Abnormal and Social Psychology*, 1957, 54, 98–102.

Feather, N.T.: Cigarette smoking and lung cancer: A study of cognitive dissonance. *Australian Journal of Psychology*, 1962, 14, 55–64.

Festinger, L.: *A Theory of Cognitive Dissonance*. Stanford: 1957.

—— *Conflict, Decision, and Dissonance*. Stanford: 1964.

—— and Walster, E.: Post-decision regret and decision reversal. In: Festinger, L.: *Conflict, Decision, and Dissonance*, Stanford: 1964, 100–112.

Frey, D.: Zwei aktuelle Forschungsrichtungen in der dissonanztheorie: "Selective exposure to information" and "Misattribution of arousal". In: Eckensberger, L.H. (eds): *Bericht über den 31.*

Kongreß der Deutschen Gesellschaft für Psychologie in Mannheim 1978, vol. 1, Göttingen, Toronto, Zürich: 1979, 362–364. (Two current research directions in dissonance theory: "Selective exposure to information" and "Misattribution of arousal". In *Report on the 31st Congress of the German Company for Psychology in Mannheim 1978*).

—— Postdecisional preference for decision-relevant information as a function of the competence of its source and the degree of familiarity with this information. *Journal of Experimental Social Psychology*, 1981a, 17, 51–67.

—— *Informationssuche und Informationsbewertung bei Entscheidungen.* Bern, Stuttgart, Wien: 1981b. (*Information which is Sought and Information Estimation in Decisions*).

——, Irle, M., Möntmann, V., Kumpf, M., Ochsmann, R. and Sauer, C.: Cognitive dissonance: Experiments and theory. In: Irle, M. (ed.): *Studies in Decision Making—Social Psychological and Socio-Economic Analyses.* Berlin, New York: 1982, 281–310.

—— and Benning, E.: *Informationssuche von Konsumenten nach Entscheidungen.* Marketing, ZFP, 1984, 6, 107–113. (*Information that is Sought from Consumer to Decisions*).

—— and Gaska, A.: Die theorie der kognitiven dissonanz. In: Frey, D. and Irle, M. (eds): *Theorien der Sozialpsychologie, vol. 1: Kognitive Theorien* (2nd edn). Bern, Göttingen, Toronto, Seattle: 1993, 275–326. (The theory of cognitive dissonance. In *Theories of Social Psychology, vol. 1: Cognitive Theories*).

—— and Irle, M. (eds): *Theorien der Sozialpsychologie, vol. 1: Kognitive Theorien* (2nd edn). Bern, Göttingen, Toronto, Seattle: 1993. (*Theories of Social Psychology, vol. 1: Cognitive Theories*).

—— and Irle, M. (eds): *Theorien der Sozialpsychologie, vol. 2: Gruppen- und Lerntheorien* (2nd edn). Bern, Göttingen, Toronto, Seattle: 1993. (*Theories of Social Psychology, vol. 2: Group Theories and Trained Theories*).

Heider, F.: *The Psychology of Interpersonal Relations.* New York: 1958.

—— *Psychologie der Interpersonellen Beziehungen.* Stuttgart: 1977. (*Psychology of Interpersonal Relations*).

—— *The Notebooks* (edited by Marjiane Benesh-Weiner), vol. 4. *Balance Theory.* München, Weinheim: 1988.

Irle, M.: *Lehrbuch der Sozialpsychologie.* Göttingen, Toronto, Zürich: 1975. (*Textbook of Social Psychology*).

—— Die Theorie der kognitiven dissonanz: Ein resümee ihrer theoretischen entwicklung und empirischen ergebnisse, 1. Theorie. In: Irle, M. and Möntmann, V. (eds): *Leon Festinger, Theorie der Kognitiven Dissonanz.* Bern, Stuttgart, Wien: 1978, 274–303. (The theory of cognitive dissonance: A resume of its theoretical development and empirical results, 1st theory. In *Leon Festinger, Theory of Cognitive Dissonance*).

—— (ed.): *Studies in Decision Making—Social Psychological and Socio-Economic Analyses.* Berlin, New York: 1982.

—— Konvergenz und divergenz in gruppen. In: Frey, D. and Irle, M. (eds): *Theorien der Sozialpsychologie, vol. 2: Gruppen- und Lerntheorien* (2nd edn). Bern, Göttingen, Toronto, Seattle: 1993, 39–64. (Convergence and divergence in groups. In *Theories of Social Psychology, vol. 2: Group Theories and Trained Theories*).

—— and Möntmann, V. (eds): *Leon Festinger, Theorie der Kognitiven Dissonanz.* Bern, Stuttgart, Wien: 1978. (*Leon Festinger, Theory of Cognitive Dissonance*).

Joule, R.-V. and Beauvois, J.-L.: Cognitive dissonance theory: A radical review. *European Review of Social Psychology*, 1998, 8, 1–32.

Krasser, N.: *Kritisch-rationales Management.* Wiesbaden: 1995. (*Criticisms of Rational Management*).

Liljander, V. and Strandvik, T.: The nature of relationships in services. *Advances in Services Marketing and Management*, 4, Greenwich, CT: 1995, p. 143.

Mills, J.: Avoidance of dissonant information. *Journal of Personality and Social Psychology*, 1965a, 2, 589–593.

——— Effect of certainty about a decision upon postdecision exposure to consonant and dissonant information. *Journal of Personality and Social Psychology*, 1965b, 2, 749–752.

Möntmann, V.: Die theorie der kognitiven dissonanz: Ein resümee ihrer theoretischen entwicklung und empirischen ergebnisse 1957–1976, 2. Empirische untersuchungen. In: Irle, M. and Möntmann, V. (eds): *Leon Festinger, Theorie der kognitiven dissonanz*. Bern, Stuttgart, Wien: 1978, 303–363. (The theory of cognitive dissonance: A resume of its theoretical development and empirical results 1957–1976, 2: Empirical investigations. In *Leon Festinger, Theory of Cognitive Dissonance*).

Pitz, G.F., Downing, L. and Reinhold, H.: Sequential effects in the revision of subjective probabilities. *Canadian Journal of Psychology*, 1967, 21, 381–393.

Raffée, H., Sauter, B. and Silberer, G.: *Theorie der Kognitiven Dissonanz und konsumgütermarketing*. Wiesbaden: 1973. (*Theory of Cognitive Dissonance and Consumer Goods Marketing*).

Walster, E.: The temporal sequence of post-decision processes. In: Festinger, L.: *Conflict, Decision, and Dissonance*. Stanford: 1964, 112–128.

5 *The Theory of Psychological Reactance*

Theory

The theory of psychological reactance is a motivation theory that describes how people react to perceived constriction of their freedom to act. Reactance is the motivation to reestablish constricted or eliminated freedom to act. Prerequisites for the arising of psychological reactance are a) to have the notion that one can operate according to the freedom to act, b) considering this freedom to act to be reasonably important, and c) perceiving threat to or the elimination of this freedom to act. The theory of psychological reactance can be traced back to Brehm (1966), and a new presentation of it is given by Dickenberger, Gniech and Grabitz (1993).

The freedom to act consists of all subjectively expected behavioral alternatives, regardless of whether these are actually available to the given person at the moment or in the future. The freedom to act does not therefore only consist of the freedom that the person actually possesses, but additionally consists of that freedom to act a person believes that they possess. Freedom is not just considered within the context of observed behavior. The freedom to hold certain opinions is also included.

POSSIBILITIES OF FREEDOM CONSTRICTION

A person's freedom can be constricted in that their spectrum of possible behaviors and opinions is cut back, in that certain alternatives are no longer available. A certain amount of freedom is lost. The other way that freedom can be constricted arises from a given person having modes of action or opinions imposed upon him or her.

To instantiate, three possibilities of threatening or eliminating freedom can be differentiated:

a) Social influence primarily involving communication.
b) Situationally determined circumstances and/or developments that do not directly have to do with the person.
c) The person's own behavior, that is, the decision for one alternative versus another one.

Social influence or communication will be experienced as constricting when it a) is seen as one-sided and unfair, b) the recipient of the communication assumes that the communication is systematically weighted with incorrect information that involves preferring the position of the sender of the communication, c) it entails consequences not comprehensible to the recipient, d) the intention to influence the recipient is recognized as exceeding a level acceptable to the recipient, and e) the sender of the communication can exercise a high degree of self-interest from the preferred position (Brehm, 1966, pp. 3–8). Every proposition a person may initiate, in order to execute certain actions, represents an attempt to constrict the freedom of action of the opposing side. The more intense this influence is perceived to be, the greater the reactance or resistance will be with regard to this influence.

Situationally determined circumstances that limit freedom through the physical unattainability of certain actions, may not be so relevant to marketing. In this context it could however be thought of as restrictive legislation with regard to, and as scarceness or expensiveness of products.

One's own decisions limit freedom because clearly by making a decision the number of previously existent decisions has been thereby constricted. Many decision-making weaknesses in management can be explained by this, as can decision-making weaknesses on behalf of customers in sales talks.

INTENSELY EXPERIENCED PSYCHOLOGICAL REACTANCE

It remains to be explained upon what the intensity of psychological reactance is dependent, together with the intensity of the motivation to reestablish threatened or eliminated freedom to act.

The intensity of psychological reactance is dependent upon conviction that freedom to act is possessed, on the importance, and on the extent freedom to act is restricted in relation to the amount of available alternatives (Brehm and Brehm, 1981, pp. 37–56).

Furthermore the intensity of reactance is influenced by the competence or expertise of the person being influenced. The more competent a person estimates themselves to be, the more sensitively they will react to attempts at influencing themselves and to possible constrictions of their freedom to make decisions. On the other hand, the more similar the influenced person perceives the alternative decisions to be, the less sensitively the person will react to freedom constricting attempts to influence him or her. In the case of very similar perceived alternatives freedom constricting communication will tend more to be understood as an aid to decision-making (Clee and Wicklund, 1980).

POSSIBLE REACTANCE EFFECTS

We come to possible effects of reactance, or in other words the question of in what ways people strive to reestablish freedom to act (Brehm and Brehm, 1981, pp. 98–117; Dickenberger, Gniech and Grabitz, 1993, pp. 247–254). Psychological reactance is a motivation to reestablish eliminated or threatened freedom and as such is deprived of direct observation. We cannot observe motivation, only consequences. For this reason a clear differentiation should be made between the existence of reactance effects and the existence of reactance. If no reactance effects can be observed that does not mean that no reactance is aroused. This is worth mentioning because reactance effects can also be encountered later than that point in time in which reactance has been aroused. The theory does not specify which reactance effects might arise, leaving all possibilities open. This means that reactance effects could include aggression displayed toward other people, for example, toward communicators, managers, institutions, or uninvolved people, or effects could take the form of simple physiological tension, which could partly be measured in the form of an increased pulse. Apart from these, changes in point of view are conceivable as a consequence of reactance. The prerequisite for encountering the reactance effects elucidated below is that the given person has learned in the past that they possess freedom. Consumers who have not learned in the past to choose between certain consumer goods will not experience reactance if they do not receive certain articles. This could be a case of lack of buying power for example. Brehm and Brehm (1981, pp. 98–117) supply the following classification of possible reactance effects:

1. Direct reestablishment of freedom via corresponding behavior.
2. Indirect reestablishment of freedom (implicit reestablishment of freedom).
3. Subjective responses (change of attraction, change of opinion).
4. Attempting to deny the recent freedom constriction, not taking responsibility for it.
5. Switching to another area of freedom, that is, that contains the same freedom value.

1. Engaging in behavior that appears to be the most effective way to reduce reactance, in defiance of constriction, threat or devaluation of freedom by other people. This alternative is available for acting on if the person is not faced with any or with not a sufficient degree of penalty threat. In the latter case the person will compare the attractiveness of the threatened mode of behavior with possible penalties they may be faced with if they engage in the behavior anyway. This is particularly the case in commercial marketing when reactance is triggered by marketing communications, because as a rule suppliers do not have power to impose penalties.

2. Often a direct reestablishment of freedom is not possible, or the consequences of doing so are seen as too prohibitive. Threatened freedom could then be reestablished via indirect actions: The affected person prompts other people to engage in the behavior.

An alternative to this is the formulation of the assumption that in similar situations in the future freedom will be exercised. This can be encountered for example when a buyer perceives a purchase decision to be settled. The no longer attainable alternative product thereby gains in attractiveness according to the assumptions of the theory of psychological reactance. According to the assumptions of the theory of cognitive dissonance a state will certainly come about via selective gathering and processing of information, whereby in the long run the chosen alternative will gain in appeal while the rejected alternative loses its appeal.

Let's take one of the animal fables of "Aesop" (a person associated with early Greek folk tales, in whose name over 500 fables were gathered). In one of these tales a hungry fox shows up, who is walking along a narrow pass, where he comes upon a bush with grapes that he would like to eat (foxes will also eat grapes and berries, and so on, in an emergency). Unfortunately he is unable to reach the branch, and in this Aesop fable the fox thinks to himself: "They're sour anyway", and goes grumpily on his way. This was a way of behaving similar to what dissonance theory predicts. From a dissonance theory point of view "it can't happen that I am unable to obtain something that I want". The dissonance that thereby arises when I want something but cannot have it can be reduced by devaluing the desired thing. From the point of view of reactance theory however the unobtainable grapes have to become increasingly attractive. Forbidden friends, toys, or fruits always have the tendency to become more attractive. A sociological experiment would have to place many foxes in this situation and then later put them along this path again, at which point the bush will have grown, the grapes will be hanging down, within reach. If dissonance theory is correct the foxes (just as hungry as the last time) would predominantly have to turn their noses up at the grapes and walk on. If the grapes get eaten this time, then it has to be admitted that last time there was a failure to reach them. This dissonance can be reduced through disdain for the grapes. If reactance theory is correct, our foxes would have to ravenously dart toward the grapes and gobble them up. In experimental social psychology both theories have been tested. The results are not clear-cut. Obviously there are personality factors. Apparently there are people (perhaps also foxes) who can more easily live with discrepancies than can others, who in other words possess a tolerance to dissonance. Specific situational conditions may also apply (intensity of hunger), and perhaps the "victory of dissonance theory or reactance theory" also depends on the given object. It follows therefore that marketing professionals who are not operating in accordance with exact information will have to keep both theories in consideration.

3.   A very common effect is change of opinion in opposition to the communication: As a consequence of the arising of reactance the appeal of forbidden or devalued avenues of action increases. There additionally arises the possibility of "indirectly reestablishing freedom". This takes place in that people share devalued, in the sense of repressed, modes of behavior with others, that is, they not only express their own opinion in opposition to the communication but also attempt to correspondingly win others over to their point of view. From the point of view of marketing these people are known as "negative multipliers".

Aggression toward the communicator is also a factor (less relevant for marketing).

4.   Similar to the dissonance theory view, in reactance theory warped information processing and gathering can also be encountered. Brehm and Brehm (1981, pp. 111 and 112), conducted experiments in which test subjects did not perceive the constriction or threat to their freedom. Here both theories come to the same conclusions.

5.   Reactance can also be processes such that the given person sees another alternative as if it were the one that was originally intended. For marketing this allows a product to be presented as an alternative to an excluded product, that is, offering a certain form of reactance reduction by supplying a corresponding product choice.

The consequences for marketing are primarily in the area of communications. Advertising and sales talks from the outset are recognizable as targeted attempts at influence. It can be fundamentally assumed the more intensely certain modes of behavior are rewarded at the outset, the more reactance effects will be encountered, and the more intensely intent to influence will be perceived. Those communications measures that are normally seen to be neutral clearly are especially subject to reactance effects. Empirical studies conducted by Bussmann, Schwarz and Kumpf (1980) show that communications in the area of public relations or in the press, as far as product publicity is concerned, lead to reactance effects especially quickly if they too obviously contain an attempt to influence. For productive goods marketing this fact is of great significance, in that informative contributions to professional publications in the technical sector can be an important instrument of marketing communication, whose presentation should involve an approach that gives reactance factors special consideration.

In general it is a worthy target in the formation of communications measures to reduce possible perception of pressure toward change of opinion. The theory of psychological reactance very clearly encourages a predominance of so-called "soft selling" methods as opposed to the "hard selling" concept. Reactance effects will have to be dealt with to a greater extent, the more important the product area is (high involvement) and the more competent the communication recipient considers him or herself to be. Incidentally the implementation of the above is summed up as recipients-as-variables acting as an influencing factor on their own credulity. There is less credulity in the case of greater professional competence. This is very relevant in the productive goods market. Reactance effects can always be reduced when the persons making the decisions at least have a limited number of alternative choices other than their own choice open to them. Ideally it will work in a sales talk to always make sure there are a few alternatives available for the decision.

Even completely settled solutions to problems (which are not normally considered to be disadvantageous) can trigger reactance, because there are no decisions that can be made anymore one way or the other, for or against something. From the point of view of reactance it can make sense in the productive goods sector to present to the customer recognizable room to maneuver, or to at least project the feeling that one has made decisions alone.

Dickenberger (1979a and 1979b) has put forward an expansion of reactance theory. When Brehm (1966) proceeds according to the assumption of threatened, anticipated or real constriction of freedom, freedom or non-freedom is being made into a dichotomous operation. Either the person feels themselves to be free or not. Reactance intensity is determined according to the importance of the threatened freedom. Dickenberger assumes that, similar to dissonance theory, the person proceeds according to the hypothesis that they have freedom to choose between alternatives. The person is more or less certain with regard to this hypothesis. If the person's freedom to choose in the direction of one alternative is constricted, the person apprehends that they, in contrast to their original hypothesis, no longer has or has less freedom to choose. The described reactance effect is then no different than an instance of dissonance reduction.

According to this theory reactance intensity is a function of an original subjective certainty, of possessing a now threatened freedom to choose. The intensity of reactance influences the motivation toward reestablishing this freedom.

Dickenberger's thesis does not contradict Brehm's approach to reactance intensity. Both approaches complement each other. Both the significance of the threatened freedom, and the subjectively experienced certainty that freedom is possessed, influence the reactance intensity.

The Ambivalence of Influence and Reactance Effects

In communications there is an ambivalence problem: In accordance with reactance theory we can say: The greater the perceived influence, the greater the reactance triggered and the less effective the influence will be. On the other hand a recognizable form of influence can be necessary, in order for there to be any kind of effect at all. This is the "influence effect", the persuasive character of the communication activated by the communication's influence, for example, a change of viewpoint or a purchase intention in favor of the communication. So what is at hand is an influence effect in favor of the communication and a reactance effect in opposition to the communication,

Reactivity trigger	Reactivity intensity determination	Reactivity effects
1. Social influence	1. Conviction of possessing freedom	1. People do the opposite
2. Setting	2. Importance and extent of constricted freedom	2. Opinion change to the contrary
3. Own decision	3. Self-estimated expertise	3. Individual reestablishment of freedom
	4. Perceived similarity of alternatives	4. Aggression

Figure 5.1   Overview of the Theory of Psychological Reactance

where both effects may end up compensating each other. A communication will trigger a maximal change in viewpoint if the difference between influence effect and reactance effect is maximal. This is presented in Figure 5.2 (see Dickenberger and Gniech, 1982, p. 329). The ordinate indicates the intensity of perceived influence, and the abscissa the consequences of influence. In the positive area an increase in value indicates an increasing effect in keeping with the communication, for example, compliance with the encouraged behavior in a percentage of influenced people, or the intensity of motivation on behalf of influenced people toward displaying the encouraged behavior. P1 indicates the minimum level of perceived influence effect that needs to be achieved in order to achieve any kind of effect. P2 indicates the level of perceived influence intensity that, with regard to influence and reactance effect, will achieve the maximal effectiveness. To the right of the highest value the influence begins to decrease again, whereupon the reactance effect kicks in, compensating the influence effect. In the negative area at P3, an increasing value indicates an increasing readiness to display opposing behavior, or an increasing percentage of people willing to display opposing behavior. As of P3 the reactance effect is greater than the influence effect. If viewpoints are changed in the direction of opposing the communication, then this is referred to as a "boomerang effect".

Next to the perceived intensity of influence, the perceived discrepancy between the viewpoint of the recipient and the attempted viewpoint change is also presumably worked out "... since discrepant communications with increasing discrepancy will become more and more counterattitudinal, the greater the discrepancy between an initial attitude and the position being advocated, the greater reactance aroused" (Brehm and Brehm, 1981, p. 125).

In the case of a concrete communications measure, the ambivalence that arises makes it difficult to develop clear propositions with regard to the occurrence and extent of influence and reactance effects. With the increasing importance of the given set of conditions and/or the more target group decision-making competence is assumed,

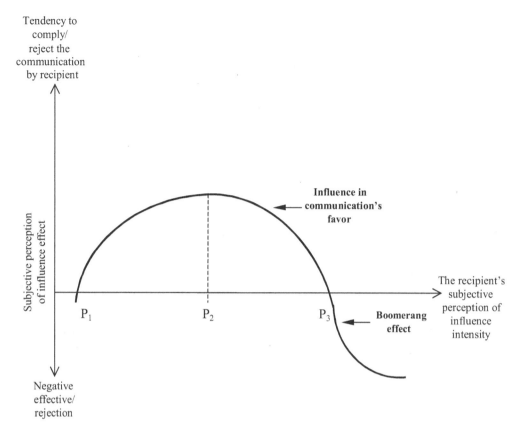

Figure 5.2   Communications effectiveness in relation to perceived influence (Dickenberger and Gniech, 1982, p. 329)

the more reactance effects will be encountered. In the case of less important products a recognizable influence pressure may be perceived, without however this leading to difficult reactance effects.

All told, this insight into these two mutually counteracting effects can be of use in that actual, specific instances of market research can be conducted on the basis of it, in order to at least roughly arrive at the optimal level of influence pressure.

Applications

MARKETING

Marketing communication

Changes of viewpoint with regard to products has a particularly high level of significance in marketing communication. Consumers are meant to find the products particularly attractive. If the intent to influence stands out too obviously, the target group will feel constricted with regard to their freedom to choose; this can lead to a weaker communications effect, or possibly even to a change in their view of the product's attractiveness in the opposite direction, or in other words to a boomerang effect.

As a marketing communications instrument, advertising is especially recognizable for primarily being an attempt at targeted influence, and for being a case where the goal of this kind of influence is relatively easy to discern. It can be fundamentally assumed that as far as advertising effect is concerned, reactance effects will be more prevalent the more intense the intent to influence is perceived to be and the more intensely very particular modes of behavior stand out and are touted via the communication as being desirable. In practice it is often attempted to get around obvious intent to influence in advertising through the use of product publicity or product placement. Bussmann, Schwarz and Kumpf (1980) tested the hypothesis, among other things, of whether similar communications have varying effects on viewpoint when they are presented on the one hand as advertising and on the other hand as neutral information. In doing this, they presented advertising communications both with a moderate influence intensity, and with an extreme influence intensity. The same communication content was presented in the form of an editorial product description, which likewise was given according to a moderate and extreme influence intensity.

Influence intensity clearly has a different effect in the case of advertising from that of apparently neutral communications (in editorial form). In the case of neutral communications there is greater difference between varying intensities of intent to influence than is the case with advertising communications. With apparently neutral communications like product publicity a recognizably intense intent to influence has a more negative effect on the success of influence than is to be expected in advertising. These effects are presented in a rough, simplified form in Figure 5.3.

	Advertising	**Product publicity**
High influence intensity	Somewhat low, medium results	Very low results
Low influence intensity	Somewhat high, medium results	Very high results

Figure 5.3   Communication results in relation to influence intensity and type of communication effect

This can be explained by the fact that with recognizable advertising communications an intent to influence is always being dealt with, yet with recognizable advertising communications the results can be reduced due to a very pronounced attempt to influence. In their influence success neutral communications are rather superior to pure advertising communications. This is based on the reactance effects that result from obvious intent to influence. If however an obvious, intense attempt to influence is present within a neutral communication, the reduction of influence success is significantly greater than is the case with advertising communications.

There are a number of techniques of reducing the perception of intent to influence, which also apply to advertising communications.

A certain amount of deflection or diversion can lead to an improvement in results in that the intent to influence is not perceived as being such, therefore triggering less reactance. Empirical work conducted by Festinger and Maccoby (1964) proves that this is possible. The fact that people are often diverted by other activities like eating or some form of entertainment while perceiving TV or radio advertising, can work to the advantage of the communications success, although this assumes that the diversion is not too pronounced. The choice of advertising media type is a matter for consideration here.

Some creative possibilities include humor, music, and image-oriented communication. All of these are oriented toward concealing the intent to influence, where they also simultaneously contain the danger of too drastically diverting from the actual communication. By way of avoiding this danger, humor, music and image elements can be worked into the communication to form a creative unit (see for a more thorough treatment, Unger and Fuchs, 1999, pp. 137 and 453).

Kroeber-Riel and Meyer-Hentschel (1982, pp. 104–113) recommend, from the point of view of reactance theory, refraining from:

- Pointing out freedom of choice.
- Emphasizing the meaning of freedom of choice.
- Creating the illusion of freedom via clever verbal formulations ("You conduct yourself the way it suits you, without clichés, without conventions. You live the way you want ...").

In any case, to go on about freedom in the context of communication that is targeted at influencing always introduces the danger of sensitizing the targeted individuals.

Product choice

Clee and Wicklung (1980, p. 394) perceive a connection between pricing and product choice: "when a price increase constitutes a barrier to free choice and reactance is aroused, the threatened choice alternative (the product) tends to increase in attractiveness". Another possibility in keeping with reactance theory is that rising product attractiveness may stem from restrictive marketing. If a product is only available in "specially selected shops", its attractiveness rises along with the increase in the difficulty of obtaining it. Both effects might also be triggered by assumed higher quality (which is assumed because of higher price or exclusive marketing).

Legal measures can also trigger reactance. If certain products are limited in their consumption by law their attractiveness may thereby be increased, which then works against the desired goals (for example, environmental protection). One need only think of the downright irrational discussions that come up now and again with regard to speed limits on the streets. This has to do with freedom and constriction just as in the context of consumption. We want to keep the potential efficiency that is there the way it is, but would lower speed limits really limit freedom all that much in the light of current traffic volumes, as debates like these tend to try and justify? What we see here is that in reality it has to do with perceived rather than actual freedom, and with its perceived constriction.

Occasionally, and increasingly in recent times, the attractiveness of products is increased by feigned shortage. Special series, or products, that are only sold for a certain time (as long as supplies last) appear to gain in attractiveness.

Personal sales

Influence is a factor in communications campaigns, but is also found in all forms of personal sales, in business conducted between commercial buyers and workers in the field, as well as in direct consumer sales. The problem as far as influencing is concerned is similar here to that encountered in advertising campaigns. It also involves the tendency for reactance effects to counteract influence effects.

There have been a few experiments along these lines (see Clee and Wicklund, 1980 and Brehm and Brehm, 1981). It was consistently found that hard sell methods yielded greater reactance effects than soft sell methods. Within a low range of influence intensity the test subjects predominantly complied with the influence. With increase in the perceived influence intensity reactance effects were increasingly encountered, in that the test subjects felt more and more that their freedom to choose between alternatives was being threatened due to the influence intensity (Brehm and Brehm, 1981, pp. 334–337; Clee and Wicklund, 1980, pp. 391 and 392). Reizenstein (1971) varied influence intensity in a fashion that did a good job of imitating a sales communication that might take place in a shop. The successful influence fell from 73 percent without reactance to 13 percent with pronounced reactance. In the study influence intensity was increased by degrees.

PERSONNEL POLICY

In the context of personnel politics it is important to point out again that reactance effects have nothing to due with whether or not constriction of freedom of whatever kind is assessed as legitimate or not. Even constriction of freedom that is viewed as legitimate can trigger reactance.

This has important consequences for personnel politics: Personnel management that is associated with constriction of freedom is less successful than personnel management that comes off as less constricting of freedom. This does not quite mean that a management style that is connected with a high degree of freedom constriction is crippled, or that it will devalue the personalities of employees. Resources are available for the implementation of freedom constriction. Necessary constrictions of freedom that can be justified will normally be accepted. In providing goods and services certain corresponding practical constraints can be introduced which impact work time. Here a compromise tends to be achieved.

Reactance theory is certainly relevant with regard to regulating work time and in the context of "employee instructions" and the checks and balances associated with them. Reactance theory effects are closely connected with the assumption of an inefficient, free time constricting management style.

QUESTIONS FOR DISCUSSION

1.   Elaborate on the theory of psychological reactance and compare it with cognitive dissonance theory.
2.   What are some examples in marketing to reduce psychological reactance?
3.   Discuss situations in your organization or university where personnel policy has been influenced by the perceived constriction of freedom. How was it resolved?
4.   What are negative multipliers and how can their prevalence be reduced?

Bibliography

Brehm, J.W.: *A Theory of Psychological Reactance*. New York, San Francisco, London: 1966.

Brehm, S.S. and Brehm, J.W.: Psychological reactance: *A Theory of Freedom and Control*. New York, London, Toronto: 1981.

Bussmann, W., Schwarz, N. and Kumpf, M.: *Psychologische Reaktanz in der Anzeigenwerbung kein Problem?* Vortrag auf der 22. Tagung der Experimentell Arbeitenden Psychologen. Tübingen: 1980. (*Psychological Reactance in Advertising: No Problem?* Presentation at the 22nd Conference of the Experimental Working Psychologist).

Clee, M.A. and Wicklund, R.A.: Consumer behavior and psychological reactance. *Journal of Consumer Research*, 1980, 6, 389–405.

Dickenberger, D.: Vergleich zweier theorien: reformulierte theorie der kognitiven dissonanz und erweiterte theorie der psychologischen reaktanz. In: Eckensberger, L.H. (ed.): *Bericht über den 31. Kongreß der Deutschen Gesellschaft für Psychologie in Mannheim: 1978*. Göttingen, 1979a, 375–376. (Comparison of these theories: Reformulated theory of cognitive dissonance and expanded theory of psychological reactance. In *Report on the 31st Congress of the German Company for Psychology in Mannheim: 1978*).

—— *Ein neues konzept der wichtigkeit von freiheitskonsequenzen für die theorie der psychologischen reaktanz*. Weinheim: 1979b. (*A new concept on the importance of freedom consequences for the theory of psychological reactance*).

—— and Gniech, G.: The theory of psychological reactance. In: Irle, M. (ed.): *Studies in Decision Making—Social Psychological and Socio-Economic Analyses*, Berlin, New York: 1982, 311–341.

——, Gniech, G. and Grabitz, H.-J.: Die Theorie der psychologischen reaktanz. In: Frey, D. and Irle, M. (eds): *Theorien der Sozialpsychologie, vol. I: Kognitive Theorien*. (2nd edn), Bern, Göttingen, Toronto, Seattle: 1993, 243–273. (The theory of psychological reactance. In *Theories of Social Psychology, vol. I: Cognitive Theories*).

Festinger, L. and Maccoby, N.: On resistance to persuasive communications. *Journal of Abnormal and Social Psychology*, 68, 359–366.

Frey, D. and Irle, M. (eds): *Theorien der Sozialpsychologie, Band I: Kognitive Theorien* (2nd edn), Bern, Göttingen, Toronto, Seattle: 1993. (*Theories of Social Psychology, vol. I: Cognitive Theories*).

Irle, M. (ed.): *Studies in Decision Making—Social Psychological and Socio-Economic Analyses*. Berlin, New York: 1982.

Kroeber-Riel, W. and Meyer-Hentschel, G.: *Werbung—Steuerung des Konsumentenverhaltens*. Heidelberg: 1982. (*Advertising—Control of Consumer Behavior*).

Reizenstein, R.C.: A dissonance approach to measuring the effectiveness of two personal selling techniques through decision reversal. In: *Proceedings*, F.C. Alvine (ed.), *American Marketing Association*, 1971, Chicago, 176–180.

Unger, F. and Fuchs, W.: *Management der Marktkommunikation* (2nd edn), Heidelberg: 1999. (*Management of Market Communication*).

CHAPTER 6 *Attribution Theories*

Theory

NAIVE PSYCHOLOGY

"The fundamental attribution error stems from the human tendency to overestimate the significance of personality and dispositional factors compared to the significance of situational or environmental influences when describing and explaining the causes of social behavior" (Aronson, 1994, p. 170). We would like to go into this in greater detail.

People try to explain the world. They are constantly enquiring into the origins of occurrences of all kinds. The motivation for this is based on the subjectively experienced necessity to react appropriately within the environment. As far as that is concerned the focus is not on objectively correct attempts at explaining events, but is rather on what are subjectively experienced as correct attempts. These kinds of attempts at explanation also involve explanations of one's own behavior. This activity also supports one's self image (the ideas of oneself that one holds to be true, and the assessment of same) in opposing devaluations or by further enhancing self image (self worth enhancement). This field is explored by a whole range of attribution theories. They explain what is known to the layman as "common sense".

Attribution theories impressively demonstrate that this "common sense" need not be oriented toward delivering usable explanations taken from out of everyday life. In this regard a mirror is held up to managers as decision-makers and observers. In everyday life we are all "naïve scientists" whose attempts at explanation differ from scientific explanations in that they are conducted according to a much narrower systematics. Heider (1958) has also called his corresponding theory "naïve psychology". In everyday life people are satisfied with less information and tend to prefer certain explanations (for example, self-worth enhancement). Aside from that naïve scientists seek certainty; they want the validity of their assumptions to be confirmed. As science is viewed as the search for insight, there is a systematic attempt to come up with better explanations via the uncovering of errors. In the following we want to present some of the most important attribution theories, whereby there is no particular attribution theory that presides over the others, there instead being a whole range of attribution theories that have been developed relatively independently from each other, which differentiate between various particular areas of enquiry (Heider, 1958, 1977; Jones and Davis, 1965; Kelley, 1967, 1972, 1973 and Bem, 1967, 1972). Newer approaches are presented by Hewstone (1983 and 1989).

PERSON AND ENVIRONMENT AS EXPLANATORY GROUPS OF FACTORS

We will first turn our attention to the earliest approach: Heider (1958). The question is asked whether a particular result of action X can be traced back more to factors that can be seen to reside within a person, or to those within his environment or inherent within the action situation.

$X = f (ff \text{ Person}; ff \text{ Environment})$.

"*ff* Person" signifies a group of personality characteristics, and "*ff* Environment" signifies a group of environmental factors, which in either case may constitute that which triggers the action result (and so $X = f (....)$).

It is enough if the factors from one of either group of factors are operative, in other words if from the point of view of the attributing person the action result can exclusively be traced back to either personality or environmental factors. It is conceivable that a person may think an action result can exclusively be traced back to his own or to an observed person's abilities. The action result can also exclusively be traced back to the perhaps randomly encountered operation of environmental factors perceived as being completely independent of the abilities of an acting person. The acting person in this case then has nothing to do with the occurrence. Actually here it is then not admissible to speak of an action result. From the point of view of observing and attributing people, a particular mode of behavior and an occurrence that has been encountered have nothing to do with each other.

It is stated again and again within industrial psychology that performance results with regard to personality factors can be traced back in essence to motivation and ability. Heider (1977, p. 103) takes this into account and divides the groups of personality factors into two subgroups: Ability and motivation. This yields:

$X = f (\text{Motivation}, \text{Ability}, \text{Environment})$.

If the group of personality factors is to be in any way brought in to explain the action result, motivation and ability must now be placed in a multiplicative relationship with each other. Without some ability motivation is not effective; without some motivation ability cannot be effective.

Here are some examples to illustrate this concept:

T hits B, because he is easily irritated (P) or because B angered him (E).

F is nice to A, because he is a friendly person (P) or because he wants something from A (E).

X passed the exam because she is talented (P) or because the tasks were especially easy (E).

It is assumed here that the factor "ability" is constant in the midst of many situations and throughout time and space. The factor "motivation" is subject to great fluctuation. Environmental factors can also be divided into constant and inconstant groups of factors. In the environment, for example, the task difficulty may have been settled upon, which counts as constant, but then enters in the inconstant factor of "chance", Weiner, 1972; Weiner et al., 1972).

Where factors of self-worth are concerned, people tend more to attribute their own success to themselves, and their lack of success to environmental factors, for example, task difficulty. As far as other people are concerned, again in the case of self-worth factors, people tend to do the reverse: The success of others is tended to be seen as the result of their environment ("The task was easy. I could have done that too."), and lack of success tends more to be attributed to the people doing the acting (see aspects of work motivation, Vroom, 1964, p. 129).

The initial thesis of tracing back the action result to environmental or personality factors ($X = f$ (ff Person, ff Environment) has led to the development of further approaches. A widespread thesis is that of Jones and Nisbett (1972, p. 82) whereby people overestimate environmental factors and underestimate personality factors with regard to their own behavior, at the same time as underestimating environmental factors and overestimating personality factors in the observation of other people. Farr and Anderson (1983, pp. 47–55) strongly criticize this thesis; it does not have a lot of empirical support (see also Hewstone and Antaki, 1992, p. 129), although a certain amount of plausibility cannot be denied. Watson (1982) qualifies Jones and Nisbett's (1972) thesis insofar as he simply has found that people value circumstantial factors less with regard to their own behavior than they do with regard to observed people. This can be traced back to the fact that with regard to our own behavior we naturally know more about our own inner motives, anxieties, the goals of our striving—in short about our personality factors, than we do in the case of observed people (Hewstone and Antaki, 1992, p. 130). This would seem to be the case regardless of a person's cultural background.

This is a possible explanation for the "fundamental attribution error" that we presented as an "introduction" into this chapter; in other words the fundamental overestimation of behavioral dispositions and the underestimation of circumstantial factors: "Our exploration of the intuitive psychologist's shortcomings must start with his general tendency to overestimate the importance of personal or dispositional factors relative to environmental influences" (Ross, 1977, p. 164).

An attribution's mode of differentiation, the way that success and lack of success are varyingly attributed, depending on whether it has to do with one's own or another's success or lack of success, is very likely motivated by protection of self esteem. In the case of his own success a person tends more to see personal factors as a pronounced influence and circumstantial factors as a less pronounced influence. With regard to lack of success the influence of circumstantial factors are valued more highly over personal factors. The attribution process proceeds in exactly the opposite way when foreign behavior is observed and the consequences of that behavior attributed. Now success tends more to be attributed to environmental factors, lack of success to personal factors (Snyder, Stephan and Rosenfield, 1976). Further empirically substantiated examples of various attribution patterns can be found in Herkner (1980, pp. 43–45).

Kruglanski (1975) has presented the hypothesis that the differentiation into external and internal attribution only makes sense in the case of success or lack of success (that is, individual consequences of actions as occurrences), but not in the case of persistent modes of behavior, because these are always triggered by the person, or in other words are internally attributed. This is not logically consistent. A mode of behavior that has persisted for a long time may also be activated either by inner motivation or by outer circumstances, like for example the presence of other people, by external reward or pressure (in the extreme: The acting person is being blackmailed).

IN SEARCH OF MOTIVES

People often approach the question, in various ways, of why a person originates a given action, or why certain action results have been achieved. The way in which people believe others have developed their structures of motivation, is explained in Jones and Davis's (1965) attribution theory. It is assumed that observed behavior along with the intent that has led to this behavior is the key to people's stable personality characteristics. In the context of the attribution process, people conclude that observed behavior and the intentions at the basis of this behavior correspond with the stable personality characteristics of the observed people. Accordingly this is "known as the theory of corresponding conclusions" (Hewstone and Antaki, 1992, p. 14).

According to a very simple procedure, observing people can draw conclusions from the consequences encountered through an action, as to the abilities and knowledge of the people doing the acting, and from there can draw conclusions as to the intensions of the people doing the acting. The observer has to assume that the person doing the acting is aware of the consequences of his actions. This process is presented in Figure 6.1.

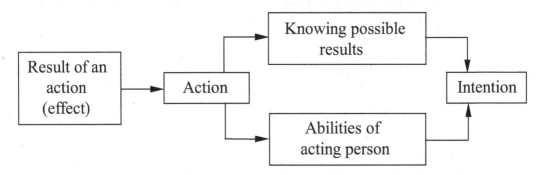

Figure 6.1   The conclusion of action consequences according to corresponding intentions

The effects of actions are intended as far as the observer is concerned, and are not activated by other factors. The ability of the acting person is discerned by observing his action, as well as his knowledge with regard to the consequences. From that the action intent is determined.

This alone—the assumption with regard to an action intention—does not yet yield a conclusion with regard to the motives underlying the intentions, or with regard to the "disposition of a person".

a) If an action is only expected to have very few consequences, in the extreme case only one, then conclusions with regard to the motives of the acting person seem to be easier than in cases where the action may trigger a great many different consequences.

b) If an action in everyday life is seen to lead to very unusual consequences (a salesperson annoys a customer), then a conclusion with regard to the motives of this person is more possible than when an action leads to what are seen as quite normal consequences (a salesperson is friendly to a customer). This is a concept from the theory of corresponding conclusions according to Jones and Davis (1965).

In this context the "social desirability" of encountered effects is relevant, along with the extent that these are seen as being "normal in general".

The fact that a customer is treated in a friendly manner, counts as being socially desirable and normal, and as such, does not lend itself to being traced back to the motives of the salesperson. If A is very angered by B and if in the end A becomes violent toward B, and B receives a broken nose, then that is not socially desirable, and will instead be assessed as being the result of unusual circumstances (for example, went on a bender last night) and also will not be viewed as normal. Looking at this situation it is not yet possible to conclude that A is in possession of a particularly aggressive motivation structure, nor is it possible to conclude that B has such a structure.

An observing person's information content is high with regard to the sought for disposition of an observed person, if a person's action with regard to its consequences strongly diverges from the action consequences of the average person—and if apart from that the number of consequences of an observed action is small. Then from these few, exactly one in particular personally relevant motive will be arrived at which is not attributable to the effects of a normal everyday action. There is a "high correspondence" of action consequences with motives.

It is exactly opposite the case if the action yields many effects and if these effects can be seen as being socially desirable in general, or as stemming from normal intentions. There is a so-called "trivial ambiguity" at hand. There is no information about the specific dispositions or motives of the acting person available in this situation.

Now we are moving on from the two extreme possibilities (high information content in the situation or no information in the situation) to in between forms.

Let's assume that a mode of behavior yields many effects that are however not normal and which are not seen as socially desirable, making the situation ambiguous but allowing for conclusions to be made with regard to possibly existing motives of the acting person. This situation is known as "interesting ambiguity".

If only a few consequences, or if ideally just one consequence of a person's action is encountered, it can be assumed that this one or these few effects are motivationally based, although the certainty that people strive for in everyday life is not present. You cannot conclude that it is the result of personal motives if a salesperson is friendly to a customer, because being friendly to customers is seen as normal in general and as socially desirable. There is here a so-called "trivial clarity", which can be a confusing term, because this situation is by no means clear; it is so normal that no conclusions can be drawn and as to observing people in general conclusions also cannot be drawn. This relationship is illustrated in Figure 6.2.

There is a little more information available to an observing person if the acting person has several alternatives with varying effects: Let's assume that an alternative X yields effects a, b, c, while alternative Y yields effects a and b. If a person in this situation opts for X, then the observing person can be sure that c is not undesired, and in fact perhaps it is a desired effect. This seems clear in everyday life, but is so unclear in reality that we cannot know whether an acting person is aware of the desirable and undesirable effects of actions, or whether effects are encountered that we do not observe, or if the acting person is acting purposefully or according to routine without thought of consequences.

	Extent of the social desirability of encountered effects and extent to which these are seen as normal	
	Low	High
A few down to only one effect of an action	There is (in the extreme case) only one effect, and this one is socially undesirable and/or unusual: **High correspondence**	There is (in the extreme case) only one effect and this effect is socially acceptable, and/or normal: **Trivial clarity**
Many effects as consequences of actions	There are several or many effects, and these are socially undesirable and/or unusual: **Interesting ambiguity**	There are several or many effects, and these are socially desirable and/or normal in general: **Trivial ambiguity**

Figure 6.2   Number of normal/socially desirable or unusual/socially undesirable effects of actions and the possibilities of drawing conclusions with regard to the motivation structures of acting persons (stemming from Jones and Davis, 1965, p. 229)

All of the attributions described here depend on the prerequisite that the people doing the attributing are assuming freedom to choose between available alternatives on behalf of the acting persons.

ATTRIBUTION VARIATIONS ACCORDING SINGLE OR MULTIPLE OBSERVATIONS: THE CONFIGURATION PRINCIPLE AND THE COVARIATION PRINCIPLE

What do we believe we know about motives or other behavioral tendencies after observing someone repeatedly? By contrast what conclusions can be arrived at after observing once?

Kelly expanded upon the attribution theories that had existed up to that point by stating that attributions that are based on observing once should be set against attributions that are based on repeated observation. In the case of repeated observation the covariation principle applies, whereas in the case of observing once the configuration principle applies.

a)   The covariation principle

An effect—for example, aggression, achievement, failure, friendliness, nervousness, anxiety—is attributed to a cause with which it covaries (Kelley, 1973, p. 108), meaning that it is encountered at the same time, particularly often. Such causes can include people, time, and entities that are special factors in the situation: "The class of entities includes (constant) characteristics of the given instance, toward which the given action is oriented." Accordingly this could have to do with products that are to be sold, texts that are to be translated, or in general, problems that need to be solved.

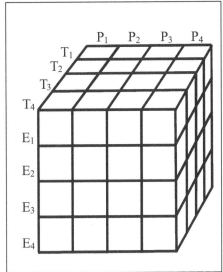

Figure 6.3a   General presentation of the covariation principle (Kelley, 1973, p. 110)

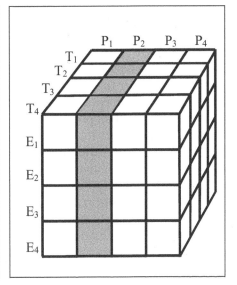

Figure 6.3b   Attributed general behavioral tendency of person (P2) in all times with regard to all entities (Kelley, 1973, p. 110)

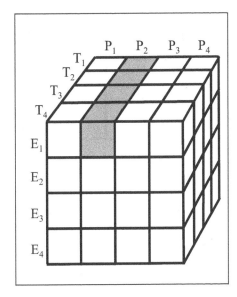

Figure 6.3c   A person's (P2) attributed behavioral tendency concerning a particular entity (E1) in all times

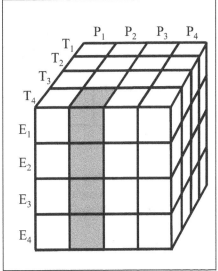

Figure 6.3d   Attributed behavioral tendency concerning many entities at a particular point in time. The situation is the cause of aggression

We would like to present and explain the diagram, based on the "Kelley Cube", using the example of aggressive behavior. This cube is defined by the dimensions of the action(s), the object(s), and the situation(s): Actor x object x situation (Ross, 1977, p. 179):

Let's assume that a person is aggressive toward many other people (entities) at many points in time. We can then conclude that there exists a behavioral tendency toward displaying aggressive behavior (Figure 6.3b). Assume that this person displays aggression toward certain entities at all points in time. Then the person seems to possess aggression oriented behavioral tendencies with regard to particular entities (Figure 6.3c). If a person reacts aggressively toward other people only at a particular point in time, then the time period and the situation native to this point in time appear to be the factors that have triggered the aggression (Figure 6.3d). Whereas if the aggressive behavior is displayed by many people toward an entity, it cannot be concluded that the observed people are in possession of aggressive behavioral tendencies (Figure 6.3e), because it could be that the entity is the cause. The situation in Figure 6.3f does not deliver any information with regard to behavioral tendencies.

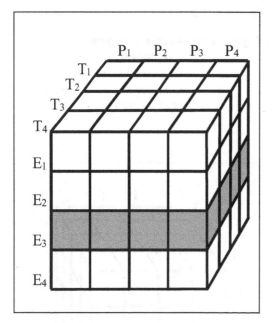

Figure 6.3e Many people are aggressive toward one entity at all times

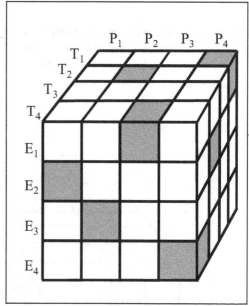

Figure 6.3f No possibility of attributing a general behavioral tendency

This procedure has been dubbed the "naïve variance analysis" because of it being reminiscent of variance analysis: The "naïve version is without a doubt a weak imitation of the scientific version—incomplete, susceptible to judgment, ready to work with incomplete fundamentals, etc. Still, there are some characteristics that it has in common with the way we scientists use variance analysis" (Kelley, 1973, p. 109).

b)   The Configuration Principle

What can an observer "know" if our person has only displayed aggressive behavior toward another person once, or in other words if only one such observation is at hand? The attribution of certain effects to certain causes proceeds according to the configuration of a situation, arising out of the existence of and relationships between various factors. This is known as the "gestalt" of a situation. From out of their everyday experience people develop ready-made opinions as to how various factors behave in relation to each other. Striving, diversion, personal problems, difficulty of tasks, work atmosphere, could all be factors that work together within a work situation that in some way simultaneously influence and, in a person's opinion, further or obstruct the performance result of another person. According to Kelley (1972) the attribution proceeds according to the principle of causal schemata, whereby people seek adequate reasons for an effect within the gestalt of a situation. This takes place according to either the value-adding or according to the devaluation principle.

The value-adding principle   Let's assume that an effect is triggered despite the influence of a counteracting factor, and then that value is added to the significance of another supporting factor: A person is biased in that they believe that people of a certain type are less able to perform well. If the person observes someone of this type performing well in a certain situation, then factors like luck, or lack of task difficulty, will be given added value.

In keeping with the value-adding principle, people may assume that several factors are necessary in order to trigger a given effect; they also may assume that there are several factors, where each one on its own is sufficient in order to trigger an effect.

The devaluation principle   This principle is clearly linked with the assumption that a person assumes an effect can be triggered by the simultaneous working of several factors. Each of the available factors is seen as possibly being a sufficient cause of a given effect. Then, whichever factors can be replaced by other more plausible factors are devalued. A person's opinions, prejudices, experiences, and so on, determine what the individual considers to be plausible factors. Thus, a personal's cultural background plays a role here.

A person might assume that a good relationship to superiors, ability, and motivation, are conducive to furthering a career. If the person then observes that a "career competitor" has received a higher paid position, they may devalue ability and motivation, because they view the factor "good relationship" to be more plausible.

The principle of causal schemata is not completely accepted. Hewstone and Antaki (1992, p. 119) are critical in that there is not yet enough evidence for the actual existence of such schemata, although it can be admitted that people act at the time "*as if* they could utilize these schemata".

WHAT CAN WE KNOW ABOUT OUR OWN MOTIVES?

How do people find out about their own orientations, motives, and emotions? People learn about their own orientations, emotions and about their other internal states in part by observing their own behavior, including the outer circumstances in which this behavior occurs. People cannot make direct conclusions as to their own motives, but rather achieve this via observing their own behavior, just as they would observe the behavior of other people. This is the starting point of Bem's (1967, 1972) theory of self-perception.

Internal signals that we use to come to conclusions as to our own motives and emotional states are often weak, ambiguous or difficult to interpret. For this reason people adopt the same position in the observation and interpretation of their own behavior that an external observer takes in observing and explaining the behavior of other people (Bem, 1972, p. 2 et seq.). We observe our own behavior and in doing so draw conclusions in a way similar to how we operate as an external observer. Accordingly, attributions can take place that are similar to those presented in the above attribution theories.

Drawing conclusions as to internal orientations, motives and emotions take place *after* actions. The mechanism is similar to that which is explained by the theory of cognitive dissonance. After an action cognitions are developed which conform to the action. The theory of self-perception claims to offer an alternative to some of the theory of cognitive dissonance's propositions. Both theories deal with the retrospective interpretation of actions. The theory of self-perception according to Bem (1967, 1972) similarly demonstrates how after an action people seek interpretations that are compatible with their self concepts. In doing this, they seek cognitive consonance and strive to avoid cognitive dissonance. Irle (1975) has shown after checking a whole range of empirical studies (which cannot be shown here due to space limitation), that claiming the theory of self-perception to be an independent alternative to the theory of cognitive dissonance is not acceptable. There are no explanations of human behavior in it that are not also to be found within the theory of cognitive dissonance. Accordingly it is simply a special application of dissonance theory. The practical conclusions coming out of the theory of self-perception are however of use.

Applications

It is easy to derive applications from out of attribution theory, both for marketing and for personnel management. Gross-Engelmann and Wiswede (1999, p. 168) complain however, that although attribution theory is presented as one of the most important theories of social psychology, it is for example hardly given any notice within consumer behavior research. They pose among others the following questions:

- To what extent can the experienced use of a product be traced back to the product?
- Can only this product provide this product use (distinctness)?
- To what extent is the perceived product use triggered by the person (or the product)?
- What is responsible for undesired occurrences (defective product, waiting time)?
- Why do certain other people also buy the product (or why not)?
- How does the person explain the reasons they bought the product?

Wiswede (1972, p. 2) has shown how attribution theories can be applied on the basis of the phases of consumer behavior:

- The phase before the decision. The evaluation of advertising statements and the content of consultation talks play a role here.

- The purchase itself. Here the assessment of sales personnel behavior is particularly relevant.
- The post-purchase phase. This revolves around retrospective explanations of one's own behavior with the aim of justifying the latter.

ACCORDING TO HEIDER (1958)

As a rule, when we advertise a product we are doing that in order to promise that it will yield a certain benefit. If the product fulfills the established expectations, then the question presents itself of whether the purchaser perceives him or herself as the cause of the successful action, or whether the success is attributed to the benefit yielded by the product. We have to assume that people tend more to attribute successful action (naturally also consumption) to their own abilities, and that in the case of lack of success they tend to attribute this consequence to the environment in the form of defective product characteristics. This is in the interests of the company that is engaged in marketing. Since human satisfaction is achieved through successful independent action, it cannot be the goal to attribute "successful consumption" exclusively to the product. This cannot be in the interests of marketing, because a certain amount of customer satisfaction is being strived for, just as it is similarly not in the interests of marketing if success is attributed solely to the person (who is here doing the consuming), while lack of success is attributed solely to the product. It may therefore be advisable within marketing to persuade the consumer that successful consumption can be traced back to a combination of one's own abilities and product characteristics: "XXX really brings out how beautiful your hair is"; "XXX allows you to bring your talents to full bloom", etc. From the point of view of attribution theory it can be advisable as a target to position products as "ideally complimenting one's own abilities" (see Schiffmann and Kanuk, 1994, p. 276, with regard to graphics programs for PCs).

This thesis of varying attributions of success and lack of success is relevant in personnel policy. It is possible that people tend more to perceive the causes of lack of success in external factors. This is also supported by dissonance theory. This means that learning processes are being obstructed. Changes of behavior appear to be unnecessary or unimportant if external factors influencing the performance result are experienced as unforeseeable or uncontrollable. It is the job of managers to work against this kind of mechanism in order to allow learning processes to activate.

ACCORDING TO JONES AND DAVIS (1965)

In marketing literature, unusual behavior is dealt with particularly with regard to marketing communication (see Schiffman and Kanuk, 1994, p. 276 or Sirgy, 1982, pp. 85–87). If, for example, a communicator expresses himself to the disadvantage of a product, then this is experienced as unusual and thereby heightens his credibility as an adviser. The fact that a salesman presents his product as exclusively positive seems trivial and tends not to be traced back to the salesman's actual motivation. At face value the salesperson seems to be assuming that a potential customer will not make the purchase as a result of the salesperson presenting the disadvantages of products. One believes that, to some significant extent, a conclusion can be arrived with regard to a motivation that likely involves giving a relatively unbiased description of a product, and really giving advice. It is being overlooked here that the salesperson could be using this as a technique to enhance his credibility as an adviser, thereby more easily making a sale.

If sales personnel display a relatively high level of effort to achieve certain sales goals which are connected with bonuses, management may adopt trivial clarity: "The only reason they are making this effort is in order to earn the bonuses." Because of this the management may additionally feel justified in the assumption that employees are only motivated by money. There may also be present an equally significant intrinsic motivation that is overlooked because of not being externally evident (see Chapter 14, "Motivation", in this book).

In general, unprofessional/unscientific observers are too quick to overlook that as a rule people behave in the way they believe they are expected to behave. As soon as people believe that they possess information as to how people expect them to behave, which they believe they have culled from experience, then we cannot say anything about the motivation underlying behavior based on such assumptions, other than that the person wants to justify this behavior according to the assumptions it is oriented toward. In marketing this is a problem with regard to market research. Test subjects should not know anything about the background of the survey (which product—which is presented in comparison with others—the test product is, which TV advertisement, or in general what advertising is being tested). Whenever test subjects possess information about what they are being tested about, positive test results may be nothing more than a record of their motivation to produce behavior that conforms to expectations. In this context market researchers are unscientific observers.

ACCORDING TO KELLEY (1967, 1972, 1973)

Attribution theory according to Kelley is relevant whenever people attempt in everyday life to explain the objects in their environment: If a product has been used again and again in many situations by many different people, then "it must be good". This can be utilized as an advertising strategy (We can think of the advertising campaign in Germany for Jägermeister®: "I drink Jägermeister® because ...". Jägermeister® is depicted being enjoyed by every possible type of person in every possible situation).

Kelley's attribution theory can elucidate the most varied range of managerial interpretations of employee behavior. Let's assume that manager F observes employee M who successfully fulfills a task for the first time. This could be taken to be chance by F, since up to now M has had no success in similar situations. It remains unrecognized that following the success M might himself attribute the success to chance circumstantial factors, and thus meet with lack of success again in the future due to expectation of failure. It can easily be imagined how F would interpret the performance behavior if they had themselves instructed M (the success would be traced back to the excellent training) or if F holds prejudices with regard to M due to gender, age or other personal characteristics (positive or negative). Extending this list is only a matter of creativity.

Weiner's theory of performance behavior is also relevant with regard to work behavior (1972, 1992, p. 232 et seq.). According to Weiner people attribute performance in relation to "locus of control" (external or internal) and "stability" of influence factors. Performance results can arise from the person ("locus of control" is internal) or from circumstantial factors ("locus of control" is external). In the case of internal control, influence factors (that is, influence of the person) can additionally arise from "ability" (stable factor) or from "effort/motivation" (variable factor). In the case of external control the stable factor is "task difficulty" and the variable factor is "chance".

There is also the factor of whether the person assumes that the cause of performance can be controlled or not. Aptitude and fatigue are not in the area of control, whereas long-term and temporary efforts are.

	Internal	External			Stable	Unstable
Stable	Ability	Task difficulty	Uncontrollable		Aptitude	Fatigue
Unstable	Effort	Luck/chance	Controllable		Long-term effort/comfort level	Temporary effort

Figure 6.4   An attribution pattern according to Weiner (1986, pp. 46 and 49; 1992, pp. 250 and 251)

Depending on the type of performance attribution with regard to one's own success/lack of success, different behavioral tendencies will manifest in the future. As a consequence of corresponding attributions, people can learn to arrive at success via effort, or in other words when success can be traced back to effort; similarly people can learn to "self-consciously" process tasks if they have learned to attribute performance success to their own abilities. "Learned helplessness" (Seligman, 1975) can also be a consequence of attribution; that is, if people believe that their performance success is the consequence of chance or is dependent upon uncontrollable external factors.

People can also over or under estimate their own abilities. According to Weiner (1985) one's own success can be explained by a multitude of external or internal variables. Along these lines it might depend on very individual attribution tendencies whether or not the self concept with regard to performance ability is appropriate or not (Brandstätter, 1998, p. 220).

An element of Kelley's attribution theory is the principle of value-adding or devaluation. If people learn that regular external rewards will be encountered as a result of strived-for success, then "a behavior may develop with a high likelihood of appearance ...", but which is externally motivated. As consequence of the attenuation principle, already existent intrinsic motivation can be undermined via reinforcement (Herkner, 1980, pp. 72 and 73). The behavior will become more and more intensified in relation to the prospect of an external reward. Management concepts in personnel management can involve a combination of external and (with emphasis on) internal rewards.

ACCORDING TO BEM (1967, 1972)

Bem's theory of self-perception is disputed and is perhaps superfluous on the basis of the propositions and applicability of the theory of cognitive dissonance. However there are examples in commerce that illustrate the theory (if the theory of cognitive dissonance can simultaneously explain these examples, then it is not relevant). Accordingly the goal of every marketing measure has to be to get consumers to attribute their consumer behavior to product characteristics, and less to the situation: discount price, time pressure, and a lack of purchase alternatives. In keeping with this an increase in positive product orientation is expected as well as a higher future purchase probability. This is especially relevant for measures having to do with encouraging sales. Potential customers are here influenced particularly through discount prices, contests, and special placement. The theory of self-perception demonstrates that for a long term effect it is especially important to integrate well-positioned product characteristics into a concept for encouraging sales. In this way, success can be had in establishing long term success.

In professional life, it makes sense for managers to give employees the possibility of attributing their performance to their own motivation rather than to outer pressure. It is then more likely that longer-lasting, more continuous motivation will come about. This proposition can naturally also be derived from the theory of psychological reactance, as well as, obviously, from the cognitive dissonance theory.

The above-presented attenuation of intrinsic motivation is also compatible with Bem's theory.

PSYCHOLOGY OF PREDICTION

In Ross (1977, p. 197 et seq.) we find summary presentations of some attribution theory essays which take prediction as their theme. Practically the same mechanism underlies people's predictions as retrospective explanations. If we believe that it just so happened that an easily completed task was the cause of our success, then a lower probability of success in the future will be predicted than if we assume that ability as the stable internal factor of success was applicable. Expectations of success that arise in this way unconsciously influence possible management behavior and again (at least as a tendency) the consequent performance behavior.

Another prediction error stems from the fact that observers come too quickly to conclusions as to causes based on given correlations (Kelley's attribution theory, when all is said and done, stems from nothing other than correlations). Correlations that have been identified lead easily to seemingly correspondent dependencies attributable to the future. As it is often said with financial investments, past performance is not necessarily an indicator of future results!

"COMMON SENSE", "SOCIAL REPRESENTATIONS" AND ATTRIBUTION IN SOCIETY

Hewstone (1989, p. 205 et seq.) proceeds in accordance with a fundamental presentation of causal attribution explanations of mass phenomena. In society "healthy common sense" is understood to be that which the majority considers it to be. A society can consist of the people of a nation, a region, or of an organization. "Common sense" is defined by Fletcher (1984, p. 204) in the following way:

Common sense is a set of shared fundamental assumptions about the nature of the social and physical world.

Common sense is a set of cultural maxims and shared beliefs about the social and physical world.

Common sense is a shared way of thinking about the social and physical world.

"Common sense" is a form of thinking originating in society, wherein it is ubiquitously distributed and wherein it is seen as normal in general. From out of "common sense" certain contents of thought and its results (ideas), and connections between ideas, arise; for example religion influences politics and its policies. We can certainly also assume that society is impacted by "social representations", which in turn influence "common sense".

Social representations ... concern the contents of everyday thinking and the stock of ideas that gives coherence to our religious beliefs, political ideas and the connections we create ... They make it possible for us to classify persons and objects, to compare and explain behaviors and to objectify them as parts of our social setting. (Moscovici, 1988, p. 214)

"Social representations" manifest themselves, among other areas, in fashion, tradition and culture.

From out of the existence of social representations, Hewstone (1988, p. 211) has derived the possibility of explaining common sense using attribution theory, since social representations provide a category that is determined by the perception and processing of social information. If a certain category of thinking is shared by a society, this leads to concurrently operating interpersonal attributions within that society. This leads in turn to similar assumptions about reality, which are all the more likely to be considered "true", the more people there are that share them. Based on this, Hewstone (1988, p. 213) has developed notions of an "attributing society". Naturally this does not mean that there is an "attribution of a society". A society cannot think and therefore also cannot attribute. It is certainly always individuals who perform attributions; but they do this predominantly in the same way as each other, within a society impacted by social representations. This is how generally accepted assumptions in society arise, about the causes of unemployment, wealth, poverty, societal disturbances, health risks, etc.

These mechanisms are relevant with regard to the managers of an organization. Managers in organizations often believe they can fall back on the generally shared opinions of "their" organization. From the point of view of attribution theory this is a rash judgment.

We can also consider the development of stock markets. If enough investors come to the same conclusions in accordance with the same assumptions, then this becomes a facet of market reality, thus triggering corresponding market reactions. This also applies for other price reactions.

It makes sense at this point to point out that Festinger (1957, pp. 200–202, 246 et seq., 247 et seq., 250 et seq., 258 et seq.) has explained mass phenomena in a similar way: within society there is a shared experience of cognitive dissonance and concurrently operating mechanisms of reduction and avoidance of cognitive dissonance. It certainly is not a problem if various theories are in a position to explain a given theory.

QUESTIONS FOR DISCUSSION

1. Explain how culture can influence what is seen as "common sense" for a given society.
2. Discuss the relevance of Kelley's cube for determining the probability of a given variable being influenced by time and the environment.
3. How can attribution theory be used to predict behavior considered normal, and how might the theory be incorrectly utilized for this purpose?
4. Discuss how the concepts outlined in this chapter can be used to help your organization's market segmentation and customer orientation efforts.

Bibliography

Aronson, E.: *Sozialpsychologie—Menschliches Verhalten und gesellschaftlicher Einfluß*. Heidelberg, Berlin, Oxford: 1994. (*Social Psychology—Human Behavior and Social Influence*).

Bem, D.J.: Self-perception: An alternative interpretation of a cognitive dissonance phenomena, *Psychological Review*, 1967, 74, 183–200.

—— Self-perception theory. In: Berkowitz, L. (ed.): *Advances in Experimental Social Psychology*, vol. 6. New York: 1972, 1–62.

Brandstätter, H.: Persönliche verhaltens- und leistungsbedingungen. In: Schuler, H. (ed.): *Organisationspsychologie* (3rd edn). Bern, Göttingen, Toronto, Seattle: 1998, 213–233. (Personal behavior conditions and achievement conditions. In *Organization Psychology*).

Farr, R.M. and Anderson, T.: Beyond actor-observer differences in perspective: extensions and applications. In: Hewstone, M. (ed.): *Attribution Theory—Social and Functional Extensions*. Oxford: 1983, 45–64.

Festinger, L.: *A Theory of Cognitive Dissonance*. Stanford: 1957.

Fletcher, G.J.O.: Psychology and common sense. *American Psychologist*, 1984, 39, 203–213.

Groß-Engelmann, M. and Wiswede, G.: Attribution und kundenverhalten. *Jahrbuch der Absatz-und Verbrauchsforschung*, 1999, 45, 168–194. (Attribution and customer behavior).

Heider, F.: *The Psychology of Interpersonal Relations*. New York: 1958.

Herkner, W.: *Attribution—Psychologie der Kausalität*. Bern, Stuttgart, Wien: 1980. (*Attribution—Psychology of Causality*).

Hewstone, M. (ed.): *Attribution Theory—Social and Functional Extensions*. Oxford: 1983

Hewstone, M.: *Causal Attribution—From Cognitive Processes to Collective Beliefs*. Oxford: 1988.

—— and Antaki, C.: Attributionstheorie und soziale erklärung. In: Stroebe, W., Hewstone, M., Codol, J.-P. and Stephenson, G.M. (eds): *Sozialpsychologie* (2nd edn). Berlin, Heidelberg, New York: 1992, 112–143. (Attribution theory and social explanation. In *Social Psychology*).

Irle, M.: *Lehrbuch der Sozialpsychologie*. Göttingen, Toronto, Zürich: 1975. (*Textbook of Social Psychology*).

Jones, E.E. and Davis, K.E.: From acts to dispositions: The attribution process in person perception. In: Berkowitz, L. (ed.): *Advances in Experimental Social Psychology*, vol. 2. New York: 1965, 219–266.

——, Kanouse, D.E., Kelley, H.H., Nisbett, R.E., Valins, S. and Weiner B. (eds): *Attribution: Perceiving the Cause of Behavior*. Morristown: 1972.

—— and Nisbett, R.E.: The actor and the observer: Divergent perceptions of the causes of behavior. In: Jones, E.E., Kanouse, D.E., Kelley, H.H., Nisbett, R.E., Valins, S. and Weiner, B. (eds): *Attribution: Perceiving the Cause of Behavior*. Morristown: 1972, 79–94.

Kelley, H.H.: Attribution theory in social psychology. In: Levine, D. (ed.): *Nebraska Symposium on Motivation* (vol. 15). Lincoln: 1967, 192–238.

—— *Causal Schemata and the Attribution Process*. New York: 1972.

—— The process of causal attribution. *American Psychologist*, 1973, 28, 107–128.

Kruglanski, A.W.: The endogenous-exogenous partition in attribution theory. *Psychological Review*, 1975, 82, 387–406.

Levine, D. (ed.): *Nebraska Symposium on Motivation* (vol. 15). Lincoln: 1967.

Moscovici, S.: Notes towards a description of social represenations. *European Journal of Social Psychology*, 1988, 18, 211–250.

Ross, L.D.: The intuitive psychologist and his shortcomings: Distortions in the attribution process. In: Berkowitz, L (ed.): *Advances in Experimental Social Psychology*, vol. 10. New York: 1977, 173–220.

Schiffman, L.G. and Kanuk, L.L.: *Consumer Behavior* (5th edn). Englewood Cliffs: 1994.

Seligman, M.E.P.: *Helplessness: On Depression, Development, and Death*. San Francisco: 1975.

Schuler, H. (ed.): *Organisationspsychologie* (3rd edn). Bern, Göttingen, Toronto, Seattle: 1998. (*Organizational Psychology*).

Snyder, M., Stephan, W.G. and Rosenfield, D.: Egotism and attribution. *Journal of Personality and Social Psychology*, 1976, 33, 435–441.

Sirgy, M.J.: *Social Cognition and Consumer Behavior*. New York: 1982.

Stroebe, W., Hewstone, M., Codol, S.-P. and Stephenson, G.M. (eds): *Sozialpsychologie* (2nd edn). Berlin, Heidelberg, New York: 1992. (*Social Psychology*).

Vroom, V.H.: *Work and Motivation*. New York: 1964.

Watson, D.: The actor and the observer. How are their perceptions of causality divergent? *Psychological Bulletin*, 1982, 92, 682–700.

Weiner, B.: *Theories of Motivation: From Mechanism to Cognition*. Chicago: 1972.

—— *An Attributional Theory of Motivation and Emotion*, New York, Berlin, Heidelberg: 1985.

—— *Human Motivation—Metaphors, Theories, and Research*. Newbury Park, London, New Delhi: 1992.

——, Heckhausen, H., Meyer, W.-U. and Cook, R.E: Causal ascriptions and achievement behavior: A conceptual analysis of effort and reanalysis of locus of control. *Journal of Personality and Social Psychology*, 1972, 21, 239–248.

Wiswede, G.: *Soziologie des Verbraucherverhaltens*. Stuttgart: 1972. (*Sociology of Consumer Behavior*).

7 *Cognitive Response*

Theory

OUTLINE

The focus of the cognitive response approach is the direction and intensity with regard to the processing of persuasive information. By "direction of information processing" is meant to what extent the processing proceeds in the direction of the (persuasive) influence—which is prerequisite for the success of the influence—or whether the influence causes a reversal of its intended effect. The latter is known as the boomerang effect. Intensity of information processing is decisive for the stability of the influence. This topic is the subject of the cognitive response theory (Petty and Cacioppo, 1984, 1986), whereby the possibilities of information processing are presented in the form of a model, known as the elaboration likelihood model (ELM). Basic to this is a differentiation into two different forms of information processing: A central route to persuasion, and a peripheral route to persuasion.

THE MODEL

The central route can lead to a more stable, longer, continuous influence, and the peripheral route to a superficial, temporary influence (see Figure 7.1).

People process information with more or less intensity, and more or less in relation to the facts. Of central importance are people's cognitive reactions during the presentation of a communication. This can involve argumentative, cognitive contentions having to do with the communication, or associations that have more or less, or even no discernable objective, logical connection to the communication. Such associations may be product-related memories concerning earlier advertisements. Advertising involving particular emotions can lead to associations regarding advertising for other products that utilize similar emotions. From the cognitive response research we know that apart from perceivable and perceived elements of the communication itself, all of the continuing cognitive reactions may also be responsible for the influence, even if these do not reveal a discernable direct connection to the communication. This is how even communications that are seemingly low in information content but rich in impressions can result in a strong influence.

The fact that cognitive reactions are emotional reactions at the same time is dealt with in Chapter 16, "Power". In this model the effects of persuasive communications depend on two factors: The intensity of the cognitive response, or in other words, the process of information processing, and the relative frequency of positive (from the point of view of the communication), or experienced as emotionally positive, reactions on the one hand, and the negative, or perceived as emotionally negative, reactions on the other hand.

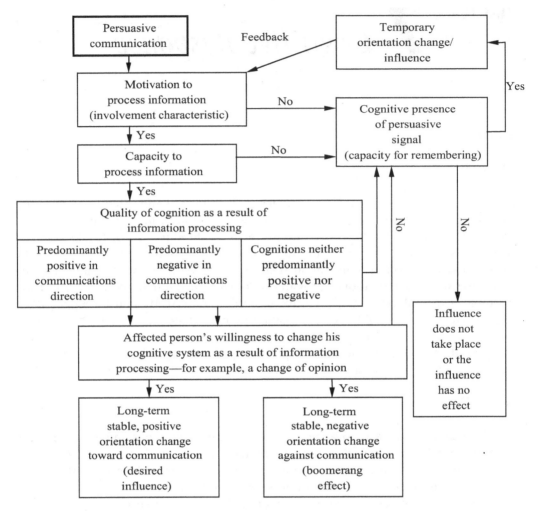

Figure 7.1   The cognitive response model (Petty and Cacioppo, 1984, p. 6; 1986, p. 4)

Long-term, stable changes of orientation only take place after extensive information processing. If there is only a superficial processing then only a temporary and unstable influence can be expected. The former is known as the central and the latter as the peripheral route to persuasion. Petty and Cacioppo's (1984; 1986, p. 4) ELM demonstrates which factors are causative with regard to the two routes.

Ability and motivation as the first prerequisites for information processing

Two factors are the initial prerequisites in order to arrive at an active and intense processing of information: Motivation and Ability. Motivation is basically determined by interest in the product and/or communication, or via the question of whether there is high involvement or low involvement (see section "Theory of Social Judgment Formation", Chapter 2, pp. 24–27). In a high involvement situation, people are motivated toward an active search for product and marketing information, whereas the information processing in low involvement is very limited. If the desire is to draw people into a high involvement situation in order to induce a change in opinion and finally a change in behavior, in-depth engagement with the communication is necessary. Having said that, it also has to be factored in that the affected people might develop counter arguments during the presentation of the message in order to defend their viewpoint, to justify—especially to themselves—their present mode of behavior. By contrast, in a low involvement situation people take in information that contradicts their opinions more passively. They only engage themselves to a small extent. Therefore instances of influencing are more difficult to achieve with high involvement than with low involvement. If however an influence is managed within high involvement—and all other prerequisites for high involvement have been met—then this will be a more essentially stable achievement than is the case on the basis of the superficial processing within low involvement.

In the high involvement area, it is disputed whether or not argumentative communication, and in the low involvement area image accentuated communication (visual or acoustic) should be implemented. There are studies that also support the advantageousness of using image accentuated communication with high involvement (Kroeber-Riel and Weinberg, 1999, p. 342 et seq.). Jeck-Schlottmann (1988) have disputed the theory that with low involvement, a) contact with the advertising medium is broken off earlier, b) contact with the advertising medium is shorter in general, c) images are more preferred, d) emotional images are preferred over factual presentations, and e) advertising text is more superficially perceived than is the case with high involvement. Accordingly, high involvement also leads to early break of contact, to short contact with the advertising medium, to preference of images in general and emotional images in particular, and to superficial perception of text.

On the other hand, in practice there is evidence of how insufficient a communication strategy that is exclusively based on emotional images is in the case of high involvement. Few of the arguments involving information overload and emotional image accentuation are applicable.

The ability to actively process information is determined by personality factors and circumstantial factors, especially those in the media environment. There is the danger of diversion in radio and TV, together with the lack of a possibility of repeat perception, even in the case of aroused interest. When interest is aroused, the users of printed media can determine themselves the frequency and duration of information intake. If attention is captured "at first sight" then theoretically a longer subsequent period of observance is possible. However, the likelihood of this is to this day overestimated within the practice of marketing.

So there is debate as to what prerequisites need to be present at the outset in order to make in-depth information processing at all possible, and as a result to achieve a long term stable influence. If these prerequisites are not present, an effect is still possible, but this will be very unstable in nature and will only be operative as long as the communication is remembered. If a communication is superimposed over this first communication, the latter will be rendered inactive. Biologically there is no forgetting. Whatever is saved once in memory (aside from sickness or accident) will not be lost. The communications that have been "forgotten" in this way can be reactivated later via other communications and corresponding associations. This is by no means an unimportant distinction for market communication. If a communication is not erased, but has merely been obscured, then it can more easily be reactivated by short, concise new communications, than would be the case if completely erased communications had to be newly implanted into memory.

The quality of information processing

In the following section, the influences that may be encountered are determined by the kind of information processing. These cognitive responses can be positive or negative with regard to the communication, or they could also be neutral. This could involve an active engagement with the arguments, or a relatively uncritical perception and processing. Seemingly illogical passing thoughts are also relevant for the influence. In this regard one's own arguments either supporting or rejecting the communication, as well as memories or moods, may be aroused. Decisive for the possible influence are the number and direction of cognitive responses.

If positive cognitive responses dominate, then a lasting effect in favor of the communication is possible; if negative cognitive responses dominate, then a boomerang effect is to be expected. An activation of psychological reactance (Brehm, 1966) can also take place when negative cognitive responses come about.

If neutral cognitive responses dominate, or if rejecting and supporting thoughts stand in a balanced relationship to each other, then a communication effect is very uncertain. If there is an effect, it will be short term and will be of unstable effectiveness.

The cognitive system's readiness to change

Whether or not a positively or negatively processed communication actually leads to a change of orientation depends on the person's overall cognitive system. According to the theory of cognitive dissonance (Festinger, 1957) people strive to maintain their cognitive system in a state of equilibrium. Additionally, all relationships between cognitions that a person subjectively understands as relevant and meaningfully related have to remain free of contradictions. In a comparative analysis of the theory of cognitive dissonance with the information theory of Rény (1966), Möntmann (1985) has shown that every new item of information (which according to Rény, 1966 can only be new if it complements our existing knowledge, or if through our acceptance of the information we are persuaded to revise our existing knowledge) initially places a person's cognitive system in a state of cognitive dissonance. Whether the person understands the new information as an information gain and integrates it into his own cognitive system, or whether the new information is distorted or denied, depends on the structure of the relevant cognitive system. A new item of information will be integrated if the subjectively experienced cognitive effort is assessed to be less than the just as subjectively experienced information gain. If acceptance of the new communication would necessarily lead to changing assumptions, opinions, etc. that are anchored in the person's worldview to a significant extent, in other words if it affects important life and cultural areas, then the person may assess the gain in information as not being worth the effort of changing their mind. On account of its central positioning in the cognitive system, the effort of changing the mind will be seen as too much and the new information will be denied or conveniently reinterpreted. It requires a great deal, or correspondingly significant, undeniable information, in order to change these kinds of central assumptions. In that regard, an exclusive feeling targeted, or affect oriented advertisement will presumably by itself hardly be sufficient. If it is not desirable, for whatever reason, that advertising deliver an informative communication, then other instruments in the communications mix can take over this function. Then advertising may just serve to create an affective, positive orientation, or to arouse interest. The function of changing behavior can be increasingly encouraged through sales talks, which are more suited to presenting information.

Summary

We can now summarize the cognitive response approach and the ELM. There are two routes to influence or persuasion: A central and a long-term route. In correspondence with certain prerequisites, the central route leads to a long-term and stable communication effect. The peripheral route leads to a short-term and unstable effect. The first prerequisite for the central route of persuasion is the presence of ability and motivation with regard to in-depth information processing. Motivation is largely determined by the involvement. Ability largely depends on the specific media conditions. The type of information processing can be defined according to the intensity and quality of the cognitive responses that are encountered. A change of mind takes place in keeping with a preponderance of positive or negative cognitive responses. A prerequisite for this is the person's willingness to accept the communication. This aspect is very much determined by dissonance theory.

Figure 7.1 makes clear that the peripheral route to persuasion also allows for the possibility of influence. However this is only effective in the short term. A long-term influence requires a continuous repetition of the communication. Subsequent communications have to reach the recipient while the previously achieved, short-term, unstable influence is still in effect. In this way the influence can be intensified in small increments. This is a typical situation within mass media advertising for most consumer goods of everyday life.

The boomerang effect that can occur within the central route of influence is not very likely within the peripheral route due to the superficial nature of information processing.

Applications

MARKETING COMMUNICATION

Cognitive response research supplies advice for the formation of marketing communication concepts, particularly with regard to the high involvement versus low involvement aspect. In high involvement conditions we can aim for sufficiently intense and positive associations toward attaining long-term and stable influence success. On the other hand the prerequisites for this are clearly rarely present.

In the area of low involvement the focus is on being present before the target group at a sufficiently high frequency, as continuously as possible. Advertising pauses are inadvisable. The advantage of relatively low involvement is a relatively low readiness to become critically engaged with the communication: "Advertising with low involvement requires frequent repetition of the information, but it slips past the cognitive control of the recipient" (Kroeber-Riel and Weinberg, 1999, p. 329). A long-term, intense communication pressure is a significant success factor. Low involvement therefore requires relatively high communication budgets.

This has been confirmed by cognitive response research. Affect encouraging image communications promise greater influence success than argumentative marketing communication formations, if no motivation for processing is present. Complex chains of argumentation are meaningless in that case. This leads to the conclusion that with low involvement the solely emotional presentation of brands is more significant than the communication of complex patterns of quality. The diverse ramifications of the communication, leads to activation of a large number of associations. The content of all communication influences the content of associations. Integrated communication (Bruhn, 1995) undergoes just such a psychological communications support.

It is similarly the case with regard to Kroeber-Riel (1993) and Kroeber-Riel and Weinberg (1999, p. 342 et seq.) in their significance accentuated image communication. Images are more easily perceived in periods of information overload than summarizing text communications. Intense images can trigger intense associations. Images only have the disadvantage that how they will be interpreted cannot always be predicted. Looking into this could be a task for advertising effect research. Additionally, the direction of image processing can be directed by subtitles.

The not always shared effort to avoid negative elements within the practice of marketing (fear inducing communication, shocking communication) has at the same time a significant justification. Reputation and sympathy are important prerequisites for breaking in a brand in the sense of market share. A commonly heard sentiment in the advertising scene is: "The most important thing is that they talk about us ...", which is incorrect. That there be positive cognitive connections with regard to brands and marketing communication is also very much an issue.

Manifestations of communications concepts over time

From the insight that the existence of short-term, unstable influences direct the processing of later, subsequent influences, can be derived the idea that communications campaigns are coordinated *vertically* (presiding over all communications measures in the moment) as well as in the long term (over time), and thus the conception of an integrated market communication has arisen (Bruhn, 1995). From learning theories we can derive the idea that signals from the environment, especially symbolical signals like brands, will be recognized more easily, the more trusted they are. Trust also creates value relevance and increases the likelihood of processing. As a rule the perception of advertisements in print media takes place only very briefly, and in TV and radio it often only takes place in a superficial manner. For this reason, rapid and unambiguous recognition is of inestimable significance.

On the one hand, repetition of statements leads to redundancy, and so has a negative effect. In this regard communications concepts with an eye to the long term attempt to utilize the positive learning effect via habituation. At the same time there is the task of avoiding the redundancy effect encouraged by repetition. This is achieved by maintaining a long-term communications strategy that straddles all marketing functions, and which is marked by easily perceivable key stimuli. The avoidance of redundancy can be attended to within the communications strategy by sufficient variation in presentation.

According to these standpoints one ought to attempt to stick with certain central compositional elements as long as possible, and at first without any changes. In the context of an ongoing long-term main communications strategy (for example, "integrated communication"), at some point certain necessary changes of form will take place, which however can consistently proceed by building systematically on the given learning effects. We can think here of successful marketing communication concepts like Marlboro®, and of the problems experienced because of changing a marketing strategy, as in the case of Camel®.

That having been said, when is it time to change a campaign, and to what extent can a subsequent campaign be changed without endangering the desired learning effect or recognition? Naturally a theoretical model, even if it has frequently been verified, cannot sufficiently provide a sure answer here. This is exactly the task of market research. Constant checking of market communication's effect provides the necessary information as to when it is time to vary the communication concept.

MARKET RESEARCH

Cognitive response research is a proven instrument in the context of communications research. Its significance for controlling the whole marketing mix is still considerably underestimated.

Studies conducted by Petty and Cacioppo (1986, pp. 131–133) demonstrate how the relative frequency of positive and negative responses change after several repetitions of communications.

Practical experience has shown that within marketing practice advertising and communications measures tend more to change too soon rather than too late. The task of marketing research then could be to a) not only test advertising measures before implementation (pretest) but to continuously conduct tests, and b) to continuously measure the quantity and relation to each other of positive and negative cognitive responses in the context of an ongoing campaign testing process. This can reveal whether the communications measures are still being sufficiently observed (the quantity of cognitive responses being the indicator) and whether the quality of the cognitive responses has developed in a sufficiently positive direction (in relation to the quantity of positive to negative cognitive responses).

In practice, a counter argument is leveled at advertising effect research (before the implementation of the advertisement in the market), which states that pointedly creative new compositional elements are initially rejected by test subjects because they first need to get used to the new advertising statements. Pointedly creative market communication would suffer in making this assumption. The problem is not so easily dismissed but it can be mitigated via the appropriate advertising effect research procedures (see Unger and Fuchs, 1999, p. 509 et seq.). In any case, an ongoing advertising effect research testing process accompanying a campaign provides the opportunity to check whether creative advertising increases in appeal after a certain amount of time. At regular intervals a check can be made as to which associations activate instances of brand recognition and confrontation with communications measures.

Lastly, cognitive response research also allows for the possibility of conducting ongoing pretests not only with regard to measuring perception or intensity of attentiveness, but also with regard to the processing that proceeds from the perception, which can also be relevant to communications success.

Job advertisements can also be checked with the help of free association. On the one hand these results provide hints toward the optimization of these advertisements. They also provide information concerning the image of the organization as an employer.

On the basis of free association, communication research accompanying the campaign can, depending on the circumstances, provide information as to which instruments within communication policy (event marketing, advertisements, sponsoring, product placement) on the one hand, and which instruments in marketing on the other hand (product policy, sales policy) are causative with regard to particular image components. The type of associations can provide information in this context. This is how cognitive response research provides advice toward the targeted optimization of marketing measures. This certainly requires a proportioning of the given associations (positive or negative) between the various marketing measures. It needs to be decided which statements are presumably founded in certain statements within the context of market communication, which statements have their origin presumably in product characteristics or in packaging, which statements might possibly have been triggered via commerce, and finally, which statements can be traced back to the measures undertaken by the competitors. The direct operations of free association provide valuable information because the answers are not structured by the formation of questionnaires or other test procedures; thus, the possibilities of cognitive response research extend much further than communications research.

The methods within cognitive response research are simple and have long been proven within social research. The work with free association or with memory protocols can be traced back to Otto Selz, as is evident from a biographical note written for his one hundredth birthday (Frijda and de Groot, 1981; see also Selz, 1991). Petty and Cacioppo (1986, pp. 35–44) describe some of these types of techniques in more detail. Apart from cognitive protocols that could occur both freely and according to predetermined structures, studies were also undertaken on the basis of electrophysiological methods, which however did not prove fruitful.

The study participants receive instructions as to whether they should report:

a) All thoughts called up by the communication.
b) General thoughts concerning the communication subject.
c) All thoughts which arise during the presentation of the communication, whether they have anything to do with the communication or not (see Six and Schäfer, 1985, p. 51; see also Petty and Cacioppo, 1986, p. 38).

In order to confine the number of expressed thoughts within memory protocols to those triggered by the communication, a time limit can be given and/or structured protocol forms can be implemented, which simply contain a confined number of fields in which the study participant can make entries. In the case of audio recordings the introduction of a time limit is sufficient.

QUESTIONS FOR DISCUSSION

1. Discuss the various forms of marketing communication appropriate for low involvement recipients.
2. Discuss the various forms of marketing communication appropriate for high involvement recipients.
3. Given the discussion in this chapter, outline the most appropriate marketing mix for your organization.
4. Discuss how time and frequency impact cognitive response.

Bibliography

Brehm, J.W.: *A Theory of Psychological Reactance*. New York, San Francisco, London: 1966.

Bruhn, M.: *Integrierte Unternehmens-Kommunikation* (2nd edn). Stuttgart: 1995. (*Integrated Enterprising Communication*).

Festinger, L.: *A Theory of Cognitive Dissonance*. Stanford: 1957.

Frijda, N.H. and de Groot, A.D. (eds): *Otto Selz: His Contribution to Psychology*. Paris, New York: 1981.

Jeck-Schlottmann, G.: Anzeigenbetrachtung bei geringem involvement. *Marketing ZFP*, 1988, 8, 33–43. (Viewing advertisements with slight involvement).

Kroeber-Riel, W.: *Bildkommunikation*. München: 1993. (*Picture Communication*).

—— and Weinberg, P.: *Konsumentenverhalten* (7th edn). München: 1999. (*Consumer Behavior*).

Möntmann, V.: *Kognitive Dissonanz und Gewinn von Information als Konsequenz eines Kognitiven Hypothesentests*. Pfaffenweiler: 1985. (*Cognitive Dissonance and Profit of Information as a Consequence of a Cognitive Hypothesis Test*).

Percy, L. and Woodside, A.G. (eds): *Advertising and Consumer Psychology*. Lexington: 1984.

Petty, R.E. and Cacioppo, J.T.: Central and peripheral routes to persuasion: Appplicaton to advertising. In: Percy, L. and Woodside, A.G. (eds): *Advertising and Consumer Psychology*. Lexington: 1984, 3–23.

—— *Communication and Persuasion—Central and Peripheral Routes to Attitude Change*. New York, Berlin, Heidelberg: 1986.

Rény, A.: *Wahrscheinlichkeitsrechnung*. Berlin: 1966. (*Probability Calculus*).

Selz, O.: *Wahrnehmungsaufbau und Denkprozeß* (von Métraux, A. and Herrmann, T. eds). Bern, Stuttgart, Toronto: 1991. (*Perception Construction and Thinking Process*).

Six, B. and Schäfer, B.: *Einstellungsänderung*. Stuttgart, Berlin, Köln, Mainz: 1985. (*Attitude Change*).

Unger, F. and Fuchs, W.: *Management der Marktkommunikation* (2nd edn) Heidelberg: 1999. (*Management of Market Communication*).

8 *Theories of Information Processing*

Processing and Retention of Marketing Information

THE CONCEPT AND ITS RELEVANCE

In this chapter, human memory will be examined from the perspective of the so-called information processing approach. This point of view defines cognitive processes primarily as a special form of transformation (processing) of information. By the idea of memory this approach means the capacity of an organism to take in information, to store it, and to call it back up on demand. It is assumed that these processes operate within a memory system consisting of stored memories (Zimbardo and Gerrig, 1999, p. 234). At the moment psychology differentiates between two different models of memory, the multiple memory model and the single memory model, which attempt to shed light on information processing from various perspectives.

The multiple memory model assumes there to be three "types" of memories as separate repositories which operate between control processes geared toward regulating information flow (Hobmaier, 1994, p. 123; Mayer and Illmann, 2000, pp. 182–184).

The sensorial memory

Information that an organism is exposed to is first of all registered by the sensorial memory (SM). The duration of the memory imprinting takes only a fraction of a second (0.1 to 1.0 second). One also speaks of an ultra short memory. During this time period it will be decided by various control processes, whether an instance of information will be forwarded along or not. From out of the large amount of information that affects an organism, only that which wins attention and has significance will be saved as long-term memories.

The unique qualities of the sensorial memory are used to advantage in film and television. A film consists of a sequence of single pictures that are shown in very quick succession (24 pictures per second). During the transition from picture to picture there is objectively nothing there to be seen. But the sensorial memory passes over or edits out the very short time period between the individual pictures, and so it appears to the observer to be an unbroken continuum of motion.

The short-term memory

The short-term memory (STM) accesses the combined reservoir of impressions available within the sensorial memory (SM). In doing this it only operates with a limited amount of what the SM takes in. In contrast with the SM, the memory imprinting here takes up to a minute. The STM is also known as the working memory. On the one hand it draws information from the SM, and interprets and processes the given information before forwarding it on to the long-term memory (LTM). On the other hand the STM calls up information from the LTM. In a manner of speaking, it takes a go-between position between the two memory systems.

The long-term memory

Only very little of the information in the STM is admitted to the long-term memory. If however a particular item of information makes it into the long-term memory it will be saved there permanently. The LTM operates according to an almost unlimited storage capacity, and can be equated with people's own memory.

Normally a rough differentiation is made between an explicit (declarative) and an implicit (non-declarative) memory (www.morschitzky.at):

- The explicit memory entails conscious memory, in the form of free memory, memory with recall help or recognition—as can be examined in the context of diagnostics. This has to do with conscious memory of representative information and includes personal experiences that are determined by space and time, as well as our knowledge that exists independently of such time and space oriented connections (episodic memory).
- In the case of implicit memory, the focus is on unconscious behavioral changes conditioned by experience. What is understood by this is a very heterogeneous group of capacities; for example, the tendency to complete words—that one has dealt with before—which one only is provided with the beginnings of, without being given any additional memory cues, as well as the faster recognition of images one has already seen (priming phenomenon).

Figure 8.1 demonstrates memory's various system divisions.

Over the course of the last few years a new point of view has developed amongst some scientists. It has to do with an approach that postulates a single memory. Accordingly separate memories are no longer assumed as in the multiple memory model, and instead various levels within one large unit, the long-term memory, are postulated. Between these levels—like in the multiple memory model—next to automatic coding processes, information processing control processes within memory operations are assumed to be present (Kluwe, 1990). The system is marked by absolute flexibility and adaptation to context relevant information. Its flexibility also shows itself in the productivity of the whole system, which is continuously forming new constellations. These are dependent upon the given interaction of the individual with regard to the context of the individual system. The formation of conceptual processes is influenced by past experiences, as well as by existent knowledge (Malter, 1996, pp. 273–274).

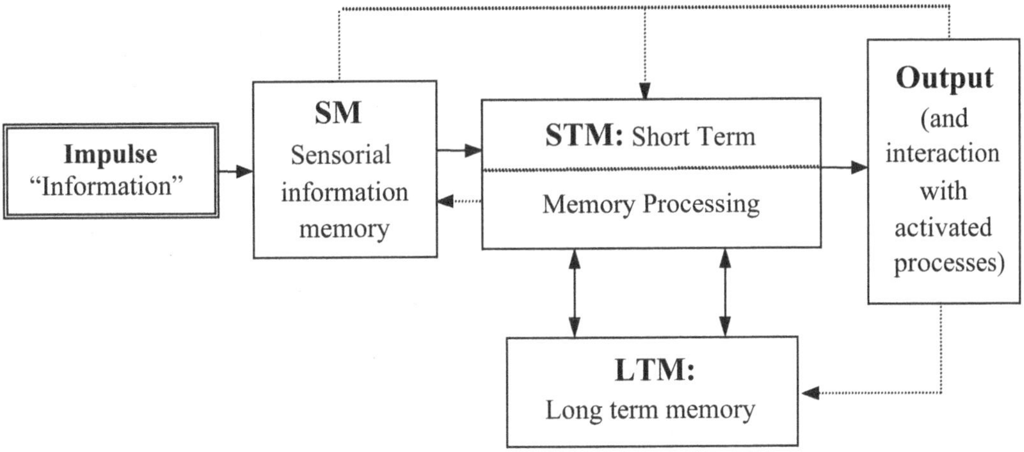

Figure 8.1 Multiple memory model of human memory (Kroeber-Riel and Weinberg, 1999, p. 225)

The fact that regardless of which memory system is being used, the ability is there to use information at a later point in time, implies that three cognitive processes are in operation: Encoding, storage, and retrieval (Zimbardo and Gerrig, 1999, p. 235).

- Encoding is the initial processing of the information, leading to representation in memory.
- Storing (storage) is the maintenance of encoded materials over time.
- Retrieving (retrieval) is calling stored information up again at a later point in time.

The relevance of information processing as a subject is easily transferable to economic topics. The success of companies today depends to a decisive extent on customers, who permanently select information that to them is interesting and important, store it, and retrieve at a certain time. Therefore an adequate and substantial offer of information that is tailored to the given customer is an indispensable prerequisite toward having the wherewithal to influence the customer's decision behavior. In this context, it must however be pointed out that the cognitive processing system displays a limited capacity, and therefore the entirety of perceived information cannot be processed. As a consequence of this, customer oriented information should be provided from the supplier's side. As a rule customers focus only on information that evokes interest and which exerts upon them a certain amount of attraction. A key element here has to do with the creative presentation of advertising media, which will be more thoroughly explained with practical examples in the following chapters (Mayer and Illmann, 2000, pp. 198–199).

RETAINING AND FORGETTING

As has already been indicated, long-term memory is marked by a very large capacity and storage time. Long-term storage of information proceeds according to the formation of material memory traces or through the setting-up of new circuits or connections. Protein synthesis appears to be necessary for the formation of a long-term memory (Lindsay and Norman, 1981, p. 326). The time necessary for the formation of a permanent memory trace—the period of time from the first imprint up until it becomes a permanent memory—is called the "consolidation phase". Only after this consolidation phase has taken place is it possible to measure a long-term memory. Before it has taken place one can only encounter the short-term memory (Kroeber-Riel and Weinberg, 1999, p. 351).

According to a leading theory of forgetting (interference theory), the later retrieval of information is therefore restricted due to the fact that previously stored information is superimposed upon subsequently stored information, thereby detracting from the memory. Memory research calls this phenomenon interference. A differentiation is also made between memory inhibitions that arise with regard to previously stored information (proactive inhibitions) and those that arise with regard to subsequently learned material (retroactive restrictions). A cause of forgetting other than interferences is thought to be that the brain simply exchanges already stored information for new information (Loftus and Loftus, 1980, p. 251). Apart from this there are clues indicating—though this is difficult to prove—decomposition as well as change of memory imprints over the course of time (Lindsay and Norman, 1981, p. 251).

Current studies are concerned primarily with the question of how access to stored—that is, actually retained—information is possible and how this can be facilitated (Kroeber-Riel and Weinberg, 1999, p. 351). In the following section, some important insights within memory research concerning the storage, retention, and forgetting of information are more thoroughly explained (Hobmaier, 1994, pp. 124–128):

- Simple repetition increases the retention of information in short-term memory over the course of several minutes (www.morschitzky.com). If one wants to remember a telephone number the way this is done is often to repeat the number in order to maintain it in short-term memory. When we come to the conclusion that we can bring up the number at any time without much thought, then it has been passed on to the long-term memory. This fact is put to good use within so-called tandem-spots. First the actual spot occurs, and then a little later an abbreviated reminder comes up. Studies have revealed that this technique significantly facilitates recall (Brosius and Fahr, 1996).
- The conscious implementation of memory strategies has a very decisive influence on retention and performance. These are target-oriented measures for improving memory performance. The ability to store and when needed to recall information differs considerably from person to person. Some have no problem committing information to memory and bringing it up when desired, whereas in others this process is very lacking. This fact is often attributed to "good" and "bad" memories. However, studies have revealed that the cause of poor retention and retrieval is not limited memory capacity, but rather that "people who cannot remember well" do not use their memories to an optimal extent because they do not use enough memory strategies.
- Emotionally colored information is more easily retained than "neutral" information, and pleasant more than unpleasant. A tendency is indicated whereby retrieval of information proceeds more easily if there is not a big difference between the physical or psychic state during learning and during recall. If one learned something while in a happy state of mind, it will be more difficult to remember this thing while in a sad state of mind, and vice versa.

- An uncompleted task is more readily remembered than a completed task. This fact is known in psychology as the "Zeigarnik effect". One continuously remembers a task that has not been completed yet. To some extent this hangs at the back of one's mind like a guilty conscience does, whereas completed tasks are already processed and considered done.
- Insightful, meaningful, well-articulated and structured learning material is more easily retained than meaningless and barely understandable learning material that is lacking in insight. The typical course of the forgetting curve for meaningless and meaningful contents sheds light on this (see Figure 8.2).

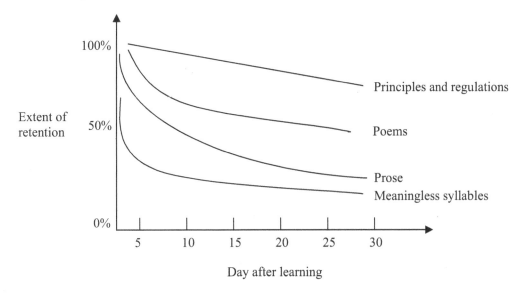

Figure 8.2   The forgetting curve for meaningful and meaningless contents (Michel and Novak, 1990)

- Noticeable information, for example, statements in bold, or that are color contrasted, are more readily remembered. This is all the more applicable if the statements are found at the beginning or end (position effect).
- Descriptive or graphic information is more easily remembered than abstract information.
- A strong inner motivation certainly also encourages the retention, storage, and retrieval of information. Content that is interesting to one is more easily and longer maintained than information that is less interesting.
- A good physical and psychological constitution (with regard to feelings, needs, well-being) on behalf of the learner or recipient has a pronounced effect on what is forgotten or retained.
- A calm working environment without fuss, noise, music, or hastiness, has a positive effect on retention.
- Shocking experiences lead to information being partially forgotten or incorrectly remembered. People who have been in a car accident often do not remember how it happened afterward.

- Anxiety can block the memory. People often have the experience of "drawing a blank" during examination situations, even though they actually have a firm command of the examination content.

MEASUREMENTS OF THE MEMORY

The measurement of stored information is to this day caught up in difficulties. How can one determine which items of information are actually retained and which are forgotten? Basically it is exceedingly problematic to objectively access retained information because every recall process entails a particular cognitive operation that both quantitatively and qualitatively changes the retrieved memory material (Kroeber-Riel and Weinberg, 1999, p. 352).

The first tested approaches to measuring stored items of information have been divided into direct and indirect measurement procedures. The direct measurement procedures attempt to bring up the stored items of information. The indirect procedures are based on the insight that the effort necessary to learn verbal or visual material again clearly depends on how much of that material still resides in memory. The retention or forgetting is therefore indirectly measured through the effort that must be exercised to learn the material again.

In consumer research, the main methods used are free recall, aided recall, and recognition (Kroeber-Riel and Weinberg, 1999, pp. 352–353).

In the free recall method, the test subject has to produce the learned material freely and without help. In aided recall, memory aids are given in the form of hints about the context of the learned material. In recognition, the subject is presented with the learned material together with other material. Memory capacity (with regard to the material the person is remembering) is here the focus of study. As a criterion for differentiating between the different procedures, it can be concluded that recognition results have a tendency to yield higher remembrance values than recall results. Moreover the forgetting curve in measuring retention via recognition proceeds along a more even plane than is the case with free and supported recall. As far as the recall method is concerned there is still doubt among experts as to what extent these procedures actually yield a unified retention performance or various aspects of retention.

Nevertheless, recall measurements that take place 24 hours after the presentation of the advertisement are quite widespread. Test subjects are called up for example a day after the television advertisement and asked whether they remembered it, and if so, which aspects they remembered, for example the slogan, brand name, etc. An advantage here is that the long-term memory is actually being tested. Apart from that recall reveals active brand awareness. The consumer has to be in a position where he is able to actively remember a product or particular product performances. A related aspect of this is that increase in demand for the product is associated with active market awareness. Furthermore methods of this kind are suited to the routing out of advertising that yields little or no persuasive power. It remains to be noted however that these measurement measures do not reveal the behavioral changes in test subjects that lead to purchase and therefore to advertising success.

Brand recognition yields information with regard to passive brand awareness. The consumer only remembers a brand when he sees the product or the brand name.

An example for this is that consumers only recognize certain products if they receive a list that presents the names of products (Kroeber-Riel and Weinberg, 1999, pp. 353–354).

INNER IMAGES AND MEMORY PERFORMANCE

The research basically differentiates between two types of inner images:

- Perception images and
- memory images.

A perception image is spoken of if the subject matter or a representation of the subject matter—for example, a photograph—is present and perceived by the person. On the other hand a memory image represents a mental vision that is supplied in the subject matter's absence. This is understood to be a learned (stored) perception image. In both cases it involves visual imaging. This reveals itself as an encoding of information in memory, in a non-verbal format (Kroeber-Riel and Weinberg, 1999, p. 343).

Inner images induce cognitive as well as emotional effects that exercise a direct influence on cognitive information processing and storage. Among other things they determine our preferences for people and for different subject matters. In the context of consumer research, studies have shown that a customer's preference with regard to a product, business or service essentially depends on the vividness of the consumer's inner image. The experts understand by this the clarity and significance with which the image resides before the observer's inner eye. The more vivid the inner image is, the greater an influence it has on behavior (Kroeber-Riel and Weinberg, 1999, p. 344). Among other things this depends on the image that the recipient has previously taken in and stored. In general a repeated presentation of corresponding attractive elements is necessary in order to form a clear imagined image of a product. Moreover it has to stand out from competing images (Kroeber-Riel and Weinberg, 1999, p. 345). Another key element is revealed in the vividness of the image. This is decisive for the consumer's ability to remember.

Studies have revealed that memory of image information is in general better than memory of verbal information. This applies to simple as well as to complex verbal and image elements. This insight can be used in various areas, for example, in the development of brands and in the formation of advertisements (Kroeber-Riel and Weinberg, 1999, pp. 345–351).

The pictorial vividness of information is also important with regard to how well consumers can remember the extent to which they have engaged in consumer spending. In the context of an experimental study in which people went around a shopping mall with a shopping cart as part of role play situation, it came out that memory performance with regard to the extent of consumer spending was significantly lower in the use of credit cards than it was in the use of cash. Credit card users were found to underestimate their expenditures considerably more often than were people with cash. What was interesting here was also that consumers were not aware of this problem. In the survey that followed the study, participants were asked how sure they were in their estimation of their expenditures. This revealed that credit card users held the same degree of subjective certainty as did cash users (Raab, 1998, pp. 162–166). Therefore credit card users assume a relatively high ability to estimate their expenditures, which does not correspond with reality (illusion of expenditure control). One could explain this illusion of expenditure control by pointing to people's desire to possess control over their expenditures (see the contribution on control theories (Chapter 17) in this book).

Information Processing and Purchase Decision Determinants

As a rule, a whole range of influences exercise an influence on the information processing of consumers. Variations in perception and processing of brand information may take place depending on information quantity, decision time, the form of presentation, sequence of information processing, and consumer specific characteristics. (Mayer and Illmann, 2000, p. 184).

INFORMATION QUANTITY

Within the purchase decision process the customer is often engaged with a great deal of information. The actual need for information is here dependent upon the respective consumer's perception of purchase risk. The greater the perceived purchase risk is, the greater will be the impulse toward additional information (Kroeber-Riel and Weinberg, 1999, p. 249). As an example we can cite the very pronounced customer need for information when purchasing an automobile or family house. As the recent housing boom and bust in the United States will attest, the availability of information does not necessarily imply that it is fully processed by the consumer prior to making a decision.

Not all of the information can be taken in and processed in order to avoid cognitive overload on the part of the customer. Therefore consumers seek to combine maximum decision success with a minimal decision effort. This occurs on the one hand in that the customer compares similar products and decides for the product with the greatest amount of advantages, and on the other hand on the basis of key information like brand name, price, characteristics, and the quality of the products (Coupey and DeMoranville, 1996, pp. 228–229; Fritz and Thiess, 1986, p. 146).

DECISION TIME

An essential element in the purchase decision is the decision time. In this regard Helgeson and Ursic (1994) differentiate between an affective oriented and a cognitive decision. In an affective decision, the customer's decision proceeds more automatically. This kind of decision will be made when the desire is to avoid a larger expenditure of time. In a cognitive decision the decision that is reached has its basis more in the customer's conscious engagement with the product's characteristics. Here a longer expenditure of time is a prerequisite.

PRESENTATION FORM

In decisions as a rule the available information is not modified but is rather directly perceived (Stoddard and Fern, 1996, p. 215). Many studies of information processing in this regard underestimate the influence of the outer format of information (Eckmen and Wagner, 1994). In order to trigger attentiveness in the consumers, and to then capitalize on it and thereby to attain the prerequisites for an efficient intake, processing and storage of product information, this should be "packaged" in a stimulating manner. Furthermore it should be formed such that it will in a very definite way be understood to be in accordance with the marketing objective, and so that it is built into the customer's cognitive system of relations. Organizational characteristics like color, text format, images, as well as ad placement, all play a decisive role (Weinberg, 1992). Von Keitz (1986, p. 115) for example, with regard to the color aspect, has come to the conclusion that color advertisements attain higher appeal values, and in comparison to black and white advertisements lead to better memory performance. With regard to text format and the use of images it can be said that in particular, good readability in the form of a contrast-rich, pleasant text size as well as a clear structure of images, increases the consumers' readiness to more intensively engage themselves in the information being offered (von Keitz, 1986, p. 115). Experts see the right side as being better than the left side as far as advertisement placement is concerned (Jeck-Schlottmann, 1988, pp. 38–40).

SEQUENCE OF INFORMATION PRESENTATION

A lot of information is as a rule sequentially perceived by consumers rather than simultaneously, for example, the spots in an advertising segment. Here the following rule of thumb applies: In serially presented information the first and last units in the sequence are more advantageous. This is known as the "primacy-recency-effect". The primacy-recency-effect phenomenon is explained on the one hand by interference and on the other hand by limited short-term memory capacity. The initial items of information encounter and empty working memory, and therefore have a relatively high chance of making it into the long-term memory. The more information that comes in, the greater the strain will be on the working memory. This is intensified if the items of information are experienced as being similar to each other. Interference occurs; information items become mixed up. An example that can be mentioned is that of several spots for a product class. The person has three spots in memory, which however can merge into two or one. Later on the consumer can only remember the last one. The last-mentioned information is then no longer hindered from being taken up by the working memory, because the working memory is no longer taking in data flow. The information contained therein can now be processed without interference (Felser, 1999, p. 62).

CHARACTERISTICS SPECIFIC TO THE CONSUMER

Information processing is often dependent on particular consumer criteria. As an example gender can be mentioned, as well as any special (expert or lay) knowledge the consumer may have concerning the various characteristics of a product.

With regard to gender-specific characteristics, men tend more to make cognitive oriented decisions, whereas women primarily display the affective aspect of decision-making (Helgeson and Ursic, 1994, p. 504). Additionally, a difference in information processing strategy has been proven to exist. In comparison to men, women tend to have a narrow processing threshold. This shows itself in that they engage themselves more intensely with the content of a communication and therefore develop a greater sensitivity for the particulars. With men on the other hand the total message comes more to the fore. Details are focused on less (Meyers-Levy and Maheswaran, 1991, p. 67). Figure 8.3 can serve to illustrate this.

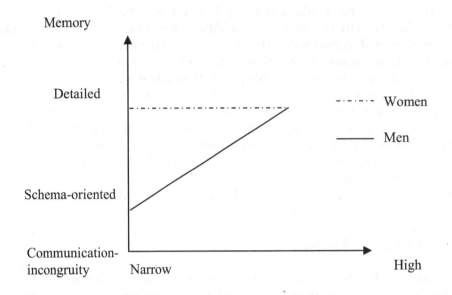

Figure 8.3 Influence of communication incongruence on memory performance (Meyers-Levy and Maheswaran, 1991, p. 67)

Information processing is moreover dependent on whatever knowledge the consumer has concerning particular products. Studies have revealed that the information processing of experts and laymen differs on the basis of various memory structures. The results have led to the conclusion that experts posses a more elaborate memory scheme than do laymen. Depending on the contextual conditions, they will call up differing product information, information that is considered to be important with regard to the given factual content. With laymen this calling up of information does not occur to this extent (Cowley, 1994, pp. 60–61). With regard to attributing cause in the case of product failure, it can also be concluded that consumers who operate on the basis of a large amount of product knowledge will also adduce a greater number of possible reasons for product failure. Due to their more complex knowledge structure, a more efficient information processing and reproduction takes place (Somasundaram, 1993, p. 217). From this we can see why laymen with a more complex decision task are more likely not to make an independent decision and will instead primarily seek information from experts or other sources (Moorman and Rindfleisch, 1995, p. 564). Publications to aid the consumer with the opinions of experts, such as *Consumer Reports*, help to provide evidence for this view.

Summary

As the above presentations demonstrate, the topic of information processing is certainly applicable to economic contexts. The success of companies today depends to a decisive extent on the customers, who select information that is permanently interesting and important to them, save it in memory, and then call it up again at some point in time. An adequate, useful presentation of information that is oriented toward the customer is an indispensable prerequisite: This is the only way the decision behavior of customers can be influenced to the provider's advantage.

QUESTIONS FOR DISCUSSION

1. Discuss the differences among the three forms of memory and how each can best be accessed.
2. Discuss how the Zeignarik effect can be utilized by marketers in an effort to increase brand and product awareness.
3. Explain how the information process affects the purchase decision determinants.
4. Provide some examples of marketing communication where both perception and memory image were utilized effectively.

Bibliography

Brosius, H.B. and Fahr, A.: *Werbewirkung im Fernsehen. Aktuelle Befunde der Medien-forschung*. München: 1996. (*Advertising's Effect on Television. Current Conditions of Media Research*).

Coupey, E. and DeMoranville, C.W.: Information processability and restructuring. Consumer strategies for managing difficult decisions. *Advances in Consumer Research*, 1996, 23, 225–230.

Cowley, E.J.: Recovering forgotten information. A study in consumer expertise. *Advances in Consumer Research*, 1994, 21, 58–63.

Eckmen, M. and Wagner J.: Judging the attractiveness of product design: The effect of visual attributes and consumer characteristics. *Advances in Consumer Research*, 1994, 21, 560–565.

Felser, G.: Zur psychologie der informationsverarbeitung. In: Felser, G., Kaupp, P. and Pepels, W. (eds). *Käuferverhalten*. Köln: 1999, 49–68.(On the psychology of information processing. In *Buyer Behavior*).

Fritz, W. and Thiess, M.: *Das Informationsverhalten des Konsumenten und seine Konsequenzen für das Marketing*. Heidelberg: 1986. (*Information Behavior of the Consumer and its Consequences for Marketing*).

Helgeson, J.G. and Ursic, M.L.: The role of affective and cognitive decision-making processes during questionnaire completion. *Psychology & Marketing*, 1994, 11, 5, 93–110.

Hobmaier, H.: *Psychologie*. Köln: 1994. (*Psychology*).

Jeck-Schlottmann, G.: Anzeigenbetrachtung bei geringem involvement. *Marketing*, ZFP, 1988, 10, 1, 33–43. (Viewing advertisements with slight involvement).

Kluwe, R.H.: Gedächtnis und wissen. In: Spada, H. (ed.). *Allgemeine Psychologie*, Bern, Stuttgart: 1990, 115–188. (Memory and knowledge. In *General Psychology*).

Kroeber-Riel, W. and Weinberg, P.: *Konsumentenverhalten* (7th edn). München: 1999. (*Consumer Behavior*).

Lindsay, P.H. and Norman, D.A.: *Einführung in die Psychologie: Informationsaufnahme und Verarbeitung beim Menschen*. Berlin: 1981. (*Introduction to Psychology: Information Reception and Processing in Humans*).

Loftus, E.F. and Loftus, G.R.: On the performance of stored information in the human brain. *American Psychologist*, 1980, 35, 409–420.

Malter, A.J.: An introduction to embodied cognition: Implications for consumer research. *Advances in Consumer Research*, 1996, 23, 272–276.

Mayer, H. and Illmann, T.: *Markt- und Werbepsychologie* (3rd edn). Stuttgart: 2000. (*Marketing and Advertising Psychology*).

Meyers-Levy, J. and Maheswaran, D.: Exploring differences in males' and females' processing strategies. *Journal of Consumer Research*, 1991, 18, 63–70.

Michel, C. and Novak, F.: *Kleines psychologisches Wörterbuch*. Freiburg im Breisgau: 1990. (*Small Dictionary of Psychology*).

Moorman, C. and Rindfleisch, A.: Divergent perspectives of the role of prior knowledge in consumer information search and processing. *Advances in Consumer Research*, 1995, 22, 564–565.

Raab, G.: *Kartengestützte Zahlungssysteme und Konsumentenverhalten*. Berlin: 1998. (*Card Support Payment Systems and Consumer Behavior*).

Somasundaram, T.N.: Consumers reaction to product failure. Impact of product involvement and knowledge. *Advances in Consumer Research*, 1993, 20, 215–218.

Stoddard, J.E. and Fern, E.F.: The effect of information presentation format and decision on choice in an organizational buying context. *Advances in Consumer Research*, 1996, 23, 211–217.

von Keitz, B.: Wahrnehmung von informationen. In: F. Unger (ed.). *Konsumenten-psychologie und Markenartikel*. Heidelberg: 1986, 97–121. (Perception of information. In *Consumer Psychology and Brand-Name Products*).

Weinberg, P.: *Erlebnismarketing*. München: 1992. (*Experience Marketing*).

Zimbardo, P. and Gerrig, R.: *Psychologie* (7th edn). Berlin: 1999. (*Psychology*).

9 *Judgment Heuristics*

The All-Too-Human Errors in Economic Judgment

THE CONCEPT AND RELEVANCE OF JUDGMENT HEURISTICS

In many situations human behavior is characterized by the need to make decisions under uncertain conditions. For instance, a consumer has to come to a decision as to which washing machine is the best for them, and an entrepreneur might be faced with the decision of whether to introduce a new product onto the market at a given time or not. The uncertainty in such situations comes from the fact that too little information relevant to the decision is available, or from the fact that the situation is especially complex, and future developments have to be predicted and/or a decision has to be arrived at under time pressure. Results of experimental psychology studies have shown that so-called judgment heuristics are often used in decisions involving uncertainty (Kahneman and Tversky, 1973; Kahneman, Slovic and Tversky, 1982; Tversky and Kahnemann, 1974). A judgment heuristic is understood to be a general, easily used, and usually unconscious rule that permits judgments and decisions to be made quickly and relatively accurately under less than optimal information conditions (Stephan, 1999, p. 103). However, judgment heuristics involve the disadvantage that these rule-based judgments and decisions are often connected with errors.

The relevance of judgment heuristics lies in the fact that they constitute further evidence of the limited validity of the homo economicus model. People operate in accordance with a limited perceptual capacity and with limited information processing capacity, and as such are far removed from the economic model of the error free operation of a utility maximizing machine. These notions were already demonstrated over 50 years ago in the psychology of Herbert Simon (1957), who won the Nobel Prize for economic science for his "bounded rationality" concept that grew out of these ideas. In making economic decisions, people and organizations (for example, companies) do not normally take all conceivable alternatives into account, and these alternatives may only be judged according to a few relevant characteristics. The decision-making process will generally be ended when a satisfying alternative is found. Judgment heuristics underscore the bounded rationality of human behavior in many situations.

Moreover, its relevance is evident in that judgments and decisions based on judgment heuristics will under certain conditions involve negative consequences. In this vein, a consumer might decide on a washing machine that upon closer inspection would reveal itself to be the more expensive alternative, and an entrepreneur might decide for the early introduction of a new product, even though a later entry into the market might have resulted in greater profit. Questions arise here as to which judgment heuristics are implemented, when they are implemented, and under what conditions does this lead to negative consequences. These points will be addressed in the following chapter.

FORMS OF JUDGMENT HEURISTICS

Among the most well known judgment heuristics are availability heuristics, anchoring and adaptation heuristics, and representative heuristics. Because of their high practical significance, the first two types of heuristics will be dealt with in the following, along with the distortions connected with them. Availability heuristics, which are used particularly with regard to estimating frequency and probabilities, will be elucidated first. Subsequently anchoring and adaptation heuristics will be described, which are of significance in the most varied range of judgments and decisions.

Availability heuristics

Availability heuristics use the degree of ease with which information is generated or called up from memory to estimate the frequency or probability of occurrences. The more easily we call up a memory and the more examples that occur to us, the more frequent and probable this occurrence will seem to us, as long as no objective information is available or is not used due to time factors (Kahneman and Tversky, 1982, p. 11). The concept of availability heuristics is, however a somewhat unfortunate choice of term. Modern memory psychology differentiates between information that is present in memory, which is in principle available, and the actual accessibility (availability) of information. Everyone knows the situation where one is actually sure that one knows something, and yet in a real situation (for example, an examination) one cannot call up or generate this knowledge. In availability heuristics the primary focus is on the accessibility and capacity to generate information (Herkner, 1991, p. 202).

Retrievability and availability heuristics

If one asks a group of the unemployed to estimate how high the level of unemployment is in their area, one will receive a considerably higher average estimation than if one were to ask a group of employed people in the same area. The cause of these varying estimations is that in a short time, in accordance with the availability heuristic, the unemployed are able to call on many examples of unemployment in their awareness. Similar results will be obtained if one asks people in Cologne and Wolfsburg, how high is Ford's market share in Germany. Due to Ford's having its German headquarters in Cologne, and due to the favorable conditions available for employees with regard to the purchase of a Ford® brand car, Ford® cars are particularly prevalent in Cologne. It stands to reason that the situation in Wolfsburg, known for being home to Volkswagen's headquarters, would be represented differently. In accordance with availability heuristics, if one asks people in Cologne, they will immediately think that there are more drivers of Ford® cars, and thus the prevalence of this brand in Germany will correspondingly be assessed at a high level.

It is clear from the examples of availability heuristics explained above that these heuristics can lead to approximately correct judgments in many cases. If the people of Cologne are just asked how high they would estimate Ford's market share in Cologne, then the ease with which they retrieve the corresponding examples is a good indictor of the brand's actual frequency. Availability heuristics is then a reversal of a fundamental insight in memory psychology with regard to the relationship between a stimulus' frequency of appearance and memory events that arise without difficulty, that as a rule are instances that occur with a high degree of probability. Availability heuristics leads to errors when the individual is not aware that their experiences (observations) only represent a sample of what is there, and that these experiences do not necessarily represent the actual frequency of occurrences.

Tversky and Kahneman have run a whole series of experiments toward the end of confirming availability heuristics and the estimation errors associated with them. In the context of one simple experiment people had to indicate whether five consonants occurred with greater probability as the first or third letter of words. Consonants were chosen that actually occur in the third position much more often than in the first position. However, most of the people (70 percent) were of the opinion that the letters occurred more often in the first position. This result made it clear that the ease with which the corresponding words could be called up from memory influenced the estimation of frequency. Since the beginning letter represents a better retrieval cue as the same letter in the third position, people could more readily remember words that begin with the respective consonants than words where the consonant is in the third position, and thus the frequency was overestimated (Tversky and Kahneman, 1973).

In another experiment Tversky and Kahneman (1974) presented people with a list of names of men and women, asking them to estimate the number of men and women. A group of people was read a list of 19 well-known men and 20 unknown women. A second group was presented with 19 well-known women and 20 unknown men. Since it is easier to remember well-known names and these are more quickly available than unknown names, it was expected in the first instance the number of men and in the second the number of women would be overestimated. The results confirmed this assumption exactly.

Stephan (1993) carried this experimental approach over to the assessment of market reports. In his experiment the focus was on the influence that familiarity (reputation) had with regard to public company names in a market report in the assessment of stock market trends. To this end a market report was created with the profit and loss of 51 public companies at the end of an imaginary stock market day. Twenty-five of the companies were very well known to the people and 26 were less known. In one version of the market report (market report A) two thirds of the 25 well-known companies were noted as gainers and the other third as losers. The average profit and loss of the market was at five percent. In the group of 26 less well-known companies the relationship between profit and loss was reversed. The market report had the following form: 25 well-known companies (17 gainers, 8 losers) and 26 less known companies (8 gainers, 18 losers). An undistorted memory of the relationship between gainers and losers should have reflected a basically even distribution or slight prevalence of losers. The second version of the market report (market report B) was the same as the first version with the exception that the relationship between gainers and losers was reversed. The market report consisted of: 25 well-known companies (8 gainers, 17 losers) and 26 less known companies (18 gainers, 8 losers).

A recording of the market reports was played for the two groups. After they had listened to the market report they were asked whether there were more gainers or losers in the 51 companies. Sixty-seven percent of the people who had listened to market report A falsely believed that it contained more gainers than losers. Sixty-one percent wrongly assessed market report B (see Figure 9.1). In both cases the higher cognitive availability of the well-known companies led to estimation error (Stephan, 1999, p. 125). It is noteworthy that this involved people who were senior students engaged in business sciences. It can be assumed therefore that the study participants had some familiarity with regard to market reports. Nevertheless, varying availability led to this effect.

	Memory of test subjects		
	More gainers	More losers	Total
Form A (More losers)	67%	33%	100%
Form B (More gainers)	39%	61%	100%
Total	54%	46%	

Figure 9.1 Availability heuristics and the assessment of market reports (Stephan, 1999, p. 125)

Generation and availability heuristics

In the above-described experiments the focus is on retrieving information from memory and then making an assessment of frequency based on it. There are also many situations where the retrieving of information is not enough. In these tasks what is called for is not only calling up information from memory, but rather calls for the cognitive generation of a solution. Imagine that you are the project leader in a company. The project team consists of ten employees. What do you think, how many different two-person groups can you make? How many eight-person groups can you make?

According to Kahneman and Tversky's (1973) results the number of two-person groups was estimated to be 70 on average and the number of possible eight-person groups was on average estimated to be 20. In actuality the number of two-person groups is the same as the number of eight-person groups. In both cases 45 groups can be formed. Naturally no one expects that people not educated in combinatorics would be able to provide exact calculations. What is interesting is the big difference between the two estimations.

The reason for the incorrect estimation that many more two-person groups could be formed is according to Kahneman and Tversky (1973) again a matter of cognitive availability. In the formation of differing groups the respective individual cases cannot be retrieved from memory; they have to be mentally generated. Two-person groups are more easily imagined than eight-person groups. Ten people can directly be split into five two-person groups without overlap, but not even one eight-person group without overlap (or extras). The ease with which groups can be mentally constructed serves as an indicator of the possible number of combinations.

Our ability to imagine particular things, in addition to influencing our estimation of group sizes and frequency, also influences the estimation of the probability of individual occurrences. In many situations where we have to or want to make decisions, we can only subjectively estimate the probability of individual occurrences. For example, we expect a certain high degree of reliability in buying a certain vehicle, and in purchasing investment shares we hope for a particular return on the capital we invest. In these situations we are often making our decisions in dependence on how well we are able to imagine the results and on how familiar we are with the subject matter. For example Americans have a pronounced preference for the shares of their local telephone companies. The total investment portfolio cannot be justified when considered rationally and when measured against recommended risk distribution yielded by a theoretical examination of the portfolio (Huberman, 1998). Even professional investors prefer companies within their countries that lie within their immediate area (Coval and Moskowitz, 1996). Familiarity and the ease of imagining particular events connected with it, influence our decisions. Companies, especially those companies whose service areas involve offering things that are immaterial in nature, should try to provide customers with information that allows them to form a "picture" of the given product and company. The results of the above-presented experiments furthermore show that too high a level of complexity with regard to product presentation and pricing is problematic. It seems to make little sense to offer customers a multitude of product variations if they cannot actually visualize the combinations. A possibility for example is allowing customers to envision how they would outfit a vehicle via the Internet, an approach that has already been adopted by some automobile dealers.

Anchoring and adaptation heuristics

Anchoring and adaptation heuristics maintain that in all manner of judgments people begin with the estimation of an initial value (anchor), which is then adapted to up until the final judgment is reached. Regardless of whether the initial value is defined by the given problem, is freely chosen by the person, or is randomly given, in every case an adaptation in the direction of the initial value takes place, which often is inadequate. Inadequate in the sense that too pronounced an adaptation in the direction of the initial value takes place (Strack, 1993, pp. 261–262).

Let's imagine that you have to calculate the answer to an arithmetic problem by rough estimate, because you only have five seconds per task. The task consists of finding the answer to the following multiplication: $8 \times 7 \times 6 \times 5 \times 4 \times 3 \times 2 \times 1$. A variation of the task consists of reversing the order of the numbers: $1 \times 2 \times 3 \times 4 \times 5 \times 6 \times 7 \times 8$. Tversky and Kahneman (1974) used exactly these two examples to study anchoring and adaptation heuristics. For the first task they obtained an average result of 2,250 and for the second task an average result of 512. The actual answer of 40,320 was significantly underestimated. How can one explain these results? In order to solve the tasks in the given time the first two or three calculations were made, thereby formulating an initial value (anchor), and on this foundation the end result was estimated. As the results show this kind of adaptation is completely inadequate, especially if the initial value is especially far removed from the end result.

There have been many other experimental studies that confirm the assumptions of anchoring and adaptation heuristics. From these it can also be shown that this effect also occurs in situations in which the anchor value has no factual connection with the question and where the person is also not aware of this. Anchor effects are here not consciously perceived by the decision-maker and as such are difficult to control.

One might be of the opinion that such effects are observed in the context of scientific studies, but that they vanish when people are in possession of know-how and experience with regard to the given subject matter they are judging. However, this is not the case. Northcraft and Neale (1987) came up with a field experiment in which real estate agents were asked to estimate the value of a house. The agents were given a booklet on the house, which also included information about other houses in the neighborhood, and all participants visually inspected the house. In order to study anchoring and adaptation heuristics, groups of real estate agents were formed that varied only in that the catalogue price of the house given in the booklets differed; the agents were all operating on the same information then, with the exception of the catalogue price. Before the appraisal all of the agents were of the opinion that the catalogue price had no relevance with regard to a correct appraisal of the house, and that they would not allow themselves to be influenced by the catalogue price in any way. In actual fact, the agents' appraisals were heavily weighted in the direction of the catalogue price (anchor). The same result was found in a comparison group of students. While the students acknowledged the influence of the catalogue price after the results were presented to them, the real estate agents argued against any influence the catalogue price might have had on their appraisal.[1] Given the influence that real estate agents have with many home buyers, the anchoring effect helps to explain how high sales prices prevailed until the recent market correction in the United States.

The effects described have also been observed in other forms of economic judgments and decisions. In a study conducted by Stephan (1992) students of business sciences had to submit predictions regarding what the value of the dollar exchange rate, the Deutsche Aktien-index (DAX), and the price of gold would be in seven weeks' time. Information concerning actual development of rates over the preceding six months was graphically presented to the participants. In this way, the information possessed by participants before beginning the study was homogenized, and prediction uncertainty was reduced. In order to study the anchoring and adaptation heuristics the participants were asked at one stage to give a rough estimate. One group was asked whether the dollar exchange rate would be more or less than 1.50 DM, the DAX more or less than 1,600 points, and the price of gold more or less than 16,000 DM per kilogram bar.[2] The other group was also asked to give a rough estimate, and here the deceptive values were dollar exchange rate of 1.70 DM, DAX 1,800 points, and price of gold 18,000 DM. The two groups differed from each other therefore in that one group was given low and the other high anchor values. The participants' predictions based on their rough estimates differed significantly and were biased in favor of the given anchor values. The average predictions for the dollar exchange rate were a revealing 1.53 DM versus 1.58 DM, for the DAX 1,719 points versus 1,764, and for the price of gold 16,670 versus 17,082 DM. These differences are highly significant and meaningful.[3] The same results came up with regard to predictions provided by professional currency dealers in an international broker firm, concerning the Dow Jones share index, the exchange rate of the English Pound, and the price of gold (Kiell and Stephan, 1997). The above findings are evidence that even people who have a

---

1   The denial that the catolog price had any influence can be explained with the help of the theory of cognitive dissonance. See (Chapter 4, pp. 43–57) in this book.

2   At the time of prediction the dollar exchange rate was 1.52 DM, the DAX 1,750 points and the price of gold 16,900 DM.

3   Regarding the discussion of methods for revealing the significance of empirical results, reference can be made to the book by Bortz and Döring (1995) as well as Cohen (1988).

high degree of professional know-how and experience in the given task area operate also according to anchoring and adaptation heuristics.

As is evident from the preceding studies, anchoring and adaptation heuristics possess a high degree of practical relevance. It is obviously of crucial significance to what extent bank employees, in evaluating developments in rates, rely on initial rough estimates that are completely uninformative with regard to providing sound predictions. This could lead to the bank having less success in its own dealings, or in customers changing banks because of being poorly advised. In this context, recommendations concerning the purchase and sale of shares also appear in a new light. The fundamental problem with these recommendations has recently been discussed. It is a fact that many underwriting banks make recommendations that are more than problematic to companies they have brought to the stock market (Heise, 2000, pp. 178–184). Recommendations like these that assert rate developments and/or specific price levels, function as anchor values. Connected with this is the fact that private, and also institutional investors, which of course are constituted by people, also have to make certain estimates that, as has been shown, again involve anchoring and adaptation heuristics, in that judgments are oriented toward these anchor values thereby leading to an incorrect evaluation of the situation.

Other interesting areas of application are price management and product management. In the context of pricing policy one entrepreneurial strategy is that of price bundling. By price bundling it is meant a situation where several products and/or services are offered for one price. McDonald's® has been very successful with package offers in the USA and in Germany, where a hamburger and fries are offered together with a beverage (Simon and Dolan, 1997, pp. 247–248). Another variation of price bundling is found in the area of cellular phones. Here commercial companies offer cellular phones at a very low price or even free of charge. The purchase of one of these devices is contingent on agreeing to a long-term contract with a service provider. Here too the customer only has to pay one price for a package or framework of services. Of interest in this connection, is that in its advertisement the company especially emphasizes the device, in other words the actual, tangible product, as well as the attendant low price.

The strong emphasis and the fact that the additional use and set-up costs are first mentioned in following text, lead to the price of the cell phone acting as an anchor, whereby the total price of the package is distorted in the direction of this anchor value. The same might apply to insurance policies in Germany. In their advertising, German private health insurance companies emphasize in particular the lower contributions they ask for in comparison to other providers and to the public health insurance companies. Additional costs, for example, for spouses, possible children, the significant increase in contributions with regard to certain previous illnesses, and the usual increasing contributions with risk and old age, are all mentioned, but are more likely to be found in small print. The customer is therefore as a rule not in the position to take into consideration all immediate as well as future factors and information, which may in the long term influence the total price.[4] Furthermore, we cannot objectively evaluate certain developments, just as experts in this field cannot. The initial contribution (anchor) will accordingly lead to an adaptation in the direction of the initial value when considering additional factors. Substantiated studies concerning the effects described here have not yet been carried out with regard to pricing policy.

---

4   A particularly good reference with regard to limited information processing capacity is Kroeber-Riel and Weinberg (1999). See also the contribution on information processing (Chapter 8) in this book.

A central element of product management is brand policy (Bruhn, 1999, p. 131; Nieschlag, Dichtl and Hörschgen, 1997, p. 234). Here it might be particularly fruitful to examine anchoring and adaptation heuristics within the context of umbrella brand name strategies and brand family strategies. Umbrella brand name strategies connect the company name with the company's combined offering of products and services (corporate logo). The company name acts as the umbrella brand even if very divergent service and product offers are present in the market (for example, Siemens®, Sony®). Brand family strategies put forward a unifying label for a product group, whereby various individual products are offered under this one name (for example, Milka®, Nivea®) (Bruhn, 1999, pp. 150–151; Meffert, 2000, pp. 861–862). These kinds of brand families often come into being because of a situation where successful individual brands are developed into brand families. The individual brand represents the seed brand (mother brand) around which the new products (brand children) are grouped. A classic model for this kind of strategy is the brand Nivea®. In this case it worked to develop a whole range of new products (for example, Nivea® Visage, Nivea® hair care, Nivea® body care) around the mother brand Nivea® Cream, thereby engaging in a very successful brand transfer (see Figure 9.2). Both the mother brand and the corporate logo function as anchor values. As long as the customer identifies quality and price with the mother brand or corporate logo, this might also lead to judgments regarding new products and brands that are biased in the direction of the given anchor values. Many companies are at least implicitly aware of the significance of this function. For example the chairman of the board of directors of the company Beiersdorf AG, Rolf Kunisch (2000, p. 20) stated in an interview concerning the company's brand strategy: "And the brand is even more important—as an anchor for trust".

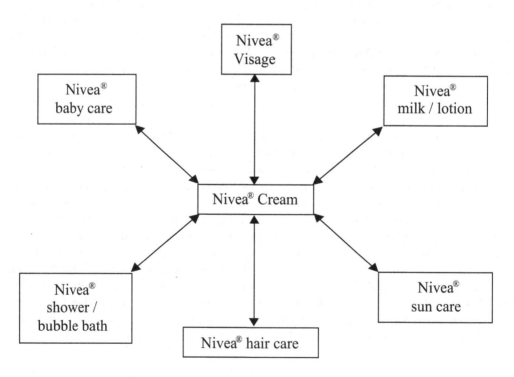

Figure 9.2   Brand family strategy with Nivea® as an example (Becker, 1994, p. 479)

Summary

The information presented above makes it clear that people often make judgments and decisions on the basis of judgment heuristics. As a result of these judgment heuristics, incorrect estimations with negative consequences often come about. Knowledge and understanding of these heuristics allow for better explanations and understanding of people's behavior. This knowledge can be of use with regard to practical problems. For example, the consumer can be sensitized to this problem on the basis of this knowledge. Companies can take these insights into consideration, for example, in product management and in pricing policy.

Judgment heuristics and the errors connected with them are certainly not anomalies, as is often assumed; rather they indicate the norm, the rules governing human thought (Kruglanski and Ajzen, 1983). Heuristics often function relatively well and lead to useful results. In many cases they are also reasonable strategies; if a decision has to be made quickly and/or without available objective information, then there is hardly any other alternative. However, the decision-maker should be aware of the risks.

QUESTIONS FOR DISCUSSION

1. What are judgment heuristics and how can their study be useful for marketers?
2. Discuss the concept of anchoring heuristics and how these are useful in branding strategy for your organization.
3. How might marketers utilize availability heuristics to gain market acceptance for their companies' products and services?

Bibliography

Becker, J.: Typen von markenstrategien. In: Bruhn, M. (ed.). *Handbuch Markenartikel*, vol. 1. Stuttgart: 1994, 463–498. (Types of brand-name strategies. In *Handbook of Brand-Name Products*).

Bortz, J. and Döring, N.: *Forschungsmethoden und Evaluation*, (2nd edn). Berlin: 1995. (*Research Methods and Evaluation*).

Bruhn, M.: *Marketing*, (4th edn). Wiesbaden: 1999.

Cohen, J.: *Statistical Power Analysis for the Behavioral Sciences*. New York: 1988.

Coval, J. and Moskowitz, T.: *Home Bias at Home: Local Equity Preference in Domestic Portfolios*. Working paper. New York: 1996.

Heise, S.: Vorsicht falle! *WirtschaftsWoche*, 2000, 36, 178–184. (Caution trap!).

Herkner, W.: *Lehrbuch Sozialpsychologie*, (5th edn). Bern: 1991. (*Textbook of Social Psychology*).

Huberman, G.: *Familiarity Breeds Investment*. Working paper. New York: 1998.

Kahneman, D., Slovic, P. and Tversky, A. (eds): *Judgment under Uncertainty: Heuristics and Biases*. Cambridge: 1982.

—— and Tversky, A.: On the psychology of prediction. *Psychological Review*, 1973, 80, 237–251.

—— The simulation heuristic. In: Kahneman, D., Slovic, P. and Tversky, A. (eds). *Judgment under Uncertainty: Heuristics and Biases*. Cambridge: 1982, 201–208.

Kiell, G. and Stephan, E.: *Urteilsprozesse bei Finanzanlageentscheidungen von Experten. Abschlußbericht einer Experimentellen Studie mit Professionellen Devisenhändlern*. Köln: Universität zu Köln, Institut für Wirtschafts- und Sozialpsychologie: 1997. (*Judgment Processes in Financial Decisions of Experts. Conclusion Report of an Experimental Study with Professional Foreign Currency Dealers*).

Kroeber-Riel, W. and Weinberg, P.: *Konsumentenverhalten* (7th edn). München: 1999. (*Consumer Behavior*).

Kruglanski, A.W. and Ajzen, I.: Bias and error in human judgement. *European Journal of Social Psychology*, 1983, 13, 1–44.

Kunisch, R.: Tanz um das goldene haar. *Werben & Verkaufen*, 2000, 35, 70–72. (Dance around the golden hair).

Meffert, H.: *Marketing* (9th edn). Wiesbaden: 2000.

Nieschlag, R., Dichtl, E. and Hörschgen, H.: *Marketing* (18th edn). Berlin: 1997.

Northcraft, G.B. and Neale, M.A.: Opportunity costs and the framing of resource allocation decisions. *Organizational Behavior and Human Decision Processes*, 1987, 37, 28–38.

Simon, H.A.: *Models of Men*. New York: 1957.

—— and Dolan, R.J.: *Profit durch Power Pricing*. Frankfurt am Main: 1997. (*Profit through Power Pricing*).

Stephan, E.: Zur rolle von urteilsheuristiken bei finanziellen entscheidungen. In: Montada, L. (ed.). *Bericht über den 38. Kongress der Deutschen Gesellschaft für Psychologie*, vol. 1, p. 711. Göttingen: 1992. (On the role of judgment heuristics in financial decisions. In *Report on the 38th Congress of the German Company for Psychology*).

Stephan, E.: If we're so dumb, how come we made it to the moon?. Vortrag für den 3. Kongreß der Schweizerischen Gesellschaft für Psychologie: 1993.

—— Die rolle von urteilsheuristiken bei finanzentscheidungen. In: Fischer, L., Kutsch, T. and Stephan, E. (eds). *Finanzpsychologie*. München, 1999, 101–134. (The role of judgment heuristics in finance decisions. In *Finance Psychology*).

Strack, F.: Urteilsheuristiken. In: Frey, D. and Irle, M. (eds). *Theorien der Sozialpsychologie, vol. 3: Motivations- und Informationsverarbeitungstheorien*. Bern, 1993, pp. 239–268. (Judgment heuristics. In *Theories of Social Psychology*, vol. 3: *Motivation Theories and Information Processing Theories*).

Tversky, A. and Kahneman, D.: Availibility: A heuristic for judging frequency and probability. *Cognitive Psychology*, 1973, 5, 207–232.

—— Judgment under uncertainty heuristics and biases. *Science*, 1974, 185, 1124–1131.

On the Development of Personality via Perception and on Through to Memory

10 *Developmental Psychology*

Customer Behavior as a Life-Long Development Process

CONCEPT AND RELEVANCE

Modern developmental psychology is concerned with the life-long development of people, where this includes the interaction of the individual with the environment (Hinde, 1992, p. 1019; Montada, 1995, pp. 1–24). Developmental psychology takes into consideration the influence of both genetic disposition and environmentally determined factors on the development of human thought, feeling, and behavior. In this context it is asked again and again to what extent certain capacities and behavioral tendencies are inborn or acquired. We do not want to deal here with this discussion (the nature versus nurture debate), because it has been discussed over a long period of time in various sciences, like in biology, philosophy, psychology, and sociology. In brief, and this is really inarguable, people do come into the world with certain genetic predispositions. A completely different question is how these predispositions or preconditions get used. Heredity provides the potential, and experience and engagement with the environment bring out the manner in which this potential gets used.

No one is born with a Nike® gene or a Starbuck's® gene. The attitude toward these and other brands, as well as the preference for these is much more the result of development or socialization.[1] What is inborn is, among other things, the need for approval in the social community. This need and the human behavior deriving from it is not a characteristic of twentieth- and twenty-first-century humanity; rather it can be traced back to the very origins of humanity (Gerloff, 1947; Sahlins, 1972; Schmölders, 1966). This fact is documented by the clothing and forms of jewelry of earlier epochs. The essential difference between the past and the present is that now these needs are increasingly being used and encouraged by business interests.

The relevance of developmental theories and insights lies in the fact that they can be utilized by various institutions (for example, companies, consumer organizations, schools), and are being used, to optimally adapt their respective services to the given developmental level of customers, consumers, or students. Use of these insights is here especially furthered in that companies have identified children, teenagers, and seniors as particularly interesting target groups. In the past few years companies have taken up developmental psychology insights with regard to the catch phrases of child and teenager

---

1   Due to consideration of life-long developmental processes and of the influence of the environment in modern developmental psychology, differentiation between the concepts of development and socialization is very difficult (Prenzel and Schiefele, 1986, p. 122).

marketing (Dammler, Barlovic and Melzer-Lena, 2000; Zanger and Griese, 2000), and senior marketing (Meyer-Hentschel and Meyer-Hentschel, 1991; Lewis, 1997). As a result of the pronounced significance of these customer groups, application of these insights will increase. The significance of these customer groups stems from the fact that among other things, children and teenagers have command of an enormous purchase potential, and in many instances influence the purchase decisions of adults. It comes as no surprise therefore that companies regularly conduct extensive studies with regard to the interests and attitudes of these groups, that countless market research institutes have specialized in these groups (for example, iconkids and youth), and that big advertising agencies have founded special departments or subsidiaries (for example, Saatchi and Saatchi, McCann-Erickson). This also applies to elderly consumers due to the increasing number of seniors in society and their corresponding purchase potential.

THEORY AND APPROACH

It would be presumptuous to believe that one could merely present the main features of developmental psychology in a market psychology textbook. Thus we will focus on three theories that elucidate the fundamental considerations of developmental psychology.

Piaget's theory of cognitive development

Cognitive development entails all cognitive processes—perception, thinking, imagination, and problem solving. A large portion of modern research in cognitive development is based on the research work of the psychologist Piaget (1974). He was above all interested in the nature of change that the way children think is subject to, in the course of cognitive development. Knowledge and understanding with regard to economical relationships and business decisions are also subject to these changes, presupposing a developmental or socialization process. Children know relatively little about economical matters like money, price and interest. Differentiated knowledge can first be assumed at around the age of fourteen (Kirchler, 1995, p. 64). Piaget's theory of cognitive development offers the possibility of describing and explaining the development of economic knowledge. Toward this end we want briefly to explore the central aspects and insights of this theory.

The core of development is in the individual's adaptation to the demands of the environment. Adaptation to the environment involves the two elementary processes of assimilation and accommodation. Through assimilation, information taken in by the individual is changed such that it is blended with available sensory motor and cognitive structures (schemata). Through accommodation, the schemata themselves are changed so that they match the information and do not come into opposition with other schemata in the total structure. As a result of these two processes the child is less and less dependent on unmediated perception and more dependent on cognition. Cognitive development therefore involves the transition from trust in appearance to trust in rules. The sensory motor structures, the action schemata of infants, are dependent on the immediate reality of things, whereas after this stage the cognitive structures increasingly contain symbolic representations of the external world that allow them to perform operations that are more and more complex. Piaget (1974) here differentiates between four qualitatively different phases of cognitive development:

The sensory motor phase (until the age of two)

By the age of two the capacity to symbolically represent objects that are not immediately present is clearly developed. The child operates according to an inner image of an object, and can deal with this object mentally, without it having to be physically present.

The phase of preoperational representation (second to seventh year)

Preoperational thinking is characterized by a centralizing; the child's attention is focused on a single subject or characteristic. The child cannot focus on more than one aspect. The following task illustrates this: A thread with 20 wooden pearls, of which 17 are black and three are white, is placed before some children. They are then asked whether the thread contains more wooden pearls or more black pearls. The children are of the opinion that the black pearls are in the majority. This results from the fact that children at this stage of development subtract the black pearls from the given amount of pearls, and in making a comparison in order to judge whether there are more wooden pearls or more black pearls, only take into account the remainder, the white pearls. Children at this stage of development cannot think abstractly. They are not in the position to note the amount of black pearls and then to mentally compare these with the total number of pearls. They therefore can only take into consideration the characteristic of color and for this reason come to an incorrect conclusion.

The concrete operation phase (seventh to eleventh year)

Children at this stage can mentally transform information and can even reverse the cognitive processing stages. They rely more on concepts than on what their perception allows them to see or feel. If the same amount of liquid is poured into two glasses, five-, six-, and seven-year-old children all report that both glasses contain the same amount of water. However, if the liquid is poured out of one of the glasses into another higher and thinner glass, the opinions as to whether there is still the same amount of liquid, begin to diverge. The five-year-olds know that it is still the same liquid, but they believe that it has increased in volume. The six-year-olds are unsure, but they also say that there is more in the tall glass. The seven-year-olds on the other hand know that there is no difference with regard to the amount of liquid. The younger children concentrate their attention only on one aspect to determine the amount of liquid, the height of the glass, while the children at the formal operation stage are in the position to take into consideration both the height and width aspects.

The formal operation stage (eleventh to fifteenth year)

At the stage of formal operation the adolescents can think in abstractions, pose hypothetical questions, and derive logical proofs for abstract problems. A classic example for this phase is that an individual at this phase is able to solve problems via a systematic approach. While children at the stage of concrete operation will for example ask the question again and again as to whether the given animal is a cat, the adolescent forms superordinate categories or questions (for example, mammal, pet) which lead to answering the actual question.

In the Piaget tradition of developmental psychology, a whole range of empirical studies have been conducted with regard to the development of understanding in the area of economic relationships and concepts. A fundamental assumption in these studies, has been that this development proceeds parallel to the cognitive development as Piaget (1974) understands it. Burris (1983) asked children in the age groups of four to five, seven to eight, and ten to twelve, among other things, about their knowledge of goods, prices, work, and possession. Four- and five-year-olds thought that the price of goods depended on size. A diamond therefore costs much less than a clock. To the seven- and eight-year-olds, price seemed to be dependent upon the goods' use. A clock cost more than a diamond or a book, because one can read the time with it. Other concrete aspects that are used as criteria for the price include the longevity of the products, or the fact that they are more fun than other products. Children between ten and twelve consider how substantial the effort to produce the product was, and posit the price to be dependent on that (Kirchler, 1995, p. 66). These findings have been supported by other studies (Claar, 1996; Berti and Bombi, 1988; Reisch, 1996) and they underlie the assumption that children proceed from a diffuse and global knowledge on to a more differentiated knowledge of economic relationships and concepts. This evaluation was also arrived at by Lea, Tarpy and Webley (1987, p. 326) on the basis of older studies in various countries.

The relevance of developmental stages is documented by the fact of how difficult children find it to recognize advertisements as advertisements and a radio or TV program as a radio or TV program. This is supported by a study conducted by the radio advertising regional office (*Landesanstalt für Rundfunkwerbung*) of Nordrhein-Westfalen and the umbrella organization of the German advertising industry (*Zentralverband der deutschen Werbewirtschaft*) (1995). In this study 38 percent of four- to six-year-olds could not differentiate between advertising and programs, even though the advertising on TV always has to be identified as such. Of the seven- to ten-year-olds, a fifth of them still had difficulty differentiating. Furthermore children under six years old are unable to see through advertising concepts like product placement or so-called program length commercials, like the Smurfs, Alf, or Sponge Bob Squarepants, which are produced for the primary purpose of marketing toys of all kinds based on them (Müller, 1997, pp. 44–45).

According to Piaget's (1974) theory of cognitive development, formal operative thinking is the last phase of cognitive development. Formal thought operations arise in the context of active processes, on the basis of biological changes determined by age and through the use of experiences with regard the environment, like those offered up by school or family. Certainly the problems that an adult is normally confronted with often do not have the clear structure of the tasks Piaget used to study formal operative thinking. In the adult age group a less abstract and less absolute form of thought is called for, a form of thought that can deal with contradictions and multiple meanings. This pragmatic way of thinking has been labeled post formal thinking (Basseches, 1984; Labouvie-Vief, 1985).

Another interesting area of enquiry in developmental psychology is the question regarding to what extent cognitive efficiency decreases with age. In contrast to the widespread misconception that the mental abilities of older people decrease, studies have shown that only five percent of the population suffers a loss of cognitive functioning.

Studies have furthermore shown that older people who are engaged in a high degree of stimulation with regard to the environment maintain a high degree of cognitive efficiency (Zimbardo and Gerrig, 1999, pp. 471–473). This means that older people who are introduced to new technologies or products (for example, the Internet), in a way that is oriented toward their needs and abilities, will also understand them. Experiences have proven this to be true, for example the presentation of and instructions for automated bank teller machines (Adams and Thieben, 1991).

The relationship between sensation seeking and age

Sensation seeking has to do with the tendency of people toward obtaining new, varying, and intense sensory impressions, or toward creating such experiences.[2] In a comprehensive study involving over 900 people, Zuckerman, Eysenck and Eysenck (1978) looked into whether this tendency changes over the course of the life span. The results show a highly significant age effect (Zuckerman, Eysenck and Eysenck, 1978, p. 147). With increase in age the optimal level of sensation lowers (see Figure 10.1). This substantiates the findings of earlier studies, which however were based on smaller and non-representative samples (Blackburn, 1969; Brownfield, 1966; Kish and Busse, 1968).

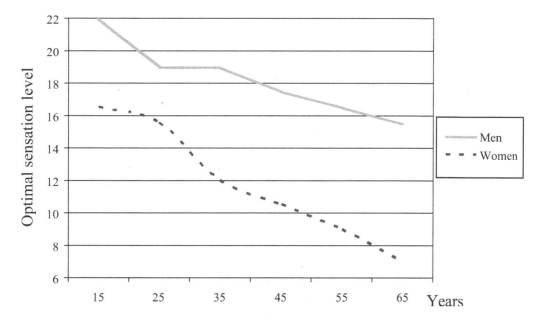

Figure 10.1 Sensation seeking and age (Zuckerman, Eysenck and Eysenck, 1978, p. 3)

Two things are revealed by the above results concerning the development of sensation seeking. One thing is that one's optimal experienced level of sensation lowers with age, and the other is that it seems that the younger generation requires more and

---

2   See also the contributions on personality theory in Chapter 11 in this book, "Sensation Seeking", (pp. 154–156).

more intense sensations in order to achieve a satisfactory level of activation. When one considers the development with increasing age, certain practical recommendations for action can clearly be derived. In presenting goods and organizing stores with regard to the senior citizen target group, one should stick with stimuli of a moderate intensity level. In terms of the presentation of floors, walls and ceilings, colors should be used that contain a relatively high proportion of white. If one wants to use more potent colors, then the wall and ceilings should be presented with the same color. In this way the room will come across as relatively calm, despite the stimulating color. One should also limit the number of colors to just two or three. This also applies to textures. It is also advisable here to limit things to just a few textures, in order to avoid too strong of a stimulation (Meyer-Hentschel, 1990, p. 195). The insights into the development of sensation seeking with age could and should also be used in the organization of Internet sites.

The Family Cycle and Consumer Behavior

The life cycle is a concept whereby people's life span is spit up into different phases like childhood, youth, marriage, family, etc. If one looks at the phase of the life cycle that has to do with being a member of a family, then one speaks of the family cycle. Each stage in the family cycle is a demographic variable that stands in close relationship with other variables (for example, attitudes, behavior) and can therefore be used to determine the behavior of consumers (Kroeber-Riel and Weinberg, 1999, p. 438).

The phase divisions of the family cycle that are used in research and practice differ significantly from each other in terms of the number of individual phases. Depending on the division criteria being used, the phases vary from two to twenty-four (Kirchler, 1989, p. 185; Schneewind, 1995, p. 138). Engel, Blackwell and Miniard (1993) start with the family in their model of new life cycles. The different stages will be described in brief below (Meyer and Illmann, 2000, pp. 340–341):

- **Single stage** Although a single has a relatively small income, he/she has the freedom to act at his/her disposal. A part of the income will typically go to acquiring an automobile and toward furnishing an apartment. He/she is fashion and free time oriented, and spends a large proportion of money on clothing, alcoholic drinks, luxury items, going out to dinner, vacations, etc.
- **Recently married couple** A recently married couple do not have any children, and so are in better financial shape than before, since the woman is often also working. A large portion of the money will be spent on a vehicle, clothing, on vacations, and on other free time activities. There will additionally be large expenditures made on costly purchases (things for the house). They appear to be particularly given to the influence of advertising.
- **Full nest I** With the birth of the first child the woman typically gives up her employment and the family income decreases. Reallocation of the household tasks takes place. The pair moves into a bigger house, new furniture becomes necessary, especially for the child. A washing machine, a dryer, and other large appliances are purchased. The many demands on the family budget lead to a reduction in savings, and the parents tend more often to be unhappy with their financial situation.

- **Full nest II**   In this phase the child is at least six years old or older. The father's income has increased and the mother is employed again. The family income increases. The structure of consumption is to a large extent determined by the needs of the child. A pronounced tendency to buy large packs of certain products arises (for example, detergent).
- **Full nest III**   Over the years, the financial situation of the family improves. The mother is working and her salary increases over the course of time. The children also contribute from time to time. Individual bits of furniture will be replaced, a new vehicle will be purchased, and various luxury items will be acquired. A large part of the income will be spent on the children's education.
- **Empty nest I**   In this phase, the family is mostly satisfied with its financial situation and with the amount of savings it has accumulated up to this point. The children are out of the house. Cosmetic adjustments are undertaken within and around the house, luxury items can be afforded, and a large part of the disposable income is spent on vacations, travel, and recreation.
- **Empty nest II**   At this point, the father has left work life and the family consequently feels the effects of a reduced income. The expenditures for health and old age provisions grow. One considers moving into a smaller house or to a region with a more pleasant climate.
- **Remaining employed survivor**   If the person still left living in the family is still employed, then that person enjoys his or her good income. Under these circumstances he/she will buy a house, spend more on vacationing, recreation, and products that are conducive to his/her health.
- **Remaining survivor with pension**   The retired widow(er) is similar to the consumption model that was just described, though at a lower level in keeping with the reduced income. There are increased needs with regard to benefits, sympathy, and security.

A weakness of the family cycle approach lies in the fact that it is not a theory in the true sense, but rather is only a description of sequentially occurring phases. Furthermore the family cycle increasingly proceeds in a way that is less in keeping with what were once considered "normal" phases. From the individual phases certain behavioral modes can be inferred which have a practical relevance; however, often these generalized descriptions prove to be inadequate. It is certainly helpful for a bank to refer to customer segmentation based on the life cycle (see Figure 10.2), because this is easily imagined and provides clues as to which products are of particular relevance to the respective customer groups. This kind of classification generally only gives advice as to whether certain products will be bought or not, but does not say anything with regard to the choice of a given product and/or of a given bank. If a couple has a child there arises the need for housing financing in order to get more living space. In this situation the family cycle model makes a clear differentiation between purchasers and non-purchasers of housing financing. Why the family might choose an actuarial loan over bank credit, in order to finance more living space, is however not discernible from the phases of the family cycle. In this case, psychological variables like for example personality characteristics need to be taken into consideration, in order to better explain the behavior (Klingsporn, 1996, pp. 34–35).

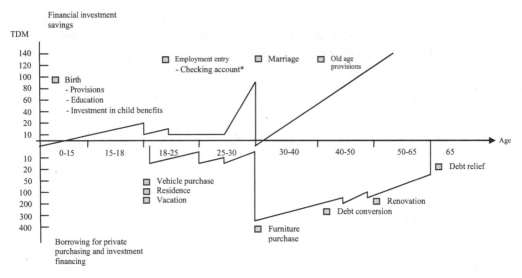

Figure 10.2 Life cycle or family cycle and the demand for financial products (Klingsporn, 1996, p. 39)

This also applies to the group of seniors. It is indisputable that this group makes up a growing proportion of the total population and that on average they possess a high degree of financial clout; to what extent certain products and/or companies profit from this fact depends primarily on what needs and attitudes these people have. More exact correlations between the objective situation and behavior can only be made when precise insight has been obtained into the psychological variables involved (Kroeber-Riel and Weinberg, 1999, p. 444). Furthermore, continuous change is at the basis of the family life cycle concept. In place of the traditional family there is ever more pronounced initiation of alternative life styles, which in Germany among other things are shown by a decrease in the marriage rate, an increase in one-person households, and in a decrease in the birth rate (Schneewind, 1995, p. 147). New approaches are trying to come to terms with this increasing proliferation of lifestyles (Wilkes, 1995).

Children and Teenagers as Consumers

Children and teenagers are consumers. In the following sections, we would like on the one hand to explore the significance this group has for companies, and how organizations address this customer group. On the other hand we want to describe an approach that has the goal of encouraging the young to approach money and consumption consciously and critically. The relevance of this kind of encouragement is made obvious by the increase in debt and excessive debt (*Arbeitsgemeinschaft der Verbraucherverbände & Deutsches Rotes Kreuz*, Team of the Consumer Councils and German Red Cross, 1999; Neuner and Raab, 2001) as well as by the increase in compensatory and addictive purchasing behavior (Black, 1996; Raab, 2000; Scherhorn, Reisch and Raab, 2001).

CHILDREN AND TEENAGERS AS A MARKETING TARGET GROUP

Children and teenagers as customers

The economic interest of companies in children and teenagers in particular results from this group's impressive purchasing power. The available cash resources of 6 to 17-year-olds in Germany, adds up to nearly 20 billion DM (Dammler, Barlovic and Melzer-Lena, 2000, p. 16). Children between the ages of 6 and 14 already command financial resources to the tune of 6 billion DM. Allowance, contributing 2.8 billion DM, only makes up a part of this. In this regard it should be noted that children are to a large extent themselves in charge of what they do with their allowance. Between the ages of 12 and 13, 87 percent are already in charge of their allowances (Zanger and Griese, 2000, p. 6). With regard to the allowance contribution, an additional 1.8 billion DM arises from erratic money allowances (for example, pocket change in the supermarket) and 1.4 billion DM from gifts of money, for example, for birthdays or for Christmas, whereby of this total amount, certainly only a portion is spent. Children save about 70 percent of this amount. Given this situation, it is understandable that banks and savings banks attend to these customer groups. This is not only limited to the development of special products and the formation of children and youth clubs; the formation of so-called youth banks has also been undertaken. Examples of this are the Jugendbank newSpark (New Youth Savings Bank) of the Kreissparkasse Mayen (Mayen District Bank) and the cashBOX of the Stadtsparkasse Magdeburg (Magdeburg Municipal Savings Bank). Banks throughout the world now offer savings accounts for minors, capitalizing on this increasingly important sub-segment of deposit balances.

Children and teenagers do not just command their own financial resources (direct purchasing power), which they command more or less depending on age; they also influence what is bought for themselves and for their family (indirect purchasing power). Atkin (1978) observed shopping parents and children between three and twelve years old in supermarkets, in front of shelves upon which cornflakes were being offered. In 66 percent of the cases the child took the initiative and pleaded for or encouraged the purchase of a particular brand. The pronounced influence of children on the purchase decision was shown in that, in 72.7 percent of the cases, parents in general, and in 63 percent of the cases in connection with the desired brand, acquiesced to the children. Only 9.1 percent of parents rejected the desires or encouragement of their children. Even in situations where the initiative was taken by the parents, the children exercised a pronounced influence on the final decision (see Figure 10.3). It is also interesting that in the context of surveys, parents significantly underestimated the influence of children in their purchase decisions. In comparison to surveys therefore, observations deliver the more reliable information. Atkin's (1978) research findings have also been supported by more recent studies, which furthermore have shown that the influence of children on purchase decisions has increased (Dammler, Barlovic and Melzer-Lena, 2000, p. 98).

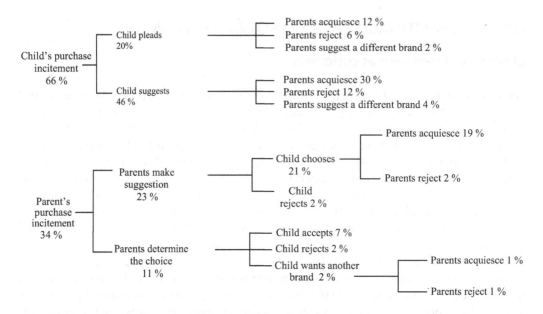

Figure 10.3 The influence of children on the decision to purchase cornflakes (Atkin, 1978, p. 43)

While children primarily influence purchase decisions with regard to products and services that they use themselves, teenagers also have a large influence on family purchase decisions. In family decisions teenagers influence with regard, for example, to the purchase of a vehicle amounts to 34 percent, of a TV set 52 percent, a stereo system 60 percent, and with regard to buying a computer 54 percent (Verlagsgruppe Bauer, 1996). Companies like Daimler, Chrysler, Volkswagen and BMW are aware of the significance of this, and accordingly conduct special market research studies involving children and teenagers. The significance of this influence is also made clear by the fact that it is assumed that children and teenagers make decisions regarding purchases to the tune of over twice that of their personal financial resources (Bastei-Verlag, Axel-Springer-Verlag and Verlagsgruppe Bauer, 1999). This constitutes an amount of over 40 billion DM.

Children and market awareness

Between the ages of two and three the process of brand commitment has already set in (Dammler, Barlovic and Melzer-Lena, 2000, pp. 99–100). As soon as kids come together with other kids, that is, shortly after infanthood, they develop awareness of the market. Children at this age already know what they want with relative precision. Between the ages of eight to ten, children have developed a clear idea of a brand and orient themselves to it according to particular social attributes (Melzer-Lena, 1996, pp. 6–9). The significance of this kind of market awareness for one thing comes from certain products and services having been developed specifically for certain age groups (as seen in any grocery check-out counter), and partly from the fact that certain products are only in demand by given age groups (Barbie®, Lego®, Playmobil®). Economic success depends on the given product being purchased by the parents. The significance also lies in the fact that the purchase of a given brand at this age leads to a high degree of brand commitment at the adult age level.

The significance for an enduring brand commitment of purchasing particular brands in youth has been substantiated by a study involving 500 people. In this study, people in their 30s were presented with collages and old songs from the time period when they were 17 years old. Over 100 different brands from 14 product areas were then presented to them, whereupon they were asked whether they used them when they were 17 and whether they still use them now. On average 52 percent still used the brands that they used when they were 17-year-olds. The market commitment of over a decade was strongest in the case of chocolate at 64 percent. But even in the areas with least loyalty like alcohol-free drinks and soap it was at around 40 percent (Dammler, Barlovic and Melzer-Lena, 2000, pp. 20–21). In the face of these numbers it is understandable why companies take the trouble to gain customer commitment as early as possible. Toward this end companies have developed various instruments. The instruments include customer clubs that are especially designed for children and teenagers (for example, ADAC-JugendClub, Barbie Fan Club, LEGO World Club, McDonalds Club, Nintendo Club), magazines (for example, of Volks-banken, *Mark*, and of Raiffeisenbanken, *Penny*), and computer games (for example, Levi's®, Playmobil®, and Expedia®'s golf and baseball games).

Figure 10.4 Milka's child-focused website (www.milka.de), accessed October 2001

A relatively new instrument for creating customer commitment is the setting up of homepages on the Internet for children and teenagers. An example of such a homepage is the one set up for Milka® (www.milka.de). Children can adopt a virtual cow on this homepage, which must be fed like a Tamogotchi®, and which also has to be milked, taken to the vet, and brought to a beauty farm. If the cow is not cared for enough, it will go back to join the herd again. On this website, there can also be found a chat room, a Milka® shop, and various online games such as an online ski jump, mountain climbing, and racing (see Figure 10.4). As useful as such instruments may be for companies, by way of criticism it needs to be mentioned that due to their psychological development children are not in a position to recognize or understand a company's intention. Moreover, the Internet offers the possibility of studying children and teenagers with regard to their consumer behavior. A US trade authority, the Federal Trade Commission (FTC) has established in a report that 90 percent of commercial Internet sites for children obtain personal information, including information regarding to the financial assets of parents (Paetsch, 2000, p. 114).

THE BANKS AND YOUTH IN DIALOGUE—AN INSTITUTIONAL APPROACH TO CONSUMER EDUCATION

The conceptual context of the approach

The central characteristic of the "Banks and Youth in Dialogue" concept is the partnership between several institutions. Up to now, concepts of consumer politics and consumer education have in general involved only one institution (for example, schools, consumer consultants, debt consultants) (Gauert, 1996). An active integration of all involved institutions, especially including companies or banks, has not taken place. The reasons for this stem on the one hand from fear of change on the part of social organizations with regard to industry, and on the other hand from industry's reserve with regard to social institutions and their objectives. In the interest of consumer education, it is certainly unavoidable that all institutions taking part develop and realize mutual concepts. In the context of this approach, this development and realization proceeds according to the following objectives:

- The encouragement and development of a competent and responsible relationship to money in the young.
- Encouragement of a partnership oriented customer relationship.
- Cooperation and integration of institutions on location (banks, schools, debt consultants, consumer consultants).

In order to realize these objectives and due to psychological insights regarding dealing with money (Claar, 1996; Furnham and Argyle, 1998; Raab, 1998; Yablonsky, 1992), the level of knowledge (cognitive level), of feelings (emotional level), and forms of behavioral control (instrumental level) are taken into consideration and the corresponding contents provided. The cognitive level contains in particular information about the forms and costs of financial services (for example, loans, investment forms, payment systems), the types and costs of insurance, the forms of building society savings, banking industry structure, and the legal aspects (for example, consumer debt law, surety). The emotional level deals with aspects of the economic and psychological functions of money, the emotional aspect of savings and debt, the material and immaterial satisfaction of needs and the compensatory function of consumption. The instrumental level involves the necessity of behavioral control or management of oneself (personal responsibility), the limits and forms as well as the instruments of behavioral control. Banks in the United States have a similar focus on educating the youth, as evidenced by the series of comic books issued by the Federal Reserve of New York that specialize in teaching teenagers the basics of things such as E-Commerce, the role of money in society, and the role of foreign trade and exchange in an economy. Private financial institutions, such as Wachovia, Bank of America, and others, offer volunteer opportunities for their employees to partner with local public schools in order to lend a helping hand.

Implementation and phases of the approach

The first phase of the approach is the initiation (initiative phase). The project can be initiated by bank employees, by teachers, or by debt or consumer advisers. Who provides the impetus depends on local circumstances, commitments, and on the time constraints of those doing the initiating. Existing local contacts should be taken advantage of (for example, local study groups), and new contacts should also be made. As a rule the initiator should take over the project management; in order to have success this is a central prerequisite. It is of utmost importance that consultation amongst each other takes place in the individual phases. The project derives its existence from all project participants coming together at one table to actively and cooperatively organize the individual phases in relation to technical content, chronological sequence, and didactic methods.

"Money and consumption" will be made into a topic in the second phase (school phase 1), subject to the students' level of knowledge and the teacher's appraisal. The content ranges from the origin of demand to the students' desires, and household planning. It has proven helpful to allocate group work according to student interests in the phase following this one, the bank phase. Here it should be taken into consideration which students have experience with regard to financial institutions, for example, via having a checking or savings account. A survey of the students concerning their attitudes in dealing with money and consumption is also part of this phase.

As part of the school phase, teenagers in the third phase (bank phase) visit a bank or savings bank for a day. This day inside a bank includes an information market, a future workshop, and a concluding group discussion. In the context of the information market the teenagers are asked questions according to chosen topics with regard to dealing with money (for example, the cost of a loan, possibilities of financial investment, the risks of a security). In order to answer these questions the teenagers will seek out the appropriate employees, usually trainees, within the respective bank departments. In preparation for the information market the bank employees of respective departments receive a catalog of questions at the beginning of the bank phase. In the future workshop the teenagers are meant to playfully and creatively engage in the topic of money. To encourage this dialogue and to bring in other possible points of view, the employees of the given bank will also take part in the future workshop. At the end of the bank phase the trainees and students organize a group discussion.

The fourth phase (school phase II) in class serves the purpose of processing the experiences and impressions of the day in the bank. Among other things ethical questions will be dealt with here, like for example the relationship between consumption and quality of life, as well as the effect consumer behavior has on the environment. Additionally in the classes further informative presentations will be given and rounds of discussion will be held, with representatives from banks, consumer advisers, and debt consultants.

Following this phase comes the fifth phase of retrospective assessment (review phase). In the context of this phase an analysis of the overall proceedings of the realized project is conducted, and perhaps a reworking or expansion. This phase may also involve a presentation of the experience involving the students and/or the institutions that took part. This presentation can for example proceed as an exhibit in the school or bank, as a contribution to the school newspaper, or as a presentation on the Internet. Experiences with realized projects so far have shown that this form of "press work" receives an impressive response from the participants and the public.

The last and *sixth* phase of the approach is the evaluation (evaluation phase). After a period of six months the students who took part in the project are once more questioned in a survey concerning their attitudes and behavior with regard to money. The goal of the evaluation is both an analysis of the project's success, and to gather information toward optimizing or expanding the approach. The projects conducted so far with over 200 students have demonstrated significant effects involving a more critical and more aware relationship to money and consumption (Peters and Raab, 2000).

Summary

The details presented above make it clear that customer behavior is a life-long development process. In this connection the insights of developmental psychology can be and are being used by various institutions. This applies for example to the development of new products, the consolidation of an enduring customer relationship, and the development of approaches that facilitate a critical and competent consumer education.

In contrast to the high interest and commitment of companies, economic science and psychology have so far had little to do with the question of how children learn to deal with money, to save, or how they can develop an understanding of economic relationships, and what changes attitudes to consumption and money undergo with age (Furnham and Argyle, 1998; Reisch, 1996). Against a background of increasing debt and addictive shopping behavior, consideration of these questions is an important future task for science. Companies would also benefit from these insights, in that responsible action with regard to customers would become a significant success factor in the future.

QUESTIONS FOR DISCUSSION

1. Discuss the different strategies of Piaget's Theory of Cognitive Development.
2. What does the relationship between age and sensation seeking imply about targeted marketing efforts?
3. What are other industries that would benefit from a consumer education approach, and are any others currently doing this?
4. Discuss the importance of the family life cycle in a marketing context.

Bibliography

Adams, A.S. and Thieben, K.A.: Automatic teller machines and the older population, *Applied Ergonomics*, 1991, 22, 85–90.

Arbeitsgemeinschaft der verbraucherverbände & Deutsches Rotes Kreuz, schulden-bericht 1999: Kredite der privaten haushalte in Deutschland. Baden-Baden: 1998. (Team of the consumer councils and German Red Cross, debt reports 1999: Credit of private households in Germany).

Atkin, C.K.: Effects of parent-child interaction in supermarket decision-making. *Journal of Marketing*, 1978, 42, 41–45.

Bassches, M.: *Dialectical Thinking and Adult Development*. Norwood: 1984.

Bastei-Verlag, Axel-Springer-Verlag and Verlagsgruppe Bauer: Kids Verbraucheranalyse 99. Bergisch Gladbach: 1999. (99th Kids consumer analysis).

Berti, A.E. and Bombi, A.S.: *The Child's Construction of Economics*. Cambridge: 1988.

Black, D.W.: Compulsive buying: A review. *Journal of Clinical Psychiatry*, 1996, 57, 50–54.

Blackburn, R.: Sensation seeking, impulsivity, and psychopathic personality. *Journal of Consulting and Clinical Psychology*, 1969, 33, 571–574.

Brownfield, C.A.: Optimal stimulation levels of normal and disturbed subjects in sensory deprivation. *Psychologia*, 1966, 9, 27–38.

Burris, V.: Stages in the development of economic concepts. *Human Relations*, 1983, 14, 791–812.

Claar, A.: *Was Kostet die Welt: wie Kinder Lernen, mit Geld Umzugehen*. Berlin: 1996. (*What the World Costs: Children Learn to Handle Money*).

Dammler, A., Barlovic, I. and Melzer-Lena, B.: *Marketing für Kids und Teens*. Landsberg: Moderne Industrie, 2000. (*Marketing for Kids and Teens*).

Engel, J.F., Blackwell, R.D. and Miniard, P.W. *Consumer Behavior*. Fort Worth. The Dryden Press: 1993.

Furnham, A. and Argyle, M.: *The Psychology of Money*. London: 1998.

Gauert, H.: *Werbung, Jugend und Konsum*. Berlin: Stiftung Verbraucherinstitut, 1996. (*Advertising, Youth and Consumption*).

Gerloff, W.: *Die Entstehung des Geldes und die Anfänge des Geldwesens*. (3rd edn) Frankfurt: 1947. (*The Origin of Money and the Beginnings of Money Exchange*).

Hinde, R.: Development psychology in the context of other behavioral sciences. *Developmental Psychology*, 1992, 28, 1018–1029.

Kirchler, E.M.: *Kaufentscheidungen im Privaten Haushalt*. Göttingen: 1989. (*Purchase Decisions in the Private Household*).

—— *Wirtschaftspsychologie*. Göttingen: 1995. (*Economic Psychology*).

Kish, G.B. and Busse, W.: Correlates of stimulus seeking: Age, education, intelligence, and aptitudes. *Journal of Consulting and Clinical Psychology*, 1968, 32, 633–637.

Klingsporn, B.: Teilmärkte bilden: Yuppi oder Skippie—wer ist Ihr Kunde. *Bankmagazin*, 1996, 7, 34–42. (Forming market share: Yuppie or Skippie—who is your customer).

Kroeber-Riel, W. and Weinberg. P.: *Konsumentenverhalten* (7th edn). München: 1999. (*Consumer Behavior*).

Labouvie-Vief, G.: Intelligence and cognition. In: Biren, J.E. and Schai, K.W. (eds), *Handbook of the Psychology of Aging*. New York: 1985, 500–530.

Lea, S., Tarpy, R. and Webley, P.: *The Individual in the Economy: A Survey of Economic Psychology*. Cambridge: 1987.

Lewis, H.: *Seniorenmarketing: Die besten Werbe- und Verkaufskonzepte*. Landsberg am Lech: 1997. (*Senior Marketing: The Best Advertising and Sales Concepts*).

Melzer-Lena, B: Frühe markenpositionierung. *Markenartikel*, 1996, 56, 1, 6–9. (Early brand-name positioning).

Meyer, H. and Illmann, T.: *Markt- und Werbepsychologie* (3rd edn). Stuttgart: 2000. (*Marketing and Advertising Psychology*).

Meyer-Hentschel, H.: *Produkt- und Ladengestaltung im Seniorenmarkt: Ein Verhaltens-Wissenschaftlicher Ansatz*. Saarbrücken: Rechts- und Wirtschaftswissenschaftliche Fakultät der Universität des Saarlandes, 1990. (*Product Formation and Shop Formation in the Senior Market: A Scientific Extension*).

—— and Meyer-Hentschel, G.: *Das Goldene Marktsegment—Produkt- und Ladengestaltung für den Seniorenmarkt*. Frankfurt: 1991. (*The Golden Market Segment—Product Formation and Shop Formation for the Senior Market*).

Montada, L.: Fragen, konzepte, perspektiven. In: Oerter, R. and Montada, L. (eds): *Entwicklungspsychologie*, (3rd edn) Weinheim: 1995, 1–83. (Questions, concepts, perspectives. In *Developmental Psychology*).

Müller, M.: *Die Kleinen Könige der Warenwelt*. Frankfurt: 1997. (*The Small Kings of the Store World*).

Neuner, M. and Raab, G. (eds): *Verbraucherinsolvenz und Restschuldbefreiung: Eine Kritische Bestandsaufnahme aus Sicht der Beteiligten*. Baden-Baden: 2001. (*Consumer Insolvency and Remaining Debt Release: A Critical Stocktaking from the Viewpoint of the Participant*).

Peters, H. and Raab, G. (eds): *Bank und Jugend im Dialog: Ein Handbuch für Banken, Sparkassen, Schulen, Schuldner- und Verbraucherberatungsstellen*. Oberhausen: 2000. (*Bank and Youth in Dialogue: A Handbook for Banks, Savings Banks, Schools, Debtor Information Centers and Consumer Information Centers*).

Paetsch, M.: Jagd auf die jungsurfer. *Der Spiegel*, 2000, 35, 114–116.(Hunting the young surfers).

Piaget, J.: *Der Aufbau der Wirklichkeit beim Kinde*. Stuttgart: 1974. (*The Construction of the Reality of the Child*).

Prenzel, M. and Schiefele, H.: Konzepte der veränderung und erziehung. In: Weidemann, B. and Krapp, A. (eds): *Pädagogische Psychologie*. München: 1986, 105–142. (Concepts of variation in upbringing. In *Pedagogic Psychology*).

Raab, G.: *Kartengestützte Zahlungssysteme und Konsumentenverhalten*. Berlin: 1998. (*Card Support Payment Systems and Consumer Behavior*).

—— Kaufsucht: Kompensatorisches und suchthaftes kaufverhalten—theorie und empirie. In: Poppelreuter, S. and Gross, W. (eds): *Nicht nur Drogen Machen Süchtig: Entstehung und Behandlung von Stoffungebundenen Süchten*. Weinheim: 2000, 147–164. (Addiction to shopping: Compensatory and manic purchase behavior—theory and evidence. In *Not only are Drugs Addictive: Development and Treatment of Addictions that are not Tied to Particular Substances*).

Reisch, L.: *Der Heimliche Lehrplan der Geldsozialisation*. Stuttgart: Universität Hohenheim, Institut für Haushalts- und Konsumökonomik, 1996, Arbeitspapier 69. (*The Secret Curriculum of the Socialization of Money*).

Sahlins, M.: *Stone Age Economics*, London: Tavistock Publications, 1974.

Scherhorn G., Reisch, L. and Raab, G.: Kaufsucht. *Bericht über eine empirische Untersu-chung*. Stuttgart: Universität Hohenheim, Institut für Haushalts- und Konsumökonomik, 2001, Arbeitspapier 50. (Addiction to shopping. *Report on an empirical examination*).

Schmölders, G.: *Psychologie des Geldes*. Reinbek: 1966. (*Psychology of Money*).

Schneewind, K.A.: Familienentwicklung. In: Oerter, R. and Montada, L. (eds). *Entwick-lungspsychologie* (3rd edn). Weinheim: 1995, 128–166. (Family development. In *Developmental Psychology*).

Verlagsgruppe Bauer: Die zielgruppe familie verändert sich erneut. *Marketing Journal*, 1996, 29, 182. (The target group family changes again).

Wilkes, R.E.: Household life-cycle stages, transitions, and product expenditures. *Journal of Consumer Research*, 22, 27–42.

Yablonsky, L.: *Der Charme des Geldes*. Köln: Edition Humanistische Psychologie, 1992. (*The Charm of Money*).

Zanger, C. and Griese, K.-M. (eds): *Beziehungsmarketing mit Jungen Zielgruppen*. München: 2000. (*Relationship Marketing with Young Target Groups*).

—— Der Kinder- und jugendmarkt und die notwendigkeit einer strategischen ausrichtung des marketing. In: Zanger, C. and Griese, K.-M. (eds): *Beziehungsmarketing mit Jungen Zielgruppen.* München: 2000, 3–19. (The child and youth market and the necessity of a strategic alignment of marketing. In *Relationship Marketing with Young Target Groups*).

Zimbardo, P.G. and Gerrig, R.J.: *Psychologie* (7th edn). Berlin: 1999. (*Psychology*).

Zuckerman, M., Eysenck, S. and Eysenck, H.J.: Sensation seeking in England and America: Cross-cultural, age, and sex comparisons. *Journal of Consulting and Clinical Psychology*, 1978, 46, 139–149.

11 *Personality Theories*

Market Behavior as a Function of Person and Environment

CONCEPT AND RELEVANCE

At the current point in time there is no generally recognized definition of the personality concept in psychology. The profusion of the most varied attempts at definition demonstrates this (Amelang and Bartussek, 1997; Fisseni, 1998). Many of these definitions are of one mind in taking the concept of personality to mean the uniqueness and the stability of structures and processes over the course of time and throughout situations, in view of which an individual's behavior should be described, explained, and predicted. Pervin has suggested a possible definition of the personality concept: "Personality represents those characteristics of a person or people in general that constitute a continuous behavioral model" (Pervin, 1987, p. 15). In this vein, there are various theoretical approaches for determining these characteristics. Some personality researchers study the biochemical and physiological personality aspects. Others focus on direct observation of behavioral patterns. Still others observe interaction processes and what role the individual takes on in society. The most fruitful approach of personality psychology lies in an interactive perspective. The interactive idea states that human behavior, including behavior with regard to markets, is determined by the interplay between person and environment. The roots of this perspective lie in the works of Lewin (1935).

On the basis of his scientific work Lewin (1935) postulated that human behavior is a function of person and environment *(B= f (P,U))*. The concept of person includes the various biological and psychological characteristics of a human being. A human can only perceive and process certain impulses due to the performance capacity of his brain and sense organs. As a result of personal interests he will also certainly often only seek certain impulses (for example, items of information) and/or will assess these on the basis of his experiences and expectations. A person's behavior will also be determined by the environment, not just by these characteristics. For example, a shopping mall's presentation and the presentation of goods have an influence on purchase behavior. This influence is however not the same with everyone. Some people's purchase behavior will be more strongly influenced than others by such environmental conditions. Many of these aspects are dealt with in this book[1] and so at this juncture we will concentrate exclusively on personality envisioned as a characteristic of people (or of a person).

Personality's relevance is demonstrated in that its significance is evident in many different areas. In the area of personnel selection it can currently be observed that personality characteristics are increasingly being brought in toward the end of successfully

---

[1]   See also Chapter 8, "Information Processing and Purchase Decision Determinants", (pp. 112–114) and Chapter 12, "Practical Application", (pp. 173–178).

filling a position (Hossiep, Paschen and Mühlhaus, 2000, pp. 44–46). This underlies the analysis of help wanted advertisements (Klinkenberg, 1994). The significance of personality characteristics is also referred to in other areas, for example, in setting up business (Müller, 2000), in insurance fraud (Fetchenhauer, 1999), and in investment behavior (Fank, 1992; Pinner, 1997). Personality also plays a role in various models for explaining consumer behavior. This applies to the older models of Nicosia (1966) and Howard and Sheth (1969), as well as to newer models, like for example that of Engel, Blackwell and Miniard (1995) (see Figure 11.1).

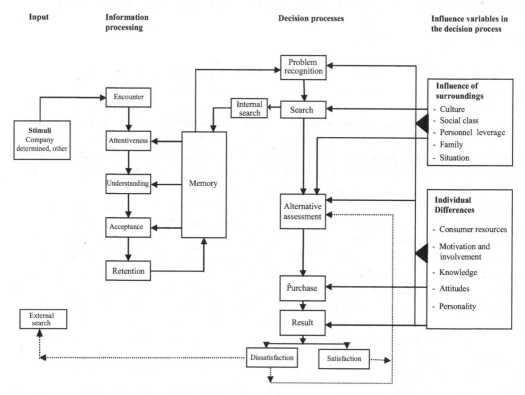

Figure 11.1 Engel, Blackwell and Miniard's model of consumer behavior (1995, p. 52)

Engel, Blackwell and Miniard's (1995) model demonstrates the complexity of consumer behavior as well as the observable relationships and influencing variables. Personality is here one of many influencing variables. Straight away two central aspects come to the fore: One has to do with explaining which personality characteristics are relevant with regard to behavior. And in the other it is of central importance to what extent behavior is determined by these characteristics. As far as the extent to which personality characteristics determine behavior is concerned, there are various empirical research findings and conceptions in practice and within science. The assumption of experts that failure within occupational circumstances and in setting up business can be traced back 90 percent of the time to personality rather than to lack of professional competence, can be doubted (Sarges, 2000, p. 17). Empirical studies have shown that only about 20 percent of self-employment success can be traced back to personality characteristics (Müller, 1999a,

p. 8). In the area of consumer behavior there are research findings according to which 10–25 percent of consumer behavior can be explained or predicted via personality characteristics (Mayer and Illmann, 2000, p. 115). The varying evaluations and results regarding what portion of behavior can be explained via personality characteristics, are due in part to the fact that in the context of economic inquiries, instruments of measurement are often used that were originally developed for the clinical area. The divergent findings are also partly due to most of the studies having lacked well substantiated theoretical integration. In the following section, some of the fundamental personality characteristics and approaches regarding them will be explained.

FUNDAMENTALS OF PERSONALITY THEORY APPROACHES

Personality theories attempt to describe and explain the structure and development of personality. From out of the many psychological personality theories three factor analysis theories will be presented, alongside the biopsychological approaches. The proponents of factor analysis personality models predominantly seek to describe people with the help of traits that are attributable to a person. "The fundamental approach here is one where each behavior can be traced back to characteristics, and is therefore predictable and explainable due to insights regarding these characteristics" (Hobmaier, 1994, p. 370). Factor analysis is used to find out these personality characteristics. This is a statistical procedure that takes a large number of characteristics or properties and reduces them to a small number of fundamental dimensions or factors. The goal here is enable a meaningful classification of individuals' various characteristics (Meffert, 1998, p. 163; Fisseni, 1998, p. 314).

The reason for choosing factor analysis personality approaches comes from the fact that these theories have strongly influenced scientific research, and forms the basis for an understanding of very practice oriented approaches. We will limit ourselves to the essential aspects of these approaches.

Cattell's theory

In order to come up with as thorough a catalog of human behavior as possible, Cattell focused on three sources of data: L-Data, Q-Data, and T-Data. He labeled these forms of data the personality sphere, which in his opinion constituted all aspects of human behavior (Pervin, 1987, pp. 307–308; Fisseni, 1998, pp. 347–348).

L-Data involves behavior in current, everyday living situations, like for example marks, number of clubs, or assessments of an individual's personality characteristics, such as emotional stability or scrupulousness. Q-Data are derived from psychometrically constructed questionnaires. They are based on self-observation, since they allow for classifying oneself. Q-Data is subject to error, for example, because of the desire to be presented in a good light. T-Data is data that is based on objective tests, research situations, and observation.

Cattell (1943) began initially with the study of L-Data. His strategy was first of all to gather L-Data, and then to develop questionnaires and objective tests that reflected these personality traits (Pervin, 1987, p. 308). The second part of his research strategy consisted of finding out whether comparable facts were present in F-Data. The main result of work with F-Data was the 16 personality factor inventory (16 PF). In constructing the

16 PF he used the personality dimensions as a basis for hypotheses or test items that he had culled from L-Data. Factor analysis brought out in the end 16 determining personality factors (Cattell, Eber and Tatsuoka, 1970). This measuring instrument also exists in a new German version (Schneewind and Graf, 1998). Each of 16 dimensions is characterized by two extremes, where every individual is placed in a very specific position between the two poles (see Table 11.1).

Table 11.1 The dimensions of 16 PF (Schneewind, Schröder and Cattell, 1994, p. 29)

Dimension	English version according to Cattell et al., 1970	German version according to Schneewind et al., 1994
1	Sizothymia vs. Affectothymia	Fact oriented vs. contact oriented
2	Low intelligence vs. high intelligence	Concrete thinking vs. abstract thinking
3	Lower ego strength vs. higher ego strength	Emotionally sensitive vs. emotionally tough
4	Submissiveness vs. dominance	Socially conforming vs. self assertion
5	Desurgency vs. surgency	Sober-minded vs. excitable
6	Weaker super ego strength vs. stronger super ego strength	Flexibility vs. sense of duty
7	Threctia vs. parmia	Reluctance vs. self assurance
8	Harria vs. premsia	Robustness vs. sensitive
9	Alaxia vs. protension	Trusting vs. skeptical attitude
10	Praxernia vs. autia	Practical vs. unconventional
11	Artlessness vs. shrewdness	Impartiality vs. judiciousness
12	Untroubled adequacy vs. guilt-proneness	Self confidence vs. solicitousness
13	Conservatism of temperament vs. radicalism	Focus on security vs. readiness to change
14	Group-adherence vs. self-sufficiency	Group-adherence vs. self-sufficiency
15	Low self-sentiment integration vs. high strength of self-sentiment	Spontaneity vs. self control
16	Low ergic tension vs. high ergic tension	Inner calm vs. inner tension

Cattell (1943, 1972) assumed that he had identified personality characteristics that allowed for a thorough description of personality. The structure of a person should be fully describable using knowledge of all important factors from these groups of characteristics. In this way one would be able to come up with a generally applicable framework of human personality. Furthermore it should be possible to make a sure prediction regarding the behavior of individuals in various situations, if one has knowledge of those factors important with regard to the specificity of character in all modalities of character traits (Brandstätter, Schuler and Stocker-Kreichgauer, 1978, pp. 175–176). To what extent a prediction and description based on the revised German version (Schneewind and Graf, 1998) of the above personality characteristics makes a contribution to the area of choosing personnel and/or customer behavior, will have to be demonstrated by future studies.

Eysenck's theory

Just as it does for Cattell (1943), for Eysenck (1970, 1990) factor analysis also serves as an important instrument for determining personality traits. Eysenck (1970) has derived three dimensions for characterizing the traits of individuals from the results of his research:

- Extraversion: To what extent is an individual outwardly or inwardly oriented?
- Neuroticism: To what extent is a person stable or labile (instable)?
- Psychoticism: To what extent is a person friendly and considerate or aggressive and antisocial?

The third dimension of psychoticism is not dealt with further in the following presentation because this later development of Eysenck's (1990) has been less influential than the original two-dimensional theory (Asendorpf, 1996, p. 128). The first two personality dimensions of extraversion (E) and neuroticism (N) form the foundation pillar of Eyseneck's personality model, which according to his conception is compatible with the ancient four temperaments personality scheme (see Figure 11.2).

According to Eysenck's conception, individuals can be placed in any of the four quadrants, indicating from a maximum of extraversion over to a maximum of introversion, as well as from the heights of lability (neuroticism) over to the heights of stability. Each position of the circle allows for a possible combination of both traits (Zimbardo and Gerrig, 1999, p. 524). According to Eysenck (1990) the difference in the fundamental dimensions can be traced back to genetic and biological causes. They account for roughly two thirds of variation within the personality dimensions. The introverted are fundamentally more affected by circumstances than are the extroverted. As a result the introverted react more strongly to sensorial stimulation. By contrast, as a consequence of their naturally low stimulation level, the extroverted seek stimulating situations (Zimbardo and Gerrig, 1999, p. 524).

According to Eysenck, people with a high neuroticism level are emotionally labile and often complain about irritation and anxieties, as well as about bodily pain. These people react quickly to stress, where the stress reaction takes longer to abate after the distress is over than is the case with more stable individuals (Pervin, 1987, p. 300). They also more easily allow themselves to become dependent, feel that they are less integrated within groups, operate with less energy and tend to limit their interests (Fisseni, 1998, p. 392).

In order to measure the various dimensions, Eysenck developed different questionnaires, of which the Eysenck Personality Inventory (Eysenck, 1964) was the most widely used. These questionnaires also exist in a German form (Eggert, 1983). Due to the fact that this measuring instrument has its roots in clinical psychological research, which to a degree is also documented in the questions, the implementation of this procedure for determining personality traits appears problematic in connection with economic questions. It therefore is not surprising if findings up to now have yielded hardly any significant explanatory contribution with regard to observed behavior (Mayer and Illmann, 2000, pp. 113–115).

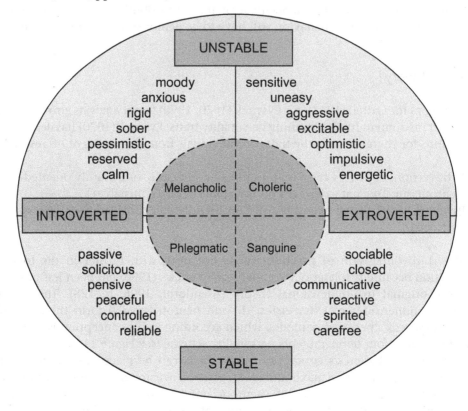

Figure 11.2 Eysenck's four quadrants of personality model (Zimbardo and Gerrig, 1999, p. 524)

Costa and McCrae's big five (1985)

At the beginning of the 1980s, Costa and McCrae (1985) looked for new important factors in the characterization of individuals' personality traits, based on Eysenck's two established factors—extraversion and introversion. In the context of these studies they found three further dimensions, which they interpreted as openness to experiences, agreeableness, and conscientiousness (Amelang and Bartussek, 1997, p. 368). In recent years an increasing quantity of evidence has been found indicating that a bigger part of the variation of differing measurement procedures can be traced back to personality on a basis of five relatively robust factors (Hossiep, Paschen and Mühlhaus, 2000, p. 116). These five factors have also been established in the analysis of observations and in differing cultural areas. It will therefore not be surprising if the five-factor model inspires numerous studies in coming years (McCrae and John, 1992, p. 177).

Costa and McCrae (1985, 1992) developed a special questionnaire in order to measure the various dimensions. Construction and further development of this was guided by both theoretical considerations and by factor analysis findings (Amelang and Bartussek, 1997, p. 370). The short form of the questionnaire was translated by Borkenau and Ostendorf (1993) for the German-speaking world. This measuring instrument, the so-called NEO Five-Factor Inventory (NEO-FFI), has so far shown itself to be a stable measuring instrument, and has proven itself in questionnaire studies and in interview evaluations. The questionnaire is comprised of 60 statements, out of which 12 at a time can be attributed to a certain factor.

Extraversion
communicative, energetic, determined   ⟷   quiet, reserved, shy

Agreeableness
dependable, friendly, compassionate   ⟷   cold, quarrelsome, remorseless

Conscientiousness
well-prepared (organized), careful,   ⟷   careless, irresponsible, frivolous
responsible

Emotional Stability
stable, quiet, satisfied   ⟷   anxious, labile, moody

Openness to Experiences
creative, intellectual, open   ⟷   superficial, unintelligent

Figure 11.3 The five-factor model of personality (Zimbardo and Gerrig, 1999, p. 525)

Figure 11.3 shows that each of the five dimensions has a bipolar configuration. Terms that closely characterize the names of the factors, describe the upper pole, whereas traits that do not, describe the lower pole of the respective dimension (Zimbardo and Gerrig, 1999, p. 525). Even though the five-factor model enjoys a wide acceptance, it must be noted that due to their abstract nature, this model and the first two approaches mentioned above are not so suitable for explaining behavioral modes within specific situations. It will therefore be necessary in the future to develop more application-oriented measuring instruments. In the areas of personnel selection and personnel development one such approach is the Bochumer Inventory for Employment Oriented Description of Personality (BIP) (Hossiep and Paschen, 1998).

Biopsychologically Based Personality Traits and Customer Relationships

In empirically oriented personality research, certain personality features arising out of the contexts of biopsychological theories are playing an increasingly significant role, and are not, or not only conceived within the context of factor analysis-based complete systems (Amelang and Bartussek, 1997, p. 381). These personality traits will be presented in the following section, "The Personality Characteristics of Company Founders" (pp. 158–162). Their relevance with regard to customer consultancy and customer commitment will also be explained.

SENSATION SEEKING

In the 1960s, Zuckerman (Zuckerman, Kolin, Price et al., 1964) focused on researching differences between individuals with regard to reaction to sensory deprivation. The theoretical starting point for these studies was the idea that there were systematic differences between individuals in how much stimulation they needed as a prerequisite to feeling good. Every individual differs in how strongly they seek such stimulation. Zuckerman called his concept sensation seeking and not stimulation seeking because it is the sensations, that is, the effects of stimuli, which influence individuals, and not the stimuli themselves. In this sense the personality trait of sensation seeking involves the tendency to obtain new, variegated, complex, and intense impressions or experiences, and so also to initiate purchase risks (Amelang and Bartussek, 1997, p. 381). Zuckerman (1994) traces the cause of this behavior back to sensation seeking being either a case of too little noradrenaline activity in the limbic brain or to its noradrenal system being sensitive with regard to stimulation. In order to obtain a medium activity within the noradrenal system that is experienced as pleasant, the sensation seeker seeks stimulation to raise the inadequate level of noradrenaline hormone concentration.

In order to measure sensation seeking Zuckerman (1964, 1994) developed a sensation seeking scale (SSS) involving multiple further developments, which yielded four underlying factors on the basis of factor analyses. These were labeled and described as given below (Amelang and Bartussek, 1997, p. 382; Pieters and van Raaij, 1988, pp. 130–131):

- **Thrill and adventure seeking (TAS)** The appetite or desire to experience excitement and adventure via risky, exciting activities like fast driving, dangerous sports, and so on.
- **Experience seeking (ES)** The craving to obtain new impressions or new experiences like for example via travel, unusual art or by fraternizing with flamboyant groups (for example, dropouts, artists).
- **Disinhibition (DIS)** The tendency to obtain stimulation via social activities (for example , parties), via disinhibition in the form of social drinking or also through sexual contact.
- **Boredom susceptibility (BS)** Intolerance with regard to repetitive experiences, for example, routine work or also with regard to boring people. This susceptibility to boredom shows itself in aversion toward monotonous situations or in restlessness.

These four factors are to be seen as primary factors in the sense of being special aspects of sensation seeking in general. For this reason, the sensation seeking scale has been configured as to be capable of yielding a general (global) value and four values for the underlying scales (Zuckerman, 1994, pp. 52–56). This very extensive analysis of the differences between people with high and low sensation seeking levels has provided complete and certain results, which are presented in very rough form in the table below (see Table 11.2):

Table 11.2 Differing results between people with high and low sensation seeking levels (Amelang and Bartussek, 1997, p. 384)

Activity area	Sensation seeking: Low	Sensation seeking: High
Readiness to take risks	Lower; higher assessment of risk, more anxiety with regard to the unknown	Higher; lower assessment of risk, less anxiety with regard to the unknown
Sports preference	Tends to avoid dangerous sports	Prefers dangerous sports
Employment	Prefers employment with predictable demands	Prefers employment involving change and challenges
Social behavior	Social contact that is too close and too long is experienced as uncomfortable	Seeks social contact, is open, dominant, and expecting of openness
Partnership behavior	More oriented toward enduring relationships	More oriented toward variation in partnerships
Smoking	Less likely	More likely
Alcohol and drug consumption	Less	More

The relevance of sensation seeking can be seen in connection with, for example, financial assets. In the context of an empirical study Harlow and Brown (1990) were able to show that sensation seekers chose more risky forms of investment. Results like this could be used in the context of talks with customers. As of 1 January 1995, according to § 31 of the German Securities Trade Act, general rules of conduct apply to financial service providers in their dealings with securities customers. The banks and asset consultants are hereby compelled to give advice that is fair with regard to investors (Frei-Gebele, 1996, p. 14). There is similar legislation in other developed countries such as the United States and the United Kingdom. The goal of a financial consultant is to allow for an investment recommendation that is in keeping with customer needs. In this vein, financial service providers must obtain data from the customers regarding their financial circumstances, investment goals, readiness to take risks, and must obtain experiences as well as insights regarding the intended investment businesses. Excepting the readiness to take risks, all the other items of information are relatively easy to obtain. An investor's readiness to take risks is a personality trait that has to be determined. Neither the customer nor the investment consultant is in a position to objectively evaluate this trait. Nevertheless, it is important; because the success of a financial investment depends on to what extent the investment product is in tune with the customer's readiness to take risks. The insights culled from fundamental research can here be practically implemented, by the development of well-founded measuring instruments for discovering readiness to take risks. An example of this is Union Investment's investment risk test (in Germany), as well as a similar test from Vanguard Investments (in the United States).

Another application of sensation seeking would be to put these insights to use toward a more individual orientation of Internet sites. If we know as a result of sensation seeking findings that older people experience less stimulation as pleasant, and furthermore if we know that there are individual differences as far as sensation seeking is concerned, then these facets ought to be used in the formation of Internet sites. Thus for customer groups with a pronounced level of sensation seeking it would be possible to develop sites such that this need for stimulation would be satisfied. This can be accomplished, for example, through the use of moving images, a contrast rich assortment of colors, and through the use of music. For customer groups with a less pronounced sensation seeking level on the other hand, a calm image with a more discreet color arrangement would be more advantageous. This would result in an increase in the duration of stay at, and in the readiness to return to, the given sites. Against a background of information overload due to the intense increase in the number of Internet sites, this aspect could become increasingly significant for companies in the future.

VARIETY SEEKING

Variety seeking has attracted increasing scientific attention in recent years and is the subject matter of many empirical studies. "Variety seeking is the phenomenon whereby consumers display a need for change in their product choice behavior, that can be traced back to a desire for variety" (Haseborg and Mäßen, 1997, p. 164). This appetite for variety has led to variety seeking being identified as an essential factor in the explanation, prognosis and control of consumer behavior.

The tendency toward variety seeking is to be understood as a personality characteristic of consumers, which shows itself as a "desire for a new and novel stimulus" (Hoyer and Ridgway, 1983, p. 115) (individual specific definition). From this it can be inferred that variety seeking represents a variation of the phenomenon of sensation seeking. As has already been indicated, a person strives in his behavior for a level of inner stimulation that is experienced as satisfying or pleasant. With sensation seeking, a fundamental appetite for stimulation is assumed to be present as a prerequisite. Successful stimulation is afforded by new, variegated, and intense impressions. In the context of consumer behavior the stimulation and its satisfaction is aroused by the consumer's appetite for change with regard to the use of a variety of products. The consumer who is striving to attain their optimal inner level of stimulus will search their environment for stimuli that will serve the satisfaction and attainment of this stimulus level. The various products that characterize their stimulus environment allow him to attain, change, and satisfy his inner stimulus level. With variety seeking it is possible for the consumer to bring back in balance motives like, for example, curiosity, boredom (satiety), or the desire for uniqueness or exclusivity (McAlister and Pessemier, 1982, p. 312).

Apart from variety seeking behavior being displayed according to individual specific aspects, it is also born out in relation to products (product specific definition). It has been observed that the appetite for variety seeking tends to be more strongly pronounced, the greater is the number of product alternatives, the smaller is the perceived difference between products, the less pronounced is market trust, and the smaller is the perceived product risk (Hoyer and Ridgway, 1983, pp. 116–117).

From there the possibility of a product feature specific analysis arises (product feature specific definition). "For an individual consumer, certain product features will be more likely than others to result in satisfaction of their appetite for variety. Thus a consumer, in their choice and consumption of soft drinks, can for example on one occasion opt for a fruity drink, and another time opt for a less fruity drink, where however in each case the drinks ought to be caffeine free" (Haseborg and Mäßen, 1997, p. 165). Also, if the significance of variety seeking can vary in the purchase situation and product category it is subject to, then it here indicates a relatively stable personality characteristic (Bänsch, 1995, p. 342; Haseborg and Mässen, 1997, p. 165).

The variety seeking approach offers an explanatory approach for the fact, often observed in reality, that customers will often change the product or provider even if they are happy with this product or provider (see Figure 11.4). Accordingly it can be shown via research focusing on a well-known German automobile manufacturer that variety seeking exercises a highly negative effect on customer commitment (Peter, 1998, pp. 77–79). A pronounced emphasis with regard to the personality feature variety seeking therefore leads to these customers changing the given product or provider even when there is a high level of customer satisfaction. Thus for a company it is of decisive importance how many of its customers are variety seekers and/or to what extent the given product encourages variety seeking. A stable relationship to customers is not obtained in this case by optimizing customer satisfaction, but is instead encouraged much more by measures that technically, economically and/or psychologically (for example, emotionally) commit the customer, so that this commitment overcomes the desire for variety.

Technical commitment of the customer can involve a large time expenditure and high cost connected with changing a product. In situations like this the customer will not simply change, just because she wants to try something new. A technical commitment like this is not possible in many fields, particularly with regard to consumer goods. Economic instruments for customer commitment attempt to get the customer to commit by granting financial advantages. The system of discount coupons, widespread in the USA, is just one example of these. In Germany the pay back card (Paybackkarte) is a successful recycling of the good old coupon booklet. The instrument of quantity discounts is being used to an increasing extent by service provider companies to encourage customer commitment. A well-known example of this is the German airline Lufthansa AG's frequent flyer program (Vielfliegerprogramm) Miles & More. In the context of this program with each Lufthansa flight, or with a Staralliance partner flight, the miles flown are credited to a personal account. Beginning at a minimum account level these miles can be traded against various bonuses like free flights or free stays at partner hotels, whereby these bonuses can also be transferred over to other people. In an increasingly competitive and challenging industry, most airlines now are equipped with this program.

In recent years, the emotional commitment of customers in particular has become the center of interest. This kind of customer commitment can take various forms. The goal here is to decrease the readiness to change via a personal relationship between company and customer and/or via preferential treatment for the customer by the company (Nieschlag, Dichtl and Hörschgen, 1997, p. 125). This can be achieved by inviting the customer to certain events (for example, tennis tournaments, sailing regattas) and/or through customer clubs, customer advisers, and company advisers. Many providers in various fields are already taking advantage of the customer club model to encourage customer commitment, as is evidenced by the Ikea Family, Metro Club, Porsche Club and Harley Owners Group (Kotler and Bliemel, 1999, pp. 71–81; Rapp, 2000, pp. 140–145; Schneider, 2000, pp. 41–42). The members of such groups enjoy advantages in the form of events, club magazines, discounted prices, and delivery service. Customer club offerings are often enhanced by so-called affinity cards. These cards are credit cards given out by financial institutions in cooperation with the company (Raab, 1998,

p. 51). The advantage of these instruments for inducing customer commitment consists in the customer becoming emotionally attached to the company and in the appetite for variety (variety seeking) being satisfied by bonus experiences like club events.

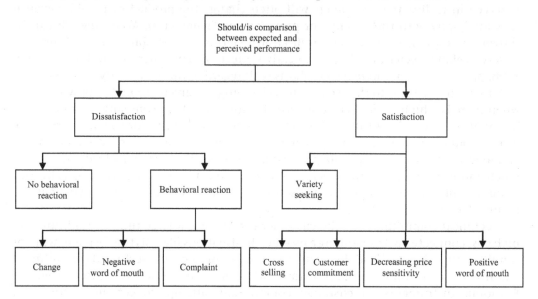

Figure 11.4 The reactions of customers to satisfaction and dissatisfaction

The Personality Characteristics of Company Founders

INFLUENCE FACTORS IN THE SUCCESSFUL STARTING UP OF COMPANIES

The founding of companies can be influenced by countless factors. It is important for people to have capacities, skills, competencies, and characteristics that support independent entrepreneurial thinking. In public discussion it is often said that so-called objective factors, for example economic or legal factors, are the decisive ones for the success of company founders. Although these factors are doubtless important for the economic health of a company, this viewpoint remains incomplete if how these factors are individually perceived, psychologically transformed, and engaged with by the founder in concrete actions, remain unobserved (Müller, 1999a, p. 3). The personal qualities of the founder or founders are already at the beginning phase nearly synonymous with those of the company being founded, that is, with the company's strengths and weaknesses (Szyperski and Nathusius, 1977, pp. 35–36).

An entrepreneur's personality interacts with all of the objective determinants, deciding how the founder handles and engages them, as is shown in Figure 11.5 below. The entrepreneurial personality is, so to speak, a filter that influences all objective factors in their effect on company success.

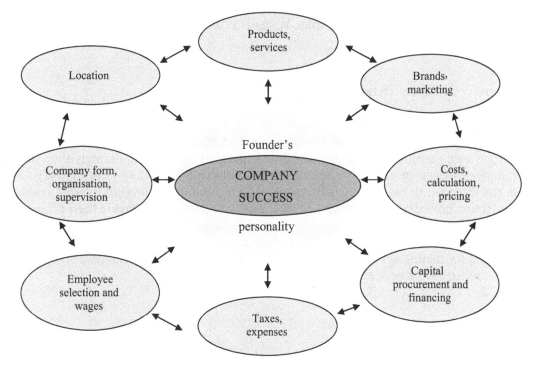

Figure 11.5 Interactions between objective factors, the company founder's personality and the influence on company success (based on Conrad, Müller, Wagener et al., 1998, p. 4)

In the analysis of determinants in the success of founding a company, the effect of the founder's personality should certainly be considered and studied. Only this approach can provide information about the actual factors of company success.

RELEVANT PERSONALITY FACTORS OF COMPANY FOUNDERS

Personality factors relevant with regard to independence are capacities and characteristics that, spanning across fields, regions, and demographic particularities, remain relatively stable over time as items that can be drawn on for predicting company behavior (Müller, 1999a, p. 3). In the section below, an overview will be given of relevant personality characteristics that have often been named in empirical studies (Conrad, Müller, Wagener et al., 1998; Klandt, 1984; Lumpkin and Dess, 1996).

Performance motivation

Performance motivation can be understood as the desire to work better, more efficiently or more quickly (Klandt, 1990, p. 88). The founder's performance motivation is characterized by the willingness and readiness to get a handle on tasks that correspond to his own competencies and inclinations, that are challenging, and which at the same time appear like they could be successfully realized. At the same time coping with the task in itself acts as incentive for the founder, in that the performance itself becomes the wellspring of effort and satisfaction (Conrad, Müller, Wagener et al., 1998, p. 9; Müller, 1999a; Müller, 1999b, p. 175).

Internal control conviction

People with a pronounced level of this characteristic see themselves as initiators of events in their field of action. Professionally they also tend to attribute work results to the effect of their own contribution (Bonnet and Furnham, 1991, p. 473). Accordingly they strive to actively engage in what is happening at work and to influence the way things are going in the direction of their own goals. People with a pronounced level of internal control conviction understand the changes to their professional career as having been caused by themselves, ascribing these changes to their own decisions. Internal control conviction turns people into actors who strive for independence, because in their work they do not gladly allow themselves be domineered by others (Conrad, Müller, Wagener et al., 1998, p. 9; Müller, 1999a, p. 3; Müller, 1999b, p. 175).

Readiness to take risks

In the discussion about the characteristics of entrepreneurial behavior the undertaking of risks is a criterion that is often considered (Brockhaus, 1980, pp. 509–513; Sexton and Bowman, 1985, p. 131). Entrepreneurial activity can hardly take place without risk. On the other hand, taking too much of a risk is also not a good idea. Entrepreneurs' appetite for risk has bearing particularly in situations that are full of risk. If an entrepreneur then gambles everything, they could lose their business (and possibly personal assets if these were taken as collateral by the bank for start-up proceeds). Therefore, it seems that in self-employment, an appetite for risk that is somewhere in the middle is best, rather than being as voracious as possible. A mid-range of character expressions points to calculated risk, ruling out forms of anxiety-ridden avoidance of risk as well as modes of behavior that are too risky (Conrad, Müller, Wagener et al., 1998, p. 9; Müller, 1999a, p. 3; Müller, 1999b, p. 175).

Not only the material aspect of risk should be focused on in the analysis; founding a business is equally connected with a psychological risk (Rispas, 1997, p. 188). The founder develops an emotional relationship to the company being founded, which often is thought of by him as his life work. Failure can be experienced by the founder as personal lack of success and thus lead to a considerable weakening of his self confidence (Klandt, 1984, p. 169). Due to the amount of time spent there is a risk with regard to the family (Klandt, 1984, p. 168); due to the large expenditure of time demanded of the founder it is significantly more difficult to maintain relationships with family and friends.

Problem orientation

The intellectual ability to tackle planning and control tasks is of particular significance for the successful company founder, since entrepreneurial activity as a rule demands the performance of many mental tasks. In order to handle mentally challenging tasks, the capacity to process information is an especially important characteristic (Hussy, 1991, pp. 314–315); it influences cognitive performances, for example, in making important decisions or in planning far-reaching action strategies.

People who are active as self-employed entrepreneurs need to have strong problem orientation because of their activity, which necessitates a pronounced capacity to process information. People who have this disposition see the challenges of life as solvable problems, trusting themselves to be up to the occasion. Thus they are also in a position to be able to handle the countless "non-routine" tasks that come up, which often go hand in hand with self-employment (Müller, 1999a, p. 4).

Ability to be assertive

This has to do with a social potential factor, whereby the focus is on the behavior and attitude with regard to interpersonal relationships or interpersonal orientation. Just as in the readiness to take risks, also with this characteristic the midrange is optimal. In order to set business ideas against competitors, self-employment necessitates a certain amount of dominance and social independence. A disposition like this is an advantage especially in the beginning phase. Certainly it is also a fundamental prerequisite not to be too overbearing with people, since cooperative behavior can also be decisive in getting along with customers or with co-workers (Müller, 1999b, p. 177).

Tolerance of uncertainty

Different levels of this personality characteristic demonstrate on the one hand preferences for regulated and well coordinated work procedures, or on the other hand for unstructured and loosely organized procedures. Entrepreneurs often find themselves in situations where unexpected circumstances arise. People who are tolerant of uncertainty here find it easier to react appropriately. They feel themselves to be suited for unstructured matters, assess the information content, and have little trouble dealing with such situations. People who are not tolerant of uncertainty by contrast feel uneasy and tend to react inappropriately, for example, defensively; they seek to avoid unstructured circumstances (Müller, 2000, p. 2).

The practical utility of the above-described personality characteristics consists in advising prospective entrepreneurs on the basis of a well-substantiated presentation of these characteristics. It goes without saying that an economically feasible business plan forms the foundation of the successful founding of a company. Still, even the best business concept is worthless if the personal prerequisites for implementing it are not there. The analysis of personality potentials aids company founders in recognizing their strengths and weaknesses and in assessing them accordingly. Insights like these are also of central significance for entrepreneurial seminars, and for the advisory aspects of industrial and trade organizations, as well as for banks. It is therefore astonishing when banks and venture capital organizations invest large sums without having implemented well-substantiated and evaluated instruments for finding out personal capacities. It is furthermore of note that this information is of increasing relevance for companies. If companies operate in certain areas as profit centers or subsidiaries, then this leads to the development that these companies must in the future more vigorously recognize, encourage, and develop entrepreneurial capacities. And finally, the company will not be able to limit itself to these areas. In order to obtain the ability to compete it will be much more necessary for employees to act altogether more as entrepreneurs within the company (Intrapreneurship). This is emphasized in a statement of the management and personnel development leader of Lufthansa: "In order to survive in global competition, we need entrepreneurial types who are ready to take risks."

Summary

It can be useful to take into consideration personality characteristics in connection with economic questions. Here it must always be kept in mind that behavior is determined by the characteristics of the person and by the environment. The person and the environment stand in a reciprocal relationship to each other. Thus it cannot be expected that personality characteristics would be capable of essentially explaining and predicting the behavior of for example consumers and/or investors. However, these characteristics constitute a decisive contribution toward a better understanding. This certainly assumes that those personality theory approaches will be used that involve a high level of practical utility, and that corresponding measuring instruments will be developed and implemented.

Sensation seeking and variety seeking belong to this type of approach. It will not come as a surprise, therefore, the significance of this approach for studying consumer behavior will increase (Kahn, 1998; Tscheulin, 1994; van Trijp, 1995). Further studies involving researching those personality characteristics relevant for successful entrepreneurs will also experience increased attention within science and practice, owing to the economic significance for the founding of companies.

QUESTIONS FOR DISCUSSION

1. How does culture influence personality via the environment?
2. How can variety and sensation seeking theory be helpful for marketers?
3. Think of some well-known entrepreneurs. What qualities of personality helped to make them successful?
4. What are some personality traits that are not desirable for company founders?

Bibliography

Amelang, M. and Bartussek, D.: *Differentielle Psychologie und Persönlichkeitsforschung*. Stuttgart, Berlin, Köln: 1997. (*Differential Psychology and Personality Research*).

Asendorpf, J.: *Psychologie der Persönlichkeit*. Heidelberg: 1996. (*Psychology of the Personality*).

Bänsch, A.: Variety seeking—marketingfolgerungen aus überlegungen und untersuchungen zum abwechslungsbedürfnis von konsumenten. In: *Jahrbuch der Absatz- und Verbrauchsforschung*, 1995, 4, 342–365. (Variety seeking—marketing conclusions out of considerations and investigations to the change of consumer needs. In: *Annual Review of Research and Consumption Research*).

Bonnet, C. and Furnham, A.: Who wants to be an entrepreneur? A study of adolescents interested in a young enterprise scheme. *Journal of Economic Psychology*, 1991, 12, 465–478.

Borkenau, P. and Ostendorf, F.: NEO-fünf-faktoren-inventar (NEO-FFI). Göttingen: 1993. (NEO-five-factors-inventory).

Brandstätter, H., Schuler, H. and Stocker-Kreichgauer, G.V.: *Psychologie der Person*. Stuttgart: 1978. (*Human Psychology*).

Brockhaus, R.H.: Risk taking propensity of entrepreneurs. *Academy of Management Journal*, 1980, 23, 509–520.

Cattell, R.B.: The description of personality: Basic traits resolved into clusters. *Journal of Abnormal and Social Psychology*, 1943, 8, 476–506.

Cattell, R.B.: The 16-PF and basic personality structure: A reply to Eysenck. *Journal of Behavioural Science*, 1972, 1, 169–187.

Cattell, R.B., Eber, H.W. and Tatsuoka, M.M.: *Handbook for the Sixteen Personality Factor Questionnaire (16PF)*. Champaign: 1970.

Conrad, W., Müller F.G., Wagener, D. and Wilhelm, O.: *Psychologische Beiträge zur Analyse Unternehmerischer Potentiale bei Angehenden Existenzgründern*. Mannheim: Veröffentlichungen des Instituts für Mittelstandsforschung Nr. 36—Universität Mannheim: 1998. (*Psychological Contributions to the Analysis of Entrepreneurial Potential Among Prospective Business Owners*).

Costa, P.T. and McCrae, R.R.: *The NEO Personality Inventory Manual Form S and Form R*. Odessa: 1985.

—— *Revised NEO Personality Inventory and NEO Five-Factor Inventory*. Odessa: 1992.

Eggert, D.: *Eysenck-Persönlichkeits-Inventar*. Göttingen: 1983. (*Eysenck's Personality Trait Inventory*).

Engel, J.F., Blackwell, R.D. and Miniard, P.W.: *Consumer Behavior* (8th edn). Fort Worth: 1995.

Eysenck, H.J.: *The Eysenck Personality Inventory*. London: 1964.

—— *The Structure of Human Personality*. London: 1970.

—— Biological dimensions of personality. In: Pervin, L. (ed.). *Handbook of Personality Theory and Research*. New York: 1990, 244–276.

Fank, M.: *Strukturanalyse zum Umgang mit Geld aus Verhaltenstheoretischer Sicht*. Frankfurt am Main: 1992. (*Structural Analysis of the Contact with Money in View of Behavioral Theory*).

Fetchenhauer, D.: Zur psychologie des versicherungsbetrugs. In: Fischer, L. Kutsch, T. and Stephan, E. (eds). *Finanzpsychologie*. München: 1999, 188–213. (The psychology of insurance fraud. In *Finance Psychology*).

Fisseni, H.: *Persönlichkeitspsychologie: Auf der Such nach einer Wissenschaft*. Bern: 1998. (*Personality Psychology: In Search of a Science*).

Frei-Gebele, P.: Persönliche risikobereitschaft richtig einschätzen. *Bank Magazin*, 1996, 12, 14–16. (Correctly estimating personal willingness to take risks).

Harlow, W.V. and Brown, K.C.: Understanding and assessing financial risk tolerance: A biological perspective. *Financial Analysts Journal*, 1990, 50–63.

Haseborg, F. and Mäßen, A.: Das phänomen des variety-seeking-behavior: Modellierung, empirische Befunde und marketingpolitische implikationen. *Jahrbuch der Absatz- und Verbrauchsforschung*, 1997, 2, 164–187. (The phenomenon of variety seeking behavior: Modeling, empirical conditions and the marketing and political implications).

Hobmaier, H.: *Psychologie*. Köln: 1994. (*Psychology*).

Hossiep, R. and Paschen, M.: Bochumer inventar zur berufsbezogenen persönlichkeitsbe-schreibung (BIP). Göttingen: 1998. (Bochumer's inventory for occupation related personality descriptions).

—— and Mühlhaus, O.: *Persönlichkeitstests im Personalmanagement*. Göttingen: 2000. (*Personality Tests in Personnel Management*).

Howard, J.A. and Sheth, J.N.: *The Theory of Buyer Behavior*. New York: 1969.

Hoyer, W.D. and Ridgway, N.M.: Variety seeking as an explanation for exploratory purchase behavior. In: Kinnear, T.S. (ed.). *Advances in Consumer Research*, 1983, 114–119.

Hussy, W.: Eine experimentelle studie zum intelligenzkonzept "verarbeitungskapazität". *Diagnostica*, 1991, 37, 314–333. (An experimental study to the intelligence concept of "processing capacity").

Kahn, B.E.: Dynamic relationships with customers: High-variety strategies. *Journal of the Academy of Marketing Science*, 1998, 26, 45–53.

Klandt, H.: *Aktivität und Erfolg des Unternehmensgründers: Eine Empirische Analyse unter Einbeziehung des Mikrosozialen Umfeldes*. Bergisch Gladbach: 1984. (*Activity and Success of the Company Founder: An Empirical Analysis Including the Microsocial Background*).

—— Das leistungsmotiv und verwandte konzepte als wichtige einflußfaktoren der unternehmerischen Akitivität. In: Szyperski, N. and Roth, P. (eds). *Entrepreneurship: Innovative Unternehmensgründung als Aufgabe*. Stuttgart, 1990, 88–96. (The achievement motive and related concepts as important influential factors of entrepreneurial activity. In *Entrepreneurship: Innovative Business Foundation as a Task*).

Klinkenberg, U.: Persönlichkeitsmerkmale in stellenanzeigen für qualifizierte fach- und führungskräfte. *Zeitschrift für Personalforschung*, 1994, 4, 401–418. (Personality features in job advertisements for qualified specialists and management).

Kotler, P. and Bliemel, F.: *Marketing-Management* (9th edn). Stuttgart: 1999.

Lewin, K.: *A Dynamic Theory of Personality*. New York: 1935.

Lumpkin, G.T. and Dess, G.G.: Clarifying the entrepreneurial orientation construct and linking it to performance. *Academy of Management Review*, 1996, 21, 135–172.

Mayer, H. and Illmann, T.: *Markt- und Werbepsychologie*. Stuttgart: 2000. (*Marketing and Advertising Psychology*).

McAlister, L. and Pessemier, E.: Variety seeking behavior: An interdisciplinary review. *Journal of Consumer Research*, 1982, 9, 311–322.

McCrae, R.R. and John, O.P.: An introduction to the five factor model and its applications. *Journal of Personality*, 1992, 60, 175–215.

Meffert, H.: *Marketing: Grundlagen Marktorientierter Unternehmensführung* (8th edn). Wiesbaden: 1998. (*Marketing: Foundations of Market Oriented Business Management*).

Müller, G.F.: Persönlichkeit und selbständige erwerbstätigkeit: Messung von potentialfak-toren und analyse ihres einflusses. *Wirtschaftspsychologie*, 1999a, 6, 2–12. (Personality and independent employment: Measurement of potential factors and analysis of their influence).

—— Dispositionelle und biographische bedingungen beruflicher selbständigkeit. In: Moser, K., Batinic, B. and Zempel, J. (eds). *Unternehmerisch Erfolgreich Handeln*. Göttingen: 1999b, 173–192. (Dispositional and biographical conditions of professional independence. In *Entrepreneurially Successful Actions*).

—— Fragebogen zur diagnose unternehmerischer potentiale. Landau: Hochschule Landau/Koblenz (Arbeitspapier): 2000. (Questionnaire for the diagnosis of entrepreneurial potential, Working Paper).

Nicosia, F.M.: *Consumer Decision Processes: Marketing and Advertising Implications*. Englewood Cliffs: 1966.

Nieschlag, R., Dichtl, E. and Hörschgen, H.: *Marketing* (18th edn). Berlin: 1997.

Peter, S.: Kundenbindung als marketingziel. *Absatzwirtschaft*, 1998, 7, 74–80. (Customer loyalty as a marketing goal).

Pervin, L.A.: *Persönlichkeitstheorien*. München: 1987. (*Personality Theories*).

Pieters, R. and van Raaij, W.F.: The role of affect in economic behavior. In: van Raaij, W.F., van Veldhoven, G.M. and Wärneryd, K.E. (eds). *Handbook of Economic Psychology*. Dordrecht: 1988, 108–142.

Pinner, W.: *Die Verrückte Börse: Eine Einführung in die Börsenpsychologie*. Düsseldorf: 1997. (*The Crazy Stock Exchange: An Introduction to Stock Exchange Psychology*).

Raab, G.: *Kartengestützte Zahlungssysteme und Konsumentenverhalten*. Berlin: 1998. (*Card Support Payment Systems and Consumer Behavior*).

Rapp, R.: *Customer Relationship Management*. Frankfurt: 2000.

Rispas, S.: *Entrepreneurship als Ökonomischer Prozeß: Perspektiven zur Förderung Unter-nehmerischen Handelns*. Wiesbaden: 1997. (*Entrepreneurship as an Economical Process: Prospects for Promoting Entrepreneurial Activity*).

Sarges, W.: Einleitende überlegungen. In: Hossiep, R., Paschen, M. and Mühlhaus, O. *Persönlichkeitstests im Personalmanagement*. Göttingen, 2000, 15–19. (Initiating considerations. In: *Personality Tests in Personnel Management*.).

Schneewind, K.A. and Graf, J.: *Der 16-Persönlichkeits-Faktoren-Test*. Revidierte Fassung (16 PF-R). Bern: 1998. (*The 16-Factor Personality Test*. Revised version (16 PF R)).

—— Schröder, G. and Cattell, R.B.: *Der 16-Persönlichkeits-Faktoren-Test (16 PF)*. Bern: 1994. (*The 16-Factor Personality Test (16 PF)*).

Schneider, W.: *Kundenzufriedenheit*. Landsberg: 2000. (*Customer Satisfaction*).

Sexton, D.L. and Bowman, N.: The entrepreneur: A capable executive and more. *Journal of Business Venturing*, 1985, 1, 129–140.

Szyperski, N. and Nathusius, K.: *Probleme der Unternehmensgründung: Eine betriebswirt-schaftliche Analyse unternehmerischer Startbedingungen*. Stuttgart: 1977. (*Problems of Business Foundation: An Economic Analysis of Entrepreneurial Start-up Conditions*).

Tscheulin, D.: Variety-seeking-behavior bei nicht-habitualisierten konsumentenentschei-dungen. *Zeitschrift für betriebswirtschaftliche Forschung*, 1994, 1, 54–61. (Variety-seeking-behavior in habitual consumer decisions).

van Trijp, J.: *Variety-seeking in Product Choice Behavior*. Wageningen: 1995.

Zimbardo P.G. and Gerrig, R.J.: *Psychologie* (eds.). Heidelberg, Berlin, New York: 1999. (*Psychology*).

Zuckerman, M., Kolin, I., Price, L. and Zoob, I.: Development of a sensation seeking scale, *Journal of Consulting Psychology*, 1964, 28, 477–482.

Zuckerman, M.: *Behavioral Expressions and Biosocial Bases of Sensation Seeking*. Cambridge: 1994.

12 *The Psychology of Perception*

Perception as the Basis of Economic Action

CONCEPT AND RELEVANCE

The concept of perception is understood to be a process of information assimilation or processing utilized by an individual to obtain insight into themselves and their environment (Kroeber-Riel and Weinberg, 1999, p. 265). Within their everyday situation, a human being is confronted with an unrelenting flood of environmental impulses that are continuously stimulating their sense organs. The reception or processing of these items of information is influenced by three different aspects: Subjectivity, selectivity, and activity (Kroeber-Riel and Weinberg, 1999, p. 266). Subjectivity means that every person individually perceives their own environment. Most people are of the opinion that they are perceiving reality the way it actually is. Many experiments have shown however that the result of perception only partially reflects the actually existent reality. The consequence of this is that one person's perceived environment can significantly differ from another person's. Furthermore the human information system perceives selectively. We are very particular in how we filter the flood of information confronting our sense organs. What we see, hear, smell, or taste is therefore not an actual representation of reality. Perception is faced with many different factors that it can distort or falsify. And finally, the concept of activity denotes people's active reception and processing of stimuli and information.

Business professionals are increasingly recognizing the relevance of perception as a topic, and they have been attempting to utilize the insights gleaned from it toward achieving their goals. The intention here is a direct influence on the attitude and thus behavior of a person by the implementation of particular communication mediums.

In order for a person to adequately interpret and perceive information that is deemed necessary by him, corresponding reactions also need to take place in the body. The body's sensory cells have to convert foreign physical and/or chemical stimuli into endogenous physiological impulses. These finally result in psychologically meaningful quantities, like for example sensations. Thus the human perceptual process is made up of three components (Felser, 1997, p. 72):

- A physical, or chemical component: for example, the wavelength of light, the intensity of sound, the frequency of a vibration, the concentration of a scent.
- A physiological component: the specific activity of nerve cells.
- A psychological component: for example, color sensitivity, loudness, the pitch of a tone, odors, instances of contacts.

In this chapter, we will mainly consider the psychological component. The physical and physiological areas will be explained in more detail only as it is conducive to a better understanding of psychological processes of perception.

ACTIVATION AND INFLUENCING FACTORS OF PERCEPTION

The effects of activation

We obtain information about our environment via our sensory organs. These certainly only have a limited effectiveness and therefore can only filter a portion of what we perceive in reality. As already indicated, people perceive selectively. Items of information come into contact with our sensory organs in the form of stimuli, for example, electromagnetic waves, mechanical vibrations, or chemical changes. Stimuli are energies coming out of the environment that trigger certain sensations via their effect on our sensory organs. The intensity of sensations depends on the intensity of the received stimuli. Stimuli that are relatively weak or that are not intense enough, as a rule do not provoke any sensation. The person cannot perceive them. For example the ultrasonic cannot be perceived by humans; if the tone is too high or too deep it cannot be heard, or if a teaspoon of sugar is dissolved in ten liters of water it cannot be tasted (Hobmaier, 1994, p. 82). Thus there is an absolute threshold to perception. It can here be fundamentally established that individuals tend mainly to activate those stimuli that have a high stimulus level or high stimulus potential (Gröppel, 1991, p. 115).

In science the effect of a stimulus or the effect of activation on a person's performance is demonstrated by the Lamda-Hypothesis. By performance is meant all the processes in operation in an individual, like perception, thinking, learning, retention, and so on (Kroeber-Riel and Weinberg, 1999, p. 80). The "Lamda-Hypothesis", empirically substantiated up to a reversal point, states that with increasing intensity of activation, or of a stimulus, an individual's performance increases. Once a certain level of activation or stimulus intensity has been reached, the consequence is a decrease in the function (Kroeber-Riel and Weinberg, 1999, p. 78). As is clear from Figure 12.1, a medium intensity of activation is seen as optimal. The reader should note this from personal experience. The more alert and focused you are, the better is your overall performance. If you become too excited or nervous, your performance is likely to deteriorate.

Factors influencing perception

Sight is the most complex, the most highly developed, and the most important of human senses. In the perceptual process the eye has the function of collecting light, focusing it, and converting it into signals that are then forwarded to the brain (Zimbardo and Gerrig, 1999, p. 151). The main objective lies in coming up with an exact image of the environment. Ambiguous stimuli and deceptive perceptions clearly make perception into a complex task. The bringing together of sensory impressions often leads to the brain having various possibilities of interpretation and thus to variations in identification and categorization. An example of this is the case of optical illusions. Our senses demonstrably deceive us by incorrectly experiencing a particular stimulus (Zimbardo and Gerrig, 1999, pp. 149–151). They suggest an image that cannot be there according to objective insight.

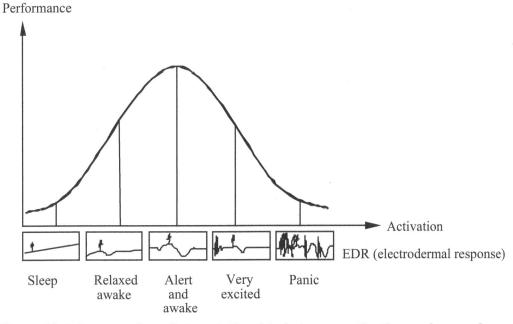

Figure 12.1 Presentation of the relationship between activation and arousal (Kroeber-Riel and Weinberg, 1999, p. 79)

Figure 12.2 Cylinder illusion (Frisby, 1983, p. 16) and the deceptive grid (Kebeck, 1994, p. 27)

Figure 12.2 first shows the so-called "cylinder illusion" (Frisby, 1983, p. 16). A vertical line crossed by a horizontal line of equal length, seems to be much longer in comparison to the line that is on top of it. Next, the deceptive grid is shown. Here we believe after brief observation that we are seeing gray flecks at the cross points of the white stripes (Kebeck, 1994, p. 27).

By way of another perceptual deception, we are presented with multiple images via one illustration. However, our brain only allows us one interpretation at a given time for each stimulus example. In Figure 12.3, this is either an old woman or a young woman, never both at the same time (Kebeck, 1994, p. 40). We are however as a rule able to purposefully influence what we want to perceive (Felser, 1997, p. 76).

There can be several reasons for these deceptions. Some are due to psychological mechanisms, while others have physiological causes. The case of the deceptive grid for example is of physiological origin. The deception arises here from a lateral hesitation of the network of cutaneous cells (Kebeck, 1994, p. 27).

Figure 12.3 What do you see? An old woman or a young woman (Zimbardo and Gerrig, 1999, p. 148)

On the basis of these examples, we can infer that we do not always see in the outer world what can be physically determined to be there. Social and cultural factors often play a role as well, for example, ideas of values and of what are normal behaviors in a given society, or also attitudes and preconceptions which play a decisive role in the perceptual process. In the context of social perception theory, Bruner and Goodman (1947) did research regarding the assumption that with the increasing value of objects and with increasing desire for these objects, an overestimation of object size increases. Their experiments demonstrated children overestimating the size of coins, whereas this effect did not occur with pieces of cardboard. The overestimation of size here increased as the nominal value of the coins increased, and was more pronounced in children of a lower class (Lilli and Frey, 1993, p. 52). And finally our perception is also influenced by other people or groups. The way others can alter our perception was impressively demonstrated by an experiment conducted by a psychologist by the name of Asch (1951):

The research subjects should say here which one of the three comparison lines on the right side corresponds with the line on the left side.

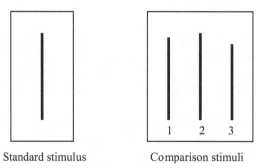

Standard stimulus   Comparison stimuli

Figure 12.4 The experiment's lines of comparison

Some of the people taking part were not research subjects in reality, but in fact were co-designers of the experiment. In their estimation of the lines of comparison they had to say that line one corresponded in length with the line on the left side. The majority of the actual research subjects adapted themselves to the judgment of these other people, that is, they viewed the first line to be the same length as the line on the left side. They evidently trusted the judgment of the majority of other participants more than their own perception.

THE ORGANIZATION OF PERCEPTION

Apart from perception being limited due to the nature of the sensory organs and due to the influence of social and individual factors, it is structured by certain rules and enhanced via certain constancy phenomena (Hobmaier, 1994, p. 88).

Rules of perception

Reality is often ordered according to certain regulating patterns. The idea is that with the help of perception, order is brought to the multitude of stimuli which people are inundated with. Psychology deals with this topic under the heading of "gestalt psychology". The gestalt psychologist sees people as having an underlying impulse toward the "good gestalt", where the individual stimulus is fundamentally encouraged to enter into an aggregate relationship. This then explains the human tendency toward a certain order, conciseness, harmony, or meaningful form (Felser, 1997, p. 78).

The most widespread gestalt laws are:

- **The Law of Similarity** Similar figures are perceived as belonging together. In the following arrangement the observer as a rule sees columns and not rows. From this it can be concluded that similar stimuli are seen to belong together.

```
O N O N O N O N O N O N O N O N
O N O N O N O N O N O N O N O N
O N O N O N O N O N O N O N O N
O N O N O N O N O N O N O N O N
O N O N O N O N O N O N O N O N
O N O N O N O N O N O N O N O N
O N O N O N O N O N O N O N O N
O N O N O N O N O N O N O N O N
```

Figure 12.5 An example of the Law of Similarity

This fact also explains for example how dancers who make the same movements are perceived as belonging together, even though they may not necessarily be near each other. It is only in this way that an individual can recognize a dance group as being an artistic figure (Felser, 1997, p. 79). The fact that we attribute specific characteristics to certain nations, minorities, or social classes, can also be traced back to the law of similarity. In fact, many cultural theories center on geographic or nationalistic factors. One example is the cultural cluster approach, which groups cultural patterns based on geography. Another is the Low-Context, High-Context approach (Hall, 1976), which groups via national lines.

- **The Law of Figure and Ground** The visual system has the ability to identify certain elements as a "figure" and to interpret the rest of the visual field as background. This figure-ground differentiation is an element of the perceptual system that affords the individual rapid and secure orientation (Kebeck, 1994, p. 39). An interesting example of this is the "Rubinsche Becherfigur". This is an illustration with two opposing head profiles that appear to be a vase with reversal of figure and ground.
- **The Law of Proximity** According to this theory, stimuli that are close to each other are perceived as belonging together. The law of proximity is often so pronounced that it can even take precedence over other perceptual habits. The following figure illustrates this:

```
N  E  U
A  S  T
S  E  E
E  L
```

Figure 12.6 An example of the Law of Proximity

This demonstrates that the spatially close together word columns as a rule get read first, taking precedence over the normal linear reading direction (Felser, 1997, p. 80).

- **The Law of Unity** This law points out the fact that we would rather see figures as a unity. From this it can be concluded that individuals tend to perceive unfinished stimuli as finished or completed stimuli. An example of this would be that we see figures that demonstrate irregularities or gaps as unities.

We do not see points or dashes here, but rather a circle or four-sided figure, despite the gaps. Thus the principle whereby an individual strives for the "good gestalt" or "unity" is demonstrated.

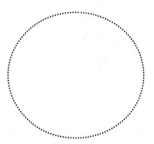
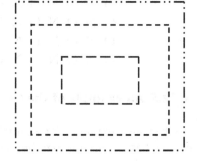

Figure 12.7 An example of the Law of Unity

- **The Law of Continuity** This demonstrates how impulses that appear to be a continuity of preceding impulses are perceived as belonging together. From this a meaningful whole arises for the individual. An example of this can be seen in the fundamental principle of film, which consists of many single pictures that are brought together into a unity, that is, as a film, due to logical succession and high speed.
- **The Law of Motion** We often see impulses that are moving in the same direction as belonging together, and according to many studies objects that are in constant motion attract more of people's attention. Department stores make use of this by the use of a special arrangement of display windows or sales areas. For example small ventilators might here keep the hair or clothing of display window puppets in motion. With advertising posters one can emphasize motion in the form of spirals or waves (Felser, 1997, p. 88).

Perceptual constants

Constancy phenomena are characterized by a perception staying constant, unchanged, despite varying conditions. The three most significant of these are presented below:

- **Size constancy** This phenomenon is that whereby objects are viewed as being the same despite varying distance. Of note here is the fact that the bigger a thing is, the more attention the person focuses on it. However, there is not a 1:1 relationship between size and increase in attention. According to Mullan and Johnson (1990, p. 18) an advertisement that is twice as big only promises an increase in effect at a factor of 1.4, and one that is 4 times as big only promises a doubling of the effect.
- **Constancy of form** What is meant here is the fact of objects being perceived as always having the same form from varying perspectives (Hobmaier, 1994, p. 91). One correctly perceives the actual outline of an object even if it is turned away from the observer, so that the outline's image on the network of cutaneous cells looks very different from how the object is actually formed. For example, a rotated circle being viewed by an observer casts an elliptical image on the retina, and a rotated rectangle casts a trapezoidal image. Nevertheless both are correctly perceived as being a circle and rectangle respectively (Zimbardo and Gerrig, 1999, p. 141).
- **Color constancy** What is meant here is the color of objects being perceived as being the same even with varying illumination. The differentiation of color tones into a manifold of shades is one of the most significant abilities of the visual system (Kebeck, 1994, p. 39). For example snow remains white to us in our perception even as twilight comes on, resulting in a darker image forming on the network of cutaneous cells.

Practical Application

ARRANGEMENT OF SALES AREAS

In recent years there have been an increasing number of studies concerned with finding out how the way a business arranges its space, and the resultant store atmosphere, affects the purchasing behavior of consumers. The following points have been taken into consideration as influencing variables (Weinberg, 1992, p. 164):

- Store layout,
- decoration,
- choice of colors,
- environmental design.

Each individual point can contribute to the extent that it is correctly worked with, toward the end of communicating to the customer a store atmosphere in which they feel at ease. An atmospheric effect that is perceived by the customer as pleasant has in turn an influence on how the consumer behaves while shopping. In an empirical study into store atmospheres test subjects were asked about their impressions and reactions immediately after their visit to a store. The following behavioral values were measured (Kroeber-Riel and Weinberg, 1999, p. 425):

- The perceived "rate of information" of the environment: This reports the stimulus strength of the store's arrangement.
- The emotional impressions within the store, which comprise the test subjects' arousal and desire.
- The attraction and avoidance behavior in the form of outwardly expressed behavioral intents.

The most important findings of this analysis can be summarized as follows:

- The store atmosphere resulting from the store arrangement mainly showed itself in the emotional impressions of "enjoyment" and "arousal".
- The sensation of enjoyment was the most pronounced in its determination of how customers behaved in the store. It was reflected in the intent to stay in the store and spend more money than was originally planned.
- If the store was in general positively assessed, then the intent to spend more time in the store increased with the rise of activation (arousal).
- The perceived size of the store influenced the customers' length of stay. The bigger the store is perceived to be, the longer the stay will be.

Recent research in this area has furthermore asserted that it is important to know customers' psychological ordering system. This includes the question of what customers give precedence to on the shelves, for example, names of manufactures, sizes, colors, taste, and on the basis of which characteristics they orient themselves within the store.

Sommer and Aitkens (1982) have attempted in a study to determine according to what criteria customers classify pre-given products on the shelves with the use a floor plan. It came out here that customers were mainly able to specify the location of products that were on the outskirts of the store. The goods that were placed in the inner part of the supermarket were by contrast less readily identified (Gröppel, 1991, p. 118). This could be explained in that as a rule, striking markings that would remain in the memories of customers and/or would catch the eye, were lacking in the inner part of the supermarket, for example, being high enough, colored surfaces, or posters. In fact, it is exactly these aids to orientation that support a customer's ordering system and which have a positive effect on the subjectively perceived pleasantness of shopping (Gröppel, 1991, p. 118). Kirchler (1995) went further with this approach. He assumes the chance of a product being purchased depends on whether it can be perceived and grasped without difficulty. Thus products that are less easily sold should be placed at eye level, while popular goods should be placed somewhat lower. Grossbart and Rammohan (1981) have conducted some empirical analyses. They have demonstrated that internalized knowledge concerning the location of products or businesses can considerably increase the level of shopping comfort in the eyes of the customer. These results could prompt businesses to apply more effort to the communication of verbal and visual information, toward the end of enhancing the perception as well as the inner orientation of customers.

Perceptual and orientational pleasantness with regard to customers is also influenced by whether the customer's course through the store corresponds with natural behavioral patterns. Empirical studies regarding the course that customers take through stores (Barth, 1975, p. 94; Berekoven, 1990, p. 295) have shown that:

- Customers generally traverse the shopping location in a counterclockwise direction.
- Customers usually tend to be oriented on the walls, and so prefer the outer edges of the store.
- Customers follow a certain speed rhythm (fast—slow—fast).
- Customers avoid 180 degree turns and the corners of the store.
- Customers tend more to direct their attention (gaze and grasp direction) to the right hand field of placement.
- Customers prefer levels that are close to the entrance.

Various shopping zone values result from this customer behavior:

"High quality shopping areas"	"Shopping areas of inferior quality"
- Store main routes - Sales areas to the right of the customer's path - Surfaces one comes upon, which the customer automatically looks at - Aisle intersections - Cash zones (in case the customers have to wait) - Zones dedicated to giving directions regarding elevators, stairs, etc.	- Aisles - Sales areas to the left of the customer's path - Areas one comes across or walks into, which are quickly passed by - Shopping area cul-de-sacs - Areas behind the cash counters - Higher and deeper levels

Figure 12.8 The value of shopping areas (Gröppel, 1991, p. 64)

The psychology of perception is not lost on real estate developers. Buildings that contain retail businesses should be on the "going home" side of the street, and have convenient ingress and egress to allow customers to "drop in" to the locations at a moment's hesitation. This is contrasted with office buildings, which typically do not have the same level of urgency for convenient access. Office properties are destination or appointment-oriented, and thus, are not dependent on spur-of-the-moment decisions by customers, as is the case with retail properties.

THE PERCEPTION OF PRODUCTS IN ADVERTISING

Perception of products in advertising is influenced by clever placement in the right context. Companies here use the insights from psychology into people's perceptual capacities in a targeted manner. In the end the goal is to awaken attentiveness in customers. Only those stimuli that generate attentiveness will consciously be perceived by customers and efficiently processed further. Many experiments have shown that customers mainly perceive those stimuli that correspond with their needs and desires. Therefore advertising has to fulfill several basic functions (Felser, 1997, pp. 7–9; Kroeber-Riel and Weinberg, 1999, p. 583):

- It should inform.
- It should entertain.
- It should be emotional.

Information: advertising is helpful if the customer is in fact looking for information that will facilitate his purchase decision. For example advertising is informative regarding the offers of competing products and services, or also the material constituents of particular goods. In the purchase of computers, customers are often interested in finding out what components are included in the purchase price of a computer being offered. A representative of the "German Direct Marketing Association" (Deutschen Direktmarketing Verbands—DDV) sums this up: "You won't find anyone who will spontaneously say that they love brochures, but the fact is that an increasing number of households react to the offer, actually buying according to the information in the advertised offer" (Ehm, 1995, p. 130).

Entertainment: Advertising often serves chiefly as entertainment for customers. The consumer is amused and relaxed if they see an advertisement that corresponds with their taste. This customer goal is often underestimated or overseen in the formation of advertising (Kroeber-Riel and Weinberg, 1999, p. 584).

Emotion: in connection with the entertainment use, also decisive with regard to the customer are the communication of emotional experiences. A significant proportion of advertising is only perceived because it communicates an emotional experience to them. This applies above all to advertising containing a large amount of images. Emotionally arousing images can for example be beautiful landscapes or erotic individuals. The consumer here reacts almost automatically, even when they should not be interested or affected by the content (Kroeber-Riel and Weinberg, 1999, p. 584).

PERCEPTION OF PRICE AND PRICE ASSESSMENT

The effect of price on the customer is of decisive importance for a company with regard to its pricing strategy (Simon, 1992, p. 591). In principle, a product's price can be perceived in various ways by the consumer. On the one hand it is information about the product that follows the price-quality-rule. The higher the price is, the higher the quality. For others it is defined according to the respective utility. The lower the price is, the greater is its utility. Which of these two definitions applies depends on the level of knowledge of the given customer with regard to the product. For example, a customer who has not had any experience with a product and who is afraid to make a mistaken purchase would be more likely to subscribe to the first definition. If a customer knows a lot about a product and is aware that they cannot make a mistake in their purchase, they will be more likely to lean toward the second way of perceiving. Here is an example (Felser, 1999, pp. 63–64): A non-professional wants to buy a computer. In assessing what computer they should choose, they take the price among other things into consideration. This gives them a reference point for assessing which ones of the available models are of high quality and which of them are of low quality. On the other hand an expert generally knows what they can expect from a certain type, even without knowing the price. From this we can conclude that people with a high level of expertise in the respective area view the price more as an extra help.

Clear and simple rules of assessment: products with very simple functions can generally be very easily assessed without extra help. For example, staple foods can be assessed without the consumer having the feeling that they have to pay attention to the price in order to get an idea of hidden product characteristics.

Negligible subjective risk due to market saturation: now and then the buyer might experience there to be a low purchase risk without having a specific look at the criteria by which the product is assessed. This can be the case if for example friends or product tests have indicated that one really cannot go wrong here in making a purchase. The consumer is convinced by this, and so the price is only of peripheral interest to them.

The control of assessment and perception of price, in order to dispose the consumer toward purchasing products, has to be one of a company's fundamental goals. Toward the end of directly influencing consumer behavior, what mainly comes into consideration are non-price-related marketing instruments like advertising, personal selling, or product placement. When considering the narrower area of pricing as an instrument, assessment and perception of price can be influenced via the organization of the price structure, payment modalities, and by the tactic of price changes (Simon, 1992, p. 599). In the context of a study regarding knowledge of price in the area of grocery shopping, Müller-Hagedorn (1983) arrived at the finding that consumers possessed a realistic idea of price level within individual grocery stores or departments, despite not having an exact knowledge of price with regard to individual products (Simon, 1992, p. 595). Accordingly it is only possible for the company to influence consumers' perception of price to a certain extent.

As far as pricing is concerned, it is noteworthy that with price increase, sales quantity does not decline in a continuous manner, but does so in stages. One example of this comes from the "society for consumer research" (Gesellschaft für Konsumforschung) (Högl, 1989), regarding the price of margarine. The price of Rama® was experimentally varied in different supermarkets: DM 2.19 presented as "on special", DM 1.99, and DM 1.79. This analysis revealed that sales were significantly better once the price went below the threshold of DM 2.00. By contrast there was hardly any improvement in the decrease from DM 2.39 to DM 2.19. A further increase in sales was noted at the decrease from DM 1.99 to DM 1.79. Presumably there is another price threshold at DM 1.80. These price thresholds as a rule turn out to be round numbers, for example, in this case 2.00 or 1.80. Optimal profit is achieved if one stays just under these assumed price thresholds. The consumer sees the product as at a psychologically lower price level, since companies do receive an optimum yield at these levels (Simon, 1992, p. 602). One therefore usually sees DM 1.99 rather than DM 2.00 on the price tag.

It should however also be looked into whether or not the use of broken prices can also damage the relationship with the customer. Diller and Brielmaier (1996) for example found that almost three-quarters of those asked experienced round prices, that is, sums rounded to increments of 10, to be more honest, and expressed their opposition, saying that broken prices should be rounded up. In this connection a possibility has arisen for companies with the introduction of the Euro. Companies had to specifically change their prices in the switch over from DM prices to Euro in order maintain current broken prices, in particular the dominant end numeral of nine. Companies who did not take the Euro switch-over as an opportunity to raise prices, could attract the special interest of the customers (Kotler and Bliemel, 1999, p. 789). The drug store chain, dm, indicated that it would round prices to five or ten cent increments, thereby limiting the use of broken prices (Hoffritz, 1998, pp. 72–75).

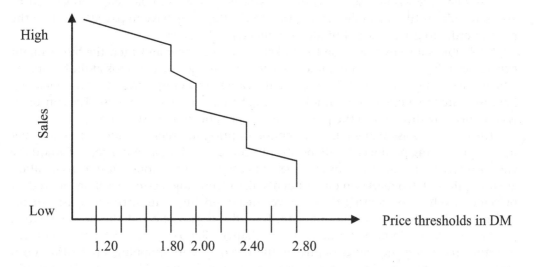

Figure 12.9 Threshold prices for margarine (Högl, 1989, p. 372)

Summary

Perception plays a decisive role in a person's life. Without it experience and behavior would not be possible at all. Perception serves the function of generating information necessary for survival, so that a person can orient themselves within their environment and behave appropriately. The high value of perception has increasingly been recognized by business professionals. In the current context of more pronounced customer orientation, the significance of perception—as shown in the above examples—is coming under ever greater scrutiny.

QUESTIONS FOR DISCUSSION

1. Elaborate on the factors that influence perception. How might culture influence perception?
2. What are the rules of perception and how might these be utilized in marketing communication?
3. How has the Lambda Hypothesis been used in advertising campaigns in recent years?
4. What determines successful product perception in advertising?
5. How has the perception of price been utilized in advertising campaigns in the following industries: automobiles, grocery, oil and gas, banking.

Bibliography

Asch, S.: *Effects of Group Pressure on the Modification and Distortion of Judgements.* Pittsburgh: 1951.

Barth, K.: Die warenpräsentation in einzelhandelsunternehmen. In: Sundhoff, E. (ed). *Mitteilungen des Instituts für Handelsforschung an der Universität zu Köln*, 1975, 7, 93–97. (The store presentation in the single trading company. In *Communications of the Institute for Trade Research at the University of Cologne*).

Berekoven, L.: *Erfolgreiches Einzelhandelsmarketing.* München: 1990. (*Successful Retail Trade Marketing*).

Bruner, J. S. and Goodman, C.: Value and need as organising factors in perception. *The Journal of Abnormal and Social Psychology*, 1947, 42, 33–44.

Diller, H. and Brielmaier, A.: Die wirkung gebrochener und runder preise: Ergebnisse eines feldexperiments im drogeriewarensektor. *Zeitschrift für Betriebswirtschaftliche Forschung*, 1996, 7/8, 695–710. (The effect of broken and round prices: Results of a field experiment in the drugstore goods sector).

Ehm, P.: Großer wurf mit database. *Werben and Verkaufen*, 1995, 27, 130–133. (Great hit with the database).

Felser, G.: *Werbe- und Konsumentenpsychologie.* Stuttgart: 1997. (*Advertising and Consumer Psychology*).

Felser, G.: Zur psychologie der informationsverarbeitung. In: Felser, G., Kaupp, P. and Pepels, W. (eds), *Käuferverhalten*, Köln, 1999, 49–68. (On the psychology of information processing. In *Buyer Behavior*).

Frisby, J.P.: *Sehen: Optische Täuschumgen, Gehirnfunktionen, Bildgedächtnis.* München: 1983. (*See: Optical Illusions, Brain Functions, Photographic Memory*)

Gröppel, A.: *Erlebnisstrategien im Einzelhandel.* Heidelberg: 1991. (*Experience Strategies in Retail Trade*).

Grossbart, S.L. and Rammohan, B.: Cognitive maps and shopping convenience. *Advances in Consumer Research*, 1981, 8, 128–134.

Hall, E.: How Cultures Collide, *Psychology Today*, July 1976, 67–74.

Hobmaier, H.: *Psychologie.* Köln: 1994. (*Psychology*).

Högl, S.: Preisschwellen und preispolitik. Teil 1: Grundlagen und ergebnisse eines feldexperiments. *Planung und Analyse*, 1989, 10, 371–376. (Price thresholds and pricing policy. Part 1: Foundations and results of a field experiment).

Hoffritz, J.: Die kosten der neuen einheit. *Wirtschaftswoche*, 1998, 16, 72–75. (The costs of the new unit).

Kebeck, G.: *Wahrnehmung: Theorien, Methoden und Forschungsergebnisse der Wahrnehmungspsychologie.* Weinheim: 1994. (*Perception: Theories, Methods and Research Results of Perception Psychology*).

Kirchler, E.M.: *Wirtschaftspsychologie. Grundlagen und Anwendungsfelder der Ökonomischen Psychologie.* Göttingen: 1995. (*Economic Psychology. Foundations and Applications of Economic Psychology*).

Kotler, P. and Bliemel, F.: *Marketing-Management* (9th edn). Stuttgart: 1999.

Kroeber-Riel, W. and Weinberg, P.: *Konsumentenverhalten* (7th edn). München: 1999. (*Consumer Behavior*).

Lilli, W. and Frey, D.: Die hypothesentheorie der wahrnehmung. In Frey, D. and Irle, M. (eds): *Kognitive Theorien*, vol. I (3rd edn). Bern, 1993, 49–80. (The hypothesis theory of perception. In *Cognitive Theories*).

Müller-Hagedorn, L.: *Handelsmarketing.* Stuttgart: 1984. (*Trade Marketing*).

Mullan, B. and Johnson, C.: *The Psychology of Consumer Behavior.* New York: 1990.

Simon, H.: *Preismanagement: Analyse—Strategie—Umsetzung.* Wiesbaden: 1992. (*Price Management: Analysis—Strategy—Conversion*).

Sommer, R. and Aitkens, S.: Mental mapping of two supermarkets. *Journal of Consumer Research*, 9, 1982, 211–216.

Weinberg, P.: *Erlebnismarketing.* München: 1992. (*Experience Marketing*).

Zimbardo, P. and Gerrig, R.: *Psychologie* (7th edn) Berlin: 1999. (*Psychology*).

13 *Learning Theory*

Theories

Learning is always connected with perception. Learning takes perception for granted as being indispensable. Learning is concerned with the long-term acquisition of information, that is, its storage in memory. The more superficially information has been processed, the more necessary it is that it must be processed again. The more intensively information has been processed, the more thorough is the learning process. We can easily infer this from Chapter 7 regarding cognitive response research. Communications that have been learned once, but which are then not used anymore, can be overrun by other communications or stimuli, and are then more difficult or impossible to retrieve. If the need is to reactivate apparently forgotten memory contents, it can work to associate them with other, current items of information. Let's assume that person X spent a holiday together with person Y a few years ago. Most of the details seem to be forgotten. After a few years X runs into Y, they begin to talk, and suddenly it is like it "was yesterday". X perceives Y and associates them with many details of their mutual holiday. Another example: Person X (X is from Munich) lived for some time in Hamburg, and now is back in Munich again. They would not be able to tell us the way from Hamburg main station to the hotel anymore. If they happen to find themselves in Hamburg again, they will easily be able to find their way to the hotel.

We need to attend to an important aspect in order to avoid mistakes in learning: for some time now in management theory there has been talk of the "learning organization" (Bock, 2000; Bertels, 2000 or Walz and Bertels, 1995). What is meant here is an evolutionary development within organization, acquisition of knowledge, and the ability to flexibly react to the demands arising from the organizational environment. Learning psychology theories often mean the acquisition and stabilization of patterns of behavior. Here learning is often the increase of an action's likelihood of occurrence, that is, exactly the opposite of flexibility. The laboratory rat that acquires the experience of the cheese being down the left corridor, and of their being a slight electric shock down the right corridor, will often very quickly seek the left corridor and avoid the right. The likelihood of occurrence of the "left corridor" will, from a start of presumably 50 percent, increase to extremely close to 100 percent. This is the opposite of flexibility.

Thus, it is just when new behavioral patterns are encountered that management theory and learning psychology mean the same thing.

STIMULUS-REACTION THEORIES

Stimulus-reaction theories have to do with conditioning (see Atkinson, Atkinson, Smith, Bem and Nolen-Hoeksema, 1996, pp. 228–253). Basically two classes of theories can be differentiated: Classical conditioning (Pavlov, 1927) and operant conditioning (Skinner, 1938, 1953).

Classical conditioning dates back to Pavlov's (1927) experiments. At first there is an unconditioned stimulus to which any given living entity (human or animal) automatically (according to Pavlov's assumption, reflexively) reacts in a biologically determined manner (a healthy dog normally reacts by salivating in the presence of food). This reaction proceeds reflexively without any preceding learning processes. If a neutral stimulus happens at the same time often enough, or if it is interjected directly before the unconditioned stimulus, according to Pavlov the new neutral stimulus will become superimposed reflexively onto the reaction of the unconditioned stimulus, thus becoming a conditioned stimulus (in the case of Pavlov's study what was regularly heard before food was given was first an attendant, and then later a bell). The dog reacted to the conditioned stimulus by excreting saliva, just as it did before in the presence of food.

Interestingly enough, the more current views within psychological research are hardly addressed at all in the marketing literature. In the more current behavioral research it is now much more assumed that it is not about an automatically occurring reflex outside of cognitive control; rather, the focus is on a cognitive, expectant attitude (so-called appetence) that is completely accessible to thought processes. "They are completely correct when they say that Pavlov was mistaken in believing that the salivation of dogs was a conditioned reflex; we have known for a long time now that it is a conditioned appetence (that is, a cognitive attitude of expectation, the assumption of experience)" (Riedl, 1985, p. 61, in Popper, Sexl, Riedl, et al., 1985). Thus the assumption of automatic reflexes proceeding reflexively has been discarded. "Pavlov's famous dog, who presumably learned via a conditioned reflex was—like all dogs—actively interested in his food. If he had not been interested in his food, he would not have learned anything. Thus he came up with a theory: When the bell rings, the food comes. That is theory, not a conditioned reflex" (Riedel, 1985, p. 5). These statements are important with regard to what image of a human being we hold. Riedel has come to the conclusion that there are no reflexes or automatically occurring associations.

Popper and Eccles (1987) take it even further, in that they even take the differentiation between conditioned and unconditioned reflexes severely into question. While in the above quoted discussion conditioned reflexes are understood to be expectant attitudes, now the very existence of unconditioned reflexes is being debated: The dog "develops the obvious theory or expectation that there is food when the bell rings. This expectation triggers his saliva—just as the optical perception or smell of the food would similarly arouse this expectation" (p. 175). This latter reaction is also based on experiences and the formation of theories. Reactions to bells, attendants, or the sight of meat are at the basis of the same mechanisms. "The reflex theory at the basis of behavior with regard to the stimulus-reaction scheme, is wrong and should be discarded" (ibid., p. 177). In any case, we can assume that reflexes, if they exist, play a relatively minor role with regard to human behavior, and that we can explain neither consumption nor work behavior on the basis of them. Given the inadequacy of the classical conditioning concept, it seems peculiar how uncritically this approach is still being presented in modern literature regarding consumer behavior (see also, for example Wells and Prensky, 1996, p. 292). Wilkie (1994, pp. 268 and 269) also relates the concept of classical conditioning uncritically, "supporting" the concept with examples: "Coca-Cola® pairs a positive phrase and photo with its brand name in order to have consumers develop an association between Coke and fun" (ibid., p. 269).

On the contrary, this does not prove anything. If correct conclusions are drawn from a set of conditions, in this case the advertising with positive moods, this does not constitute evidence for the accuracy of the original set of conditions. It is certainly possible to arrive at useable conclusions by way of false assumptions (see likewise in Albert, 1972, p. 13).

Operant conditioning originates with Skinner (1938 and 1953). This involves the positive reinforcement, the negative reinforcement, and the extinction and punishment of behavioral patterns.

Positive reinforcement is based within a neutral situation. As the result of a certain form of behavior, a reward is given—the positive reinforcement. This in turn increases this behavior's likelihood of occurrence, which constitutes the learning of that behavior. The typical Skinner experiment consists of a rat having various ways it can choose from in a labyrinth. For many rats the probability of certain ways being chosen is the same for all alternatives. Certain ways are rewarded with food, where the food is the positive reinforcement. This increases the likelihood of these ways being chosen.

In negative reinforcement the beginning situation is negative; for example a stressful feeling, experienced as unpleasant, may be present. When a certain kind of behavior is displayed the stressful situation goes away. The indicated behavior is learned on this basis. Let's assume that there is a rat sitting in a cage, the grid of which is slightly electrified. The rat experiences this as uncomfortable. The rat activates a switch accidentally, turning the electricity off. Finally the rat learns to hit the switch whenever it experiences the electricity (Lefrancois, 1986, p. 36).

Positive reinforcement is differentiated from negative reinforcement in that a positive stimulus is interjected (reward as a positive reinforcement), whereas with negative reinforcement an unpleasant stimulus is eliminated (reward as a negative reinforcement).

Whenever an unpleasant stimulus is interjected, or in other words when a punishment is given after a certain behavior, that behavior is unlearned, in that its likelihood of occurrence declines.

It has been established that learning processes are more likely to be activated via positive reinforcement. The second best learning result is triggered by the mechanism of negative reinforcement. Presumably stress (the elimination of which is the negative reinforcement) hinders learning. The least successful is learning through punishment. In accordance with the punishment, a particular behavior is extinguished, but the desired behavior is not indicated.

A learned behavior's probability of occurrence falls when a behavior that used to be reinforced is suddenly not reinforced anymore. The behavior becomes unlearned. This process has been labeled the extinction of a behavioral pattern. With extinction, the behavior is displayed, but is not reinforced anymore.

Forgetting occurs if a behavior is not displayed anymore after a long period of time. A reason for this could be the lack of an opportunity that yields this behavior, so that it also cannot be reinforced. The process of forgetting takes place over a longer period of time than the process of extinction.

The most important elements of the operant conditioning learning theory therefore are: Positive reinforcement, negative reinforcement, punishment, extinction, and forgetting.

Also of interest are the various so-called levels of reinforcement (Lefrancois, 1986, pp. 39–41). A behavior is more quickly learned if the reinforcement takes place immediately after its occurrence. This is for example relevant in business, within performance incentive systems. Field service performance that has to take place for a year before a reward is received, hardly leads to any learning of modes of behavior. Behavioral modes are more readily learned if they are performed over a time period of eight to twelve months and then immediately rewarded afterwards.

The second aspect relating to levels of reinforcement is the question of how regularly behavior is rewarded. A behavior that is irregularly rewarded is learned more slowly, but will remain relatively stable even after the occasional lack of a reward. It is only after the reward is absent for a long time that the behavioral pattern slowly begins to disappear. The fact that irregularly reinforced behavior becomes especially stable has been explained by societal socialization. If we behave in a way that is considered socially acceptable in a culture, this behavior is not always reinforced and not always right away, but certainly it is reinforced again and again. In this way the arising of behavioral patterns that are typical for a given culture can be explained.

The critique that was leveled against Pavlov above, also equally applies to Skinner, if it is assumed that the reinforcement and extinction of behavioral patterns proceeds without any cognitive control. "A behaviorist attitude toward humans and animals entails thinking the whole time according to ideas of an absurdly simple reflex process of stimulus and response, and then with operant conditioning to think that the character of how the nervous system functions comes into play" (Popper and Eccles, 1987, p. 595). The consequence is the same; we have to begin with the assumption of more complex cognitive processes than those which have been associated with operant conditioning, and than those associated with classical conditioning. It is now assumed that learning is based, to a much larger extent than was originally thought, upon cognitive processes. This also applies if the reactions to be learned subsequently occur outwardly very quickly, which after superficial observation could be attributed to a reflexive automatism.

It should however be pointed out that Skinner understood himself just as an observer. The label "S-O-R" was put forward. S stands for stimulus, R for response. Skinner observed these relationships. O stands for the object of research—the laboratory rat, the human or other subject of research. Behaviorism does not include any theory that explains what happens in O. Complex cognitive processes are also compatible with behaviorism. Perhaps the criticisms presented here should be leveled at later interpretations and premature applications (among others, in business sciences), rather than at the original statements (of behaviorism).

COGNITIVE LEARNING THEORIES

In psychology the "gestalt psychology approaches", which can be traced back to Wertheimer (1925), Köhler (1947) and Koffka (1950), have been identified as cognitive learning theories. The following gestalt psychology thesis is very popular: "The whole is more than the sum of its parts". Accordingly, it is not only the individual parts that are important in perception, but also their relationship to one another. As indicated by the name, this learning theory places more emphasis on cognitive processes than the preceding theories.

The theory is best presented on the basis of individual laws (Irle, 1986, pp. 129–134):

What is Perceived Conforms to the Law of Conciseness

According to this law, the precepts of the perceptual act assume the best possible gestalt. "Best possible" means here simple and clear structures that are in accordance with the principles of "unity", "continuity", of "similarity", or of "proximity". The law of conciseness is therefore a kind of "overarching law".

a) **The principle of unity** states that incomplete stimuli will be perceived cognitively as unified, completed stimuli. The more stimuli are well known, like for example brand symbols, the more the principle of unity will apply with regard to incomplete stimuli material. Misperceptions are also possible which are not always in accord with the stimuli being perceived as a unity. What a person believes they are perceiving depends on their personal familiarity with the given stimuli. A North Saxon politician may well perceive the letters "C...U" as CDU, whereas a Bavarian politician might see them as CSU. This just goes to show the advantages to a very independent presentation of companies, products, and advertising messages

b) **The principle of continuity** states that the perceived stimuli will be perceived as continuous, even if perceiving stimulus material in this way cannot occur without the addition of something. The implications are similar to the law of unity. The problem here is that possible idiosyncrasies of the stimulus material's individual constituents do not get perceived.

c) **The principle of similarity** states that similar individual stimuli are perceived as a unity. In Figure 13.1 one tends more to see 4 rows of the same letters than to see 10 columns of varying letters.

$$a\ a\ a\ a\ a\ a\ a\ a\ a\ a$$
$$c\ c\ c\ c\ c\ c\ c\ c\ c\ c$$
$$e\ e\ e\ e\ e\ e\ e\ e\ e\ e$$
$$s\ s\ s\ s\ s\ s\ \ s\ s\ s\ \ s$$

Figure 13.1 The principle of similarity (Lefrancois, 1986, p. 99)

In accordance with the principle of similarity, many individual cherries will be perceived as "a dish full of cherries". In the process differences between individual cherries are overlooked. The same goes for products, other people, etc. Nothing is ever referred to negatively in advertising productions, as legal problems with consumers are avoided at (almost) any price.

d) **The principle of proximity** entails that a relationship is established between two stimulus objects that are relatively close to each other. With an eye on profits, this is taken very seriously into account by the world's biggest consumer goods company, Proctor and Gamble: Meticulous attention is paid to assuring that anything that could in any way be negatively judged, never becomes associated with this company's brands. Companies within the production goods areas could also learn from this.

e) Within memory what is perceived may also be altered in the search for a good gestalt. This includes the processes of adaptation, of generalization, of accentuation, or of normalization.

- In accordance with the principle of adaptation individual, completely different objects will increasingly be remembered as similar. In memory a company's various product releases will be adapted to the most concise, the most frequent, or to the middling products. The principle of adaptation is similar to the principle of generalization: "In generalization there is the factor of applying earlier behavior to new situations similar to earlier ones in which the behavior was first learned" (Lefrancois, 1986, p. 44).
- In accordance with the principle of accentuation a memory impression will adapt to an especially extreme variant. Along these lines, a very bad experience with a product could color the perception and memory of subsequent product experiences.
- In accordance with the principle of normalization the memory impression will be adapted in memory to stored prototypes differing from it.

Which of these principles actually gets applied within memory simply depends on what mechanism is found to be applicable in each case for the person. There are no generally applicable laws regarding the preference of this or that principle.

Learning can be hindered by numerous similar communications regarding differing objects. The more similar communications are, the more difficult it is for the person to differentiate them from each other. This phenomenon, known as interference, leads to similar communications of competing providers not being perceived as unique. Stimuli that differ objectively are reacted to identically due to presumed equality (interference). We can certainly establish that there is a difference, with regard to this phenomenon, between a market leader imitating the communication of a smaller competitor, and a challenger imitating a market leader.

Let's assume that a smaller challenger is trying to tackle the market leader with a new product. A strong market leader can readily attempt, informatively and with product cunning (with a very similarly crafted product), to imitate the challenger's product and, on the basis of its established power as the market leader, it can appropriate the product field for itself. By contrast, the challenger has to sharply differentiate itself from the market leader, since potential buyers will otherwise be more inclined to remain with the trusted brand. In this case the principle of discrimination applies. "Discrimination is a process complementary to generalization, whereby differentiation must be made between two similar situations, so that the reaction is accurate with regard to each of them" (Lefrancois, 1986, p. 44).

On the other hand this phenomenon can be of use if the task is to offer individual products under the umbrella of one brand. The characteristics of the brand will then also be attributed to new products. In this case the above-presented generalization applies.

People also make things easier for themselves by identifying stimuli through learning categories, under which they can subsume sets of stimuli (for example, products). Origins, price class, materials used, brands, or the presence of particular quality standards, can all lead to products being seen by the customer as belonging to certain categories. Various stimuli will also be similarly reacted to in this case. Certainly here, the perceiving people are cognizant (in contrast to the phenomenon of interference) of this phenomenon of various stimuli being summarized, and they react in the same way or certainly in very similar ways.

Cognitive networks, discussed below, are more important as an aspect of cognitive learning theory, and are more relevant for marketing. It may seem immediately plausible for the reader that we can better retain complex things if we cognitively structure and make networks out of them. Let's assume that you have to memorize the following images: 1. Wristwatch; 2. Bicycle; 3. Cigar; 4. Umbrella; 5. Football; 6. Top Hat; 7. Sunglasses; 8. Ape. The difficulty of remembering all of these things, which do not have any apparent connection to each other, is obvious. Let's now assume that you are given a single picture to look at. A cigar-smoking ape wearing a top hat and sunglasses, is riding a bicycle that has a basket with a football in it, while holding an umbrella with one hand, on the wrist of which is an idiosyncratic wristwatch. The chances of you remembering all of these things have now substantially increased, due to there now being a relationship between the different things, albeit a relationship that is also structured somewhat unusually. A task of market communication can be seen to be the realization of such cognitive networks toward the end of facilitating the learning of its statements.

Constituents of memory that may be particularly important for marketing are product characteristics, experiences in using the product, and knowledge regarding existing product alternatives. There are possible connections between these memory contents, which might bring together product characteristics, product experiences and product expectations/demands. In this regard Grunert (1990 and 1991) differentiates between three types of cognitive connections: a) Characteristics can be linked to instances of using the product in relation to product expectations/demands; b) characteristics may be linked to alternatives in relation to knowledge regarding the products; c) instances of using the product can be linked with product alternatives in relation to product experiences. These cognitive links can be more or less intensive (see Figure 13.2).

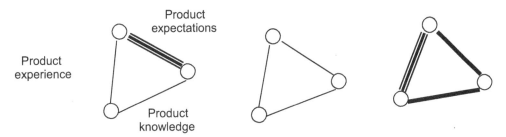

Figure 13.2 Cognitive connections and varying intensity of these connections (see Grunert, 1991, p. 13)

These cognitive connections can be influenced via appropriate market communications measures, particularly with regard to their intensity. The cognitive connections operate with more or less pronounced cognitive effort. They certainly could be the subject matter of learning processes. The sequence of such learning processes could also be a habit. Three levels of the habituation process can be differentiated:

- Extensive problem solving behavior.
- Limited problem solving behavior.
- Routine problem solving behavior (Grunert, 1990, p. 73).

At the beginning of the habituation process there is a diversity of focus on product uses and known product alternatives. After individual alternatives have been tried, diverse features will also be known. The cognitive connections have become more numerous. Toward the end, individual products will be purchased with increasing frequency, individual cognitive connections will become more and more intensive, until the purchase proceeds as if it was a routine.

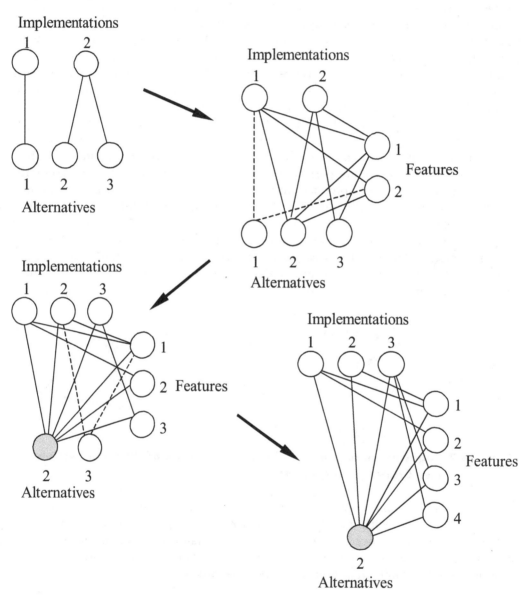

Figure 13.3 Development of habituation (modified from Grunert, 1990, p. 74)

Grunert (ibid., p. 75) demonstrates how the process of individuation comes to fruition in the course of four stages:

1. **First phase** At the beginning there is a slightly developed cognitive structure. What is known are desired product uses and some product demands. With regard to product alternatives, developing attitudes consist exclusively of assumptions.
2. **Second phase** Product standards and product knowledge dominate. Due to some consumer experience there is knowledge regarding individual product features; these features are contrasted with product standards.
3. **Third phase** After several consumer experiences, a "balanced cognitive structure" will have formed. Now product standards, relevant product features, and foreseeable applications will all be equally considered as a basis for making a decision.
4. **Fourth phase** After frequently using the product, the habit of using the product becomes fixed. Actual product experience exceeds the significance of implementations and individual features.

PERCEPTION AS THE CONSEQUENCE OF LEARNED HABIT

We now come back to a behaviorist approach, in which the habit is likewise the main focus: Hull (1952) and Spence (1960). Learned habits can influence the potential to react to a stimulus. We can certainly refine this relationship. Apart from the habit intensity, stimulus intensity, intensity of desire, and motivation play a role. In this regard Hull's (1952) concept suggests itself:

$$E = H \times D \times V \times K$$

E indicates the reaction potential, or the potential to react to a stimulus in a certain way (response). H indicates the habit intensity, that is, the frequency with which the external stimulus in question has been reacted to in this form. H is a learned quantity. D (drive) indicates the desire intensity, for example, the extent of hunger. V (vector intensity) indicates the stimulus intensity, and in the tradition of social psychology means the force with which an external stimulus influences a given behavior. K indicates the incentive or motivation to react to the particular stimulus in the learned fashion. What is also meant is how high the given desire and its satisfaction are assessed. In the language of behaviorism K is also understood to be an expected intensification.

These quantities can complement and also be superimposed on each other. If we have not drunk anything for some time (strong desire), and if we are used to drinking a certain kind of beer (H), and if upon wandering into a bar we discover a big keg of this beer, and are encouraged by friends to have a seat and drink beer, then it will not be difficult to predict E. However, perhaps we are aware of many types of beer. Which one will we consume? The most obvious one, which we have drunk more often, which has immediately caught our eye? Or will we drink an unknown alcohol-free beer, since later we have to drive and therefore our motivation to drink alcohol is small? We are assuming that the person here will drink beer in any case; though what might happen if our person is equally used to drinking wine, cola, or juice?

We can now apply ourselves to an expansion of this. All purchasing activities are the same in that they involve a price. If we want to change a behavior in social marketing, for example, to have less aggressive behavior in traffic, then additionally there is the necessary task encouraging "gentler behavioral patterns". In both cases there may be a hesitation I with regard to expressing the behavior being encouraged through marketing. Accordingly the reaction potential E will be reduced by this value (inhibition factor I):

$$E = H \times D \times V \times K - I$$

The multiplicative combination adopted in Hull's (1952) system results in behavior not being possible if only one of the variables has a value of zero.

A student of Hull, Spence (1960), introduced an additive combination:

$$E = H \times (D + K)$$

Now it is possible for a reaction to be expressed if one of the two variables, desire intensity or incentive, has a value of zero, as long as the habit intensity is pronounced enough. Certainly expression of a new behavioral pattern would be completely impossible if H were zero in this case. For Hull, just as for Spence, a new behavioral pattern was only possible if it was composed of other already learned behavioral patterns.

In light of the set of difficulties with regard to information in modern industrial societies, the stimulus intensity (vector intensity V) and the inhibition factor should be emphasized, in particular for marketing. This yields the following formula:

$$E = H \times V \times (D + K) - I$$

Here we are assuming a stimulus intensity for V that is above a given necessary threshold. A reaction is not to be expected if the habit intensity is not present or if the stimulus intensity is not high enough. For desire and incentive the above specifications apply. A reaction is however only to be expected if the product of $H \times V \times (D + K)$ exceeds the inhibition factor I.

Accordingly, with regard to the expected reaction, it is advisable within marketing to take habit intensity, stimulus intensity, desire intensity, incentive, and possible behavioral obstacles (inhibition) equally into consideration.

SOCIAL LEARNING THEORY

The social learning theories we will deal with here do not involve any new laws for learning. But they do elucidate that aspect of learning that does not necessarily presuppose one's own behavior. We also learn by observing other people. The most well known advocate of this approach is Bandura (1976 and 1979). His most significant contribution can be seen in the explanation of social learning by way of imitation. Both in classical conditioning and in operant conditioning it is not strictly necessary that the person doing the learning expresses the behavior to be learned. It is enough if the person can observe the process of reinforcement. To a considerably greater degree than it implies reflexivity, observation implies cognitive processes.

Reinforced behavior can be imitated. A person observes how another person displays a particular behavior and is rewarded for it. The person can learn that behavior.

Behavior that is frequently observed might possibly be adopted because of the engagement of a habituation process, independent of a possible reinforcement. Learning by imitation is influenced by attentiveness, speed, quantity, and the complexity of the stimuli being presented to the observer (Bandura, 1976, p. 125; Bandura, 1965). And finally behavior can be learned via observation if the people being observed serve as role models or as representatives of positively regarded role model groups. These considerations go beyond Bandura's learning theory however.

At this point we can point out the fact that the often-disputed theory (by representatives of the media) of how children learn violent behavior, is lent credence by Bandura's research:

Children learn violent behavior by observing the use of violence on TV shows where violence appears to have been "worth it", that is, if violence lead to attaining the goal (Bandura, 1973). Children also learn that consumption of certain products solves problems in a simple way.

People are often rewarded when they imitate a particular behavior. Already as children and adolescents we are rewarded for imitating our parents' behavior. It seems to be worth it to imitate the behavior of people residing at hierarchically higher levels. Thus adolescents learn consumer habits from their parents or from role model groups at their peer level. According to experience the latter has greater relevance.

Very clear imitations can result in rewards. A person observes a behavior, imitates it, and receives a reward. "A child who has learned to say milk, this being the result of the fact that it has heard their mother saying milk 40 times a day for 3 years, is not acquiring the praise of proud parents, but is rather actually acquiring milk as a result of expressing this word" (Lefrancois, 1986, p. 199).

Lefrancois (1986, p. 198) assumes that learning by imitation is the prevailing form of learning in highly developed societies. Furthermore there is a mechanism that Bandura (1979, p. 192) has dubbed "reciprocal determinism". The role model, and the observing person mutually influence each other. A person who displays behavior "to be emulated", and notices that others are imitating this behavior, will note that that this behavior exercises power over these observers (in social psychology power means any potential to influence the behavior of other people). This is a pleasant realization and will be experienced as reinforcement; thus the role model learns that his very behavior is being imitated by others. The role model can work at finding out in what other situations this role model function can hold sway. At some point those behavioral patterns will be displayed because it is believed they will very likely be imitated. This is how mutually qualifying behavioral patterns arise in society.

Applications

Classical conditioning has influenced consumer goods marketing to some extent, especially advertising.

In marketing literature (as representative reference see Kroeber-Riel and Weinberg, 1999, p. 130) it is assumed that classical conditioning is useful in market communication. If emotionally unconditioned stimuli are paired often and regularly enough with emotionally neutral stimuli, the emotional reaction will carry over reflexively to the neutral stimuli (for example, products). This simple mechanism is not to be assumed in light of the critical further developments in this regard from within learning psychology. This is certainly not to say that via emotional, experience-rich images, products cannot be successfully associated with the corresponding emotions. "If advertising repeatedly presents a ('neutral') brand together with emotional stimuli, the brand can be imbued with an emotional experience" (Kroeber-Riel and Weinberg, 1999, p. 130). We are however assuming that "this learning process demands from people a modicum of individual cognitive participation..." (ibid.). What is essential is the question of what cognitions are engaged with the associations being encountered.

Operant conditioning has also found its way into personnel management. In principle all performance incentives (bonuses, etc.) that are given out after certain goals have been attained can be seen as reinforcement. Performance bonuses can function both as positive and as negative reinforcement. Within the sales force performance, bonuses could for example be given out as result of having achieved the goals of the sales plan. Often the fulfillment of the plan's tasks discloses a performance level that is seen as standard. The attainment of bonuses is practically seen as an expected performance. Until the field agents have attained this goal they are under considerable pressure to perform, which pressure then vanishes when the goal is achieved. Thus, in fulfilling the sales task a negative reinforcement is triggered. If by contrast bonuses are viewed as a special performance reward for some kind of exceptional result, then this effect can be compared with that of positive reinforcement. Commission plays a special role in controlling the sales force. This is a remuneration for performance that is given out for very particular performance results (sales volume, profit contribution), but it lacks a connection to a definite performance level, because commission is paid out continuously, that is, in percentage of profit or of contribution to profit. Commission is thus not particularly suited as an instrument for the learning of behavioral patterns (regarding control of the sales force see Unger, 1998). In the area of performance we must by all means keep in mind that it cannot revolve around reflexive learning processes. Cognitive processes, like assessment of success probability, the comparison with other people's performance results, and general experiences with the incentive system, have a lasting influence on performance behavior (see Chapter 14, "Motivation").

The origin of purchasing habits oriented toward particular consumer goods has been explained through operant conditioning. A particular brand is acquired, is consumed to satisfaction or successfully used. It is perceived as a "satisfying experience"; the behavior is positively reinforced. Through repeated similar experiences a consumer habit is established (see Wilkie, 1994, p. 271). Again it is definitely advisable to also take cognitive processes into consideration. The origination of purchasing habits has also been explained via the development of cognitive networks, as Grunert (1990 and 1991) has demonstrated. The principle of proximity states that brand articles should in all cases be kept away from negative sets of conditions. According to this theory's view, advertising involving uncomfortable stimuli (shock advertising) should also be avoided.

Other cognitive learning theories are relevant for marketing, particularly the law of conciseness, as the marketer should strive for clarity in the message being communicated. The principle of unity can be of use in brand strategy, and demonstrates how important it is to continuously and unchangingly communicate brand images over a very long time period of time. Due to the very pronounced information overload in practically all developed industrial societies we only perceive many communications in a scattered form. Concise communications lead to the consequence that even separate bits are perceived as wholes. The principle of adaptation results in various objects within a group being perceived as increasingly similar to one another, more so than they actually are. This is the fundamental principle behind various products being positioned under the umbrella of one company brand. The quality levels of especially good products are carried over by consumers to other products. This applies equally to exceptional quality and to the quality problems of individual products. Brand image results in all products being rated at the same level of quality. Thinking in categories leads to consequences analogous to those of market leadership.

Cognitive networks arise via applications (instances of using the product), product features, and from known product alternatives. These networks can form out of product experiences and intensify, such that habitual purchasing behavior is triggered. It is certainly possible to explicitly emphasize and accelerate these cognitive processes in market communication. The emphasis on very particular product uses of a brand, on the basis of very particular features, can constitute a long-term communication strategy, for example, in the context of an integrated communication.

It is especially easy to imagine applications for Bandura's imitation learning. Just the presentation of products being used in TV advertising can alone satisfy its implications. Interesting applications arise from product placement, especially in the presentation of brand articles as items in TV movies. Here actors use brand articles in movies, which can also be reinforced via the movie's action. Sponsoring can also be thought of along these lines: Athletes can use brand articles as sports equipment. Each success comes across as an observed reinforcement of the behavior to be imitated (use of the product) (see for more detail Unger and Fuchs, 1999, pp. 257–274). As an example, the success of tennis stars Roger Federer and Raphael Nadal have been linked in a marketing context to their use of Wilson® and Babolat™ tennis rackets, respectively. The message is that if you want to hope to play tennis like them, you must purchase what they use on the court. It is equally easy to carry imitation learning over to personnel management. For example role models could be presented in meetings, and their way of working can be documented. It should however be kept in mind that in accordance with the theory of social comparison, the level of performance of chosen role models should not be too far beyond the performance level that is achieved on average. The attempted comparison will not be taken seriously by most people, and in fact will even be rejected.

The imitation learning in highly developed societies emphasized by Lefrancois (1986) discloses the possibility that consumers can learn particular consumer behavior patterns through the observation of others. In child and teenager marketing for example an attempt is made to equip role models from the youth scene with brand articles in order to accelerate this kind of imitation learning, not always successfully however. The reason for this could be found within the theory of social comparison processes. Perhaps such fortunate teenagers are experienced as diverging too much from their own peers for them to be taken seriously as consumer role models.

QUESTIONS FOR DISCUSSION

1. What are some examples of both positive and negative reinforcement by management in your firm or university?
2. Elaborate on the individual laws of cognitive learning theories, and their importance in a marketing context.
3. How can social learning theory best be utilized when designing personnel incentive plans?
4. Describe the four stages of the process of individualization, provide examples of specific products where this has occurred in your experience.

Bibliography

Albert, H.: Theorien in den sozialwisenschaften. In: Albert, H. (ed.): *Theorie und Realität* (2nd edn). Tübingen: 1972, 3–25. (Theories in social sciences. In *Theory and Reality*).

Albert, H.: (ed.): *Theorie und Realität* (2nd edn), Tübingen: 1972. (*Theory and Reality*).

Atkinson, R.L., Atkinson, R.C., Smith, E.E., Bem, D.J. and Nolen-Hoeksema, S.: *Hilgard's Introduction to Psychology* (11th edn) Fort Worth, Philadelphia, San Diego: 1996.

Bandura, A.: Influence of models' reinforcement contingencies on the acquisition of imitative response. *Journal of Personal and Social Psychology*, 1965, 1, 589–595.

—— *Agression: A Social Learning Analysis*. Englewood Cliffs: 1973.

—— *Lernen am Modell*. Stuttgart: 1976. (*Learning the Model*).

—— *Sozial-kognitive Lerntheorie*. Stuttgart: 1979. (*Social-cognitive Trained Theory*).

Bertels, T.: Die lernende organisation: Modell für das management des wandels im wissenszeitalter. In: Kremin-Buch, B., Unger, F. and Walz, H. (eds): *Lernende Organisation. Managementschriften*, vol. 1 (2nd edn), *Sternenfels*: 2000, 53–112. (The learning organization: Model for the management of the change in the science age. In *The Learning Organization. Management Writings*, vol. 1).

Bock, F.: Lernen als element der wettbewerbsstrategie. In: Kremin-Buch, B., Unger, F. and Walz, H. (eds): *Lernende Organisation. Managementschriften*, vol. 1 (2nd edn), *Sternenfels*: 2000, 9–52. (Learning as an element of competitive strategy. In *The Learning Organization. Management Writings*, vol. 1).

Grunert, K.G.: *Kognitive Strukturen in der Konsumforschung: Entwicklung und Erprobung eines Verfahrens zur Offenen Erhebung Assoziativer Netzwerke*. Heidelberg: 1990. (*Cognitive Structures in Consumption Research: Development and Testing of a Procedure Dealing with the Open Investigation of Associative Networks*).

—— Kognitive strukturen von konsumenten und ihre veränderung durch marketingkommunikation — theorie und meßverfahren. *Marketing ZFP*, 1991, 13, 11–22. (Cognitive structures of consumers and its variation through marketing communication—theory and measurement procedure).

Hull, C. L.: *A Behavior System*. Hew Haven: 1952.

Irle, E.: Lerntheorien. In: Unger, F. (ed.): *Konsumentenpsychologie und Markenartikel*. Heidelberg, Wien: 1986, 122–140. (Trained theories. In *Consumer Psychology and Brand-name Products*).

Koffka, K.: *Principles of Gestalt Psychology*. London: 1950.

Köhler, W.: *Gestalt Psychology. An Introduction to New Concepts in Modern Psychology*, New York: 1947.

Kremin-Buch, B., Unger, F. and Walz, H. (eds): *Lernende Organisation. Managementschriften Band 1* (2nd edn). Sternenfels: 2000. (*The Learning Organization. Management Writings*, vol. 1).

Kroeber-Riel, W. and Weinberg, P.: *Konsumentenverhalten* (7th edn). München: 1999. (*Consumer Behavior*).

Lefrancois, G.: *Psychologie des Lernens* (2nd edn). Berlin, Heidelberg, New York: 1986. (*Psychology of Learning*).

Pawlow, I.P.: *Conditioned Reflexes*. London: 1927.

Popper, K.R. and Eccles, J.C.: *Das Ich und Sein Gehirn* (2nd edn). München: 1987. (*You and Your Brain*).

—— and Lorenz, K.: *Die Zukunft ist Offen*. München, Zürich: 1985. (*The Future is Open*).

Popper, K.R., Sexl, R. Riedl, R. Wallner, F. and Weingartner, P.: Wissenschaft und hypothese. In: Popper, K.R. and Lorenz, K.: *Die Zukunft ist Offen*. München, Zürich: 1985, 47–73. (Science and hypothesis. In *The Future is Open*).

Skinner, B.F.: *The Behavior of Organisms: An Experimental Analysis*. New York: 1938.

—— *Science and Human Behavior*. New York: 1953.

Spence, K.W.: *Behavior Theory and Learning*: Selected papers. Englewood: 1960.

Unger, F. and Fuchs, W.: *Management der Marktkommunikation* (2nd edn). Heidelberg: 1999. (*Management of Market Communication*).

Unger, F.: Die mitarbeitersteuerung. In: Pepels, W. (ed.): *Absatzpolitik*. München: 1998, 318–358. (Colleague control. In *Sales Politics*).

Walz, H. and Bertels, T.: *Das Intelligente Unternehmen: Schneller Lernen als der Wettbewerb*. Landsberg am Lech: 1995. (*Intelligent Business: Learn More Quickly than the Competition*).

Wells, W.D. and Prensky, D.: *Consumer Behavior*. New York, Chichester, Brisbane: 1996.

Wertheimer, M.: *Drei Abhandlungen zur Gestalttheorie*. Erlangen: 1925. (*Three Treatises on Gestalt Theory*).

Wilkie, W.L.: *Consumer Behavior* (3rd edn). New York, Chichester, Brisbane: 1994.

III Motivation and Emotion

14 *Motivation*

If there are enough reasons that would result in the attainment of what is desired through one's own actions, after an initial stage of motivation in which desires are assessed and elaborated upon with regard to their desirability and plausibility, then the formation of an intention, of an act of volition, will come about. As soon as an appropriate opportunity arises, intention is given access to action, and intention will then direct the given action until the goal has been attained (Heckhausen, 1989, p. 4). The formation of an intention has been dubbed volition within motivation psychology. Volition is formed, via expectations with regard to the consequences of one's own behavior, among other things. People assess the consequences of their action (A). Furthermore people foster assumptions concerning the instrumentality of a particular behavioral pattern, in connection with a targeted benefit (I), and they live with certain expectations of success (E). This outlines Vroom's (1964) assessment-expectation approach to motivation. Behavioral intention or intent to act (B) is therefore dependent upon assessment, expectation and instrumentality.

$$B = f (A \times I \times E)$$

However, this alone does not yet explain the numerous possible behavioral variations. In Vroom's model, questions regarding how expectations are formed, and what role earlier experiences, self worth, situational factors, and management style play, are left open (see Weinert, 1981, p. 276).

Theory

The same behavior can result from various causes. People acquire a particular car because they want an especially safe vehicle, for general reasons of prestige, for economic reasons, because they want to impress a certain person, out of habit (brand loyalty), because the trunk is of a certain size, or for a simultaneous mixture of various reasons. "Reasons" are the assumed causes of behavior which in common speech tend to be referred to as "motives". "However, the reference to its function in the formation of behavior is not enough to have the motivation concept be separated from other psychological constructs," (Thomae, 1983, p. 1), because perception, thinking, and learning are all included as causes of behavior. In keeping with the currently prevailing view, motives explain the intensity, direction, and form of behavioral patterns. They explain: a) individually different reactions to the same external impulses in the same situations; b) an energy input sustained over a long period of time; c) and why a person displays the same behavior again and again in varying situations.

a) A person basically does not react to certain forms of performance incentives; or a person might always react very intensely to certain performance incentives.

b) An adventurer always climbs "the highest mountains".
c) Regardless of where a person finds themselves, they always immediately check out certain sightseeing locations.

The similarity of these items to the covariation principle according to Kelley (1973) is obvious.

Behavior is not only triggered by motives. Instincts, drives, emotions, needs, single-mindedness, capacities, or experiences, and especially desires, can also influence behavior.

Resolution is practically a synonym for decision. A decision is the consequence of possible motives. We view intentions in a similar way. An intention is however not seen as being as concrete as a decision. We might have the intention to buy a new car, and then decide on a particular type or for a certain brand, or no brand at all.

Single-mindedness, or purposefulness, is closely related to motivation. It can be a particularly intense version of motivation.

According to the psychological terminology drives denote behavior triggering factors whose cause is primarily biologically determined. By contrast it is assumed that motives and needs are to a large extent learned during the course of a person's social development. And along these lines there are also culturally specific differences which are hardly present in the case of drives. If drives are seen as being biologically determined, then being able to influence them via marketing and personnel management is not to be expected. Marketing and personnel management tend to be oriented more toward drives.

MOTIVATION AS THE CAUSE OF CHANGE AND OF MOTION

Thomae (1983, p. 2) presents the aspect of behavioral change in connection with motivation: "Differing motivation concepts arise from different aspects of behavioral change being placed in connection with motivation variables." Motives and motivation are seen as being causes of motion and change.

Motivation implies energy and arousal; it directs a given energy potential, which was initially without direction, toward a particular goal. Motivation therefore has a guiding function.

THE IMPETUS FUNCTION OF MOTIVATION

Motivation also has an impetus function (see Atkinson, Atkinson, Smith, et al., 1996, p. 335 et seq.). Hull's (1952) learning concept is also considered to be a motivation concept (on the basis of the significance of the "factors drive" in his model).

Motives can also be brought in to describe human behavior. Motives are the basis of intensity (that is, "impetus function"), direction (that is, "guiding function"), form and of the goal orientation of possible activities. Behavior is always a function of environment and personality variables, or behavior within a real situation is triggered both by the environment and by a person's personality. Kroeber-Riel and Weinberg (1999, p. 142) have derived the following from this:

Motivation = fundamental impetus strength + cognitive goal orientation.

The fundamental impetus energies arise from emotions (see Chapter 15) and drives. Given this we can present the motivation concept in accordance with Figure 14.1:

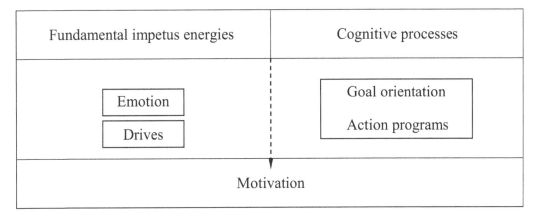

Figure 14.1 The concept of motivation according to Kroeber-Riel and Weinberg (1999, p. 142)

STIMULI ARISING FROM THE ENVIRONMENT, MOTIVATION AND BEHAVIOR (S-O-R)

A person's environment consists, among other things, of all perceived signals. If some of these signals are in any way behaviorally relevant for the given person, they will become stimuli. Everything that a person perceives from the environment is a signal, and out of these signals some are of value and can trigger behavior—these are so-called stimuli. The task of personnel policy and marketing is to see to it that their own communications are attributed with enough relevance that they become stimuli. Gebert and von Rosenstiel (1996, p. 19) have added to the S-O-R paradigm, focusing on expected consequences:

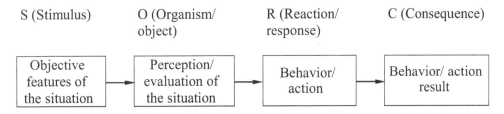

Figure 14.2 The S-O-R paradigm according to Gebert and von Rosenstiel (1996, p. 19)

Not everyone reacts to the same stimuli in the same way. Varying intensity and type of reaction to certain stimuli can be explained via differing motivational dispositions. Thus the well-known S-O-R chain can also be explained thus: Stimuli are perceived by a person (object/organism) and are internally processed (motives have an effect here) and lead to an external behavior, the reactions (or to be psychologically correct, "responses").

In this vein motives are also known as "interceding variables". It should be mentioned that perception itself is already influenced by motivation.

MOTIVATION AND ACTIVATION THEORY

The human brain, originating at the backbone, is constantly supplied with energy via a network of neural tissue. This energy current flows continuously. It is guided on the one hand via hormones, and on the other hand by external stimuli that make it to the brain. Stimuli that are strong enough to make it to the brain, if they have significance, lead to an intensification of brain activity and thus to an intensification of processing. Perceptual and processing performance increases with increasing activation at first, reaches its highest point with medium activation, and then in a state of panic decreases again to a very low level. At the middle level of activation processing, quality and influence strength are at their highest. Kroeber-Riel and Weinberg's (1999, p. 78 et seq.) thesis concurs that we can hardly be seeking to induce panic with marketing statements, since marketing measures are directed toward inducing the maximum level of activation possible.

If motivation was exclusively attributed the function of triggering reactions, then due to the statements of activation theory it would be rendered redundant, because activation theory explains everything that such a limited motivation theory would also explain. The change of activation comes across as more than just the triggering of a reaction, and as the description of reaction intensity, also having a qualitative dimension that describes the content of the reaction (including the perceptions). Motivation theory cannot be replaced by the seemingly "objectively" graspable activation. Here market research, as conducted within marketing practice, tends to see activation as being more precisely measurable with regard to intensity and time, via measuring electrical skin resistance, in contrast to motives and motivation which in general are barred from precise measurement due to their admittedly less precise contents. However, a psychological construct does not derive its relevance from its being more easily measured than another construct.

> *The motivation concept is not necessary in order to explain the triggering of behavior, but fresh indications keep arising regarding connections between motivation variables and changes of behavior, concerning intensity, direction and form* (Thomae, 1983, p. 19).

MOTIVATION AND NEEDS

Needs are felt states of deficiency connected with the desire to alleviate these same states. Such states of deficiency can be of a biological nature (hunger, thirst, sexuality, motion), but they can also be of a social nature (recognition, alleviation of cognitive dissonance, striving for performance, defense of the freedom to act, attribution of success and lack of success). The breakdown into biologically caused or socially caused needs is not obvious. All known biologically triggered needs are to some extent also subject to social influence; in developed cultures this even applies to hunger and thirst to some extent. To what extent the striving for psychological equilibrium (avoidance of cognitive dissonance), for freedom, for performance, or also to what extent certain attribution mechanisms, are partly also biologically determined, will not be further discussed here, as this debate exceeds the scope of a psychology of marketing textbook.

Since needs also arise via socialization, it is conceivable that there is an unlimited number of identifiable individual needs (see Thomae, 1983, p. 15). Motives are necessary from the point of view of motivation psychology, in order to understand why people behave in a particular manner in a given situation, or why they are oriented toward the satisfaction of a particular need. For example performance motivation entails a fundamental personality disposition that can apply to many different situations. It does not entail behavior that is oriented toward a very definite target level, up to the point that this target is attained.

We have a need for nourishment; because we experience hunger, we eat, until that hunger is sated. If a fundamental performance motivation is present, then the person will not just perform until a certain performance goal has been attained and the performance motivation fades due to not having importance for the moment. A person who is motivated to perform will very quickly find new challenging tasks to apply themselves.

If, on the other hand, the basic needs of hunger and thirst are sated the person will turn to completely other things. The need is no longer behaviorally relevant after it is sated. We can look to Becker-Carus (1983, p. 13) for further clarification of this: "We do not eat every time someone offers us food, and we do not drink everything that is placed before us. Or we will not play the violin for hours on end like the woman next-door does. How can we explain such variation in behavior? We establish that we eat because we are 'hungry', or that we work or practice because we are acting upon the desire for 'performance'." In the case of hunger we speak of need; in the case of performance we speak of motivation. Becker-Carus (1983, p. 17) later uses the concepts of "drive" and "motive" to make the differentiation:

a) Drives denote biological motivation and result "from the organism's fundamental needs like for those of nourishment, fluids, sleep, warmth or cooling off".
b) Motives denote psychological needs like "social recognition, security, performance, or knowledge ..."

Thus there is a need for performance!

On the other hand there is a still a question as to how long the person will remain performance motivated. Is there a limit or are they always oriented toward performance motivated behavior? According to Lewin (1982, p. 41 et seq.), performance motivation (McClelland, 1951) is simply a variant of a general need for quality that—as is the case with all needs—leads to comparison of a prior target with an achieved result (see Irle, 1975, p. 188).

According to Lewin (1926a, 1936) intention (see above) does not have its own status. We originally have the intention to make a lot of money, and develop from this a need for performance or for gambling. The "real need", the overarching goal, determines the needs that stem from it, the quasi-needs. According to this conception the motive as a theoretical construct is redundant. A quasi-need grows in strength the more closely it is connected with real needs (Lewin, 1926b). It comes as no surprise that motivation psychologists (like Heckhausen and Kuhl) are not particularly persuaded by this approach. "He has turned the actual formulation of aim, the intention ... into a *quasi-need* that is connected with real needs" (Heckhausen, 1989, p. 26). Social psychologists (Irle) have shown themselves to be more open to it.

In all cases of satisfying desires, we can refer to the homeostasis model. Here it is assumed that the behavior that follows sensed states of deficiency will involve reacting by consuming, "which then reestablishes the organism's equilibrium and/or satisfies the uncomfortable inner stimulus (hunger)" (Becker-Carus, 1983, p. 18). There is a theoretical concept that states that the homeostatic model of motivation merely involves physiological disequilibrium and its transformation into equilibrium. However, there is no factual reason for reducing homeostasis to the physiological level. That would simply constitute a definition. Definitions do not however have any value as knowledge.

MOTIVE AND MOTIVATION

We now want to explore more deeply the idea that behavior is not only triggered or influenced by a single motive. In a given situation there are normally many motives presently in operation, which simultaneously direct behavior.

We identify the activation of many individual motives as motivation (von Rosenstiel, 1996, pp. 6 and 7). According to this approach each person operates using numerous individual, latent motives; together these latent motives form a person's motive structure. Some motives are activated via stimuli. The mutually activated motives form the behaviorally relevant motivation. These interrelationships are presented in the chart below in accordance with Rosenstiel:

	Individual components	**Totality of all motives**
Latently present	Individual latent motives	Existent motive structure
Activated via external stimuli	Individually activated motives	Motivation

Figure 14.3 Interrelationships in the emergence of motivation (from Rosenstiel, 1996, p. 6 et seq.)

In our explanation of the emergence of motivation, we also need to keep in mind that stimuli are perceived in varying ways. One and the same stimulus can be perceived differently from within the same social environment or also in seemingly the same environment. Even an individual person may varyingly process stimuli that are the same when viewed objectively. To a very pronounced extent the triggered motivation depends on subjective perception and not on its objective nature. For their success, a management style, an incentive system, or an agreement, depends on the perception of co-workers. Past experience plays a decisive role here.

People can say relatively little about their own motives. They essentially experience motives by way of self-observation (introspection). Often people will only admit to those motives (and make "observations" regarding them) that they also hold to be socially desirable.

It is not just the behavior of other co-workers or managers that influences the emergence of motivation; the working situation can also have an influence. Monotony in the work life, experienced dependence or continuous overwork, have a negative effect on work motivation. A change in these kinds of environmental factors can certainly have a positive effect on work motivation.

A known lack of performance motivation can temporarily lead to an incorrect assessment of personal motivation, when in fact the real cause for insufficient motivation could be environmental factors, and not the character or work ethic of the given person.

The real mutual cause of an emerging motivation structure is the interplay of work situation and personality structure. This arises from the already mentioned interplay of environment and personality variables. To quote the economist John Kenneth Galbraith,

> ... *pecuniary compensation need not be the main motivation of members of the organization. Identification and adaptation may be driving forces* (Galbraith, 1967).

Hope of success and fear of failure (Heckhausen, 1963) are essential components in the emergence of motivation.

We now want to present the conditions under which a particular performance motivation also leads to performance behavior. Kuhl (1983) has provided a thorough presentation of this. Performance oriented behavior is triggered on the one hand via the value of a goal and the subjectively sensed probability of success, and on the other hand by probability of failure.

An important personality characteristic has to do with the question of whether a person is oriented toward avoiding failure or toward seeking success. There are people who tend more to see the prospect of success with regard to a task, whereas others tend more to see the possibility of failure. Each task inevitably involves both the prospect of success and the fear of failure. The decisive question for motivation is how highly the given person assesses the likelihood of success or failure. Success oriented people tend to seek out tasks with a medium probability of success. In the case of a very high likelihood of success, possible future success may not be experienced as such, whereas a probability of success that is too small is de-motivating due exactly to this small likelihood of success. People who tend be oriented toward avoidance of failure, seek out tasks with as high a likelihood of success as possible, including when the level of standard of the given task is low. Avoidance of failure takes precedence; that is why they are known as failure avoidance oriented people (Atkinson, 1976). The task of managers within an organization is to adapt performance goals to the corresponding motivation structures, or through management behavior to influence these structures. Both of these motivational components were emphasized earlier by Heckhausen (1963) in a two-factor concept: "Hope of success" and "fear of failure" are catalysts in many human behavior patterns.

Hope of success shows itself in

- A need for performance and success.
- Instrumental actions that are oriented toward success.
- An expectation that this success will be attained (success expectation).
- Praise.
- Positive feeling.
- A stronger focus on success and a weaker focus on failure.

Fear of failure shows itself in

- A need to avoid failure.
- Instrumental actions that are oriented toward avoidance of failure.
- An expectation that failure will be experienced.
- Disapproval.
- Negative feeling.
- A stronger focus on failure and a weaker focus on success.

The tendency to seek success (Ts) on the one hand, and the tendency to avoid failure (Tf) on the other hand, can be formulated as follows (Kuhl, 1983, pp. 506 and 507; Heckhausen, 1989, p. 176; Weiner, 1992, pp. 182–187; Irle, 1975, p. 189):

$$Ts = (Ms \times Is) \times Ls$$

Ls stands for the subjective likelihood of attaining success, Is for the incentive to succeed and Ms for the personal motivation to succeed. Ms stands for an affective personality, that is disposed toward experiencing joy and success. The incentive value with success-oriented people is higher, the fewer other people attain the goal, expressed as:

$$Is = 1 - Ls$$

The tendency to avoid failure (Tf) has the following structure:

$$Tf = (Ma \times If) \times Lf$$

Lf stands for the subjective likelihood of experiencing failure, If for the incentive to avoid failure, and Ma for the personal motivation to avoid failure. Furthermore:

$$If = 1 - Lf$$

The likelihood of failure can logically be derived from the likelihood of success:

$$Lf = 1 - Ls$$

If the likelihood of failure is very high then failure is not experienced as being as grave as it would be in a situation in which failure is only experienced by a few people.

The actual tendency of behavior, the resulting tendency (RT), is the difference between Ts and Tf:

$$RT = (Ms \times Is) \times Ls - (Ma \times If) \times Lf$$

We have defined the following termini in this formula:

$$Is = (1 - Ls)$$

$If = (1 - Lf)$

$Lf = (1 - Ls)$

By substitution we get Atkinson's (1957) risk selection model:

$RT = (Ms - Ma) \times Ls \, (1 - Ls)$

In the case of the success oriented Ms is greater than Ma; because Ls and Is are complementary the maximum behavioral tendency results at a medium level of success likelihood. It can furthermore be shown that those oriented toward avoiding failure prefer situations with a very low likelihood of success or with a very high likelihood of success (see Figure 14.4).

It has however been observed that the success oriented often overestimate the chances of success, in that they are inclined to assess as 50 percent an objective likelihood of success that is roughly less than 50 percent. Atkinson (1976) has furthermore been able to demonstrate that the success oriented display greater endurance in pursuit of a goal during the course of a day.

Just this differentiation between success motivation and failure avoidance motivation is not quite enough to explain which levels of difficulty people prefer. In this regard we have to introduce the "personal level of standard" variable (Kuhl, 1983, pp. 549–552). A success oriented person with a low standard level will choose easier tasks than a person with a high personal level of standard. This seems plausible. In the case of people oriented toward failure avoidance, an interesting constellation arises. It is certainly possible for a person with a high level of standard to fear failure more than they strive for success. A person motivated by failure avoidance who has a high standard with regard to themselves will choose very easy tasks in order to exclude failure from the beginning. A failure avoidance oriented person with a low standard can also choose very difficult tasks. Due to this low level of standard, failure is unproblematic and can be identified as not being a real failure because of the previously identified very low likelihood of success, since the task was simply "too difficult". This can be seen in an example from the world of competitive tennis. If an above average player has a high level of standard and a failure avoidance motivation, then they are less likely to seek out players of equal or slightly higher abilities. They might, additionally, play someone much better than themselves, as losing to this player may not seem like a true defeat, given the low probability of success.

In order to predict behavior, on the one hand we need to know the motivation structure, and on the other hand the level of standard.

The differentiation between extrinsic and intrinsic motivation is of significance in work and organization psychology. In extrinsic motivation, behavior proceeds according to desired consequences, for example, rewards, recognition, etc. With intrinsic motivation, behavior proceeds according to self will. Performance can just proceed according to an inner motivation toward performance (performance motivation). Certainly a clear differentiation is often not easily made. A mountain climber climbs the highest mountains because he wants to reach the top, and because he wants to increase the range of his capacity for performance. Is the person extrinsically or intrinsically motivated? Important extrinsic motives are: Money, recognition, sexuality, security, power.

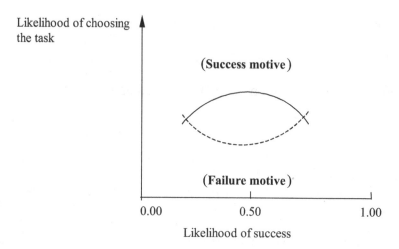

Figure 14.4 Resulting tendency with regard to people oriented toward success or toward avoidance of failure (see Kuhl, 1983, p. 507; Heckhausen, 1989, p. 177; see also Gebert and von Rosenstiehl, 1996, p. 54)

Important intrinsic motives are based on performance, social contacts that arise out of the work itself. With extrinsic motivation, an action takes place in order to attain a goal. An extrinsic motivation is present if a person engages in professional life in order to obtain monetary rewards due to hoped-for professional success, to win prestige, or to compensate for failure in private life. Managers often start by giving preeminence to intrinsic motivation. There is nothing to support this however. A pronounced emphasis on intrinsic motivation can lead to a sort of "over motivation" that can also have negative consequences for performance. At this point in our knowledge, the only statement that can be affirmed is that intrinsic and extrinsic motivations are to be judged as being of neutral value. For managers then, the nature of co-workers' motivation can initially be irrelevant.

A typical extrinsic motivation is that which is tied up with striving for income, which first takes on pronounced significance after the standard of living has reached a relatively developed level. Money does not just serve the purely material standard of living. It also contributes to further prestige and social recognition through corresponding (modes of) consumption. In times of relatively high unemployment, acquiring a secure job placement takes precedence in significance. Eventually an occupation also supplies satisfaction to the ego's needs. Friedel-Howe (1974) has asserted that sexuality can be an important extrinsic motivation, because for one thing, one's job is an important criterion for establishing oneself in preparation for getting to know future life and marriage partners. And apart from that it is the most important setting in life in which men and women can get to know each other outside of marriage or long-term relationships. This has nothing to do with sexual activity; just being observed by members of the opposite sex can thoroughly motivate performance. "The influence of sexuality on professional performance—whether it encourages or constricts—is not to be underestimated" (von Rosenstiel, 1996, p. 52).

As intrinsic motivation we are aware first of all simply of the desire for expending energy. We know that lack of activity leads to substantial dissatisfaction. Work satisfies the biological need for activity. Furthermore, many people are characterized by a highly developed need for performance. This is developed to a varying degree, on the one hand interculturally, but also individually from within a given cultural group (McClelland, 1966). McClelland discovered a whole range of factors that are responsible for the cultural and individual variations in how developed is the need for performance, which will not be gone into specifically here. It is enough to here establish that some workers do obtain satisfaction just from performance alone, which is however also needed in order to develop job satisfaction and additional motivation.

A more important insight for management is that motives can be inborn as well as learned through one's own experience. Bandura (1976) was able show that models (other people whose behavior is observed) and examples contribute to the formation of motives (see also Chapter 13, "Learning Theory"). This means that managers bear a significant amount of responsibility for the raising of employee motivation structures.

Herzberg, Mausner and Snyderman (1967) have found that two classes of factors can be assumed within performance motivation: "Hygiene" factors and motivations. During the course of empirical studies it was found that the following factors acted as triggers for satisfaction and for a positive attitude toward work: Performance results, recognition, the work itself, responsibility, and advancement possibilities. These five factors were labeled motivations by Herzberg, Mausner and Snyderman. They relate directly to the activity to be expressed, and not to the work environment. A positive, favorable prevalence of the motivations indicates satisfaction and the motivation toward performance.

Factors belonging to the work environment are: company politics, administration, management, reward, interpersonal relationships, and the external working conditions. These were labeled by Herzberg, Mausner and Snyderman as "hygiene" factors, in that they pertain to the environment and not to the work itself.

The clear split between motivations and hygiene factors has not always been apparent in later studies. Nevertheless, the following relationship is noteworthy: a negative development of the motivations is the cause of lack of motivation toward an increase in performance. In this situation, only the absolutely necessary effort is displayed. Increases in performance are not to be expected.

Only with a positive development of the motivations does above average readiness to perform manifest itself. An absolute prerequisite for this is however a positive development of the hygiene factors. If the hygiene factors are not sufficiently fulfilled, the motivations can also have no effect, due to the occurrence of an overall dissatisfaction. An inadequate development of the hygiene factors leads to dissatisfaction and to the ineffectiveness of the motivations. On the other hand a positive development of the hygiene factors does not trigger readiness to perform. The situation is merely not characterized by dissatisfaction.

Sufficiently developed hygiene factors do not lead to satisfaction; the situation is neutral. In the case of insufficient development dissatisfaction will arise.

Motivations lead to satisfaction with sufficient development and by association to greater readiness to perform, but only with simultaneously sufficient development of the hygiene factors. If the motivations are not sufficiently developed, but if the hygiene factors are sufficient, then the situation takes on a neutral value.

To conclude this section we want to explore one of the most popular of motivation theories: Maslow's (1954; 1989) hierarchy of needs pyramid. According to this well-known theory, human motivation is determined by five levels of need:

- First of all people seek basic physiological well-being (food, water, procreation).
- Second, after the first level has been fulfilled, there follows the need for security (with regard to professional life one can think of the securing of employment).
- If this security is adequately taken care of there follows as the third level, the striving for the satisfaction of social needs, the so-called need to belong.
- The fourth need is the striving for recognition (within groups that one feels one belongs to).
- The fifth need is the striving for self-actualization, which can be understood to be the seeking of freedom from any kind of external determination.

Human behavior in organizations is certainly not based on mechanisms as simple as those one might like to derive from the above hierarchical ordering of needs. Maslow himself, who developed this approach from within clinical psychology, always doubted that his pyramid of needs could be applied to management and personnel problems.

Presumably Maslow's pyramid of needs is only one of many examples of how business science often prematurely applies basic psychological research findings as solutions in practice.

It may have been noted that we have just spoken of needs, and not of motives. This has something to do with the fact that for a long time now there has not been any unity of opinion within psychological research with regard to how needs and motives may be differentiated from each other (see the above presentation concerning quasi needs).

This pyramid of needs enjoys substantial popularity within occupational psychology. The tendency here is to overlook the fact that this approach has in no way empirically proven itself within personnel management (even Alderfer's further development, 1969, was not able to stand up to scrutiny—see Bröckermann, 1997, pp. 269 and 270 for details—even though it seems to be thoroughly plausible).

Alderfer (1969) holds there to be three classes of motives:

a) **E-motives**: These are so called "existence" needs; in other words, those which are relevant for a person's subsistence, like (when necessary) nourishment, shelter, clothing and perhaps procreation.
b) **R-motives**: These are motives that are oriented around contact with other people, also known as social motives.
c) **G-motives**: The concept of growth stands for the further development of a person, and so what is meant is the motive of self-actualization.

Alderfer's (1969) motivation theory essentially consists of 7 hypotheses (cited in Rüttinger, von Rosenstiel and Molt, 1974, p. 96):

1. The less basic needs are satisfied, the more their goals will be pursued.

2. The less contact need is satisfied, the greater are the basic needs.

3. The more basic needs are satisfied, the greater contact need becomes.

4. The less contact need is satisfied, the more its goals will be pursued.

5. *The less the desire for self-development is satisfied, the greater contact need becomes.*

6. *The more contact need is satisfied, the greater the desire for self-development becomes.*

7. *The more the desire for self-development is satisfied, the more its goals will be pursued.*

The Relationship Between Performance and Satisfaction

Herzberg, Mausner and Snyderman's (1967) assumption of a direct relationship between performance and satisfaction bears closer examination. To anticipate the result: dissatisfaction very clearly leads to demotivation and so to withholding of performance. Only people with a very strongly developed intrinsic motivation structure can rise above this. As before Herzberg's statements are justified with regard to the negative effect of poor or completely inadequate hygiene factors. The direct relationship between satisfaction and positive readiness to perform has to be put into perspective. Satisfaction is then a prerequisite, which is alone not enough.

The traditional view, shared by Herzberg, Mausner and Snyderman (1967), corresponds with what is presented in Figure 14.5:

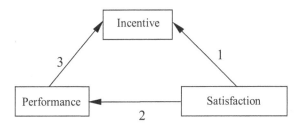

Figure 14.5 Assumed, direct and positive relationship between performance and satisfaction

Later a further quantity, performance intention, was added. Here account is taken of the fact that we can only accept the influence of psychological quantities. This is illustrated below in Figure 14.6.

The relationship between performance intention and incentive is a mutually qualifying one, as is the relationship underlying incentive and satisfaction. Performance intention and satisfaction also mutually condition each other.

Performance intention leads to performance, which conditions what is acquired of available incentives (money, recognition, advancement, etc.). Performance furthermore also directly affects satisfaction. People achieve satisfaction due to their own successful action (with reference to Scherhorn, 1992, p. 27). This insight is incidentally also of great significance for consumer criticism. However, this structure is still far from the reality. We need to take into account past experiences, personal levels of standard, attitudes toward organization and work, conflicts between non-performance oriented and performance oriented behavior, and ever present work-relevant motives. These are all addressed in Figure 14.7.

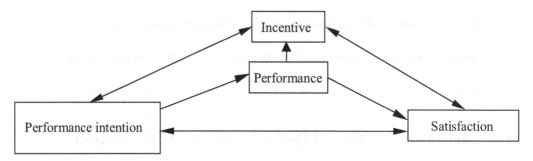

Figure 14.6 Introduction of the variable "Performance intention" (von Eckardstein and Schnellinger, 1975, p. 73)

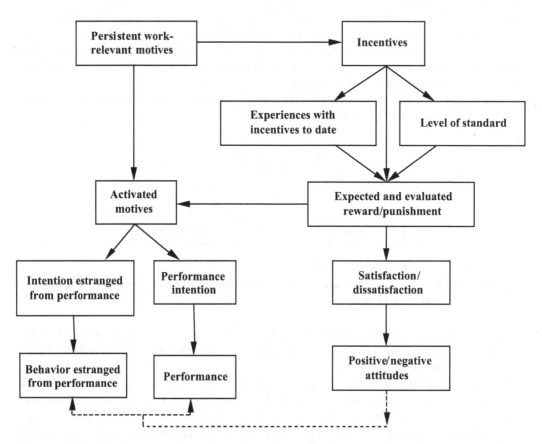

Figure 14.7 The interrelationships of work motivation, work performance, and work satisfaction (see von Eckardstein and Schnellinger, 1975, p. 70)

The starting point is the work-relevant motive structure ("persistent work-relevant motives"). These are set against the incentives. The experiences to date with incentives, together with the personal level of standard, influence expectations with regard to possible reward or punishment, where the person expects to follow particular results of behavior. Added here is the given person's subjective evaluation. A negative judgment within the work sphere (punishment) may be evaluated at a lower level than a reward in the private sphere. Official sanctions may have a lower value than recognition/rejection within the sphere of immediate colleagues. These thought structures influence the activation of motives and the anticipated satisfaction or dissatisfaction subsequent to the occurrence of rewards/punishments. This again leads to positive or negative attitudes with regard to work and organization. The activated motives and attitudes (see the next four paragraphs) influence both performance intention and performance.

Success and lack of success have an affect on future behavior. Success increases the personal level of standard, and lack of success decreases it. The actual need for performance remains the same in both cases. What changes are the quasi needs that manifest within the changed level of standard. Lack of success in an action does not reduce the inner readiness for performance, but rather leads to a change of goals (Lewin et al., 1944). The "real need" for performance still remains present, unchanged.

The conflicts being addressed here have something to do with personal intent (motivation) and with social acceptance (the social norms existing within the community of co-workers, with regard to work-relevant and other behavioral patterns). It is not infrequent to see the failure of motivation concepts due to social acceptance within the community of co-workers.

Even when management has the best of intentions, attempts to bring down barriers between staff and management often fail.

Figure 14.8 provides a concluding overview. Ability and motivation are personality factors of behavior. Social and situational indicators are environmental factors.

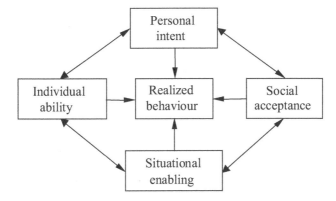

Figure 14.8 Determinations of behavior (von Rosenstiel, 1996, p. 40)

Applications

PURCHASE BEHAVIOR

Due to the multitude of varying motivation concepts there currently is no unified theory of motivation regarding purchase behavior. It seems reasonable to divide purchase behavior into consumer behavior and professional purchase behavior.

Professional purchase behavior can be directly linked to professional performance behavior. Purchasing personnel who are success oriented are more likely to be ready to try something new. Purchasing personnel who are oriented toward lack of failure will be more likely to prefer tried and true products and suppliers.

Consumer behavior and motivation

Schiffman and Kanuk (1994, p. 94 et seq.) explain the motivation of purchase behavior as an interplay between preceding concepts. These concepts are: needs, tensions, drives, learning processes, cognitive processes, tension reduction, satisfaction of needs, and observed purchase behavior.

From the concept of "motivation" as an interplay of several behaviorally relevant motives, it can be inferred that increasing the intent to purchase is possible, by simultaneously addressing several motives.

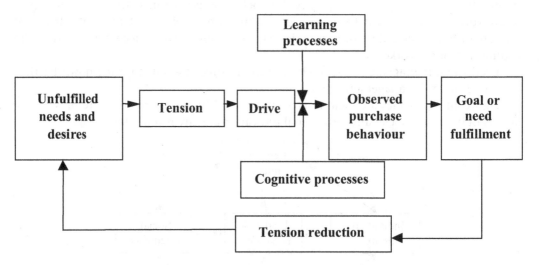

Figure 14.9 Purchase motivation as a system of psychological processes (Schiffman and Kanuk, 1994, p. 94)

The concept of quasi needs leads to similar consequences. People do not buy products for their own sake. The need for a product is a quasi need with a "real need" at its base. The more closely a quasi need or the actual product is linked with the "real need(s)" hidden in the background, the more intense will be the resulting behavior. The task therefore lies in emphasizing through the marketing mix as close a relationship as possible to real needs. We can list the following motives, relevant to purchase behavior (Based on Schiffman and Kanuk, 1994, p. 107), which in the terminology of Lewin would be the "real needs" out of which quasi needs may be derived:

Activity	Amusement
Esteem	Comfort
Possession	Thirst

Ambition	Influence over others
Refreshment	Hospitality
Security	Enjoyment
Taste	Health
Domestic Comfort	Authority
Devotedness	Courtesy
Humor	Hunger
Children's Love	Zest for life
Performance	Power
Emulation	Naturalness
Curiosity	Prestige
Religion	Cleanliness
Protection	Protection from fear/danger
Sexuality	Certainty
Sportiveness	Good will towards others
Pleasure	Trust
Warmth	Competition
Well Being	Collaboration

We need to keep in mind that these "real needs" can be quasi needs in the case of individual people.

WORK BEHAVIOR

In general it is very easy to relate the whole text regarding performance motivation to professional life or work behavior. The motivational consequences within employee behavior also depend on the whole psychological context, which can be influenced by repressive or employee oriented management styles, by trust or control, by open communication, or by very selective and one-sided communication.

Consequences in the S-O-R schema

The motivational effect of personnel strategy measures depends on how the given measures are perceived by the personnel in question. If the staff has had negative experiences in the past regarding changes, then there will (justifiably) be mistrust at first in the face of new changes, which can only gradually be assuaged.

It is very difficult within a negative environment to effect rapid improvements via incentives.

Thus, an employee oriented management style, with a lot of freedom for employees to make decisions, may be met with considerable of suspicion if personnel have experienced managers who have gladly cited employee error when poor decisions were made. The attainment of freedom from work regulations can be understood as an attempt to diminish the personnel's justifiable interest in self protection. Fixed work regulations may be extremely inflexible, but they protect the personnel from managers having expectations that are too high.

Here the influence of S and O variables on R is being addressed. Apart from that, the anticipated consequences affect R, with regard to behavior. The consequences of work behavior are directly resultant outcomes, for example, profit in sales. Moreover there are the consequences in a second stage, that being the reactions of the environment to the consequences of the first stage, for example, incentive bonuses, respect or disrespect in the social context (managers, colleagues, people in private life).

The need for performance and the homeostasis principle

McGregor (1960) asserts that managers can be divided according to what basic attitudes with which they approach their personnel. A negative basic attitude on behalf of a manager with regard to employees is indicated by McGregor as theory X, whereas a more positive basic attitude is designated as theory Y. Theory X and theory Y are layman's theories on behalf of the managers with regard to their employees' attitudes toward work.

Theory X is characterized by the following assumptions on the behalf of managers:

a) The average person has an inborn aversion to work and seeks to avoid it.
b) Since people are characterized by aversion to work, they have to be made to display the necessary performance behavior via controls, directions, and threat of sanctions.
c) People want to be led, they avoid responsibility and having to make decisions, they do not have any ambition, and they prefer security.

Theory Y is characterized by the following assumptions on the behalf of managers:

a) Mental and physical work stems from a natural need and is just as self-evident as playing and resting. Therefore one cannot proceed from the assumption of a natural aversion to work. Work can be viewed as being a means toward self-actualization and by no means has to be experienced as a punishment.
b) Management, direction, and threat of punishment—in other words heteronomy—are not the only ways of motivating people to achieve the objectives of an organization.

If people feel committed to certain goals, those goals can be achieved via independent behavior.

c) Whether or not and how strongly a person feels committed to certain objectives, depends on the value these goals hold for the person.

d) People can learn to take on responsibility and to make their own decisions.

e) It is possible for most people to learn organizational abilities, discrimination, and responsibility.

f) The abilities of the average person are only being partially utilized under the conditions of modern industrial society.

The assertions regarding the connections between motives and needs, and to a particularly pronounced extent the construct of quasi needs, strongly indicate that the idea of people which corresponds with theory Y is closer to the reality. Hence there arises the possibility, via the appropriate management style, of realizing a work environment that leads to a situation wherein personnel fulfill their own needs at the same time as exerting themselves for the goals of the organization. McGregor related to this in 1960 as the industrial society (theory Y). There is certainly no reasonable doubt regarding relating this thesis to the postindustrial service or information society.

If people display a relatively low level of standard regarding the achieving of goals this does not mean that they are not motivated toward performance. They are simply simultaneously oriented toward the avoidance of failure, and less toward the realization of success. This avoidance of failure orientation can also result in learning taking place in an organization.

Motive and motivation

From out of the interplay of motive and motivation there results a situation whereby as a rule real behavior can be influenced by the simultaneous addressing of several individual motives that exist in interdependent relationship to each other. These aspects can therefore be taken account of within personnel management's system of incentives via the simultaneous presence of many reward possibilities. A field service incentive system can address basic performance by way of "bonuses for fulfilling the plan", additional performance by "activity bonuses", and extraordinary performance can be addressed by way of special contests. Social needs or motives can be accounted for via group trips and shared events. Prestige needs or motives can be addressed by non-material incentives. Opportunities to advance and consideration of life partners, by way of incentives and work atmosphere, can offer further possibilities for motivation.

From Herzberg, Mausner and Snydermann's (1967) two-factor theory we have learned that motivations will only be effective if the hygiene factors have been satisfied. In the case of dissatisfaction (whereby hygiene factors are relevant) it does not make any sense to introduce more motivations. First consideration has to be given toward sufficient hygiene factors. In practice, it is certainly often unclear what a hygiene factor is and what is a motivation. According to Herzberg, Mausner and Snydermann's (1967) theory, in the service sector, fixed salaries are hygiene factors, and bonuses are motivations. Studies by Unger (1987) have shown that regularly awarded bonuses of a high percentage commission come to be viewed as a kind of additional fixed income. These bonuses clearly count as hygiene factors. The bonuses for special performances, group events, and performance competitions (of a partly game-like character) would be motivations.

QUESTIONS FOR DISCUSSION

1. Discuss the difference between being motivated by a hope of success versus a fear of failure. Provide examples from your working experience to clarify the differences.
2. Discuss Maslow's hierarchy of needs and its relevance for marketers.
3. Describe the relationship between performance and satisfaction.
4. Discuss the difference between Theory X and Theory Y managers. Provide some examples of how these management styles influence employee motivation.

Bibliography

Alderfer, C.P.: An empirical test of a new theory of human needs, *Organizational Behavior and Human Performance*, 1969,vol. 4, pp. 142–175.

Atkinson, J.W.: Motivational determinants of risk taking behavior. *Psychological Review*, 1957, 64, 359–372.

—— Erwartungstheorie und utilitaritätstheorie. In: Thomae, H. (ed.): *Die Motivation menschlichen Verhaltens* (9th edn), Köln: 1976, pp. 462–473. (Expectation theory and utilitarian theory. In *The Motivations of Human Behavior*).

Atkinson, R.L., Atkinson, R.C., Smith, E.E., Bem, D.J. and Nolen-Hoeksema, S.: *Hilgard's Introduction to Psychology* (11th edn). Fort Worth, Philadelphia, San Diego: 1996.

Bandura, A.: *Lernen am Modell*. Stuttgart: 1976. (*Learning the Model*).

Becker-Carus, C.: Motivationale grundlagen der nahrungs- und flüssigkeitsaufnahme. In: Thomae, H. (ed.): *Psychologie der Motive (Enzyklopädie der Psychologie)*. Göttingen, Toronto, Zürich: 1983, 12–69. (Motivational foundations of food and liquid reception. In *Psychology of Motivation (Encyclopedia of Psychology)*).

Bröckermann, R.: Personalwirtschaft—Arbeitsbuch für das praxisorientierte studium. Köln: 1997. (Human resources—Work book for study and practice).

Friedel-Howe, H.: Neue Organisationskonzepte. In: von Rosenstiel, L.; Hockel, M. and Molt, W. eds): *Handbuch der Angewandten Psychologie. Grundlagen—Methoden—Praxis*. Landsberg: 1994, VI 4.1; pp. 1–20). (New organization concepts. In *Handbook of Applied Psychology. Foundations—Methods—Practice*).

Galbraith, J.K.: *The New Industrial State*, Boston, Houghton Mifflin, 1967, sentry edition, p. 138.

Gebert, D. and von Rosenstiel, L.: *Organisationspsychologie* (4th edn). Stuttgart, Berlin, Köln: 1996. (*Organizational Psychology*).

Heckhausen, H.: *Hoffnung und Furcht in der Leistungsmotivation*. Meisenheim:1963. (*Hope and Fear in Achievement Motivation*).

—— *Motivation und Handeln* (2nd edn). Berlin, Heidelberg, New York: 1989. (*Motivation and Action*).

Herzberg, F.H., Mausner, B. and Snyderman, B.: *The Motivation to Work* (2nd edn). New York, London, Sydney: 1967.

Hull, C.L.: *A Behavior System*. New Haven: 1952.

Hunt, V.McV. (ed.): *Personality and the Behavior of Disorders*. New York: 1944.

Irle, M.: *Lehrbuch der Sozialpsychologie*. Göttingen, Toronto, Zürich: 1975.

Kelley, H.H.: The process of causal attribution. *American Psychologist*, 1973, 28, 107–128.

Kroeber-Riel, W. and Weinberg, P.: *Konsumentenverhalten* (7th edn). München: 1999. (*Consumer Behavior*).

Kuhl, J.: Leistungsmotivation: Neue entwicklungen aus modelltheoretischer Sicht. In: Thomae, H. (ed.): *Psychologie der Motive (Enzyklopädie der Psychologie)*, Göttingen, Toronto, Zürich, 1983, 505–625. (Achievement motivation: New developments out of model theoretical view. In *Psychology of Motivation (Encyclopedia of Psychology)*).

Lewin, K.: Untersuchungen zur handlungs- und affektpsychologie I.: Vorbemerkungen über die psychischen kräfte und energien und über die Struktur der Seele. *Psychologische Forschung*, 1926a, 7, 294–329. (Studies on the psychology of action and emotion I: Preliminary remarks on psychic powers and energies and on the structure of the soul.).

Lewin, K.: Untersuchungen zur handlungs- und affekt-psychologie II.: Vorsatz, wille und bedürfnis. *Psychologische Forschung*, 1926b, 7, 330–385. (Studies on the psychology of action and emotion II: Design, Will and Need).

Lewin, K.: *Principles of Topological Psychology*. New York: 1936.

Lewin, K.: Feldtheorie (Kurt-Lewin-Werkausgabe), vol. 4, von Graumann, C.-F.). Bern, Stuttgart: 1982, 41–365. (*Field Theory* (Kurt-Lewin Work edition)).

Lewin, K., Dembo, R., Festinger, L. and Sears, P.S.: Level of aspiration. In: Hunt, J.McV. (ed.): *Personality and the Behavior of Disorders*, vol. 1, New York: 1944, 333–378.

Maslow, A.: *Motivation und Persönlichkeit*. Reinbek bei Hamburg: 1989 (*Motivation and Personality*).

McClelland, D.: *Die Leistungsgesellschaft*. Stuttgart, Berlin, Köln, Mainz: 1966. (*The Achieving Society*).

McGregor, D.: *The Human Side of Enterprise*. New York: 1960.

Rüttinger, B., von Rosenstiel, L. and Molt, W.: *Motivation des Wirtschaftlichen Verhaltens*. Stuttgart, Berlin, Köln, Mainz: 1974. (*Motivation of Economic Behavior*).

Scherhorn, G.: Kritik des zusatznutzens. *Thexis*, 1992, 9. Jg., Nr. 2, pp. 24–28. (Critique of added value).

Schiffman, L.G. and Kanuk, L.L.: *Consumer Behavior* (5th edn). Englewood Cliffs: 1994.

Thomae, H.: Motivationsbegriffe und motivationstheorien. In: Thomae, H. (ed.): *Theorien und Formen der Motivation (Enzyklopädie der Psychologie)*. Göttingen, Toronto, Zürich: 1983, 1–61. (Motivation concepts and motivation theories. In *Theories and Forms of Motivation (Encyclopedia of Psychology)*).

Thomae, H. (ed.): *Theorien und Formen der Motivation (Enzyklopädie der Psychologie)*. Göttingen, Toronto, Zürich: 1983. (*Theories and Forms of Motivation (Encyclopedia of Psychology)*).

—— *Psychologie der Motive (Enzyklopädie der Psychologie)*. Göttingen, Toronto, Zürich: 1983. (*Psychology of Motivation (Encyclopedia of Psychology)*).

Unger, F.: *Marktgerechte Außendienststeuerung*. Heidelberg: 1987. (*Market-driven Steering of the Field Sales Force*).

von Eckardstein, D. and Schnellinger, F.: *Betriebliche Personalpolitik* (2nd edn). München: 1975. (*Operational Personnel Politics*).

von Rosenstiel, L.: *Motivation im Betrieb* (9th edn). Leonberg: 1996. (*Motivation in Business*).

Vroom, V.H.: *Work and Motivation*. New York: 1964.

Weiner, B.: *Human Motivation—Metaphors, Theories, and Research*, Newbury Park, London, New Delhi: 1992.

Weinert, A.B.: *Lehrbuch der Organisationspsychologie*. München, Wien, Baltimore: 1981. (*Textbook of Organization Psychology*).

15 *Emotions*

Theory

Hardly any other psychological concept is approached in as many different ways as emotion. The following approaches do have in common the assumption of an inner arousal, or a so-called affective reaction and subjective sensations. We would like to present four selected conceptions: Duffy (1934, 1962), Izard (1994), Scherer (1990), and Schachter and Singer (1962).

Emotions are often understood as complementary to cognitions. Piaget (1981) has shown that emotion and cognition are two aspects that are indivisible from all human actions. "There are neither affective states without cognitive aspects, nor are there exclusively cognitively controlled patterns of behavior" (Mandl and Huber, 1983, p. 3). The occurrence of emotion is linked to the assumption that a person has cognitive connections with the environment. "As a rule emotions are object oriented" (Meyer, Schütz-Wohl and Reisenzein, 1993, p. 26). Romantic love presumes that there already is a relationship based on good will and attraction toward another person.

According to Lazarus, Kanner and Folkmann (1980) emotions are the result of cognitively influenced transactions with the real, assumed or expected, natural or social environment; they arise out of cognitive assessments, impulses to act, and bodily reactions (Mandl and Huber, 1983, p. 25).

Other approaches categorize emotions into the three areas of experience, physiological aspects, and behavioral aspects (Meyer, Schützwohl and Reisenzein, 1993, pp. 29 and 30). Experience pertains to the subjective perception component; the physiological aspects denote bodily reactions like heartbeat, blood pressure, breathing, vertigo, changes in the visceral area, etc.; the behavior aspect pertains to mimicry, gesture, and bodily posture.

In taking a good look at emotions, it has to be taken into consideration that there are very many differing, to some extent conflicting approaches to the content of emotions. Euler and Mandel (1983, p. 7) have presented (based on Kleinginna and Kleinginna, 1981) 11 different conceptions: affective, cognitive, situational, psychoanalytical, expressive (expression oriented), disruptive (disorganizing), adaptive (need related), syndrome-like (containing several interconnected components), restrictive (which limit emotions via other conceptions), motivational, and approaches that are a consequence of diversity/dissimilarity (which fundamentally questions the value of the emotion concept).

Kleinginna and Kleinginna (1981, p. 355) have arrived at the following definition of emotion based on the approaches that have been presented:

Emotion is a complex interactive structure of subjective and objective factors facilitated by the neuronal/hormonal system, which can produce (a) affective experiences like feelings of arousal or desire/aversion; (b) which can evoke cognitive processes like emotionally relevant perceptual effects, assessments, classification processes; (c) can set in motion extensive physiological adjustments to arousal triggering conditions; can lead to behavior that is often expressive, goal oriented, and adaptive (Euler and Mandl, 1983, pp. 7 and 8).

It should be mentioned that emotion psychology is perhaps the one branch of psychology in which there is the least agreement regarding what its subject matter actually is (see Meyer, Schützwohl and Reisenzein, 1993, p. 17 et seq.). For application oriented purposes this is a problem. On the other hand it should not go unnoticed that Irle (1975, pp. 13–16) refused, in his at that time groundbreaking textbook of social psychology, to provide a conceptual description of social psychology's subject matter. These kinds of conceptual descriptions only serve to delimit the matter and have absolutely no insight value. This approach seems to be scientifically appropriate and has obviously not deterred the progress of knowledge.

We will begin our presentations with the oldest of the emotion theories here selected.

DUFFY (1934, 1962)

Duffy (1962) starts with the assumption that human behavior can be described according to two dimensions: direction and intensity. The question of which behavior pattern we are going to choose, determines the direction of our behavior. The intensity is derived from the arousal of the given person. Duffy (1962, p. 17) defines this as the "degree to which potential energy stored within the organism's tissue is released, and how it becomes expressed in activity or reaction". All of them, even the simplest cognitive processes, are accompanied by instances of arousal in the nervous system. Here emotion is simply a special case of cognitive activity: emotions can be identified as those states that happen to be in the upper range of a developing scale of arousal. It became clear later that this arousal could be determined though the measurement of electrical brain activity with the help of the electroencephalogram (EEG). From this there developed the activation theory of marketing, which is used especially by Kroeber-Riel (1975, today Kroeber-Riel and Weinberg, 1999) to explain consumer reactions to marketing communication. This approach is significant for understanding the current state of marketing studies.

The extreme one-sidedness of this approach has to be seen as problematic. After all, Duffy's approach leads to every cognitive effort that reaches a certain extent being identified as an emotion. According to this the intense attempt to remember the "train schedule information telephone number" is an emotion. Activation is a more encompassing concept than emotion: It is compatible with emotion, but there are more possibilities of activation than those that have a relationship to emotions. Emotions therefore are not always the result of activation. Activation also does not guide behavior; it can be triggered by behavior. Physiological arousal and emotion often occur at the same time. From all of these statements it can be inferred that emotional arousal and physiological activation mutually qualify each other.

IZARD (1994)

Emotions consist of three components (Izard, 1994, p. 20): a) Experience of feelings, b) Processes in the nervous system; and c) Observable expressions, especially in the face. These certainly apply to a great many human manifestations, for example to very simply manifestations, like using an electric appliance. We feel the switch, and via processes directed by the nervous system we manage to trigger the switch with a hand motion, and during this not so exciting operation we fix our gaze (facial expression) on the switch and on our hand. We hardly arrive at any thoughts here that recognize the presence of any emotional impulses. So when should we identify certain manifestations as emotional or as an emotion? It is conceivable for us to define certain states as "emotional".

Izard (1994, p. 24 et seq.) differentiates between the following emotional contents:

- interest,
- enjoyment,
- surprise and alarm,
- sorrow, pain, grief, depression,
- anger, disgust and contempt,
- fear and forms of anxiety,
- shame and shyness,
- guilt, conscience and morality.

There are subjective variations as to how these possible emotional contents are experienced. Positive emotions should be of primary relevance for marketing: Interest, enjoyment, surprise. Izard (1994, p. 244) considers interest to be the most common emotion. Interest is closely connected to visual perception. An interesting subject matter is fixed with the gaze: "As long as the gazed is fixated, the interested person is captivated and fascinated" (ibid., p. 245). This fixation triggers neurological activation. As a consequence of the directed activity of perceptual organs, activation of the nervous system comes about. Due to the stimulation of neurons impulses are "transported" to the brain and processed. Interest can be physiologically described by way of the increase in impulse frequency per time unit, that is, in that neurons more frequently stimulate the given succeeding neuron in a chain of neurons within a period of time (see Unger and Fuchs, 1999, p. 476). "The triggering of interest (on the physiological level), brings with it a slight increase in the density of neural impulses" (Izard, 1994, p. 246). An instance of information processing is then all the more "deep", the more intense was the processing. "The quality of information storage, in other words of memory, depends on the depth of information processing" (Irle, 1986, p. 122).

Interest can also be aroused via affectively operative stimuli, like through important factual information. The question is simply which component has more significance, the stronger emotional, or the stronger cognitive component. The answer to that is not at all decisive; what is essential is the insight that people can be addressed in a way such that there is emphasis both on an emotional and on a cognitive level. From this we can derive the theory that successful market communication as much as possible always tries to address both of these levels at the same time.

Emotions influence the behavior of people in many ways: Izard (1994, p. 26 et seq.) lists consciousness, marriage and partnership, parenthood, sexuality, social development, personality, bodily reaction (changes in electrical brain activity—see Duffy, 1962—heartbeat, circulation, breath), perception and cognitive processes.

SCHERER (1990)

According to Scherer (1990) emotions consist of five components that each incorporate independent functions:

- The cognitive component (this has the function of assessing impulses).
- The neurophysiological component (this has the function of "system regulation", that is, the regulation of the biological organism).
- The motivational component (this has the function of triggering actions).
- The expression component (this concerns the function of communication).
- The feeling component (this has the function of reacting to and influencing external impulses, which Scherer has called "reflection and control").

The cognitive component has to do with the positive or negative assessment of external impulses. Information processing and association play a significant roll in this. The neurophysiological component has to do with the arousal that occurs due to external impulses, which in turn determine states of feeling. Emotional states invoke a multitude of behavioral tendencies. This explains the close relationship between motivation theory and emotion theory. The expression component also plays a big role, whereby in particular the externally observable reactions of other people are attended to. Many emotional reactions can be seen to derive from mimicking other people.

SCHACHTER AND SINGER (1962)

The emotional theory of Schachter and Singer (1962), and Schachter (1978), focuses on cognitive processes (see Atkinson, Atkinson, Smith, et al. 1996, pp. 383–387). According to this theory people are physiologically aroused by external stimuli. This shows itself in increased pulse frequency, heartbeat, blood pressure, or simply in a greater activation of the nervous system. According to Schachter and Singer (1962) identical bodily reaction can be differently experienced depending on each varying situation. This cognitive explanation of bodily reactions is the emotion. We certainly experience the same sensations with regard to hunger, love, and anxiety (butterflies in our stomachs). Whether or not we experience—based on those sensations—the emotion of hunger, love or anxiety, depends on the external situation. From this can be inferred that the challenge for marketing is to trigger positive sensations, to create situations that deliver emotionally positive experiential values.

How difficult it is for people to achieve clarity with regard to their own emotions was also demonstrated in studies conducted by Valins (1966). It was shown here that the actual arousal is not a prerequisite for the occurrence of an emotion. A pseudo incitement is already enough to achieve it, for example, transmitted via false information. In experiments based on this assertion male test subjects were shown slides of scantily clad young women. At the same time they seemingly heard their own heartbeats over the loudspeaker. This information was false. The heartbeats heard over the loud speaker did not have anything to do with the test subjects. When some of the slides were shown, the perceived (false) heartbeat was increased. In conclusion, the assessment of the attractiveness of the perceived females correlated with what they perceived as the frequency of their own heartbeats. People are obviously far removed from being able to adequately perceive and assess their own bodily reactions.

In more recent emotional psychology Schachter and Singer's (1962) theory has been combined with Bem's (1972) theory of self-perception (Laird and Apostoleris, 1996; Laird and Bresler, 1992). In accordance with this, people observe their own behavior in the same way that they observe the behavior of other people. Accordingly feelings are the consequence of behavior, not the causes. Bodily reactions are not the consequences of emotions; they are much more their cause. Both the Schachter-Singer and the self-perception approaches explicitly relate back to the approach of James (1884) and Lange (1885), which later came to be known as the "James-Lange theory" (Lange and James, 1922).

"Common sense says, we lose our fortune, are sorry and weep; we meet a bear, are frightened and run; we are insulted by a rival, are angry and strike. The hypothesis here to be denied says that this order of sequence is incorrect ... and the more rational statement is that we feel sorry, *because* we cry, angry *because* we strike, afraid *because* we tremble" (James, 1884, p. 449).

There is a great deal of experimental support for this (see Laird and Apostoleris, 1996 and Laird and Bresler, 1992). If test subjects were experimentally induced to display a happy facial expression, they subsequently revealed that they felt happy; if they were caused to produce a sad expression, they subsequently revealed that they felt sad (Duclos, Laird, Schneider et al., 1989). Kellermann, Lewis and Laird (1989) found that test subjects who were induced to gaze intensely into each other's eyes for a very long time, developed signs of love. Normally, people in love gaze into each other's eyes intensely and for very long periods. Obviously a reversed sequence would seem to be realistic: intense eye contact can lead to love.

In the referenced original experiments conducted by Schachter and Singer (1962), as well those of Schachter (1964), patients were administered medication on a pretence. The test subjects received information that they were receiving a medication that a) was excitement inducing, which had the effects of increasing heartbeat, making the face warm and red (which are the correct physiological effects of adrenaline), or b) that as a consequence of this medication being administered, temporary itchiness or numbness, and perhaps a slight headache, could take place. A number of the test subjects were in reality just injected with a salt solution, and those remaining were injected with an excitement inducing medication, namely adrenaline. Afterwards all test subjects were aroused by real external manifestations, whereby another person displayed aggression triggering behavior. There were four test conditions:

1. Placebo information → A placebo was administered.
2. Medication information → A placebo was administered.
3. Placebo information → A medication was administered.
4. Medication information → A medication was administered.

The study structure can be seen in Figure 15.1.

Information		Correct information regarding the physiological effects of adrenalin	False information concerning expected, but in reality impossible, effects
Injection	Adrenalin		
	Salt solution		

Figure 15.1 The experimental setup in accordance with Schachter and Singer (1962)

In the cases where the test subjects were acting according to the information that they had received a stimulant, they did not display any aggressive behavior toward the other person; they assumed that the sensed stimulation had been caused by the medication. In the cases where the test subjects assumed that they had been administered salt they openly blamed the other person for the experienced agitation, and displayed aggressive behavior toward the person. What was decisive for the reaction was the *information* that a medication or salt had been administered, not the *fact* of having been administered a medication or salt. So what is at hand here is: a) The information that a medication has been administered or b) the behavior of the other person.

These experiments resulted in a further insight. If the physical manifestations are clear and explainable, the test subjects will hardly allow the other person (helper) to influence them, "but if they experience a strong physiological reaction whose cause is not clear, they interpret their own feelings as anger or euphoria, depending on how other people are behaving whom they assume are in the same pharmacological boat" (Aronson, 1994, p. 52). Particularly in situations they experience as unclear, people seek external explanations for experienced stimulation.

Emotive experiential values are subjectively perceived, emotive product assessments (Konert, 1986, p. 36). This experiential value can be applied to the assessment of products or shopping sites, as well as to sales talks. In markets with technically interchangeable products emotive experiential values have come to have a considerable and increasing significance. Emotionally oriented communications measures have the advantage that techniques of influence are more difficult to see through than is the case in a purely factual presentation. All emotional conceptions are in agreement that an inner stimulation is present.

Cohen and Areni (1991) set motivational reactions against affective reactions. Affective reactions are understood to be those behavioral patterns, triggered by stimuli, which trigger a mood (pleasant or unpleasant) that is experienced in a generalized way. These kinds of stimuli include music, light, and environment dominating colors, and people in the social surroundings who are friendly (or unfriendly) in general. People are often unaware of the causes of their moods.

Understanding emotional psychology is made more difficult due to the—to some extent contradictory—use of the terms "feeling", "emotion", and "affect". Mandl and

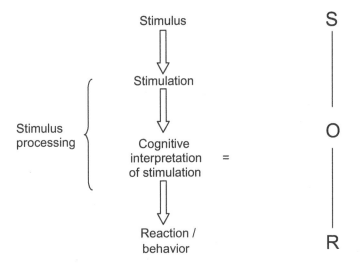

Figure 15.2 Emotion in the "S-O-R" scheme

Huber (1983, p. 5) have differentiated important concepts from each other in the following way:

Emotions are understood as a process:

They are initiated, they unfold, and they fade away.

Experiential qualifiers however are emotional reactions to cognitions, which last as long as the specific content of consciousness is present.

We experience warmth as long as we remain sitting under the heat lamp; we experience being cramped, as long as we remain in the crowded elevator. We are wont to equate experiential qualifiers of this kind with "feelings".

Moods ... yield an enduring system of relations for all information processing activities, that remain relatively unchanged over long periods of time—for example an elevated or depressed mood.

This may be relevant for shopping malls, wherein we are surrounded by pleasant light and pleasant music.

Applications

SALES MARKETING

Consumer goods marketing

As has already been mentioned, emotional approaches are of great significance in consumer goods marketing. At the fundamental level of psychological research the most varied of emotional conceptions are discussed. There is overall agreement with regard to inner (neurophysiological) stimulations playing a big role in emotional experience. In addition however there is a cognitive interpretation of this experienced arousal. We identify one and the same "feeling" as love, hunger or anxiety, depending on the context. Interest, enjoyment, surprise, fear, anxiety, shame, and shyness are, among others, all identified as emotions (Izard, 1994). In consumer goods markets, marketing should produce so-called "emotional experiential values" in particular (Konert, 1986). Weinberg and Konert (1984, p. 313) understand experiential values as "the product's contribution to quality of life as subjectively experienced by consumers. It has to do with meaningful product experiences or emotional consumer experiences, that are anchored in the consumer's real feeling and experiential world, and which make a real contribution to quality of life." What is meant by quality of life is a certain level of subjectively experienced satisfaction with life. Humor, eroticism, emphasis on images, and music, all communicate these kinds of experiential values.

Adventure	Variety	Being active
Stability	Attractiveness	Balance
Enthusiasm	Comfort	Thankfulness
Dynamism	Jealousy	Opinionatedness
Haughtiness	Relaxation	Recovery
Relief	Eroticism	Exhaustion
Exclusiveness	The exotic	Extravagance
Family happiness	Progress	Freedom
Freshness	Aid	Security
Coziness	Pleasure	Sociability
Health	Homesickness	Humor
Concern	Joy of life	Vitality
Passion	Compassion	Courage
Naturalness	Despondency	Nostalgia
Fantasy	Prestige	Trust
Romance	Calm	Malicious joy
Sensation	Self actualization	Certainty
Excitement	Fun	Intensity
Tradition	Dream world	Sadness
Trusted home	The tropics	Superiority
High spirits	Independence	Holiday
Originality	Scorn	Adoration
Appetite	Familiarity	Doubt
Warmth	Satisfaction	

Figure 15.3 Emotional experiential values (Neibecker, 1990, pp. 165 and 166)

Positively assessed experiential values are mainly what is relevant in marketing, because overall research in marketing communication has shown that negatively assessed emotions (anxiety, fear, hesitation) are detrimental to product acceptance.

Affective reactions as a result of moods can be taken into consideration as far as shopping and office spaces are concerned. If we keep in mind that according to Schachter and Singer's (1962) theory of emotions, when considered together with Bem's (1972) theory of self perception, outer circumstances can lead to bodily experiences, which are cognitively perceived as emotions, then it becomes evident that moods triggered in people by the way the shopping space has been organized, will be experienced as independent emotions. This could explain why people experience these situations as more enjoyable to shop in. Shopping behavior can be positively influenced by the surroundings within businesses, the emotional state of the consumers, and the friendliness of personnel. This is assumed to be true in general, and has been substantiated in many empirical studies (Sherman, Mathur and Smith, 1997).

Batra and Stephans (1994) were able to show that moods and emotions that have been triggered by advertising more strongly influence attitudes toward brands that fall under the category of "low personal significance" than those that fall under the category of "high personal significance". This effect comes about due to the fact that in the category of "low personal significance" critical engagement with the communication due to moods and emotions and emotions triggered by the advertising is suppressed.

In general it is assumed in practice that positive moods facilitate success in influencing. Moods influence the associations that occur during the presentation of a communication.

According to a congruence hypothesis regarding the influence of moods it is thought that the occurrence of associations proceeds in the same direction as the current mood. According to the cognitive response theory if positively assessed associations overwhelmingly occur in the person to be influenced, then the advertising has had a positive influence.

According to a motivation hypothesis, people in a positive mood due to what is for them seemingly an overall positive situation, tend to be motivated toward a simplified, universal, and less critical engagement with communications, whereas in negative moods they tend toward a more critical engagement with communications. Put another way, when you are in a bad mood, things that typically do not bother you seem to get on your nerves!

These and similar hypotheses seem to fortify the assumptions of marketing practice. Empirical studies have shown however that a more differentiated consideration and influence of moods in marketing would be advantageous. On the basis of some empirical studies Schwarz, Bless and Bohner (1991) demonstrate that positive moods reduce the amount of influence in the case of strong arguments. If we want to persuade using strong arguments, then those on the receiving end should be in a neutral mood, and certainly not in too much of a positive mood. If the basis of argument is weak, the influence success will benefit from a positive mood. Schwarz, Bless and Bohner (1991, p. 191) have traced this back to the fact that the positive mood leads to an overall more superficial level of information processing, whereas strong argumentation within the central approach to influencing, should lead to a long-term and stable influence, according to the theory of cognitive response.

Since consumer goods advertising is rarely about communicating strong arguments, but is rather oriented more toward communication that is more image saturated and emotional, the attention should generally be on positive moods, for example with regard to the content of TV advertising or within the editorial context. In other communication situations, the influence of moods may be assessed differently.

With regard to the formation of marketing communication the disinterest of the target group cannot be overestimated. Image oriented, emotional design is of great significance for this reason. Activating components are an absolute prerequisite for every attempt at influence (see the above presentations regarding emotional experiential values). Music, humor, vivid arrangement of images, unusual presentation, and eroticism are frequent design elements. Advertising has become a "world of beautiful images". On top of this there is the attempt to increase persuasiveness by way of word play. Many advertising slogans acquire a cult character. At the same time, since there is a considerable over-saturation of advertising, additional communication instruments have gained in significance. However, this has often led to a substantial lack of clarity regarding individual marketing concepts. The multitude of different media and communication instruments has led to the consequence that communication strategies having long-term validity and connection to all the different measures, have gained in significance. We are here speaking of an "integrated communication". This means a creative and substantive coordination of all of the different individual measures (Bruhn, 1995 and 1997).

According to Izard (1994, p. 26 et seq.) emotions influence human behavior in many different ways; all of these behavioral dimensions have considerable relevance for consumer behavior. Consumer decisions are influenced by behavior involving the roles taken within partnerships, behavior which is partially shaped by emotions. This means that pairs can often be more relevant target groups than those who can be described sociodemographically and psychologically as individual people. The attitude to sexuality has a very big influence on the acceptance of sexually toned marketing communication. We have already dealt with questions of personality in Chapter 11. The significance of bodily reactions is derived from Duffy's (1934, 1962) emotion theory. Bodily reactions, especially those within the nervous system, play a central role in the context of communicative influence (Kroeber-Riel and Weinberg, 1999, p. 52 et seq.; this is dealt with in detail in Chapter 12, "The Psychology of Perception").

Not only the intensity of perception, but also the quality or the content of perception is influenced by emotions. In positively charged moods information may perhaps be more positively taken in than in the case of negatively charged moods. Thus an advertising influence will take place more easily in the context of an entertaining TV program than in the context of unpleasant news. Goldberg and Gorn (1987) were able to show that enjoyable program content helped the advertising influence, and that unpleasant contents limited the influence. There are certainly many other interactive effects. Gleich (1996) has found evidence suggesting that advertising content that diverges from the program content is more effective than advertising that is adaptive to that content. In keeping with this, advertising with an emphasis on humor will have greater effect in the context of factual program content, than the same advertising would have in a context of a similarly humorous program. It should be pointed out here however, that this approach is contradicted by Piaget's (1981) above-mentioned approach; it states that emotions are responsible for the "functioning", but not for the "structuring of cognitive processes". Accordingly emotion alone does not affect cognitive structures. Piaget (1981, p. 5) compares this with the interplay of fuel and motor. Fuel activates the motor without structurally altering it; however it is necessary that it be there in order to activate the motor. Mackie, Asuncion and Rosselli (1992) have researched the various effects of weaker or stronger forms of argumentation in elevated or neutral moods.

In general, affectively loaded communications arouse attentiveness to a greater extent; affectively positive contents additionally encourage preferential perception (Isen, 1987). There is also variation in influence success, dependent upon the strength of argumentation. In neutral moods a greater degree of influence resulted in the case of stronger argumentation. People in a positive mood showed no variation in the level of influence with regard to the strength of argumentation (Isen, 1987, p. 253). In several experiments there was an increase in the amount of positive thoughts during the course of the influence, for test subjects in a positive mood. A further study showed that the relative quantity of counter arguments asserted by test subjects in a positive mood was less than in the case of those in a neutral mood.

In the end, Mackie, Asuncion and Rosselli (1992, p. 257) come to the conclusion that positive moods decrease the differentiated processing of influencing communications. At the same time, the positive processing of stimuli increases, and in turn negative stimuli processing decreases. Moods thus influence both the extent (less differentiated processing) and the content (more positive, in a more positive basic mood) of stimuli processing.

And finally, emotions are also relevant with regard to cognitive processes: Human memory, thinking, and imagining are all influenced by emotions (Izard, 1994, p. 26). In Chapter 2 ("Theories of Perception and Social Judgment Formation as Starting Points") and Chapter 4 ("The Theory of Cognitive Dissonance") it has already been made clear that there is no such thing as unbiased perception. Existent cognitive structures influence perception. Now we see that emotions also influence both perception and memory. It is becoming clearer and clearer how little we can trust our own perception, and to what a pronounced extent communicative influence is not just dependent on one's own arguments, but is additionally dependent on other factors: existent cognitive structures and the emotional tone. The latter can also be influenced by marketing, via the composition and choice of medias. Eagle (1983) has provided a selected number of relevant empirical studies. The results are partially contradictory; generally speaking, "in most cases one comes to the conclusion that affective material is better retained than neutral material, and that pleasant stimuli are better retained than unpleasant ..." (Eagle, 1983, p. 85). Marketing can stay on top of things by intense emotional content design on the one hand and via preference for content that is experienced as pleasant. In any case negative advertising content is problematic. Selective memory (preference for pleasant contents) is set against selective forgetting. There are various approaches regarding the cause of the preferential forgetting of unpleasant stimuli. A concept that is common knowledge is that of suppression, or "motivated forgetting" Freud (1901). It should be pointed out at this juncture that biologically there is no forgetting; what has been stored in our cells does not disappear. When we have "forgotten" something then the cognitive access to it has been lost. The memory contents are still there from a biological point of view, and they can be reawakened via the appropriate associations. They have merely been overrun by other memory contents.

The role of image-rich advertising also has its basis in the psychology of emotions. Brosius and Kayser (1991) have conducted research regarding the influence of emotional presentations (image-rich items of film) on information reception and on judgment formation, in the context of television—actually with regard to the news and factual programs. The initial hypothesis was that images have an especially positive influence on information reception and on understanding; if those images are designed to fit the text. Occasionally "the creative" in advertising attempt to awaken attentiveness via contradictory text-image combinations. From the point of view of communications research this appears to be a questionable undertaking. What has been substantiated is the hypothesis that "with increasing image orientation the information reception of the textually communicated news content also increases" (ibid., p. 239). Image oriented news broadcasts lead to better memory performance, whereby memory performance is equally improved in both emotional and neutral items of film.

It could not be substantiated that this effect also confirmed the hypothesis that "an increase in both the amount of film images and the amount of emotional images more strongly focused the assessment of factual content in the direction suggested by the given film" (ibid., p. 240). Therefore it is not a matter of the quantity of images!

That TV triggers emotions via its pronounced image orientation will be viewed as a given. The quality of emotions is however highly varied, and this fact is still too superficially assessed within advertising effect research. In any case, within media effect research (not advertising effect research), much more complex processes are discussed and applied than those which are to date being implemented within market research (see Mangold's 1999 overview). Bente, Stephan, Jain et al. refer to the results of media effect research, presenting the impressive finding "that even the most subtle variation of gesture and mimicry on the part of actors can noticeably influence the emotional situation of the viewer ..." (Bente, Stephan, Jain et al., 1992, p. 188). If we also take into consideration that cultural variations exist that are relevant in this regard, then discussions within marketing practice concerning the possible standardization of market communication appear oddly unrealistic. In fact, multinational firms who serve in culturally distinct markets most often have to customize market communication in order to succeed.

There is also a conditioning theory of emotion (Staats and Staats, 1958) that is referred to in consumer psychology (Kroeber-Riel and Weinberg, 1999, p. 130 et seq.). According to this theory, if in marketing communication an emotionally "neutral" stimulus (for example, a consumer good) is related often enough with an emotionally appealing stimulus then in keeping with this assumption the emotion will be transferred to the originally neutral consumer good. Therefore, in this view emotions are learnt in accordance with the classical conditioning model. We have dealt with this model in Chapter 13, "Learning Theory", and we have seen that no such thing as reflexive mechanisms are evident, rather what is much more the case is that expectation behavior patterns are learned. It is similarly the case with so-called emotional conditioning. In any case in marketing communication there still remains the possibility of establishing emotional expectation behavior patterns regarding products, brands, and companies.

That the interplay between affective and cognitive reactions is something to be taken into consideration is shown for example by a study conducted by Kempf (1999). Test subjects were confronted by an entertaining product (computer game) and by a functional product (grammar check software). The dependent variables were enjoyment, arousal, and brand attitude, subsequent to using the products. During the use of the products the affective reaction with regard to the entertainment product was higher than with the functional product. The brand attitude was however strongly influenced in using the functional product, and less so in the case of the entertainment product.

Productive goods marketing

The significance of emotional composition within marketing is no longer questioned today with regard to consumer goods marketing. It has not yet been accepted to the same extent that emotion oriented marketing is also of considerable significance within productive goods marketing (increasingly known as the "business to business field"). This is substantiated by Lasogga (1998 and 1999). Also applicable here is the effect of a change in values toward an experiential orientation, and also the information overload that no one can avoid. Lasogga (1998) has shown that after making decisions, decision makers in businesses tend to be interested in information (reduction of cognitive dissonance); in the case of less recent purchase decisions emotional advertising elements take on more significance. Experiential values like success, the future, and trust thus have more significance than informative contributions (Lasogga, 1999, p. 64). The emotional impression aspect or quality influences the product assessment and the effects on memory of future decision processes. Thus the assertions regarding emotional consumer goods communication may certainly be transferred to productive goods markets. If "advertising in the B2B field should be emotional" (Lasogga, 1999, p. 67) as well, this does not mean that the techniques of composition can be directly transferred. When in the consumer goods sector a small car (Renault Clio®) is advertised with the slogan "Made in paradise" and if as a point of focus an erotically toned "paradise scene" is chosen, then this just might be appropriate for the consumer goods sector. In the productive goods sector a similar advertisement for a commercial vehicle could with a high degree of probability trigger irritation of an undesirable variety. In these markets it involves on the one hand recognizing the necessity of the emotional composition of communication instruments, and on the other hand it involves finding composition orientations that can be concretely implemented with regard to the target specific group. This can additionally lead to there being emotional contents that differ in significance from those in consumer goods marketing. Lasogga (1999, pp. 61 and 62) asserts three product dependent experiential values:

- Products provide a very specific benefit or fulfill a very specific function. They should solve problems. From this success can be derived as an experiential value.
- The benefit of the product should be obtained over a longer period of time; from this the future can be derived as an experiential value.
- Productive goods are purchased due to economic considerations; the desired benefit is always set against a financial risk, on the basis of which trust is revealed to be an experiential value.

In order to carry out successful emotional marketing similar to that conducted in the consumer goods field, in the long term more varied emotional approaches are needed, in order to avoid the danger of interchangeable marketing conceptions. Certainly as far as presentations of success, trust, and the future are concerned, there already exists a great variety of compositional possibilities.

Product related experiential values are contrasted with self-actualization as an experiential value independent of products. We view this as unfortunate. This has to do with personal values; the search for entertainment (of what kind?); the search for excitement and enjoyment (of what kind?). All of this does not directly pertain to the common psychological concept of self-actualization. It simply has to do with personality structures, which to some extent also pertain to emotions, but also to individual motives (for example, success or lack of success orientation), presumptions, and attitudes. A difficult problem arises here for the productive goods (B2B) marketing. In consumer goods marketing we can distinguish target groups directly according to certain personality structures, whether they are more emotional or more cognitive. In productive goods marketing that is not possible. The sales person and the decision maker regarding very particular productive goods initially have only had one thing in common: interest in a very specific productive good. They often differ considerably with regard to their psychologically describable personalities and their sociodemographic characteristics, and therefore also with regard to the possibility of an emotional approach oriented toward their personalities.

The product oriented possibilities of approach and those independent of products, are codetermined by product and market characteristics. These are: market dynamics, degree of innovation of the products being attended, the policy of the providing company, and cultural factors. According to these aspects, the structure of emotional approaches within productive goods marketing can be presented in Figure 15.4.

PERSONNEL MANAGEMENT

Feelings, moods, and affects are all similarly seen as determinants of performance behavior (Engelhard, 1992, p. 1257). It can be assumed that emotions that are experienced as positive have just as much influence on performance behavior as they do on consumer behavior.

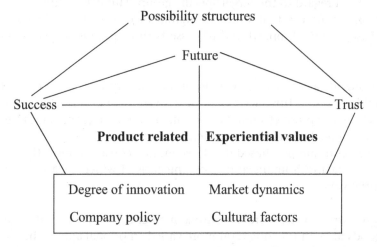

Experiential values independent of products

Possibility structures

Future

Success — Trust

Product related | **Experiential values**

Degree of innovation   Market dynamics

Company policy   Cultural factors

Figure 15.4 The structure of emotional approaches (a modification of Lasogga, 1999, p. 62)

In practical personnel management it is occasionally claimed that factual relationships and emotional relationships can be clearly separated. The above deliberations regarding the character of emotion ought to have made it quite clear how inexpert these kinds of claims are. Emotional aspects cannot be excluded from professional life to the same extent that psychological/sociological aspects cannot be excluded from general market behavior. In upholding this claim we would be expecting the same type of behavior as displayed by Mr Spock on *Star Trek*. However, there are no cognitive mechanisms without an affective element (Mandl and Huber, 1983, p. 16). A view that sees emotions as interfering with human rationality dispenses with empirical, scientific fundamentals, and cannot be justified.

Instead of wanting to exclude emotions from professional life, the case for "emotional intelligence" can be asserted. By this can be understood the ability to appreciate one's own emotions, to react to experienced emotions in a way that is appropriate to the situation, and to appreciate the emotions of others, and to react to them appropriately. Appropriateness can be understood to mean goal orientation and avoidance of interpersonal tensions.

Along with these considerations it should be kept in mind that organizations are becoming increasingly international, and thus are taking on an increasingly multicultural character. That this necessitates the utmost differentiation in dealing with emotions

---

QUESTIONS FOR DISCUSSION

1. Define emotions in a psychological context.
2. Explain differences in emotional advertising campaigns for consumer products and for business to business (B2B) products.
3. Explain the need for different advertising campaigns in culturally diverse environments.
4. Think of some successful marketing campaigns in both print and broadcast media. How was emotion communicated to the recipient?

---

requires no further argument.

Bibliography

Aronson, E.: *Sozialpsychologie—Menschliches Verhalten und gesellschaftlicher Einfluß*. Heidelberg, Berlin, Oxford: 1994. (*Social Psychology—Human Behavior and Social Influence*).

Atkinson, R.L., Atkinson, R.C., Smith, E.E., Bem, D.J. and Nolen-Hoeksema, S.: *Hilgard's Introduction to Psychology* (11th edn). Fort Worth, Philadelphia, San Diego: 1996.

Batra, R. and Stephens, D.: Attitudinal effects of ad-evoked moods and emotions: The moderating role of motivation. *Psychology and Marketing*, 1994, 11, 199–215.

Bem, D.J.: Self-perception theory. In: Berkowitz, L. (ed.): *Advances in Experimental Social Psychology*, vol. 6. New York, London, Toronto: 1972, 1–62.

Bente, G., Stephan, E., Jain, A. and Mutz, G.: Fernsehen und emotion. *Medienpsychologie*, 1992, 4, 186–204. (Watching television and emotion).

Berkowitz, L. (ed.): *Advances in Experimental Social Psychology*, vol 1. New York, San Fransisco, London: 1964.

—— *Advances in Experimental Social Psychology*, vol. 6. New York, London, Toronto: 1972.

—— *Cognitive Theories in Social Psychology*. New York, San Francisco, London: 1986.

—— *Advances in Experimental Social Psychology*. New York: 1987.

Brosius, H.-B. and Kayser, S.: Der Einfluß von emotionalen darstellungen im fernsehen auf informationsaufnahme und urteilsbildung. *Medienpsychologie*, 1991, 3, 236–253. (The influence of emotional representations on television on information reception and judgment development).

Bruhn, M.: *Integrierte Kommunikation* (2nd edn). Stuttgart: 1995. (*Integrated Communication*).

Bruhn, M.: *Kommunikationspolitik*. München: 1997. (*Communication Politics*).

Clark, M.S. (ed.): *Emotion*. Newbury Park, London, New Delhi: 1992.

—— *Emotion and Social Behavior*. Newbury Park, London, New Delhi: 1992.

Cohen, J.B. and Areni, C.S.: Affect and consumer behavior, In: *Handbook of Consumer Behaviour*, Englewood Cliffs, NJ: Prentice Hall, 188–241.

Duclos, S.E., Laird, J.D., Schneider, E., Sexter, M., Stern, L. and van Lighten, O.: Categorical vs. dimensional effects of facial expressions and postures on emotional experience. *Journal of Personality and Social Psychology*, 1989, 57, 100–108.

Duffy, E.: Emotion, An example of the need for reorientation in psychology. *Psychlogical Review*, 1934, 41, 184–198.

—— *Activation and Behavior*. New York: 1962.

Eagle, M.N.: Emotion und gedächtnis. In: Mandl, H. and Huber, G.L. (eds): *Emotion und Kognition*. München, Wien, Baltimore: 1983, 85–122. (Emotion and memory. In *Emotion and Cognition*).

Engelhard, J.: Leistungsdeterminanten. In: Gaugler, E. and Weber, W. (eds): *Handwörterbuch des Personalwesens* (2nd edn). Stuttgart: 1992, 1254–1264. (Achievement determinants. In *Handbook of the Personal Being*).

Euler, H.A. and Mandl, H.: Einleitung. In: Euler, H.A. and Mandl, H. (eds): *Emotionspsychologie—Ein Handbuch in Schlüsselbegriffen*. München, Wien, Baltimore: 1983, 1–4. (Introduction. In *Emotion Psychology—A Handbook in Key Concepts*).

Euler, H.A. and Mandl, H. (eds): *Emotionspsychologie—Ein Handbuch in Schlüsselbegriffen*. München, Wien, Baltimore: 1983. (*Emotion Psychology—A Handbook in Key Concepts*).

Freud, S.: *Psychopathology of Everyday Life*. London: 1901 (*Psychopathologie im Alltagsleben*. Berlin: 1904).

Gaugler, E. and Weber, W. (eds): *Handwörterbuch des Personalwesens* (2nd edn). Stuttgart: 1992. (*Handbook of the Personal Being*).

Goldberg, M. and Gorn, G.: Happy and sad TV programs: How they affect reactions to commercials. *Journal of Consumer Research*, 1987, 14, 387–403.

Gleich, U.: Aktuelle ergebnisse der werbewirkungsforschung. *Media Perspektiven*, 2002, 4, 190–196. (Current results of commercially effective research).

Harré, R. and Parrott, W.G. (eds): *The Emotions – Social, Cultural and Biological Dimensions*. London, Thousand Oaks, New Delhi: 1996.

Irle, E.: Lerntheorien. In: Unger, F. (ed.) *Konsumentenpsychologie und Markenartikel*. Heidelberg, Wien: 1986, 122–140. (Trained theories. In *Consumer Psychology and Brand-name Products*).

Irle, M.: *Lehrbuch der Sozialpsychologie*. Göttingen, Toronto, Zürich: 1975. (*Textbook of Social Psychology*).

Isen, A.M.: Positive affect, cognitive processes, and social behavior. In: Berkowitz, L. (ed.): *Advances in Experimental Social Psychology*. New York: 1987, 203–253.

Izard, C.E.: *Die Emotionen des Menschen* (3rd edn). Weinheim, Basel: 1994. (*The Emotions of the Person*).

James, W.: What is an emotion? *Mind*, 1984, 19, 188–205.

Kellermann, J., Lewis, J. and Laird, J.D.: Looking and loving: The effects of mutural gaze on feelings of romantic love. *Journal of Research in Personality*, 1989, 23, 145–161.

Kempf, D.S.: Attitude formation from product trial: Distinct roles of cognition and affect for hedonic and functional products. *Psychology and Marketing*, 1999, 16, 35–50.

Kleinginna, P.R. Jr. and Kleinginna, A.M.: A categorized list of emotion definitions, with suggestions for a consensual definition. *Motivation and Emotion*, 1981, 5, 345–355.

Konert, F.-J.: *Vermittlung Emotionaler Erlebniswerte. Eine Markenstrategie für Gesättigte Märkte*. Heidelberg, Wien: 1986 (*Procuring Emotional Experience Value. A Market Strategy for Satiated Markets*).

Kroeber-Riel, W.: *Konsumentenverhalten*. München: 1975. (*Consumer Behavior*).

—— and Weinberg, P.: *Konsumentenverhalten* (7th edn), München: 1999. (*Consumer Behavior*).

Laird, J.D. and Apostoleris, N.H.: Emotional self-control and self-perception: Feelings are the solution, not the problem. In: Harré, R. and Parrott, W.G. (eds): *The Emotions—Social, Cultural and Biological Dimensions*. London, Thousand Oaks, New Delhi: 1996, 285–301.

—— and Bresler, C.: The process of emotional experience: A self-perception theory. In: Clark, M.S.: *Emotion*. Newbury Park, London, New Delhi: 1992, 213–234.

Lange, C.G.: *Om Sinsbevaegelsere*. Copenhagen: 1885 (Über Gemütsbewegungen. Leipzig: 1887). (*Over Mind Movements*).

—— and James, W.: *The Emotions*. Baltimore: 1922.

Lasogga, F.: *Emotionale Anzeigen- und Direktwerbung im Investitionsgüterbereich—Eine Exploratorische Studie zu den Einsatzmöglichkeiten von Erlebniswrten in der Investitionsgüterwerbung*. Frankfurt am Main: 1998. (*Emotional Advertising and Direct Advertising in the Capital Goods Area—An Exploratory Study for the Possible Uses of Experience Value in Capital Goods Advertising*).

Lasogga, F.: Emotionale werbung im business to business-bereich. *Jahrbuch der Absatz- und Verbrauchsforschung*, 1999, 45, 56–70. (Emotional advertising in the business to business area).

Lazarus, R.S., Kanner, A.D. and Folkman, S.: Emotions: A cognitive-phenomenolgical analysis. In: Plutchik, R. and Kellerman, H. (eds): *Emotion. Theory, Research, and Experience, vol. 1: Theories of Emotion*, New York: 1980, 189–217.

Mackie, D.M., Asuncion, A.G. and Rosselli, F.: The impact of positive affect on persuasion processes, In: Clark, M.S. (ed.): *Emotion and Social Behavior*. Newbury Park, London, New Delhi: 1992, 247–270.

Mandl, H. and Huber, G.L.: Theoretische grundpositionen zum verhältnis von emotion und kognition. In: Mandl, H. and Huber, G.L. (eds): *Emotion und Kognition*. München, Wien, Baltimore: 1983, 1–60. (Theoretical foundations for the relationship of emotion and cognition. In *Emotion and Cognition*).

—— (eds): *Emotion und Kognition*. München, Wien, Baltimore: 1983. (*Emotion and Cognition*).

Mangold, R.: Zum einsatz hirndiagnostischer verfahren bei der untersuchung kognitiver und insbesondere emotionaler medienwirkungen. *Medienpsychologie*, 1999, 11, 121–142. (Use of brain diagnostic procedures in the investigation of more cognitive and especially emotional media effects).

Meyer, W.-U., Schützwohl, A. and Reizenstein, R.: *Einführung in die Emotionspsychologie*, vol. I. Bern, Göttingen, Toronto, Seattle: 1993. (*Introduction to Emotion Psychology*).

Neibecker, B.: *Wirkungsanalyse mit Expertensystemen*. Heidelberg: 1990. (*Effective Analysis with Expert Systems*).

Oatley, K.: Emotions: Communications to the self and others. In: Harré, R. and Parrott, W.G. (eds): *The Emotions—Social, Cultural and Biological Dimensions*. London, Thousand Oaks, New Delhi: 1996, 312–318.

Piaget, J.: *Intelligence and Affectivety: Their Relationship During Child Development*. Palo Alto: 1981.

Plutchik, R. and Kellerman, H. (eds): *Emotion. Theory, Research, and Experience, vol. 1: Theories of Emotion*. New York: 1980.

Schachter, S.: The interaction of cognitive and physiological determinants of emotional state. In: Berkowitz, L. (ed.): *Advances in Experimental Social Psychology*, vol. 1. New York, San Francisco, London: 1964, 48–80.

Schachter, S.: Second thoughts on biological and psychological explanations of behavior. In: Berkowitz, L. (ed.): *Cognitive Theories in Social Psychology*, New York, San Francisco, London: 1978, 433–453

Schachter, S. and Singer, J.E.: Cognitive, social, and physiological determinants of emotional state, *Psychological Review*, 1962, 69, 379–399.

Scherer, K.R.: Theorien und aktuelle probleme der emotionspsychologie. In: Scherer, K.R. (ed.): *Psychologie der Emotionen*. Göttingen, Toronto, Zürich:1990, 2–38. (Theories and current problems of emotion psychology. In *Psychology of Emotions*).

—— (ed.): *Psychologie der Emotionen*. Göttingen, Toronto, Zürich: 1990. (*Psychology of Emotions*).

Schwarz, N., Bless, H. and Bohner, G.: Mood and persuasion: Affective states influence the processing of persuasive communications, In: Zanna, M.P. (ed.): *Advances in Experimental and Social Psychology*, vol. 24. San Diego, New York, Boston: 1991, 161–199.

Sherman, E., Mathur, A. and Smith, R.B.: Store environment and consumer purchase behavior: mediating role of consumer emotions. *Psychology and Marketing*, 1997, 14, 361–378.

Staats, A.W. and Staats, C.K.: Attitudes established by classical conditioning of attitudes. *Journal of Abnormal and Social Psychology*, 1958, 57, 37–40.

Unger, F. (ed.): *Konsumentenpsychologie und Markenartikel*. Heidelberg, Wien: 1986. (*Consumer Psychology and Brand-name Products*).

Unger, F. and Fuchs, W.: *Management der Marktkommunikation* (2nd edn). Heidelberg: 1999. (*Management of Market Communication*).

Valins, S.: Cognitive effects of false heart rate feedback. *Journal of Personality and Social Psychology*, 1966, 4, 400–408.

Weinberg P. and Konert, F.J.: Messung produktspezifischer erlebniswerte von konsumenten. *Planung und Analyse*, 1984, 11, 313–316. (Measurement of product specific experience value for consumers).

Zanna, M.P.: *Advances in Experimental and Social Psychology*, vol. 24. San Diego, New York, Boston: 1991.

Zimbardo, P.G. and Gerrig, R.J.: *Psychology and Life* (15th edn). New York, Reading, Menlo Park: 1999.

IV Power, Control, and Exchange

16 *Power*

Theory

CONCEPTUAL FOUNDATIONS

"Power denotes every opportunity within a social relationship where one can exercise one's own will, including against opposition, in keeping with the nature of this opportunity" (Weber, 1972, p. 28). This assertion is scientifically neutral. According to Weber's formulation it is "amorphous".

"We can define 'b's power over 'a' ... as a quotient of the maximum possible power that b can exercise on a ..., and the maximum resistance a can muster in opposition" (Lewin, 1951, p. 336; see also Lewin, 1982, p. 361).

Power arises when there is an imbalance between participants with regard to resources pertaining to their mutual influence. "The extent of this imbalance can be identified as the power that exists between the participants. A participant is thus more powerful than the other participants if they—relatively—have control over more resources, where those resources are of interest to the other participants" (Esser, 1993, p. 347). Power then becomes a special case of mutual dependence.

This approach was already being taken by Foucault (1976). Power is no longer seen as a "top to bottom" oriented resource consisting of possibilities of influence, but as a mutual framework of relationships built into every society and thus also into organizations of all kinds. Power relationships arise between all people who come into contact with one another. This does not contradict Weber's (1972) or Lewin's (1951) approach in any way; it merely makes clear that the content of the concept "power" is to be understood as mutual or interchangeable, not as one-sided. This is necessary, because even in the case of educated laymen (for example, management) power is understood too much as a "top to bottom" relationship, and this is particularly with reference to Max Weber (Lewin is not trusted as much by educated laymen). Human relationships are not possible without power structures (Hahne, 1998, p. 200).

According to Weber (1972, p. 541) power within relationships of exchange and power within relationships of dominance need to be differentiated. Power within relationships of dominance is possible insofar as there is the potential for an authority to assert power via coercion, reward, and punishment, whereby the effectiveness of such coercion consists in the degree of subjection of people on whom the power is being exercised, in relation to those exercising the power (see also Scherhorn, 1983, p. 56).

RESOURCES OF POWER (CARTWRIGHT, 1959)

Power is founded on a range of fundamentals, described by Cartwright (1959, 1965).

Physical influence

This aspect is no longer seriously taken into consideration in free, democratically organized societies. It played a big role in earlier eras, including within commerce. Even today not all economic performance processes are free of physical influence—consider child labor. To what extent we are wont to speak here more of violence than of power, is a question posed by Luhmann's power theory. In any case, as a power factor, there does exist the possibility of exercising physical violence.

Influence on revenue and expenses, on reward and punishment

This aspect plays a considerable role in modern economic life. Incentive earnings, the assignment of pleasant or unpleasant work, the threat of job loss, the threat or promise of transfer or of career possibilities—all of these are power resources for those people who are in positions to make such decisions.

It is certainly not the case however that power within organizations always proceeds from "top to bottom", from superiors to so-called subordinates. The latter also have influence on the revenue and expenses of superiors, who desire performance on behalf of their subordinates, in order to achieve certain results, which they will experience as successful, or in the negative case as unsuccessful. In this sense they are dependent on the cooperation of others. In economic systems based on division of labor, power is always interchangeable. In this way subordinates exercise influence on the revenue and expenses, and on the expenses and revenue of their so-called superiors.

Influence via arrangement of the surroundings, or so-called "environmental influence"

The arrangement of the surroundings facilitates many behavioral patterns and hinders others. In professional life we will think first of all of safety precautions that prevent entering certain areas or premises in the first place. Much more interesting psychologically is the arrangement of sales areas in order to control the flow of shoppers. Via the arrangement of shelving, every shopper can be compulsorily caused to walk through the whole of the sales area, even if he or she only has to buy one product, in order to trigger impulse buying. In the end no one can be forced, but environmental influence at least necessitates passing by certain shelves.

In the modern information society, access to certain data is made easier for certain people, whereas for others it is made impossible. This can likewise be seen as a form of environmental exercising of power.

Internalization and identification

Internalization denotes a process whereby people take on the goals of an organization that they are a member of as their own. Clearly people take note of to what extent their personal income is dependent upon the success of the organization. The question is whether they assume that their own performance behavior is in fact codependent with regard to the company's success, or if they live according to the hypothesis that they will profit from success to the same degree if they hold back their performance behavior. If the latter hypothesis corresponds with reality, then from a purely economic perspective it can be correct to only give a minimum contribution, in order not to run the risk of being ousted from the organization. The fact that people are often more fundamentally engaged than would be expected according to these considerations reveals the problems of a so-called "pure economy". Economic behavior is social behavior and requires explanations from the viewpoint of social science. Employees are obviously prepared to internalize or can be motivated to do so. If this state of affairs is obtained, many conflicts over goals will be reduced and will even subside.

Identification has to do with the process of acquiring role models. People seek out role models and role model groups whose behavior is seen as approved behavior. The theory of social comparison (see Chapter 3) applies here. People who are chosen as role models exercise power over the behavior of other people because these other people will attempt, to a more or less pronounced extent, to imitate their role model's behavior. One can quite easily observe this influence in the everyday life occurrence of people taking on the sayings or turns of phrase of others. This can be a(n) (unconscious) sign of solidarity or of subservience. We often observe that "subordinates" imitate the sayings of their superiors.

Influence via selective communication

We must necessarily proceed according to the assumption that communication always has to be selective, as is apparent from Luhmann's (1988) contribution concerning power through communication. So from this perspective power arises through communication. The question is simply how consciously or targeted the selectivity of the communication is, and whether or not it is knowingly being engaged in as an instrument for exercising power. That information holds potential for power is common knowledge these days. In any case, the behavior of others is influenced by communication, sometimes to an extreme extent. This influence can proceed very concretely, for example in the form of commands, or it can proceed very subtly and to some in a partially unnoticed manner, like in the context of market communication: advertising, public relations, product placement, sponsoring, measures to further sales at sales outlets, and also at election campaigns and other forms of political communication, are prominent examples.

Speech (as technical language) and writing are communication based power resources. It was not for nothing that the Church suppressed the printing craft for so long, and it is not for nothing that forms of technical language have formed within many professional circles, which much more serve the entrenchment of power than they do communication.

Power via communication can to some extent take the place of power via environmental influence. A person's view regarding their situation can be changed via communication; this effect can be congruent with environmental influence measures.

Power via communication can also be exercised through communication regarding what success is considered to be. "What success is seen to be in the organization, how success is measured, and what procedures are applied in the attribution of success, varies from organization to organization" (Hahne, 1998, pp. 204, 205).

And finally a person's expectations regarding the consequences of their actions can be communicated in various ways (ibid).

Appeal to morality, and psychological pressure

There is an aspect that does not explicitly arise in Cartwright's approach: that of appealing to morality, that is, the application of psychological pressure. He may have implicitly indicated that this influence is contained within selective communication. However, the particularities of appealing to morality make giving it independent treatment seem relevant. A person who is exercising power may seek to alter what the person they are trying to influence uses to assess value, and in this effort they may refer to the common good. Politicians like to refer to the "will of the people". There is however no such thing as a "collective will of the people". There are majorities that allow for the formation in Parliament of various coalitions supporting a given administration. Even if this coalition can continue to rule after an election this does not mean that the "work of the administration" has been endorsed or approved. Nevertheless, being able to lean on the "will of the people" bestows considerable moral integrity.

A contemporary, seemingly downright grotesque example is provided by the inability to complete the Doha Development Agenda at the World Trade Organization. The most recent trade round by the WTO was started in an effort to improve the income earning potential of the world's poorest citizens, who often are victims of protectionism in agriculture in the developed world markets. The inertia was caused owing to the inability of the developed and developing world to agree on an acceptable trade liberalization agreement. Both sides were marked by their pursuit of their own protectionist interests (developed and developing world wanting to protect their domestic farmers from foreign competition, to the deteriment of the world economy at large), meanwhile evoking the interests of the "poorest people of the world", and "the interests of the common man", etc.

The assertion of a particular morality can therefore be a very effective method of exercising power, because moral assessments detract from insight; they do not lend themselves to being critically evaluated in relation to reality. There always arises the possibility that a communication that does not correspond with the truth of the matter will fail to hold up when compared with the critically testable reality. A saying like "You can't do that" in the sense of "You aren't allowed to do that" entails an absolute standard of acceptable behavior. People who are seen to hold the moral high ground can very easily exercise power through appeal to morality. This would seemingly be the basis of power in organized religion.

Formally established influence

Though not dealt with by Cartwright (1959), there is nonetheless the relevant possibility of exercising formally established power. This derives from the formal, hierarchically organized structures of entrepreneurial organizations. Formal power is that power resource that is almost exclusively used to exercise power from "top to bottom", in the hierarchical way of thinking. In this sense it seems justified to equate formal power with authority. However, the previous possibilities regarding the social exercising of power show that it is disadvantageous to exclusively rely on formally based power resources. The state also relies on the enforcement of its right to formal power.

Sexuality as a power factor

This aspect is hardly present at all in organizational literature, a fact that female scientists are certainly justified in attributing to management and science still being dominated by men. The spectrum of sexuality based exercising of power is broad (see Rastetter, 1994): Male dominated authority structures and the "male societies/boys' clubs" that derive from them (this fact would be offset with the addition of female dominated networks); performance assessment in male dominated structures; gender defined division of labor; gender specific perception of performance behavior and of behavior deemed to deviate from performance; gender specific attribution of success and lack of success; and finally to problems that stem from harassment in the workplace (Rastetter, 1994, p. 171 et seq.; and see also Stockdale's overview of the research, 1996). It is completely clear that in the case of sexual harassment, according to the approach of many theories of power, we no longer find ourselves in a power context but in the context of authority structures. The other sexually determined factors could theoretically be implemented by both sexes as a basis for power and in that sense they represent power structures. At the beginning of this millennium these factors, de facto, certainly (still) partially underlie authority structures, due to male dominance.

Behavior (B) is in general always and everywhere dependent on two groups of factors (f) that mutually influence each other: Personality factors (P) and environmental factors (E) (Lewin, 1936; 1982, p. 66).

$$B = f\,(P,E)$$

Power is always being exercised when environmental factors are being influenced. All the power resources that have been listed by Cartwright (1959) fulfill this criterion. This also applies to internalization and identification. Internalization is an example of the interchangeable influence of personality and environmental factors. The environmental factor "goal" is made into a personality factor via internalization. Identification initially starts with an environmental factor, namely a person, who serves as a role model, or a group, that can serve as a role model group. Over the course of time the affected person P takes on the behavioral patterns or even personality characteristics, which become P's personality factors. The process of adopting moral standards of assessment proceeds analogously.

According to Lewin's field theory, every person P finds themselves in a power field that influences them. This could work in favor of those conditions that P is striving for, or against them. These are the environmental factors. At the same time P continuously develops their own forces, forces that are directed toward their own goals or toward deflecting undesired conditions. P's actual behavior is the result of the total forces inherent in external influences (E) and of their own power or forces (P) (Lewin, 1982, pp. 103–126).

In order to fully understand this we need to consider that thinking, the decision-making process, opinion formation, attitude formation, etc., or in other words all conceivable cognitive processes, are all constitutive of behavior.

Social power has a certain range of influence (Irle, 1971, p. 17). What is meant by that are the areas of life that can be influenced by a certain exercising of power. The greater the amount of clout taken away from personality factors due to environmental factors being influenced by a power-wielding authority, the more we are moving away from the exercise of power to "social control". "Social control entails ... that in the formula B = f (P, E) the P factors, as determinants of B, fall to 0, whereby the E factors are nearly the sole determinants of B ..."

POWER AND COMMUNICATION (LUHMANN, ESPECIALLY 1988)

Social systems, like for example organizations, only arise via communication (Luhmann, 1988, p. 5). Communication is always selective information, since no communication can ever fully represent any given reality. The world is enormously complex, and through communication this complexity is reduced. Luhmann (1988, p. 11) sees the function of communication as the transmission of "reduced complexity". Via its selectivity, communication always holds the possibility of manipulation. In this sense communication is the basis of power. In modern societies, money is also a medium for power (Luhmann, 1996, p. 310).

People operate according to a certain quantity of behavioral alternatives. Influential communication consists of directing a possible communication partner with regard to their selection (Luhmann, 1988, p. 8). In this way power becomes a medium of communication. Because communication is always an interchange between communication partners, there arises a double-sided selectivity (ibid). According to Luhmann power only arises if there is the underlying condition that at least one of the participating communication partners experience uncertainty. The exercise of power is thus possible if a decision-maker (a person exercising power) "can dispose the *other* toward being uncertain in relation to their own decision" (Luhmann, 2000, p. 212). This clearly does not mean that there is less uncertainty for the person exercising power than for the person subject to this exercising of power. When looked at realistically, certainty is never possible; however, people sometimes are under the illusion of certainty. Thus the exercise of power, in Luhmann's sense of it, is not possible. This leads to the paradox that people who are operating according to an illusion (of certainty) are less at the mercy of power than those people who live with a realistic assumption of uncertainty.

Power via communication is exercised in that it limits the communication partner's freedom of action. "Power is greater when it controls the engagement in attractive alternatives of action or in the refraining from such attractive actions" (Luhmann, 1988, p. 9). This is plausible: if we manage to present a person with certain alternatives of action in an unattractive light, alternatives which at the outset were not being sought after, then this is not a convincing evidence of our power. If on the other hand, on the basis of our communication, what was a very attractive and coveted alternative of action is taken away, then the execution of power via communication must have proceeded quite convincingly.

Insofar as power constrains freedom of action via communication without forcing the performance of a single concrete action, power is differentiated from force (compulsion). In an extreme case an action can be brought about through the use of physical violence. Luhmann (1988, p. 21) sees a person who is subject to any kind of power as being free in their choice of action. Instruments of power may be implemented against them (via threats) in order to influence their decision. If the threat is actually carried out, the communicative structure collapses, the future condition is no longer foreseeable, and the previous condition is irreversibly destroyed. For this reason a power system contains the provision of seeking to avoid force. The formulation of power can already take on a "character of threat" (Luhmann, 1988, p. 26) and as a next step the implementation of punishments can become necessary, with their above-mentioned undesirable consequences. The explicit assertion of power and punishments is therefore avoided wherever possible. In modern societies legal claims or rights serve this function. These have the advantage of not speaking directly of power and punishment; legal rights exist implicitly.

The exercise of power is always a mutual affair. Not only those who are subject to power may be influenced with regard to their modes of behavior, but also those wielding power may be caused to use it (Luhmann, 1988, p. 21). It can be in the interest of those who, in occupying hierarchically higher positions, who have been assigned power resources, not to exercise their power, because such people have been made responsible with regard to instances of success and failure. Despite this, a person who is subject to power may opt for those alternatives that invite punishment from the person wielding the power, or they may threaten (!) this behavior, thereby forcing the power wielder to enact punishments which they in fact do not want to implement (Luhmann, 1997, p. 356). It is a question of who is wielding the power, and who is subject to the power.

"The power of superiors to assign unpleasant work with the threat that disobedience will be followed by being fired is contrasted by the power of the subordinates to withhold cooperation in cases where their superiors are dependent on such cooperation" (Luhmann, 2000, p. 201). When looked at this way, both participants are simultaneously or interchangeably wielding power and subject to power.

Luhmann's (1988) theory of power revolves around negative consequences. The central focus is on behavioral alternatives that both participants want to avoid. A power wielder threatens unattractive circumstances toward the end of assuring that certain modes of behavior are not engaged.

P1 (power wielder) threatens P2 (person subject to power) with X in order to ensure behavioral manifestation Y. They have successfully exercised power if P2 would rather avoid X, and if X is truly less attractive for P2 than Y. There arises a "connection between combinations of avoidance alternatives with a less negatively assessed combination of other alternatives" (Luhmann, 1988, p. 22). If P1 is put in a position where they have to implement X, the communication structure collapses; it turns into a system of force or violence. "Power is only in operation if, in contradistinction to a given expected circumstance, a more unfavorable combination of alternatives has been asserted" (Luhmann, 1988, p. 23).

THE CONTRIBUTION OF MOTIVATION PSYCHOLOGY TO POWER THEORY

Power is always oriented toward the utilization of the existing motives or needs of others. In this regard avoidance motives may be the focus, as in Luhmann's approach, or avoidance and attraction tendencies may equally be starting points for the exercising of power. Those exercising power will employ whatever power resources yield the best expenditure-to-benefit relationship with regard to the goals being strived (Heckhausen, 1989, p. 362). To this end, they will attempt to fashion a situation whereby (psychologically from the point of view of those subject to power) conformance, on behalf of those subject to power to patterns of behavior desired by the wielders of power, represents for the former the most advantageous expenditure-to-benefit relationship. Desired and undesired consequences of an action will also be taken into consideration, including the pros and cons of possible evasive modes of action. For example, a person can avoid performance behavior in the workplace, preferring activities in the private sphere. They will do this if the expected rewards and/or punishments in the workplace are evaluated as a whole at a lower level than the expected rewards and punishments in private life. This is driven by the existing need or motive structures of both the wielders of power and those subject to power. We are here aware that everyone participating in the power process can simultaneously be both the wielders of power and those subject to power.

The entire process of power behavior is triggered by the motivation to exercise power, or via the assumption that one's own goals can be reached by others engaging in specific behavior. Thus their behavior has to be influenced. Along these lines there are certain means of exercising power available: personal factors on behalf of the power wielder (intelligence, vitality, charisma) on the one hand, and on the other hand there are institutional factors, or in other words formally assigned roles within the organization. The exercising of power is contrasted by possible resistance on behalf of the targeted individuals, and aside from that there are reservations regarding the exercise of power. In order to employ power (despite one's own reservations and despite the resistance of those subject to power), power resources are needed (see Cartwright, 1959). There will be reactions on behalf of those subject to power. These reactions are also influenced by the personal motives and power of those subject to power, not just by those in a position of power. The result is the appearance of consequences of implemented behavior for both the wielders of power and those subject to power.

In motivation psychology, there tends to be the assumption that there is a personality specific motivation toward power. Heckhausen (1989, pp. 368–375) has presented many approaches to measuring the power motive, all of which are however still viewed very critically, and thus we will here forgo a thorough presentation. We will make do with the assumption that there is motivation toward or a need for power that varies according to how pronounced it is in the individual. People appear to be structured with regard to the motivation to exercise power in a way that is similar to general performance behavior (hope and fear within performance motivation, Heckhausen, 1963); there similarly appears to be a hope for power and a fear of losing power (Schmalt, 1987). Every implementation of power has consequences as a result that will either strengthen or weaken one's own power position. These expectations will also more or less noticeably influence the decision to implement power.

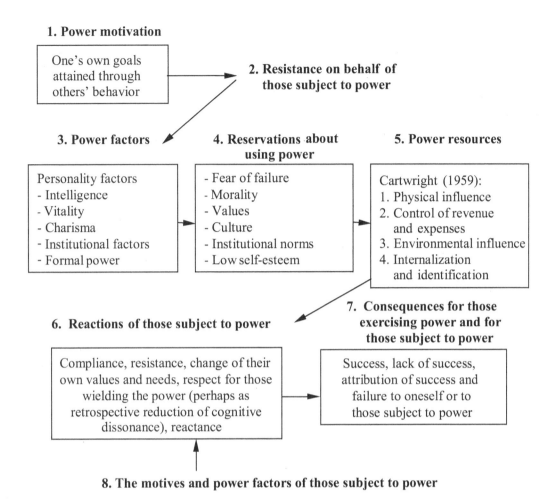

1. Power motivation

One's own goals attained through others' behavior

2. Resistance on behalf of those subject to power

3. Power factors

Personality factors
- Intelligence
- Vitality
- Charisma
- Institutional factors
- Formal power

4. Reservations about using power

- Fear of failure
- Morality
- Values
- Culture
- Institutional norms
- Low self-esteem

5. Power resources

Cartwright (1959):
1. Physical influence
2. Control of revenue and expenses
3. Environmental influence
4. Internalization and identification

6. Reactions of those subject to power

Compliance, resistance, change of their own values and needs, respect for those wielding the power (perhaps as retrospective reduction of cognitive dissonance), reactance

7. Consequences for those exercising power and for those subject to power

Success, lack of success, attribution of success and failure to oneself or to those subject to power

8. The motives and power factors of those subject to power

Figure 16.1 The process of power behavior, based closely on Heckhausen (1989, p. 365), see also Cartwright (1965) and Kipins (1974, p. 89)

Applications

LUHMANN (IN PARTICULAR 1988)

In hierarchies an asymmetrical distribution of power is assumed. "One assumes that a supervisor has more power than a subordinate, even though in bureaucratic organizations the opposite should normally be the case" (Luhmann, 1988, p. 10). From this we can infer that hierarchies are constituted by an unequal distribution of power.

Within organizations (and elsewhere) power is exercised in that the freedom of action of subordinates and supervisors is limited. In organizational practice it is assumed that managers, as those who have been favored with power, are more significant with regard to the manifesting of power than "subordinates". This assumption is incorrect; it underestimates the fact that communication and therefore the exercising of power is always interchangeable. In this regard the possibility of those who have been placed in a hierarchically higher position being controlled by those who have been assigned lower positions, has been considerably underestimated.

In Luhmann's (1988) power theory the focus is on a system of alternatives that are to be avoided. This significance of positive reinforcements, that is, of rewards, is only barely discernible within personnel management. In international politics Luhmann's theory is clearly discernible. In this case in the past we have experienced massive communication of threats, which none of those involved actually wanted to carry out. A country or system threatens (often tacitly) the use of military resources, knowing full well that it will not use them if at all possible. In the case of personnel policy the use of a one-sided orientation toward negative sanctions is more unfortunate. The promise of rewards is certainly possible. Luhmann has called that a positive point of departure, one that is based on promises (protection, affection, payment); the exercise of power then arises when certain patterns of behavior result in these positives not being obtained.

The essential difference between obtaining rewards (positive sanction) and the deprivation of what has been promised (negative sanction in the sense of Luhmann's theory) is the following: in the case of the former promises of reward, those who are subject to power may freely choose between various (positive) consequences of their actions. In the case of retroactive deprivation of promised rewards (performance bonuses, promotion), the subordinate person has already adjusted to the idea that they will receive these positives.

In any case, it seems ill advised not to see the control of rewards as likewise being a resource for the assertion of power.

The consideration of a conception of personnel management that is not based on threats can be derived from Luhmann's (1988) power theory in that, as Luhmann states, the explicit exercise of power and negative sanctions already paves the way for the collapse of power structures that are based on communication. A single occasion where force is applied or where a threat is expressed can lead to one having to continuously fall back on this form of influence. Inefficient forms of management are perpetuated and increased as a consequence. There are authorities within organizations that make decisions with regard to hiring, firing, careers, and so on. They will rarely expressly threaten with their punitive possibilities, but "there is the widespread assumption that one's own behavior (even including being sick) is significant with regard to such decisions" (Luhmann, 1996, p. 310).

The extent of power resources of this sort appears to be quite high. Accordingly there is also a similarly high potential for organizations to destroy themselves from within. The system thus serves itself by greatly reducing the open use of power, and by attempting to soften the power game via mutually respectful contacts and the avoidance of irritations that could result in possible backlash" (Luhmann, 2000, p. 202). What works within organizations regarding the use of power, or even better, the non-use of power, also works between organizations, that is, within economic systems, and similarly within society and between societies.

Attention is directed toward the fact that money is a medium of power. The allocation of budgets within organizations is also a medium of power. Budgets and the change of budgets document the significance, change of significance and the success of departments, of authorities and areas of operation (Luhmann, 1996, p. 311).

The fact that Luhmann limits the concept of power to a communication structure and sharply differentiates it from structures of coercion or force, is a question of definition. It does not matter whether we do not want to identify relationships outside of communication as power relationships, or whether we proceed according to various forms of exercising power: Power via communication (which Luhmann presents as always necessarily being selective) or via coercion (of a psychological sort, or of a physical sort, or in other words violence).

Dialectics serve as an outstanding example of power via targeted, selective communication. There is not enough space here to present dialectics in a comprehensive manner. An excellent proponent of this is Lay, who already spells out the power-wielding function of verbal communication in the titles of his publications: *Manipulation through Speech* (Lay, 1980), *Dialectics for Managers* (Lay, 1978), or *Management via the Word* (Lay, 1981). Dialectics is here understood as the art of getting your way without harming anyone: "Dialectics is the art of winning, without conquering!" (Lay, 1981, p. 20). Dialectics is understood to be a technique of viewing disputes, discussions within teams, and also presentations, as game-like verbal competitions. Lay distances himself from "higher dialectics", which will also tolerate disagreements, and which can be rejected by critical, rational thinking, with complete justification. We certainly encounter an important facet in another viewpoint: "A typical ability of those who command power is to overcome forceful resistance behavior" (Lay, 1981, p. 37). This point of view indicates the current possibilities of exercising power in modern societies, such that it may have a much more widespread influence due to its remaining unseen.

Lay (1980, p. 183) discusses the following techniques of manipulation, among others:

a) In professional life:

- Motivation toward greater performance.
- Techniques of alienation (as the corollary of self actualization).
- Techniques of inducing employee commitment.
- Solidarity with the interests of the employer/superiors.

b) Manipulation of consumers by the manufacturer or the business:

- The many forms of consumer goods advertising (which we cannot go into comprehensively, see Unger and Fuchs, 1999).
- When accustomed to prosperity, certain products will be taken for granted.
- Techniques of inducing customer commitment to the manufacturer (the brand name product), or to the business.

It is interesting to observe the obstinacy with which some members of the advertising field (the Central Committee of the German Advertising Industry, for example) resist the accusation of manipulation. Manipulation is the directing of other people's behavior to one's own advantage. Marketing communication does nothing other than this. How this is to be judged is a question of individual and societal norms.

c) There is manipulation in the religious field through the encouragement of unobtainable modes of behavior, which are then connected with the awakening of considerable feelings of guilt, and through the threat of eternal punishment and where the religion is presented as the way to eternal salvation. The power potential increases considerably if one excessively expands the catalogue of sins.

d) Raising kids according to the interests of the parents; here what is "good" is presented as what happens to be in the parents' interests: peace and quiet, what is observed as a prestigious choice of profession, a more rapid completion of education.

e) Manipulation in the political system; citizens vote for politicians on the basis of information they have received from the media. They judge policy according to these same sources. Citizens are informed very selectively: Of military dangers, or of technical dangers (atomic or having to do with genetics), or of health dangers (BSE). Parties and election programs are extremely simplified, to some extent reduced down to the pictures of the respective politicians. Elections become "media events". Presumably it is necessary to reduce political communication to buzzwords and images because citizens in modern industrial, information societies are overwhelmed with information and are disinterested with regard to political information. However, when in recent years was an attempt made to conduct an election with actual content? Could perhaps the lack of content inherent in election statements be responsible for oft-bemoaned poor voter turnout and for the disinterest? Are the parties' election strategies manipulated by self-styled "experts" from the advertising field?

In a modern information society power is wielded by whoever has control over the mass media.

"POWER AND DECISIONS IN ORGANIZATIONS" (IRLE, 1971)

In organizations there are authorities. These are positions that have the formal right to issue directives. They make decisions regarding other subordinate positions. This can take place according to direct commands or via the allocation of task categories, through the allocation of financial, personal, or tangible resources. In actual fact, higher positions can often only make decisions on the basis of information received from subordinates. Decisions in all different areas of an organization are always the result of a network of information sources spanning over many different positions. There are no autonomous decisions anymore! Perhaps there never were. The concept being outlined stems from the classical line organization (see Figure 16.2). It overtaxes those in positions of authority, whose comprehensive decision-making areas are increasing.

It has been obvious to decision-makers for some time that they are often overwhelmed. However, they are afraid of losing power. For this reason the "advisory staff unit line principle" was introduced (see Figure 16.3). Advisory staff units are administrative bodies assigned to authorities a) in order simply to provide information, b) in order to advise or c) in order to devise alternatives on the basis of which decisions can be made. The formal decisions regarding the choice of alternatives that can be brought to fruition are still made by the main line authorities.

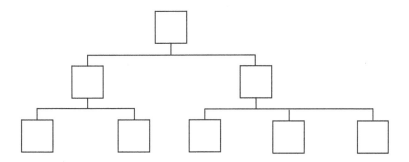

Figure 16.2 The line structure of an organization

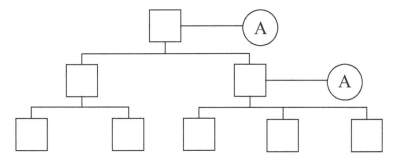

Figure 16.3 Advisory staff unit (A) line structure of an organization

Looking at the positioning of advisory staff units it can be inferred that the occupants of these units are more dominant regarding some issues than the main line authorities. This also applies if the line just has to refer to the advisory staff units because of capacity problems. However, the line does reserve the right to reject, modify or accept the information, or alternatives ready to be decided upon, supplied by the advisory staff units (Irle, 1971, p. 32). Still, in reality these units exercise power on the line.

In order to demonstrate this we will present (based on Irle, 1971) a model of the decision-making process:

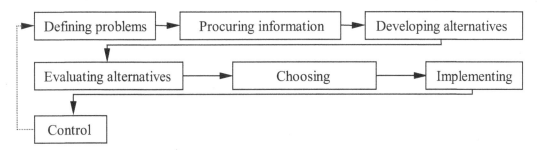

Figure 16.4 Decision-making process

Initially there is the problem definition, which is the result of a context that is perceived in a highly subjective manner, causing the problem to appear in the light of a very particular viewpoint. This context already contains a significant precondion with regard to possible alternatives, which can be perceived by the decision-makers, for solving the problem (Albert, 1978, pp. 23 and 24). The choice of problems is already influenced by habits, attitudes, and preconceptions. "Many components of these problem situations mainly remain in the background, without being elaborated, others are made explicit during the course of the attempt to solve the given problem, while others are significant right from the beginning (Albert, 1978, p. 23).

In management practice, the choice and formulation of those problems that are seen as significant is also a set of decision-making conditions that has a more or less pronounced influence on all subsequent stages of the decision process. The question of the choice of problems can never be discarded; it is inevitable. This insight enables the critical scrutinization of that initial choosing and formulation. However, due to advantages with regard to information, advisory staff units can purposely manipulate the line right at the initial phase of the decision-making processes—in other words they can exercise power. Because of unavoidable selectivity of information within communication (according to Luhmann, 1988), the exercise of power is inevitable.

They have an information advantage over the line authorities. The line can never simultaneously process all relevant items of information without making the advisory staff units redundant. Even when the advisory staff units really try to correctly inform the line they are still exercising power through the selectivity of the information that is presented. It is not possible to produce fully comprehensive information regarding a given condition. Further questions can always be posed. The possibility of comprehensive information presupposes the possibility of certainty. Both are impossible. The line cannot reconstruct the set of assumptions the advisory staff units held in formulating the problems in processing information (Irle, 1971, p. 59). Every search for information is always and generally directed and selective; it proceeds according to certain assumptions of which even the active participants are not always aware.

When advisory staff units develop alternatives for solving problems which are then presented to the line to be decided upon, they are thereby limiting the possible range of decisions. With every problem-solving endeavor there is an indefinite number of solution alternatives; the choice of an overview of solution alternatives represents an extremely selective decision.

Who establishes the final standards that will be drawn upon to evaluate the alternatives to be decided? The advisory staff "helps" here as well. In the end, a choice from the alternatives is made. This choice is reserved for the line. But what is left for them to decide, when previously it has already been decided what problem is to be solved, what information is to be included and how it is to be evaluated, what alternatives are to be developed and how those are to be evaluated? The line can only ratify what has already been established, or they can reject all of the suggestions. The latter border on being arbitrary, since the information basis for such a decision is insufficient.

Finally there is the implementation (Who gives instructions? How will the instructions be understood? Will what is understood be correctly implemented?) and control. Again there is the question of who decides when control will take place and what standards will be applied.

An important problem in this process stems from the theory of cognitive dissonance (see Chapter 4), which states that after a decision, people tend to seek those items of information that support their decision, or to correspondingly interpret information. Each phase of the decision process outlined above is its own decision-making process:

We decide what is to be defined as a problem, what information we will deal with, what alternatives we will consider, and how we will evaluate these alternatives. The further we move along in this decision-making process, the greater the pressure is to justify the decisions made in preceding stages.

> *Whoever has accepted a false hypothesis very early on has necessitated the influx into the decision-making process of more contradicting information, in order to make corrections, than is the case with someone who has not started with a false hypothesis ... The earlier one settles on an alternative as a hypothesis (= preferred alternative) after discovering a problem, the more probable it is that one will end up with an incorrect conclusion* (Irle, 1971, p. 164).

If an employee position delegates tasks this means functions will be reallocated such that they will no longer be perceived. These functions will then be taken up by subordinate staff units. In doing this those positions performing the delegating are giving up power that cannot be recovered, unless they are willing to sacrifice the authority of these advisory staff functions. One cannot delegate decision preparation activity and subsequently make independent decisions. Whoever gives away decision preparation activity is also handing over decision-making authoriy. In the law system experts in court serve an advisory function. Can a lawyer really appraise expert observations regarding the safety or risks of technologies, or appraise expert psychological observations regarding the criminal responsibility of defendants?

If, for example, a professor is to be hired by a university, initially a hiring commission is formed which then establishes the exact teaching and research parameters regarding the professor to be hired. In doing so, an extreme narrowing of the decision has been made. There then follows an invitation to applicants. Subsequently the submitted application documents will be reviewed by the commission, followed by the selection of some applicants who will be invited to give test lectures. If a short advisory statement regarding each rejected applicant is also prepared, in the form of a three to four sentence rejection, then this constitutes a further limiting, a preliminary decision, that subsequent authorities cannot seriously challenge. After the test lectures and interviews have taken place the commission presents a list of applicants in the order of their preference. The commission has no decision-making authority from a legal point of view! Finally, a formal decision is made by the faculty council. Can all of the members really question the commission's suggestions? The majority of voting members of the board are often not once in attendance at the test lectures. In the end the college parliament (or the senate), has to authorize the decision. Does the board have another choice? It can ask "critical" questions. The result depends on the adeptness with which the people who have to promote the decision present their arguments, or in other words how adept they are at working with selective communication. After the senate's conclusion the "actual" decision occurs within the appropriate department. Naturally they could formally come to another decision, but in practice this happens very rarely. The formal decision-makers are dependent upon a number of preceding decisions of which they can hardly have complete comprehension.

Solutions come about when the line management finally accepts that it must give up power, and that it in fact has already done so. Decisions can be made better in teams. "The real attainment of modern science and technology consists in the fact that one takes completely normal people, thoroughly educates them in a very focused subject, and then via appropriate organizational arrangements, makes sure that their knowledge is combined with that of others. In this way, the genius becomes dispensible" (Galbraith, 1967, p. 78). If we expand this education in a focused subject to also include the capacity to think in a way that spans many subjects, then this statement becomes a way to solve the advisory staff unit principle. In general with group decisions we have the advantage that managers are less likely to revise them than individual decisions. Galbraith's early approach has the advantage that it comes closer to the current reality of how decisions are made than the advisory staff unit principle. "Managers do not make the decisions. The actual decision takes place much further below with planners, technicians, and other specialists" (Galbraith, 1967, p. 85). Galbraith returned to the concept of organizational power in later years. He felt that those that make decisions and identify with the aims of the organization are known as "Agency Men". The more of these types of decision-makers a company has, the stronger is the organization (Galbraith, 1983).

Decisions should take place at the point where the level of information is optimal (Irle, 1971, p. 218).

The suggestion of using team structures to allay the problem of the varying specialized knowledge areas of those participating in the decision-making process, raises the question of how conflicts within teams or in two-way relationships (superiors and subordinates) are to be handled. In principle there are five possibilities here: one's own interests tend to be more or less moderately or strongly considered; the others' interests tend to be more or less moderately or strongly considered. In a "two times two scheme" this yields four possibilities, which scheme is completed by adding the fifth possibility of the compromise between the two modes of interest (see Figure 16.5).

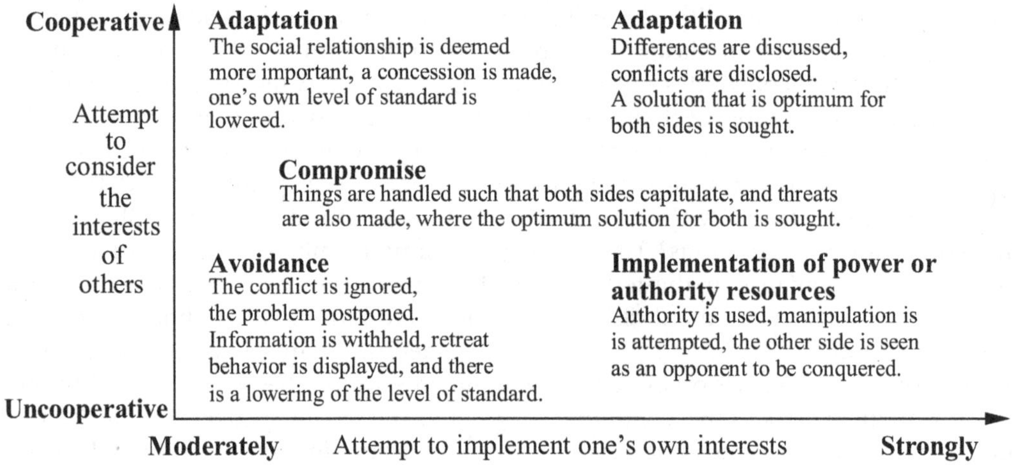

Figure 16.5 Handling conflicts (see Scholl, 1998, p. 436; Thomas, 1976)

THE FUNCTIONING OF MARKETS

The pure economy is only aware of the phenomenon of power from the side of the buyers. It is assumed that there is a large number of autonomous suppliers set against another large number of similarly autonomous buyers, and that via market mechanisms that are as free as possible they will all arrive at the maximum state of mutual welfare. Demand is seen as a quantity that is independent from supply; demand is much more in control of supply. Psychological variables are left out, just as uncertainties are left out, like the problem of an incomplete and presumably error-ridden basis for making decisions, or the question of group decisions. This kind of pure economy disregards every empirical fundamental, eluding empirical testing on the basis of its model assumptions. It presents itself as a formal scientific, tautological model, which has already been logically refuted by Morgenstern (1935) and later by Albert (1972). The assumption of complete information is alone untenable, because this also entails complete prescience. One certainly could maintain the standpoint that complete information is available (an assumption that is untenable however), and that this information however does not pertain to the future. In other words, the model has been purged of all troublesome aspects, up to the point where the desired approach has been achieved. The exclusion of psychology from the pure economy also invites criticism. A science of economic behavior, seen as a special instance of sociology, can lead to usable insights; economics is not an independent science, but rather is a social science (Albert, 1972, p. 23). The attempt to assert a perspective of scientic insight based on a pure economy, independent from all other perspectives, entails the attempt to establish an area that is protected from criticism. However, there is no separate precinct to which any one science belongs (Irle, 1975, p. 13). On the basis of these considerations we will have to say goodbye to the assumption of "consumer sovereignty", and also to the assumption of the independence of demand from supply. It is definitely true that demand can be established or influenced through the corresponding marketing activities.

Wiswede (1983, p. 183) also criticizes economics in its screening out of social science statements due to power considerations. Similar to Wiswede, Scherhorn (1983, p. 50) argues that: "If one factors out normative statements from price theory and competition theory and then merely takes into account the phrases that are empirically rich in content then, strictly speaking, one ends up with a collection of insights regarding market power."

Unequal power positions lead to the maintenance of asymmetrical mutual relationships, or in other words the benefit of the mutual relationship is greater in the long term for the side that is enjoying more power. Power also plays an essential role as a factor in competition. The more market power a supplier has in comparison to competitors, the more likely it is it can implement its interests and overcome deviating interests on the demand side (Scherhorn, 1983, p. 51). An example of this kind of market power is image advantages or trust advantages in competition. The long-term establishing of brand images becomes relevant at this juncture. Boundaries set by the market come up against boundaries established through power (ibid.). Wiswede (1983, p. 185) has contrasted possible consumer counter strategies with the above fundamentals of power according to Cartwright (1959):

a) "Affecting the interaction partner": In this regard Wiswede does not see many possibilities for influencing due to the multitude of "anonymous, depersonalized purchasing acts". The chances of consumers could be improved via coordinated patterns of behavior. Consumers could establish lobby groups to a greater extent than they have in the past.

b) "Changing to another interaction partner": This method is most similar to the conceptions held by a theory of competition, but it only works if many consumers make use of this possibility.

c) "Changing to another product class": At the change of the millenium, 2000/2001, consumers changed their purchasing habits with regard to meat to a considerable extent. This happening reached such an extent that it resulted in actually recognizable consequences for the suppliers. More recently, higher oil prices (from the point of view of environmental protection) have led to consumers choosing more oil efficient vehicles.

d) "The curbing of needs": Here the same ideas apply as in b), in that higher prices lead to a withdrawal of demand, where consumers can additionally attempt to reduce their actual experience of needing things. This serves as a reminder about the comedian George Carlin, who had a reponse to people who said that their needs weren't being met: drop some of your needs!

e) "Shifting of need": A need is reduced in order to enable the satisfaction of another need. When there is is little purchasing power consumers have little choice but to do this.

f) Consumers become habituated to an unsatisfactory situation in the course of time, for example, in the case of long-term increase in price, whereby in the course of time this becomes cognitively reinterpreted in accordance with cognitive dissonance.

Scherhorn (1983, p. 79) assumes that through suppliers' use of targeted disinformation consumers can be put in a position that bears more resemblance to an authority relationship than a mutual exchange process, in that they interpret signals from the provider more as directives, which they then obey. He proceeds according to the assumption that consumers from lower levels of society are more subject to this danger than are those occupying the higher levels.

Müller (1983, pp. 640 and 641) infers long-term disadvantages for consumers due to unequal distribution of power in consumer goods markets. At the moment the weaker side is not in a position to effectively represent its interests. For this reason a more powerful authority, in other words the state, can take on the task of representing their interests. This does not necessarily have to be seen as an "imposing of the will on mature consumers". Consumers are not really able to assess what is being consumed owing to a quantitatively limited information processing capacity.

On the provider's side there is the possibility of protecting or consolidating market power in that the competition may be reduced. This can be attempted via legal or illegal cooperation between providers; legal "protection" can be demanded. Provider power can be acquired or expanded in this way, in that individual providers select conflicting strategies and attempt to hinder competitors in their activities (see Scherhorn, 1983, p. 52).

Perhaps the most outstanding feature of consumer goods marketing is the information disadvantage of consumers in relation to providers. They are able to assess the quality of products to a much lesser extent than can the recipients of productive goods marketing. This is due to the multitude of varying products that are consumed in private households, which alone due to the sheer quantity makes coping with the flood of information—independent of intellectual capacity—virtually impossible. Although information overload is certainly not just a consumer specific phenomenon, it is of particular relevance here. In the productive goods sector the purchasing authorities concentrate on a relatively small number of different products. In the consumer goods sector private consumers have to juggle over 2,000 different products. Therefore there is necessarily the tendency to simplify purchasing and information behavior.

Governmental consumer protection can serve the function of alleviating this power disadvantage. Governmental interventions can certainly reduce the efficiency of the national economy. On the other hand, a completely free market enonomy (which is only theoretically possible; it would operate completely without any legal regulations) would bring with it undesirable circumstances. In a completely free economy children would also be able to buy alcohol, and anyone would be able to produce and distribute pharmaceutical drugs. This would certainly create more jobs, but the consequences would not be desirable. Thus protective regulations are more valued than economic advantages. The oft-heard allegation against almost all governmental regulations, that they reduce economic potency, is just as much based in ideology as the assertion of the consumer's total dependence on the provider's marketing measures. In reality the idea is simply to normatively evaluate the undesirable consequences of a relatively free market economy, and to set these against the costs of governmental interventions. The decision is then always of a political nature.

POWER IN AND BY WAY OF GROUPS

Insofar as people are oriented toward others in their behavior, these others exercise power, whether they want to or not. For example in matters of taste and with regard to normative things people are insecure and are on the look out for behavioral standards. Reference groups can deliver such standards. Reference groups are groups that the person himself is not a member of whose standards are strived for or have been adopted by the person. In marketing this effect is taken advantage of via presenting the behavioral modes of attractive groups (Engel, Blackwell and Miniard, 1993, p. 143 et seq.). People are also members of various groups; a differentiation is made between primary and secondary groups with regard to contact intenstity. Primary groups could be circles of friends or families, and secondary groups could be clubs, colleges. Further more differentiation is made between formal (family, college membership) and informal groups (circles of friends). More important is the question of what influence groups have on the behavior and values of a person. In this connection a difference is made between groups that are accepted or rejected. Acceptance does not yet mean that the behavior of members of this group serves as a measuring stick for one's own behavior. Within work groups, effects of power may be evident, based on power resources in accordance with Cartwright (1959). Additionally, Galbraith (1983) discussed the concept of countervailing power, which is an equal power response created when existing power is seen as being negatively utilized.

An interesting case is that of the influence within groups of minorities without any formal power resources. Moscovici's (1976 and 1980; see also Moscovici and Faucheaux, 1972, and Maas, West and Clark, 1993) studies deal with the influence of minorities without formal power or status in groups.

According to Moscovici the minority, who is in command of neither power nor status, has to assert his viewpoint via a particular mode of behavior. This way of behaving promises success, and is an extremely consistent insistence on their own, minority, viewpoint. They must unerringly represent their own viewpoint. They cannot diverge from their original argument in any way; they have to continuously set their arguments against those of the majority. In this connection they may not allow themselves to be influenced by the majority's pressure in any way. They must not signal a readiness to compromise in any sense. From Ricateau's (1971) work we can certainly say that the minority should not stereotypically repeat their arguments. The logical structure of the arguments has to remain the same but the verbalization should be varied. A continuous repetition of the same statements will come off as redundant and will soon be rejected. Variability in choice of words maintains the other group members' interest.

Focused insistence on a minority viewpoint in relation to the majority fulfills two functions, both of which lead to the majority becoming unsure and leaning toward a possible joining of the minority.

a) It appears to be a conflict that is at an impasse; the group structure appears unstable. The minority gives the impression of not being prepared to compromise. For this reason the existence of the group or the group climate may be appear to be in danger for the long term. To the majority it seems as if the conflict can only be solved through compromise. At least those in the group who are interested in harmony may be motivated to make some accommodations.

b) Due to their resolutely sticking to their guns, the minority gives the impression of being very convinced of their viewpoint, and seems to have good reasons for it. This increases the readiness of various members of the majority to adjust to the minority opinion. This conviction of opinion conveys the impression that they are particularly intensely focused on the subject of the conflict. Many members of the majority have only developed a superficial conviction and are therefore are more easily made to feel uncertain.

An important factor for minority success is time. In a focused manner the minority has to maintain their divergent viewpoint over a long period of time. They cannot allow themselves to give in to time pressure. Pressure to decide can become an "ally" for the minority if the majority believes it has to decide due to time pressure.

Moscovici supplemented his theory of minority influence with his conversion theory (1980). If people allow themselves to be influenced, then the question arises whether the influence has only taken place on an external level, or whether the behavioral or opinion change has taken place due to inner conviction. The result is as follows: With the influence of minorities other people will also change their inner conviction; whoever allows themselves to be influenced by majorities predominantly allow this only superficially.

The effect of allowing oneself to be internally convinced by minorities increases with the extent of whatever previous discrepancy of opinion one may have encountered, and with the extent to which the conflict has grown (with regard to the significance of this discrepancy of opinion for the individual members of the group). This can be explained with reference to dissonance theory. The more one's own opinion changes and the more significant this opinion seems to be, the greater the pressure is to justify this change of opinion to oneself, all the more so since the minority in the studies here in question were not operating according to formal power.

QUESTIONS FOR DISCUSSION

1. What are the various ways that power can be exerted?
2. Elaborate on the factors of power, the resources of power, and the reservations about using power.
3. Is power better served when used, or only when threatened for use?
4. Provide some examples of power structure and use in your organization, church, and family.
5. What form of organizational structure makes the most out of the use of power in a multinational firm?

Bibliography

Albert, H.: *Ökonomische Ideologie und Politische Theorie* (2nd edn), Göttingen: 1972. (*Economical Ideology and Political Theory*).
—— *Traktat Über Rationale Praxis*. Tübingen: 1978. (*Treatise on Rational Practice*).
Berkowitz, L. (ed.): *Advances in Experimental Social Psychology*, vol. 6. New York, London, Toronto: 1972.
—— *Advances in Experimental Social Psychology*, vol. 13. New York, London: 1980.
Cartwright, D.: A field theoretical conception of power. In: Cartwright, D. (ed.): *Studies in Social Power*. Ann Arbor: 1959, 183–220.
—— Influence, leadership, and control, In: March, J.G. (ed.): *Handbook of Organizations*. Chicago: 1965, 1–47.
Dunette, M.D. (ed.): *Handbook of Industrial and Organizational Psychology*. Chicago: 1976.
Engel, J.E., Blackwell, R.D. and Miniard, P.W.: *Consumer Behavior* (7th edn). Fort Worth, Philadelphia, San Diego: 1993.
Esser, H.: *Soziologie—Allgemeine Grundlagen*. Frankfurt am Main, New York: 1993. (*Sociology—General Foundations*).
Foucault, M.: *Überwachen und Strafen*. Frankfurt: 1976. (*Supervision and Punishment*).
Frey, D. and Irle, M. (eds): *Theorien der Sozialpsychologie, vol. II: Gruppen- und Lerntheorien* (2nd edn), Bern, Göttingen, Toronto, Seattle: 1993. (*Theories of Social Psychology, vol. II: Group Theories and Trained Theories*).
Galbraith, J.K.: *The New Industrial State*, Houghton Mifflin Company, Boston, 1967.
—— *The Anatomy of Power*, Houghton Mifflin Company, Boston, 1983.
Hahne, A.: *Kommunikation in der Organisation*. Opladen: 1998. (*Communication in the Organization*).
Halisch, F. and Kuhl, J. (eds): *Motivation, Intention and Volition*. Berlin: 1987.
Heckhausen, H.: *Hoffnung und Furcht in der Leistungsmotivation*. Meisenheim: 1963. (*Hope and Fear in Achievement Motivation*).
—— *Motivation und Handeln* (2nd edn), Berlin, Heidelberg, New York: 1989. (*Motivation and Actions*).
Irle, M.: *Macht und Entscheidung in Organisationen—Studie gegen das Linie-Stab-Prinzip*. Frankfurt am Main: 1971. (*Power and Decision in Organizations—Study Against the Line-Staff-Principle*).

—— *Lehrbuch der Sozialpsychologie*. Göttingen, Toronto, Zürich: 1975. (*Textbook of Social Psychology*).

—— (ed.): *Marktpsychologie*, 1. Halbband. Göttingen, Toronto, Zürich: 1983. (*Market Psychology*).

Kipins, D.: The powerholder. In: Tedeschi, J.T. (ed.): *Perspectives on Social Power*. Chicago: 1974, 82–122.

Lay, R.: *Dialektik für Manager*. Reinbek bei Hamburg: 1978. (*Dialectics for Managers*).

—— *Manipulation Durch die Sprache*. Reinbek bei Hamburg: 1980. (*Manipulation Through Language*).

—— *Führen Durch das Wort*. Reinbek bei Hamburg: 1981. (*Leading Through the Word*).

Lewin, K.: *Principles of Topological Psychology*. New York: 1936.

—— *Field Theory in Social Science*. Chicago: 1951.

—— Allgemeine feldtheorie. In: *Kurt-Lewin-Werkausgabe, vol. 4, Feldtheorie* (von Graumann, C.F.). Bern, Stuttgart: 1982, 39–131. (General field theory. In: *Kurt Lewin Work Edition*, vol. 4, *Field Theory*).

Luhmann, N.: *Macht* (2nd edn), Stuttgart: 1988. (*Power*).

—— *Die Wirtschaft der Gesellschaft* (2nd edn), Frankfurt am Main: 1996. (*The Economy of the Company*).

—— *Die Gesellschaft der Gesellschaft* (vol. 1). Frankfurt am Main: 1997. (*The Company of the Company*).

—— *Organisation und Entscheidung*. Wiesbaden: 2000. (*Organization and Decision*).

Maas, A., West, S.G. and Clark, R.D.: Soziale einflüsse von minoritäten in gruppen. In Frey, D. and Irle, M. (eds): *Theorien der Sozialpsychologie, vol. II: Gruppen- und Lerntheorien* (2nd edn). Bern, Göttingen, Toronto, Seattle: 1993, 13, 65–100. (Social influences of minorities in groups. In: *Theories of Social Psychology, vol. II Group Theories and Trained Theories*).

March, J.G. (ed.): *Handbook of Organizations*. Chicago: 1965.

Morgenstern, C.: Vollkommene voraussicht und wirtschaftliches gleichgewicht. *Zeitschrift für Nationalökonomie*, 1935, 6, 337–357. (Perfect foresight and economic balance).

Moscovici, S.: *Social Influence and Social Change*. London: 1976.

—— Toward a theory of conversion behavior. In: Berkowitz, L. (ed.): *Advances in Experimental Social Psychology*, vol. 13. New York, London, Toronto: 1980, 208–239.

—— and Faucheux, C.: Social influence, conformity bias and the study of active minorities, In: Berkowitz, L. (ed.): *Advances in Experimental Social Psychology*, vol. 6. New York, London, Toronto: 1972, 149–202.

Müller, G.F.: Anbieter-nachfrager-interaktionen. In: Irle, M. (ed.): Marktpsychologie, 1. Halbband. Göttingen, Toronto, Zürich: 1983, 626–735. (Supply-demand interactions. In *Market Psychology*).

Rastetter, D.: *Sexualität und Herrschaft in Organisationen*. Opladen: 1994. (*Sexuality and Domination in Organizations*).

Ricateau, P.: Processus de categorisation d'autrui et les mecanismes d'influence. *Bulletin de Psycholgie*, 1971, 24, 909–919. (Process of categorization of others and harvesting mechanisms of influence).

Scherhorn, G.: Die funktionsfähigkeit von konsumgütermärkten. In: Irle, M. (ed.): *Marktpsychologie*, 1. Halbband, Göttingen, Toronto, Zürich: 1983, 45–150. (The utility of consumer goods markets. In *Market Psychology*).

Schmalt, H.-D.: Power motivation and the perception of control. In Halisch, F. and Kuhl, J. (eds): *Motivation, Intention, and Volition*. Berlin: 1987, 101–113.

Scholl, W.: Grundkonzepte der organisation. In: Schuler, H. (ed.): *Organisationspsychologie* (2nd edn), Bern, Göttingen, Toronto, Seattle: 1998, 409–443. (Basic concepts of the organization. In *Organization Psychology*).

Schuler, H. (ed.): *Organisationspsychologie* (2nd edn), Bern, Göttingen, Toronto, Seattle: 1998. (*Organization Psychology*).

Stockdale, M.S. (ed.): *Sexual Harassment in the Workplace—Perspectives, Frontiers, and Response Strategies*. Thousand Oaks, London, New Delhi: 1996.

Tedeschi, J.T. (ed.): *Perspectives on Social Power*. Chicago: 1974.

Thomas, K.W.: Conflict and conflict management. In: Dunette, M.D. (ed.): *Handbook of Industrial and Organizational Psychology*. Chicago: 1976, 889–935.

Unger, F. and Fuchs, W.: *Management der Marktkommunikation* (2nd edn.), Heidelberg: 1999. (*Management of Market Communication*).

Weber, M.: *Wirtschaft und Gesellschaft* (5th edn.), Tübingen: 1972. (*Economy and Company*).

Wiswede, G.: Marktsoziologie. In: Irle, M. (ed.): *Marktpsychologie*, 1. Halbband. Göttingen, Toronto, Zürich: 1983, 151–224. (Market sociology. In *Market Psychology*).

17 *Theories of Control— Customers' Desire for Control*

Psychological Concept of Control

Control theoretical extensions have developed into an important research area of psychology and the behavioral sciences (Frey and Irle, 1993, p. 126; Wiswede, 1991, p. 92; Wong, 1992, p. 143). This is primarily because it has been established that psychological control research is highly useful, especially in the area of perception and since the concept of control is practiced in many different areas of life (that is, work, health) and has proved to be an important source of physical as well as psychic well-being (Bungard and Schultz-Gambard, 1990, p. 145; Osnabrügge, Stahlberg and Frey, 1993, p. 164). This research also especially concerns economic actions as economic research focuses on frequently controlled, planned and systematic behaviors. So for example consumers must have their expenditures under control, and businesses must be in a position to keep promises vis-à-vis their customers.

White (1959) performed an important contribution to the concept of psychological control. White turns against a drive theory explanation of behavior because certain manners can be explained, for example, exploring or arbitrarily changing the environment, which is insufficiently explained by the satisfaction of primary drives. These manners are driven rather from that what the individual learns to explain for themselves effectively within their environment. Hence White postulates (1959, p. 318) that an innate basic necessity exists to experience (efficiency motivation) themselves as a cause of actions and variations in the environment.

In later works, these considerations of White (1959) are taken up especially by Bandura (1977), DeCharms (1968), Lefcourt (1973) and Seligman (1975) and have become more fully developed. It is through these extensions that the perception of control leads to feelings of self-competence and self-worth and that well-being is negatively influenced by the loss of control.

Control is given most unambiguously then if objective contingencies exist between an action and its consequences. This form of control corresponds to the colloquial significance of control in the sense of a planned and driving influence. The psychological concept of control comprises in addition the subjective perception of contingencies between action and its consequence. Thompson (1981) distinguishes four possible forms of psychological control: (1) susceptibleness exists if a person perceives the possibility to be able to influence an event or its consequences through their own behavior, (2) predictability includes whether a person has information about the relevant event, (3) cognitive control comprises reinterpreting, playing down or avoiding; it enables the subject to appear as less event aversive and (4) retrospective control means the retroactive statement of causes for already entered or past events.

With the more comprehensive meaning of the psychological control concept, control can be exercised therefore not only by active exertion of influence on the environment, but rather also by cognitive processes. Verifiableness exists here that the individual can explain or predict an event. Control can be given also to persons of competence whom are held in trust, for example, management consultants, salesmen, or politicians, (a lower level of control here), because it is assumed that these individuals possess the capacity to exercise control (Rothbaum, Weisz and Snyder, 1982). These different forms of control permit the person, in an environment in which many events of direct influence are removed, to experience a feeling of control. Control loss does not exist if a person cannot exercise control in a described situation, or if control over one of the persons does not exist (Osnabrügge, Stahlberg and Frey, 1993, p. 129).

Interaction of Person and Environment

Which possibilities of control an individual in a concrete situation has available, and which of them he or she uses, will be determined by both the characteristics of the individual and of the environment. At the same time, there can become a sense of an interaction between the person and the environment, as they are mutually influencing both themselves and their environment. (Krampen, 1982, p. 78; Osnabrügge, Stahlberg and Frey, 1993, p. 138).

CONTROL AS AN INDIVIDUAL FEATURE

Although some theorists (Deci and Ryan, 2002) wish to view control as a basic need, individual differences in the amount in which a person attempts to achieve control exist nevertheless. In order to determine this personality feature, Burger and Cooper (1979) developed a scale for the detection of individual control motivations, which is known as the Desirability of Control Scale. Persons with a high control motivation are driven to exercise different areas of everyday control. They frequently attend executive functions (Burger, 1992), engage themselves in interest groups (Zimmerman and Rappaport, 1988), are less easily influenced (Burger, 1987), and have higher expectations as well as high goal achievement behavior (Burger, 1985, 1992).

In an investigation by Glass (1977) it was shown that especially type-A persons, who are marked by competition inclination, achievement orientation, permanent time pressure and hostility, show a distinct control motivation. Type-B persons are seen as being less concerned with control, and by not expressing a loss of control as threatening.. The interpretation of type-A behavior is based on Glass (1977), and is seen as a characteristic reaction style upon being threatened with control loss, which shows an especially high control motivation (Osnabrügge, Stahlberg and Frey, 1985, p. 139). If one considers that these people have an increased risk of coronary heart disease (Haynes, Feinleib and Kannel, 1980; Rosenman, Brand, Jenkins, et al., 1975), one can refer to the investigation by Glass as to the possible negative effects of having a high control motivation, with the increased stress levels contributing to heart conditions.

Another concept that has high importance in the control theory literature, is that of the locus of control of reinforcement, that was developed by Rotter in the social learning theory of personality framework (Rotter, 1954, 1966). Krampen (1982, p. 1) has introduced a framework for this as the concept of control convictions. Here one understands the expectations generalized over situations and areas of life of an individual about whether they can (internal locus of control) influence important events in their lives by their own behavior or whether they assume that these events depend (external locus of control) on other persons or on the good fortune, chance, fate or control more powerfully. Rotter (1966) developed a questionnaire for the detection of the characteristics (Internal External SCALE 2) that proposes a one dimensional, bipolar personality characteristic exhibiting extremes in both the internal and the external perspectives.

The one-dimensional estimate of the detection of the control convictions was criticized by different authors. Before this background, Levenson (1972, 1974) developed among other things a scale for the detection of three independent aspects of control convictions (internal and external control convictions, fatalistic external control convictions). In a multitude of empirical investigations, the acceptance of the multidimensionality of control convictions was able to become confirmed (Krampen, 1982). After that, differing estimates of the detection of generalized control convictions were established. Additionally, procedures for the detection of area specific control convictions were established. These procedures primarily focused on certain areas of life such as work (Hodgkinson, 1992; Spector, 1988), health (Wallston, Wallston and DeVellis, 1978; Lohaus and Schmitt, 1989), relating to alcohol consumption (Krampen and Fischer, 1988) and enterprise (Müller, 2000). A specific gauge for the detection of control convictions in the area of the consumption behavior does not yet exist.

Regardless of the social learning theory and a theoretical integration, the idea of the conviction of control has encouraged a multitude of investigations, and thus is highly important in psychological research (Hautzinger and Bommer, 1992, p. 192; Herkner, 1991, p. 127; Nelson, 1993, p. 155). The previous empirical results together appear to show, among other things, that internal control convictions stand in relation to a positive self-worth (Chandler, 1976), higher life contentment (Krampen, 1991), a higher resistance vis-à-vis influence attempts (Phares, 1976), the striving after professional independence (Müllers, 1999) and a more frequent use of cognitive control strategies (Krampen, 1982). External control convictions are connected, on the other hand, to among other things, with a higher general anxiety (Archer, 1979; Krampen, 1991; Ollendick, 1979), materialism (Hunt, Kernan, Chatterjee et al., 1990) and depression (Hermann, 1980; Krampen, 1991). Similar to the studies of control motivation, internal conviction of control can also be connected with negative aspects. Such inadequate internal control convictions exist then if a person believes they can (owing to a lost sense of reality) influence all events through their behavior.

VERIFIABLENESS AS A FEATURE OF THE ENVIRONMENT

Next to the individual features (that is, control motivation, control convictions) is the perception and/or execution of control as well as situational factors. In a series of investigations, it could be shown that different features of the environment exercise an influence on which form of control is given for an individual and which positive or negative consequences result. Out of these multitude of investigations and/or investigation extensions two are supposed to be represented as being exemplary. One documents the relevance of situational factors, while the other covers the meaning of individual dispositions.

The effects of influential situations, among other things, were examined in comprehensive experimental works on the theory of learned helplessness (Abramson, Seligman and Teasdale, 1978; Seligman, 1975). A two-phase experiment plan stands behind most experiments of this theory. In the first phase, the development of three attempt groups results. While a group possesses the objective possibility to control (susceptibleness) aversive attractions, this possibility does not exist for a second group (influentialness). The third group possesses no aversive attractions (control group). In the second phase, the effects of the different situational conditions are examined. So Hiroto (1974) in the framework of an experimental study, was able to show that persons who had no possibility in the first phase, to influence loud noises objectively, had significant difficulties in learning how to turn down the noise in the second phase through an instrumental reaction.

The central assumption of the original theory of learned helplessness, that objective uncontrollableness, when repeated, always leads to negative motivational, cognitive and affective effects, has been criticized repeatedly. The reason for this was, among other things, the observation of all daily situations that proved the existence of different reactions to uncontrollableness. Abramson, Seligman and Teasdale (1978) took this circumstance into account in their revised theory of helplessness in that they integrated attribute processes and the importance of uncontrolled events into their new extension. So Pittman and Pittman (1979) were able to show that the perception also depends on control of generalized expectations such as internal versus external control convictions, therefore on individual features.

A more practical work for the investigation of the relevance of control possibilities comes from Schulz (1976). It examined older nursing home inhabitants, who had either no control (uncontrollableness) and no knowledge of the time or the duration of a weekly social contact (visit by students) or did understand the time and the duration of the visit, but had no influence on either of them (predictability), or were able to set time and duration of the visits independently (susceptibleness and predictibility). A further group of nursing home inhabitants received no visits (control groups). The goal of this work was to examine whether some features which are observed frequently in older persons in nursing homes, such as depression, helplessness, physical troubles and physical dismantling, can at least be partially explained by loss of control. The investigation results showed that control and/or the predictibility of the weekly visits had positive effects on the subjective well-being, the activity rate and the constitution of the old persons, compared to the uncontrollableness condition and the control group. A study by Langer and Rodin (1976) reaches a similar conclusion. These positive effects were not observed in a replication study carried out in Germany (Hautzinger and Bommer, 1992). As an explanation for these deviating conditions, the authors name among other things the fact that the random sample shows a lower socioeconomic status, which could result that this group lived for years under rather dependent, less predictable conditions, and the practice of control is connected based on linking experience with stress. Also this interpretation refers last of all to an interaction of the person and the environment.

Capacity for Self-control

THEORETICAL FOUNDATIONS

The employment with theories and methods of self-regulation and self-control become more meaningful in different areas, for example in organizational psychology (Cervone, Jiwani and Wood, 1991; Kanfer and Kanfer, 1991), in saving behavior (Wärneryd, 1989) or in consumption behavior (Campbell, 1987; Hoch and Loewenstein, 1991), primarily. This importance is based upon the belief that the individual controls a series of actions that are not determined through attractions in the environment, but rather by the self-control of the subject. The following examples are primarily concerned with the works of Kanfer (1977, 1987) and Reinecker (1978, 1990) because both authors influenced the theoretical and empirical work in this area substantially.

Under self-regulation, Kanfer, Reinecker and Schmelzer (1991, p. 25) understood the fact that a person drives their own behavior with regard to self-made goals, whereby the regulation results through a modification of the behavior itself or through influencing one of the conditions of the behavior. A similar view of self-regulation was presented in Karoly (1993, p. 25). Self-regulation does not follow internal settlements that are independent from the influence of situational factors, but rather out of a dynamic interaction from external environment (alpha variable), manners and/or processes of the person herself (beta variable) and physiological as well as biological prerequisites (gamma variable). To explain this interaction Kanfer used an example: whether a person steals bread depends on what extent the alpha variables favour, for example through the easy accessibility of the bread, and the gamma variables promote this, for example through a continuous hunger condition. In this situation, the intensity of the beta variables, for example the person's attitude, can either allow them to steal, or attempts to distract them to stop the stealing behavior (Kanfer, 1977, p. 802).

The extension to self-regulation can be used fruitfully for economic questions. For some years the classic medium of cash has become increasingly replaced by card supported payment systems (that is, credit cards, customer cards). When the self-regulatoratory behavior is transferred to the situation of the purchase with card supported payment systems, clearly these payment forms ease (alpha variable) the use of financial resources, but simultaneously the understanding of the experienced expenditures and the associated costs are impeded. If one considers the natural boundaries of the human information processing system (gamma variable), card supported payment systems could lead to a higher level of abstractness in comparison to cash, and in addition the capacity to remember experienced expenditure could decrease. This assumption is based on the fact that the concreteness (graphic appearance) is also decisive for how well information is stored in the memory. (Dirx and Craik, 1992; Kroeber-Riel and Weinberg, 2003, p. 231 and p. 350; Paivio, 1971, 1986). Independent of individual and/or cognitive processes (beta variables), card supported payment systems therefore change the general conditions of self-regulatory processes. The possibility of self-regulation differs between cash and card supported payment systems additionally as the wallet can be looked at as an external information database. In a given purchase situation, this wallet permits a continuous survey with respect to the experienced consumption expenditure and the solvency of the individual, without that this information is stored in the memory and is retrievable from there. A comparable information state requires an active information processing in card supported payment systems on the other hand. Cash offers an advantage based on its concreteness and its function as external information storage with respect to self-regulatation behavior vis-à-vis card supported payment systems.

The sketched acceptances for the influence of card supported payment systems on consumption could be proven in an experimental investigation (Raab, 1998). To realize this investigation, a simulation game (department store game) was developed in collaboration with one department store. The department store game permits the simulation of a purchase situation and to examine the influence of different payments systems. The only variable, that in the framework of the investigation was different, was the form of the money. One half of the test subjects played the simulation game with cash and the other half with a customer card of the department store. Given the described control theory extensions, the hypothesis was diverted that the objective control loss is larger in payment by means of card than in cash payments, the objective loss of control is here defined as a sum of the difference between actually purchased sums and how much the subject thought that they have purchased (goodness of the estimation). In order to test the hypothesis, approximately 20 minutes after termination of the department store game, each participant is asked how much they purchased in the department store game approximately altogether. Corresponding to the hypothesis, participants who handled their purchases by means of cash, more exactly estimated the amount of their consumption than persons who handled their purchases by means of card. The average sum of the difference between actually purchased sums and sums thought to have been purchased amounted to 115 DM for participants with cash, and 207 DM for participants with cards.

Under self-regulatory viewpoints, it is of special relevance to what extent the expenditures are underestimated or overestimated This establishes that especially this can lead to a lower estimation of the expenditures, and in addition, that self-regulatory processes remain undone and if additional consumer spending are experienced that would not result in correct estimation or overestimation. Fundamentally two questions stand therefore: first, to what extent do consumers underestimate or overestimate the amount of their consumer spending, and second, do consumers with cards frequently underestimate their expenditures than does a consumer with cash? In the framework of the investigation, it could be assessed whether consumers generally underestimate rather than overestimate the amount of their expenditures. Regardless of the form of money used, the tendency seems to be therefore to underestimate rather than to overestimate the amount of consumer spending. With respect to the second question, it appeared that persons with a card underestimated their expenditures significantly more frequently than persons with cash, and in addition that the deviation of the actually purchased sum was significantly higher than that of persons with cash. Money in form of card supported payment systems influences accordingly therefore not only the accuracy of the estimation of experienced expenditure (see above), but also card supported payment systems lead to the underestimation of consumption expenditures (see Table 17.1). If the amount of the expenditure is incorrectly estimated, it is nevertheless possible that self-regulation processes can be effective. A prerequisite for this is to be sure that the person is aware that they cannot estimate and/or control the situation correctly. In many cases, people assume that they are able to control certain things, although it is objectively not possible. If a person is aware that they can a control a situation, even if this is objectively not true (illusion of control), there is missing one of the central prerequisites to self-regulation and/or self-control. This aspect is more closely discussed in the next section.

Table 17.1 Estimation of expenditure consumer spending under consideration of the payment system

	Consumption expenditure underestimated	Consumption expenditure overestimated
Cash	22 (27.5)	20 (14.5)
Card	37 (31.5)	11 (16.5)

Legend: The italic printed figures represent the amount (frequency) of the observed persons under the condition cash and card. In the parenthesis, the statistically expected frequencies are indicated.

$Chi^2 = 5.01, p < .05$

ILLUSION OF CONTROL

The illusion of control exists where individuals believe that they are able to control certain events even though this does not correspond to reality (Langer, 1975). Accordingly, many people behave in objectively uncontrollable situations as if the occurring effects resulted from their efforts, abilities or behavior: persons for example, who can chose their own ticket when playing the lottery, believe to have increased chances of winning in comparison with persons who get a ticket that was assigned to them by someone else. With this in mind, Alloy and Abramson (1979) carried out a series of experiments. The test subjects had ability to influence the lighting up of a green light. They could either press a button or opt not to press it. The test subjects estimated the degree of their control on the basis of a scale of 0 to 100 percent. At the same time, different attempt conditions appeared, and these varied with respect to the size of the contingencies and the number of the affirmations. Highly depressive people judged the objective possibilities of control very correctly. The depressed subjects did not overestimate their own control possibilities in objectively uncontrollable situations. There is a series of further investigations by Alloy (1992) with illusionary control that refer to psychic well-being and a high self-worth (Alloy and Clements, 1992; Koenig, Clements and Alloy, 1992; Taylor and Brown, 1988). For Langer (1975), a certain amount of psychic well-being and control illusion are necessary prerequisites by which result feelings of self-competence and positive self-worth. The original cause of control possibilities of the overestimation today are attributed to motivational processes (that is, influence of the self-worth) and to cognitive processes (that is processing of earlier contingency information) (Herkner, 1991; Koenig, Clements and Alloy, 1992).

Until today, control theory research has concerned itself primarily with the positive effects of the illusion of control. On the other hand, the possible negative effects of an illusion of control is given very little attention (Wong, 1992, p. 145). At the same time, the relevance for different areas of research for these negative consequences can clearly be recognized. In the previous section, it was represented that self-regulatory processes become effective only if consumers perceive that they do not estimate consumption amounts incorrectly. In the framework of the investigation of Raab (1998) it could be shown that card supported payment systems lead not only to additional expenditure, but that the capacity decreases for the accurate estimation of experienced expenditure, and that people subjectively assume that they are able to estimate the expenditures with card supported payment systems just as well as with cash. Although cards lead to an increased difficulty in the estimation of experienced expenditure, consumers experience the same degree of subjective security. This means that an increase of the illusion of the spending control leads in addition to a decrease in effectiveness of self-regulatory processes.

The phenomenon of the illusion of control can be observed also in the stock markets. In a continuous cycle of economic growth, which is connected predominantly with positive invetment experience by the investors, a feeling of control is produced (Rapp, 1997, pp. 90–91). Stock exchange participants assume to be able to control the market through corresponding strategies and technologies. Control means in this case, the capability to predict certain events. This assumes that they know the relevant market information. The necessary information is however frequently not available, or they are only accessible for a prior point in time. Investors, especially private investors, often believe nevertheless that they are able to control and/or time the market (Mass and Weibler, 1997, pp. 113–114). At the same time, it can also be observed that successes (appreciations) are frequently assumed to lead back to their own capabilities. Poor performance (losses) would be attributed, on the other hand, to unfavorable or unpredictable market developments. Herewith clear parallels to gambling appear. Given the recent increases in share trades over the Internet, it would be necessary in the future to obtain a better understanding of investment behavior (Meyer, 2000).

The illusion of control is also promoted in many cases in that certain institutions purport and probably even believe that they have the ability to be able to control certain things, that they cannot objectively control. The individuals learn a feeling of deputy control in that they trust these institutions. How deceitful and dangerous this illusion can be, as examples such as the nuclear catastrophes in Three Mile Island and Chernobyl, the development of the hole in the ozone layer, the worldwide loss of usable land through ground erosion and the recent financial crisis help to illustrate.

SELF-CONTROL AND INDEBTEDNESS

In an empirical investigation by Lunt and Livingstone (1991) it was examined which factors are seen by persons as relevant for when consumers get themselves into debt. At the same time, the other question was to observe whether both internal and external reasons are relevant. Belonging to the internal factors: lack of self-control (that is, impulsive purchase behavior, lack of self-discipline), lack of realism (that is, missing knowledge in the finance area), pleasure (that is, joy in shopping) and greed. The external reasons surround: the credit system (that is, comfort with credit cards, amount of the credit limit), commercial pressure (that is, advertising), social pressure (that is, wishes of the children) and external problems (that is, job loss). Additionally, a multitude of personal factors become eventful (that is, birth of a child, divorce, etc.). In a further investigation, the authors examined the causalities of these factors, that is, to what extent individuals go out, which certain factors are influenced by others and/or influence others. At the same time, it appeared that individuals see essential influential factors with regard to self-control in the amount of credit limit and the comfort of credit cards. The influence of credit cards was able to become also covered in a newer experimental study (Raab, 1998, pp. 166–168). In the framework of the investigation, the readiness for indebtedness increased significantly with payments by credit cards in comparison with payments in cash (see Table 17.2). If one grasps the summary results of Lunt and Livingstone (1991), consumers are influenced their individual capacity for self-control and also by institutional and/or situational factors.

Table 17.2   Readiness for indebtedness depending on the payment system

	No indebtedness	Indebtedness
Cash	*34* (28.0)	*18* (24.0)
Card	*22* (28.0)	*30* (24.0)

Legend: The italic printed figures represent the amount (frequency) of the observed persons under the condition cash and card. In the parenthesis, the statistically expected frequencies are indicated.

$Chi^2 = 4.68$, p < .05

While the preceding investigation of Lunt and Livingstone (1991) concerned itself generally with the reasons that consumers make for when persons get into debt themselves responsibly, Livingstone and Lunt (1992) examined in a further study those variables that persons distinguish from one another with and without debt. The differences in both person groups resulted on the basis of the statements of those questioned made concerning their present financial situation. Attitude proved itself as one of the central influences, especially in the amount vis-à-vis credit. For persons with debt, credit in higher amounts represented something useful as well as comfortable and was considered a part of the modern lifestyle. They wanted to satisfy their needs without saving as in consumption there is a possibility to attain recognition. The causes for the debt is both in themselves and in institutional factors. To the individual causes belong, especially the satisfaction and confirmation that is experienced in the consumption, and the loss of self-control in contact with financial matters and in purchase actions. As a central institutional influence factor, the credit system, with which possibility to be able to use, relatively easy credit, and the amount of the credit limit are named. The amount of the income does not on the other hand influence whether persons use credit. To be sure the amount of the average debt climbs with the amount of the income. Of even more relevance with respect to the amount of indebtedness, is the amount of the credit, however. With the amount of the credit taken, the indebtedness climbs. A reference could be made that that people make use of higher amounts of credit to the cover the lack of liquidity and utilize credit to make necessary interest payments on different financing sources. Through the introduction of card supported payment systems, these possibilities increase.

Using a database of a large number of borrowers from different banks, Dessart and Kuylen (1986) examined the institutional, socioeconomic, psychological and behavior related causes of problematic indebtedness situations. The amount of the credit limit proved itself as the most important influential factor. In a more exact analysis, it appeared that the probability of a problematic indebtedness situation is especially large, if there exists both unfavorable institutional factors (two and more credits) and unfavorable personal characteristics (that is, external control conviction) simultaneously. In the case of credit utilization, if there exists rather favorable individual features (that is, internal control conviction) the probability of a problematic indebtedness situation decreases to zero. These results support the thesis of an interaction between institutional and individual factors as a cause of problematic indebtedness situations.

A further interesting result of this study is the observation there exists a curvilinear relationship between the probability of running into a problematic indebtedness situation, and the state of knowledge with regard to financial questions (that is, credit forms, credit banks) (see Figure 17.1). Borrowers with a middle state of knowledge clearly show an increased risk. This result of the work of Dessart and Kuylen (1986) can be interpreted in the sense of control illusion: people with a middle knowledge overestimate their financial capacities for judging their situation. This increases their readiness to use credit and leads to an increased nature of problematic repayment. Individuals with a low or high state of knowledge on the other hand judge their situations either very carefully based on their missing knowledge or rationally based on their high knowledge, which both reduces the risk of borrowing too much. The negative consequences of a control illusion for the consumer are also here recognizable.

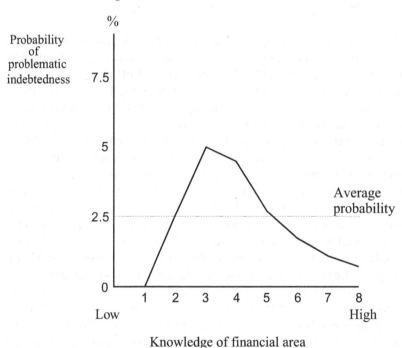

Figure 17.1 Probability of a problematic indebtedness situation and the state of knowledge with regard to financial matters (Dessert and Kuylen, 1986, p. 322)

Summary

Control theoretical extensions and insights can be used to answer many practical questions. At the same time, it is to be considered that individual differences exist with respect to the need of control. There are independent of these individual differences situational facts that lead to people learning a feeling of control. These situational facts influence our behavior. So new forms of money lead to consumers learning an illusion of control for expenditures, which is connected with higher consumer spending and a higher level of indebtedness. The knowledge of such connections can be used to develop strategies and manners for consumers, to possibly avoid these effects or at least to diminish them.

These insights are also of high relevance for business. Against the background of the increasing indebtedness as well as the overindebtedness of private households and the social responsibility of the businesses, there lies an elementary interest to avoid too high of indebtedness for their customers, and the connected possibility of the personal (and corporate) insolvency. At the same time control theory insights can also be used in other areas, for example, investment behavior or during the sales conversation. In many situations, businesses fulfill the functions of a vicarious control unit. This rests on the assumption that customer safety is suggested regarding certain product achievements, but that is not actually provided. In the sense of the construction of a profitable and durable customer relationship, based on partnership, the business must be however in a position to fulfill the customer expectations persistently, or it must lose the customers prematurely due to certain achievements that cannot be controlled or guaranteed by the business.

QUESTIONS FOR DISCUSSION

1. Explain the differences between Type A and Type B personalities, and discuss the relevance in a marketing context.
2. Elaborate on the internal and external locus of control and discuss possible marketing strategies for each alternative.
3. Discuss self-regulation as it relates to the use of cash and credit in consumer purchases.
4. Discuss how the illusion of control was involved in the recent financial crisis.

Bibliography

Abramson, L.Y., Seligman, M.E.P. and Teasdale, J.D.: Learned helplessness in humans: Critique and reformulation. *Journal of Abnormal Psychology*, 1978, 87, 49–74.

Alloy, L.B. and Abramson, L.Y.: Judgement of contingency in depressed and non-depressed students: Sadder but wiser? *Journal of Experimental Psychology: General*, 1979, 108, 441–485.

—— and Clements, C.M.: Illusion of control: Invulnerability to negative affect and depressive symptoms after labourite and natural stresses. *Journal of Abnormal Psychology*, 1992, 101, 234–245.

Archer, R.P.: Relationships between locus of control and anxiety. *Journal of Personality Assessment*, 1979, 43, 617–626.

Bandura, A.: Self-efficacy: Toward a unifying theory of behavioral change. *Psychological Review*, 1977, 84, 191–215.

Bungard, W. and Schultz-Gambard, J.: Überlegungen zum verhalten von börsenakteuren aus kontrolltheoretischer sicht. In: Maass, P. and Weibler, J. (eds): *Börse und Psychologie: Plädoyer für eine neue Perspektive.* Köln: 1990, 140–159. (Considerations for behavior of stock exchange participants in view of control theory. In *Stock Exchange and Psychology: Plea for a New Perspective).*

Burger, J.M.: Desire for control and achievement related behaviors. *Journal of Personality and Social Psychology*, 1985, 48, 1520–1533.

—— Desire for control and conformity to a perceived norm. *Journal of Personality and Social Psychology*, 1987, 53, 355–360.

—— Desire for control and academic performance. *Canadian Journal of Behavioral Science*, 1992, 24, 47–155.

—— and Cooper, H.M.: The desirability of control. *Motivation and Emotion*, 1979, 3, 381–393.

Campbell, C.: *The Romantic Ethic and the Spirit of Modern Consumerism.* Oxford: 1987.

Cervone, D., Jiwani, N. and Wood, R.: Goal setting and the differential influence of self-regulatory processes on complex decision-making performance. *Journal of Personality and Social Psychology*, 1991, 61, 257–266.

Chandler, T.A.: A note on the relationship of internality-externality, self-acceptance, and self-ideal discrepancies. *The Journal of Psychology*, 1976, 94, 145–146.

DeCharms, R.: *Personal Causation.* New York: 1968.

Deci, E.L. and Ryan, R.M.: *Handbook of Self-Determination Research.* Rochester, NY: University of Rochester Press, 2002.

Dessart, W. and Kuylen, A.: The nature, extent, causes, and consequences of problematic debt situations. *Journal of Consumer Policy*, 1986, 9, 311–334.

Dirx, E. and Craik, F.I.M.: Age-related differences in memory as a function of imagery processing. *Psychology and Aging*, 1992, 7, 352–358.

Frey, D. and Irle, M. (eds): *Theorien der Sozialpsychologie. vol. 3: Motivations- und Informationsverarbeitungstheorien.* Bern: 1993. (*Theories of Social Psychology. vol. 3: Motivation Theories and Information Processing Theories*).

Glass, D.C.: *Behavior Patterns, Stress, and Coronary Disease.* Hillsdale, NJ: 1977.

Hautzinger, M. and Bommer, M.: Die Auswirkungen von kontrolle und vorhersagbarkeit auf das befinden älterer menschen—eine replikation. *Schweizer Zeitschrift für Psychologie*, 1992, 51, 191–197. (The effects of control and prediction on the condition of older persons—a replication).

Haynes, S.G., Feinleib, M. and Kannel, W.B.: The relationship of psychosocial factors to coronary disease in the Framingham study. *American Journal of Epidemiology*, 1980, 11, 37–58.

Herkner, W.: *Lehrbuch Sozialpsychologie.* Bern: 1991. (*Textbook of Social Psychology*).

Hermann, C.: Zusammenhänge zwischen depression, ursachenerklärung und kontroller-wartungen. In: Hautzinger, M. and Schulz, W. (eds). *Klinische Psychologie und Psychotherapie*, vol. 3, 79–87. München: 1980. (Connection between depression, cause explanation and control services. In *Clinical Psychology and Psychotherapy*).

Hiroto, D.: Locus of control and learned helplessness. *Journal of Experimental Psychology*, 1974, 102, 187–193.

Hoch, S. and Loewenstein, G.: Time-inconsistent preferences and consumer self-control. *Journal of Consumer Research*, 1991, 17, 492–507.

Hodgkinson, G.: Research notes and communications development and validation of the strategic locus of control scale. *Strategic Management Journal*, 1992, 13, 311–317.

Hunt, J.M., Kernan, J.B., Chatterjee, A. and Florsheim, R.A.: Locus of control as a personality correlate of materialism: An empirical note. *Psychological Reports*, 1990, 67, 1101–1102.

Kanfer, F.H.: Selbstregulierung und selbstkontrolle. In: Zeier, H. (ed.). *Pawlow und die Folgen*. Zürich: 1977, 793–827. (Self-regulation and self-control. In *Pavlov and the Consequences*).

—— Selbstregulation und verhalten. In: Heckhausen, H., Gollwitzer, P.M. and Weinert, F.E. (eds). *Jenseits des Rubikon: Der Wille in den Humanwissenschaften*. Berlin: 1987, 286–299. (Self-regulation and behavior. In *Beyond the Rubicon: The Will in the Human Sciences*).

——, Reinecker, H. and Schmelzer, D.: *Selbstmanagement-Therapie. Ein Lehrbuch für die Klinische Praxis*. Berlin: 1991. (*Self Management Therapy. A Textbook for Clinical Practice*).

Kanfer, R. and Kanfer, F.H.: Goals and selfregulation: Applications of theory to work settings. In: Maehr, M.L. and Pintrich, P.R. (eds). *Advances in Motivation and Achievement*, 1991, 7, 287–326. Greenwich.

Karoly, P.: Mechanismus of self-regulation: A systems view. *Annual Review of Psychology*, 1993, 44, 23–52.

Koenig, L.J., Clements, C.M., and Alloy, L.B.: Depression and the illusion of control: The role of esteem maintenance and impression management. *Canadian Journal of Behavioural Science*, 1992, 24, 233–252.

Krampen, G.: *IPC-Fragebogen zu Kontrollüberzeugungen*. Göttingen: 1980. (*IPC Questionnaire for Control Convictions*).

—— *Differentialpsychologie der Kontrollüberzeugungen*. Göttingen: 1982. (*Differential Psychology of Control Convictions*).

—— *Fragebogen zu Kompetenz- und Kontrollüberzeugungen (FKK)*. Göttingen: 1991. (*Questionnaire to Competence Convictions and Control Convictions (FKK)*).

—— and Fischer, M.: Kontrollüberzeugungen in der alkoholismusforschung. Literaturüberblick und theoretische bezüge. *Zeitschrift für Klinische Psychologie, Psychopathologie und Psychotherapie*, 1988, 36, 100–117. (Control convictions in alcoholism research. Literature overview and theoretical references.).

Kroeber-Riel, W. and Weinberg, P.: *Konsumentenverhalten*. (8th edn). München: 2003. (*Consumer Behavior*).

Langer, E.J.: The illusion of control. *Journal of Personality and Social Psychology*, 1975, 32, 311–328.

—— and Rodin, J.: The effects of choice and enhanced personal responsibility for the aged: A field experiment in an institutional setting. *Journal of Personality and Social Psychology*, 1976, 34, 191–198.

Lefcourt, H.M.: The function of the illusions of control and freedom. *American Psychologist*, 28, 1973, 417–425.

Levenson, H.: Distinctions within the concept of internal-external control: Development of a new scale. *Proceedings of the 80th Annual Convention of the American Psychological Association*, 1972, 7, 261–262. Washington, DC.

—— Activism and powerful others: Distinctions within the concept of internal-external control. *Journal of Personality Assessment*, 1974, 38, 377–383.

Lewis, A.: Some methods in psychological economics. In: Earl P.E. (ed.). *Psychological Economics*, 1988, 189–210. Boston, MA.

Livingstone, S.M. and Lunt, P.K.: Predicting personal debt and debt repayment: Psychological, social and economic determinants. *Journal of Economic Psychology*, 1992, 13, 111–134.

Lohaus, A. and Schmitt, G.M.: *Fragebogen zur Erhebung von Kontrollüberzeugungen zu Krankheit und Gesundheit (KKG)*. Göttingen: 1989. (*Questionnaire for the Promotion of Control Convictions in Illness and Health (KKG)*).

Lunt, P.K. and Livingstone, S.M.: Everyday explanations for personal debt: A network approach. *British Journal of Social Psychology*, 1991, 30, 309–323.

Mass, P. and Weibler, J.: Immer unter spannung. In: Jünemann, B. and Schellenberger, D. (eds). *Psychologie für Börsenprofis*. Stuttgart: 1997, 109–122. (Always under tension. In *Psychology for Stock Exchange Professionals*).

Meyer, G.: Spielsucht—theorie und empirie. In: Poppelreuter, S. and Gross, W. (eds). *Nicht nur Drogen Machen Süchtig*. München: 2000, 1–16. (Addiction to gambling—theory and evidence. In *Not Only Drugs are Addictive*).

Müller, G.: Dispositionelle und biografische bedingungen beruflicher selbständigkeit. In: Moser, K.; Batinic, B. and Zempel, J. (eds). *Unternehmerisch Erfolgreich Handeln*. Göttingen: 1999, 173–192. (Dispositional and biographic conditions of professional independence. In *Entrepreneurially Successful Trade*).

—— *Fragebogen zur Diagnose unternehmerischer Potentiale*. Landau: 2000. (*Questionnaire for the Diagnosis of Entrepreneurial Potential*).

Nelson, E.: Control beliefs of adults in three domains: A new assessment of perceived control. *Psychological Reports*, 1993, 72, 155–165.

Ollendick, D. (1979). Parental locus of control and the assessment of children's personality characteristics. *Journal of Personality Assessment*, 43, 401–405.

Osselmann, J.: *Eine Skala zur Messung der Intrenalen und Extrenalen Verstärkungskontrolle*. Bonn: 1976. (*A Scale for Measurement of Strengthening the Internal and External Control*).

Osnabrügge, G., Stahlberg, D. and Frey, D.: Die theorie der kognizierten kontrolle. In: Frey, D. and Irle, M. (eds): *Theorien der Sozialpsychologie. vol. 3: Motivations- und Informationsverarbeitungstheorien*. Bern: 1993, 127–172. (The theory of cognitive control. In *Theories of Social Psychology, vol. 3: Motivation Theories and Information Processing Theories*).

Paivio, A.: *Imagery and Verbal Processes*. New York: 1971.

—— *Mental Representations: A Dual Coding Approach*. New York: 1986.

Phares, E.J.: *Locus of Control in Personality*. Morristown: 1976.

Pittman, N.L. and Pittman, T.S.: Effects of amount of helplessness training and internal-external locus of control on mood and performance. *Journal of Personality and Social Psychology*, 1979, 37, 39–47.

Raab, G.: *Kartengestützte Zahlungssysteme und Konsumentenverhalten*. Berlin: 1998. (*Card Support Payment Systems and Consumer Behavior*).

Rapp, H.: Der tägliche wahnsinn hat methode. In: Jünemann, B. and Schellenberger, D. (eds). *Psychologie für Börsenprofi*. Stuttgart: 1997, 75–108. (The daily madness has a method. In *Psychology for Stock Exchange Professionals*).

Reinecker, H.: *Selbstkontrolle. Verhaltenstheoretische und Kognitive Grundlagen, Techniken und Therapiemethoden*. Salzburg: 1978. (*Self-control. Behavior Theoretical and Cognitive Foundations, Technologies and Therapy Methods*).

—— (ed.): *Lehrbuch der Klinischen Psychologie: Modelle Psychischer Störungen*. Göttingen: 1990. (*Textbook of Clinical Psychology: Mental Disorder Models*).

Rosenman, R.H., Brand, R., Jenkins, C.D., Friedman, M., Straus, R. and Wurm, M.: Coronary heart disease in the western collaborative group study. *Journal of American Medical Association*, 1975, 233, 872–877.

Rothbaum, F., Weisz, J.R. and Snyder, S.: Changing the world and changing the self: A two-process model of perceived control. *Journal of Personality and Social Psychology*, 1982, 42, 5–37.

Rotter, J.B.: *Social Learning and Clinical Psychology*. Englewood Cliffs, NJ: 1954.

Rotter, J.B.: Generalized expectancies for internal versus external control of reinforcement. *Psychological Monographs* (No. 609), 1966, 80, 1, 1–28.

Rotter, J.B.: Some problems and misconceptions related to the construct of internal versus external control of reinforcement. *Journal of Consulting and Clinical Psychology*, 1975, 43, 56–67.

Schulz, R.: Effects of control and predictability on the physical and psychological wellbeing of the institutionalized aged. *Journal of Personality and Social Psychology*, 1976, 33, 563–573.

Seligman, M.: *Helplessness: On Depression, Development, and Death.* San Francisco, CA: 1975.

Spector, P.E.: Development of the work locus of control scale. *Journal of Occupational Psychology*, 1988, 61, 335–340.

Taylor, S.E. and Brown, J.D.: Illusion and well-being: A social psychological perspective on mental health. *Psychological Bulletin*, 1988, 103, 193–210.

Thompson, S.: Will it hurt less if I can control it? A complex answer to a simple question. *Psychological Bulletin*, 1981, 90, 89–101.

Wallston, K., Wallston, B. and DeVellis, R.: Development of the multidimensional health locus of control (MHLC) scales. *Health Education Monographs*, 1978, 6, 160–170.

Wärneryd, K.-E.: On the psychology of saving: An essay on economic behavior. *Journal of Economic Psychology*, 1989, 10, 515–541.

White, R.W.: Motivation reconsidered: The concept of competence. *Psychological Review*, 1959, 66, 5, 297–333.

Wiswede, G.: *Einführung in die Wirtschaftspsychologie.* München: 1991. (*Introduction to Economic Psychology*).

Wong, P.T.P.: Guest editorial: Control is a double-edged sword. *Canadian Journal of Behaviour of Science*, 1992, 24, 143–146.

Zimmerman, M.A. and Rappaport, J.: Citizen participation, perceived control, and psychological empowerment. *American Journal of Community Psychology*, 1988, 16, 725–750.

18 *Exchange Theories— Equity as a Prerequisite of Enduring Customer Relationships*

Concept and Relevance

According to the principle of classical exchange theory, people pursue that particular objective that is such that the results (output) of an interaction have an appropriate (equitable) relationship to one's own efforts (input). In this sense exchange theory is also known as equity theory.

It is assumed that each partner in an interaction makes contributions (in the form of time expenditure, monetary means, and so on) and targets results (rewards and punishments in the broadest sense). Both results and contributions can be positive but also negative. Equitability is always present when none of the partners in an interaction has unreasonable advantages or disadvantages in comparison to the others.

The relationships between the results and contributions of the partners in an interaction are of principal significance. The key thing here is not the objectively verifiable relationships, assuming that these are at all measurable or detectable, as much as it is the actual perception of each partner in an interaction. According to Adams (1965) a situation is equitable or balanced for person A if she perceives the relationship between her results (outcomes O_A) and her contributions (Inputs I_A) to be the same as the relationship between the results and contributions of her partner B. Person B on the other hand could perceive the same situation completely differently (Herkner, 1991, p. 435):

$$\frac{O_A}{I_A} \quad - \quad \frac{O_B}{I_B}$$

Proponents of exchange theory/equity theory refer to the work of Adams (1965), Homans (1958), Thibaut and Kelley (1959) with regard to the influence of social norms. This work details under what conditions an interaction takes place and what values norms take on in interaction processes. As far as the psychological components of people's interaction behavior are concerned, these scientists have made reference to dissonance theory.

As discussed earlier in Chapter 4, Festinger's (1957) dissonance theory is based on the assumption that individuals strive for an enduring balance within their cognitive system. If for example an individual's cognitions end up in an unbalanced state due to a perceived discrepancy between the contributions that have been made and the targeted results, this will lead to the interaction partner feeling upset. He experiences inconsistencies in the field of perception as psychological tensions. This then leads the person to reducing the imbalance that has been encountered, in that he will try to alleviate this discrepancy between contribution and result.[1]

An essential development of exchange theory/equity theory has been provided by Walster, Berscheid and Walster (1973). They have attempted to expand the approach within a general behavioral or interaction theory. Essentially the principle of exchange or equity theory can be extended to all possible areas, from interaction partner relationships on up to the relationships within economic interactions.

The Approaches of Various Proponents of Exchange Theory

HOMANS' EXCHANGE THEORY (1958, 1961)

According to Homans (1958, 1961) people interact with the goal such that they seek results that both pay off and that are fair. They hope to get a profit out of the interaction and they entertain expectations that are informed by normative preconceptions as far as the distribution of this profit is concerned. These expectations are informed by equivalent or distributive justice. In his original equivalent justice approach Homans proceeded from the assumption that people not only derived a benefit or reward from an interaction, but that they also had to accept a certain amount of detriment in relation to their egotistical goals. As a consequence the following relation was formulated (Müller and Crott, 1984, p. 219):

$$\text{Profit}_{(\text{Person A})} = \text{Reward}_{(A)} - \text{Costs}_{(A)} \text{ in relation to}$$

$$\text{Profit}_{(\text{Person B})} = \text{Reward}_{(B)} - \text{Costs}_{(B)}$$

Homans is of the opinion that the rewards and costs of two or more people can vary, and yet the benefit to the interaction partners is always the same. This yields (Müller and Crott, 1984, p. 219):

$$\text{Profit}_{(\text{Person A})} = \text{Profit}_{(\text{Person B})}$$

Accordingly, what is at hand is the absolute equivalence of profit regardless of the input of each interaction partner involved in the exchange, in that the same profit result arises for each. Factors conditioned by varying circumstances and individual differences are not taken into consideration here (Müller and Crott, 1984, p. 220; McClintock, Kramer and Keil, 1984, p. 201).

Homans (1961) later corrected this relatively idealistic and undifferentiated approach to an equity principle—characterized by identical results or interaction partner profit— thereby turning the principle of distributive justice into the principle of relative profit equivalence. He here began from the following consideration: a person who is in an

---

1   See Chapter 4 in this volume "The Theory of Cognitive Dissonance" (pp. 43–57).

exchange relationship with another person will expect the profits of each person to behave proportionally to their investments. The greater the investment is, the greater the profit will be (Homans, 1961). He understands investment to be characteristics that individual people bring with them into an interaction, characteristics that could be significant within an exchange, like for example age, experience, intelligence, etc. (Müller and Crott, 1984, p. 220).

This leads to another new formulation of distributive justice:

$$\frac{\text{Profit}_{(\text{Person A})}}{\text{Investment}_{(\text{Person A})}} \quad = \quad \frac{\text{Profit}_{(\text{Person B})}}{\text{Investment}_{(\text{Person B})}}$$

If the formula of equivalent justice is not maintained, for example, if one interaction partner has an advantage in the eyes of another, then the disadvantaged person will be upset and dissatisfied (McClintock, Kramer and Keil, 1984, p. 202). If the partner in this interaction assesses the relation between profit and investment to be similar, and if they also see themselves to be in a superior position compared with the other, then they will not get satisfaction from this, but instead will tend to experience feelings of guilt. Both interaction partners then feel bad about the results of the interaction. They will exert themselves in trying to restore the law of equivalent justice. This could come about for example in that the disadvantaged person could belittle the other's perceived profit or lower their own input-cost-relationship (Müller and Crott, 1984, p. 221).

THIBAUT AND KELLEY'S EXCHANGE THEORY (1959)

Like Homans (1958) theory, Thibaut and Kelley's (1959) approach deals with interaction partner exchange results and with their efforts to obtain maximum satisfaction in their interaction results in comparison with others and/or in relation to their costs (Fischer and Wiswede, 1997, p. 390). The central assertion hangs on the assumption that the likelihood of a long-term social relationship is higher if the result of an interaction is positive, or if the difference between the result (reward or benefit) and input (costs) is seen to be advantageous.

Thibaut and Kelley have tried to provide verification of the advantageousness of an interaction with the help of a pay off matrix (see Figure 18.1). It is here assumed that each interaction partner has a number of behavioral alternatives. Each alternative has a particular value (V). This value is related to benefits and costs and applies to both partners. The value of an alternative certainly does not have to be identical for the participants. Thus the different lines of the matrix reflect the various result-input-relations of one of the interaction partners, while the columns represent those of the other. The interaction partners are here influenced by both exogenous variables, like for example individual needs, and endogenous variables, which stem for example from earlier experiences. Each unit combination yields an individual result for both interaction partners (McClintock, Kramer and Keil, 1984, p. 205). This provides information regarding the satisfaction of each interaction partner and the stability of a relationship (Fischer and Wiswede, 1997, p. 390). The results allow for conclusions to be drawn as to whether mutual or separate actions will yield more earnings. In this regard it is of note that the respective individually targeted earnings can be greater and that compromises ensure a higher total sum (Wiswede, 1991, p. 102).

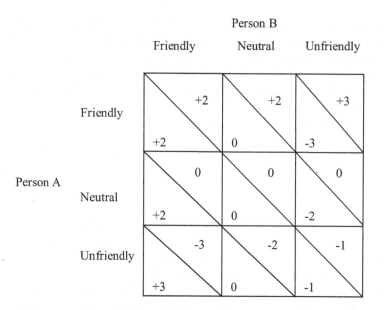

Figure 18.1 Thibaut and Kelley's pay off matrix (1959)

The decisive question now is how people manage to assess the benefit and costs relationship that they have themselves come up with. In the end the value of a relationship can only be judged by one comparative index. Thibaut and Kelley (1959) have proceeded on the assumption that individuals (for example, customers) judge a relationships value (for example, a business relationship) on the basis of two standards of comparison. The first of these is called the comparison level (CL) and is a measurement that derives from earlier experiences. With this variable the customer is referring back to experiences with the given product or company. What is being dealt with here is a sort of average measure of these experiences. This average measure is thus a measurement of the customer's expectations in relation to which it will be judged how good or bad is the current result of a relationship. Positive experiences with the product or business relationship increase the CL, while negative ones decrease them. The comparison between the value (V) of the current relationship and the comparison level (CL) is not however enough to assess whether the customer will stay in a relationship or not. In order to assess this question a second measurement has to be brought in, the comparison level for alternatives (CLalt). This measurement is an average measure of benefits and costs regarding viable alternatives, whereby the best alternative is given particular consideration. From the simultaneous consideration of V, CL and CLalt can be derived a statement regarding the attractiveness of the relationship and its dependence. Three situations have to be differentiated (see Figure 18.2).

1. The current value V is higher than CL and CLalt. The relationship is attractive to the customer since V is higher than the other attractive alternative CLalt. The customer is not dependent because of this alternative since they could switch and still be above the comparison level CL.
2. The current value V is higher than CL, making this an attractive relationship. Since CLalt is lower than CL the customer however does not have an attractive alternative, making them dependent.

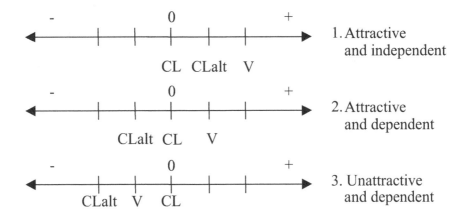

CLalt = Comparison level for alternatives
CL = Comparison level
V = Result of a business relationship

Figure 18.2 Thibaut and Kelley's pay off matrix (1959)

3. Current value V is lower than CL, making this an unattractive relationship. Since CLalt is lower than the current value V, the customer would find himself in an even worse position if they switched. They are dependent in an unattractive relationship.

Plinke and Söllner (1998, p. 60) have pointed out that the factors of attractiveness and dependence can also be used to describe the situation involving companies and customers (see Figure 18.3). In this example the company C is in an unattractive [V(C) is lower than C(C)] and dependent [Calt(C) is lower than V(C)] business relationship. The customer Cr by contrast is in what is for them an attractive business relationship [V(Cr) is higher than C(Cr)], although like the company C is dependent [Calt(Cr) is lower than C(Cr)].

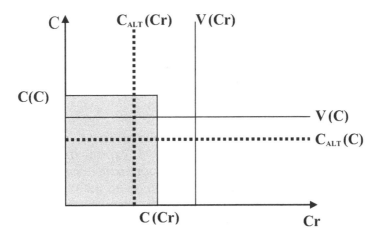

Figure 18.3 The structure of dependence in a business relationship (Plinke and Söllner, 1998, p. 61)

The described situation is thus characterized as reciprocally dependent with an uneven distribution of attractiveness. Some points of departure for improving the company's situation can be derived from this. There is a possibility of actively pursuing new relationships to alternative customers that would result in a better cost to profit relationship for the company. A further approach consists of making the customer aware of the current situation. Since the customer is in a dependent situation this increases the company's bargaining position.

WALSTER, BERSCHEID AND WALSTER'S EXCHANGE THEORY (1973)

Walster, Berscheid and Walster (1973) define equity as perception of an equivalent relationship between profit and investment, whereby profit is seen as the difference between the result and the investment. In this connection they are referring to Homans' basic assertions. Their theory consists of four central assumptions, where two of these assumptions are in accordance with Homans' original theoretical conception (Herkner, 1991, pp. 435–436; Müller and Crott, 1984, p. 224):

1. Individuals attempt to maximize their profit or results.
2. Since unconstrained striving for profit by individual people would result in many other (especially weaker) people coming to harm, groups have established norms regarding the equitable distribution of rewards and costs. One such norm is the equivalence of the relationship between profit and investment for all members. Important here is that members of this group accept these established norms, that they orient themselves toward them and maintain them. The group will reward those members who in general uphold the norms, and will discipline those people (for example, raise their costs) who behave unfairly in relation to other members.
3. If people find themselves in an unfair relationship they will feel upset, and all the more so the greater the discrepancy is in relation to the norms of justice.
4. People who find themselves in an unequal or unjust relationship will attempt to relieve their unease by reestablishing justice, and will do so all the more determinedly the greater is the existing state of injustice.

It is of note that one has to differentiate between three varying kinds of injustice. Depending on whether the inequality of profit and investment is in a person's favor or not in his favor, he may become either an exploiter (profit > investment) or a victim (profit < investment). In the first case feelings of guilt or anxiety may arise; in the second case the person will tend to become angry (Herkner, 1991, p. 436). The accompanying emotional reaction to the perception of inequity can already be found in Homans' theory. An expansion of Homans' theory—as already suggested—derives from the second assumption; Walster, Berscheid and Walster, (1973) explain that interaction partners "suffer" if all members of the group attempt to maximize their gain and are not prepared to make compromises. The group therefore attempts to motivate the members to be fair through the use of disciplinary measures and incentives (Müller and Crott, 1984, p. 225).

RUSBULT'S THEORY (1980): THE INVESTMENT MODEL

Rusbult's (1980) theory offers an expansion of the above-explained basic approaches. Rusbult (1980) is of the opinion that the equity of a social relationship is not only dependent on an interaction's current costs and earnings (satisfaction) and on the possible alternatives; its equity is additionally dependent on all previous investments in this relationship. Commitment within a relationship is thus, apart from profit, dependent on all previous investments into this relationship, minus the assumed benefit of the best of the available alternatives (Buunk, 1996, pp. 390–391; Fischer and Wiswede, 1997, p. 394). From this can be derived the following equation of an existing relationship:

Commitment to the Relationship = Benefit – Costs + Investments – Alternatives

It has been substantiated in various empirical studies that previous investments do in fact have a decisive influence, and that they strengthen an interaction's stability. From the point of view of dissonance theory, the inclusion of investments can be explained via a justification of effort and through the increase in the relationship's value entailed by this inclusion (Fischer and Wiswede, 1997, p. 394).

Examples of the Practical Application of Exchange Theory

Exchange (or equity) theory has been supported by many studies in various areas. The following elaborates on some of the relevant areas.

EQUITY AND SATISFACTION IN SOCIAL RELATIONSHIPS

According to Thibaut and Kelley (1959) the satisfaction of individuals within a relationship is dependent upon comparison level, or in other words on that degree of results that in their opinion one should be targeting within a relationship. Walster, Berscheid and Walster (1978) conducted a study along these lines:

Over 500 male and female students had to assess the extent and quality (positive or negative) of their contributions and the results with regard to their partners. They were also asked how satisfied, happy, upset, or guilty they felt, and how stable was their relationship. In agreement with the theory it came out that people in an equitable relationship were especially happy and satisfied and seldom felt upset or guilty. By comparison partners who felt themselves to be at an advantage were less satisfied. The least satisfied were partners who felt themselves to be at a disadvantage. The conclusion that can be drawn here is that equitable relationships have proven to be more stable (Buunk, 1996, p. 388; Herkner, 1991, p. 437). The following table reproduces some of the study data:

Table 18.1   Study results: Equity in relationships (Herkner, 1991, p. 437)

Type of relationship	Number of participants	Satisfied	Happy	Upset	Guilty
	64	2.7	2.98	1.98	1.39
	84	3.26	3.42	1.75	1.44
	220	3.51	3.61	1.36	1.31
	89	3.51	3.69	1.36	1.51
	80	2.91	3.06	1.54	1.83

Note: The answers were given according to a 4 point scale: 1 = Not at all; 4 = To a very high degree.

According to exchange theory, individuals are less happy in a relationship when (Buunk, 1996, p. 388),

- the relationship between contribution and result is unequal between the partners;
- a partner has received a disproportionately large amount of advantages from the relationship. They believe that they have profited more from the relationship, and feel unhappy because of feelings of guilt;
- a partner has received disproportionately few advantages from the relationship. They feel upset and hurt because they have profited less than they expected to have earned from the relationship.

More recent studies have shown that there is a direct relationship between satisfaction within a relationship and the extent of equity. According to these studies the influence of perceived equity on satisfaction within a relationship is mainly found in people who exhibit a high degree of exchange orientation. Such people expect quick and proportionate rewards for benefits that they have given others, and they do not feel satisfied if someone does them a favor that they are unable to repay (Buunk, 1996, p. 389).

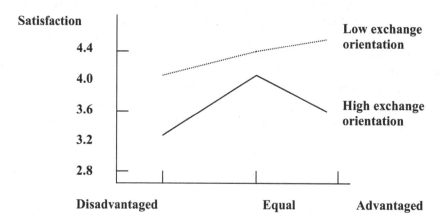

Figure 18.4   The relationship between equity and satisfaction (Buunk, 1996, p. 389)

Figure 18.4 shows that there is an upside-down v-shaped relationship between satisfaction and equity in the relationship if the given person has a high degree of exchange orientation. In the case of people with a low degree of exchange orientation on the other hand, a linear relationship is shown. These people are especially satisfied if they feel themselves to be at an advantage in a relationship. These insights could be utilized by differentiating customers on the basis of surveys and/or analysis of their behavior to date with regard to their exchange orientation. Based on this differentiation corresponding strategies could be developed. Customers with a high degree of exchange orientation in the given business relationship present the opportunity of reducing costs and the opportunity for a simultaneous increase of customer satisfaction. It goes without saying that such a strategy requires a well-substantiated analysis of the customers and of the situation regarding competitors. Still, the results indicate that not all customers are satisfied if they feel themselves to be at an advantage in a long-term partnership relationship.

EQUITY IN PERFORMANCE RELATED EXCHANGE

An application of exchange theory within this context is to attempt to explain those behavioral patterns that are triggered by over or underpayment. According to Pritchard (1969), there are five output-input variants that characterize the criteria of over- and underpayment. Accordingly, a person A will experience unfairness if they make an apparent comparison to person B as per Table 18.2 (L stands for "low", H for "high"):

Table 18.2 Output-input variants with regard to the under or overpayment of person A and B (Müller and Crott, 1984, p. 226)

L	H	L	L	H	L	L	L
L	L	H	L	L	L	L	H
L	H	H	L	H	L	L	H
H	H	H	L	H	L	H	H
L	H	H	H	H	H	L	H

Various studies support these results. Homans (1953) for example studied a range of office workers at a manufacturing plant who differed with regard to their activity within the company. During the course of these studies he established that bookkeepers assessed their status within the office organization to be higher in comparison to employees in the department who dealt with invoices, because they had completed a longer training period and were engaged in work that involved greater responsibility. Both received the same salary. Although the amount of the salary gave no cause for complaint (the company paid very well), the bookkeepers were dissatisfied with their work situation. The reason for this had to do with the discrepancy between salary and training plus responsibility. The bookkeepers perceived their activity, which demanded more responsibility in comparison to that of the employees in the department dealing with invoices, as not being rewarded well enough (Müller and Crott, 1984, p. 226).

There is a range of other studies, conducted on the basis of representative samples, which confirm that perceived unfairness regarding payment and the dissatisfaction that results from it, stems from the comparison with the income of a reference group (Furnham and Argyle, 1998, pp. 213–214). It is not the sheer amount of the income that determines the fairness of, and satisfaction with an income, but rather it is the comparison with others. It is of note that many studies have demonstrated how, in the case of underpayment, uneven output-input relationships leading to feelings of unfairness and dissatisfaction, are accompanied by patterns of behavior whose aim is to establish an equitable exchange relationship. The results in the case of overpayment are less persuasive with regard to the level of behavior. Adams (1965) has asserted the supposition that the perceptual threshold for unfairness is lower with regard to underpayment than it is in the case of overpayment (Müller and Crott, 1984, pp. 227–228). People who are overpaid are more likely to feel that it is due to their high intelligence or value to the firm, rather than to actually being overpaid. Reference groups are seldom in lower paying positions.

EQUITY WITH REGARD TO CUSTOMER RELATIONSHIPS

Implementing exchange theory in this area entails the assumption that a customer compares the relationship between the perceived costs and the anticipated benefits of a transaction, with that of certain reference persons. This means that they put their own contribution into an exchange relationship with a result that stems from a transaction, and compare this with the contribution and result of his partner in this relationship. Moreover the customer weighs their own input-output result with that of the other person and/or of the company according to fairness criteria.

In addition to price, contribution can also mean in this context values like waiting periods, or for example traveling costs. The result aspects include the value of the received service, the benefit, and the social effect. If the cost-to-benefit relationship is perceived as unfair or turns out to place the customer at a disadvantage, dissatisfaction of the customer will arise. This perception (of the cost-to-benefit relationship) will have a positive influence on customer satisfaction if the exchange is experienced as fair (Homburg and Rudolph, 1998, pp. 36–37).

The application of exchange theory to the area of customer satisfaction was first undertaken by Huppertz (1979). Further studies were conducted by Fisk and Coney (1982) as well as by Mowen and Grove (1983). They all examined the customer's experience of equity with regard to the purchase of a service. All of them came to the conclusion that the perceived equity within a transaction has a pronounced influence on the satisfaction of customers. However, to date none of these studies was able to demonstrate what emphasis experienced equity has to have within the input-output relationship in order to satisfy a customer, and to what extent experienced equity has an effect on customer satisfaction (Oliver and Swan, 1989, p. 22). A comprehensive analysis regarding these criteria—among others—would be interesting, since both the buyer and seller, as two sides of a sales transaction, represent two completely different parties, and therefore will have differing experiences of equity or fairness. While the seller sees the result of the transaction as the sale of a product or service and thus a possible commission, the buyer desires the functionality and utility of the product or service. Oliver and Swan (1989) used these criteria in a study concerning customer perception of equity and satisfaction in the purchase of automobiles. They arrived at the conclusion that equity with regard to the input-output relationship of buyers and sellers, depends on the view of the buyer in the following manner (Oliver and Swan, 1989, p. 30):

- For the buyer the occurrence of equity depends on their output. The input-output variable on the other hand appears not to have too much influence on the buyer's experience of equity.
- For the seller the occurrence of equity is by contrast relatively closely related to their input, whereas the output takes on a relatively low significance.

The perception of fairness also plays an important role in how complaints are dealt with. Customers mostly complain about problems that they see as being serious. They expect therefore a quick and appropriate reaction, or more exactly: they want justice or fairness. In this connection, they measure fairness in a threefold manner: What is the result of the complaint, how does the company proceed in their dealing with it, and how is the complainant treated? Goal oriented fairness focuses on whether or not the result is satisfactory. Typical forms are refunds, coupons, discounts, and replacement services. Procedural fairness is gleaned from the practices and regulations, as well as from the punctuality with which the complainant is dealt. Included here is that the responsibility for the mistake should be taken on, and that the complaint should be tackled immediately. A fair way of proceeding entails a flexible reaction system that takes individual circumstances into consideration and that inquires into the customer's ideas regarding compensation. The aspect of dealing with the matter is focused on how the company behaves with regard to the customer. Included here is especially polite, helpful, and upright behavior. The mistake should be explained for example, and the effort to solve the problem should be obvious. That this aspect has been neglected in the context of complaint management has been shown in an empirical study conducted by Tax and Brown (2000). In the context of this study customers were surveyed regarding their experience of and satisfaction with how fairly complaints were dealt with in various contexts (for example, restaurants, banks, airlines). It was here demonstrated that the majority found that the way their complaints were dealt with to be unfair (see Figure 18.5).

The experience of fairness with regard to satisfaction in the selling of products or regarding complaints has direct bearing on the long-term commitment of customers to a company. In support of this a study conducted by Hansen and Jeschke (1995, p. 539) demonstrated that satisfied complainants exhibited a marked loyalty to the brand and to the given company location. An internal study conducted by Volkswagen showed that 50 to 70 percent of satisfied complainants became long-term customers and that this increased to 95 percent given faster reactions (to complaints) (Bunk, 1993, p. 65). Empirical studies coming out of the Technical Assistance Research Program (TARP) give proof that the customer loyalty of satisfied complainants can even be greater than that of customers who have never experienced a problem with the products or the company (Adamson, 1993, pp. 441–443).

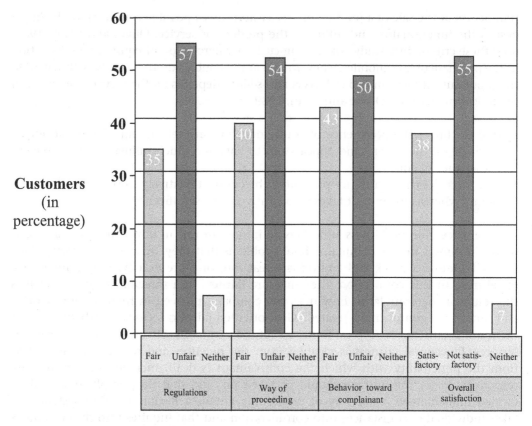

Figure 18.5 Fairness and satisfaction—complaint management in the judgment of customers (Tax and Brown, 2000, p. 104)

THE EXPERIENCE OF FAIRNESS AND THE INTRODUCTION OF THE EURO

The theoretical approaches to and empirical results of exchange theory can be carried over to macroeconomic questions. It makes sense here to differentiate between two aspects of equity: Procedural and the distributive equity (Thibaut and Walker, 1975).

Procedural equity pertains to the occurrence of an exchange of resources. The central question here is: is one personally involved in the decisions, or is the exchange partner making the decisions alone, or is there in fact a third party (for example, the state) that is making the decisions. Tyler, Rasinski and Spodick (1985) were able to show that just the possibility of being able to express a decision (for example, via a plebiscite) increases judgment regarding procedural equity, even though the influence of the individual is small. Distributive equity pertains to judgment regarding the input-output relation within a relationship. Procedural equity is important for the overall evaluation of a social system, while distributive equity is relevant for the evaluation of proceeds received by an individual or group belonging to this social system (Jacobs, 1999, p. 392).

These considerations were examined by Kiell and Müller-Peters (1999) in the context of a large empirical study concerning the introduction of the Euro. Over 15,000 people from all of the member states in the European Union took part in the study. As far as the countries within the monetary union were concerned, the significance of political participation in the experience of equity was apparent. The less perceived participation there was in the process of introducing the Euro (procedural equity), the more the attitude to the Euro was negative (r = 0.42). Some Europeans felt that the introduction of the Euro without their previous consent was most unfair. In this respect, this feeling did not stem from lack of knowledge as to whether the country belonged to the net distributors or net beneficiaries of funds within the European Union. For the most part people within the different countries know whether their country is a net distributor or a net beneficiary. In general the results of the study show that the more unfair the procedures and distribution of resources are judged to be, the more negative is the attitude towards the Euro (Kiell and Müller-Peters, 1999, p. 288).

The application of equity theory can also be carried over to areas involving other macroeconomic questions. Jonas, Heine and Frey (1999) for example have described in their model of tax satisfaction the significance of experienced fairness on the behavior of taxpayers, and consequences for taxation policy that derive from it. And equity theory can also make a contribution within the context of the currently discussed approach to corporate citizenship. If companies are understood as value adding organizations that profit from the society, who therefore should also do something for that society, then this basically involves exchange processes. Already in 1957 Bill Hewlett and David Packard, the founders of the American computer giant Hewlett-Packard, knew the significance of the company's contributions to society: "We want to fulfill our obligation to society in every country and every community we are active in, in that we want to make economic, cultural and social contributions." In 1999 Hewlett-Packard spent 58 million dollars for charitable reasons (Ramthun, 2000, p. 21). If citizens find a company's contributions to be fair, then this holds significance for that company as to an increasing degree the populace considers that company to be sharing responsibility in the solution of societal problems.

Summary

Many proponents of exchange theory attach to this approach a level of general applicability that in their opinion allows for the explanation and prediction of people's interactive behavior. The advantage of this theory mainly stems from the fact that various areas can be viewed according to one perspective—that of distributive justice. At the moment in economic life interaction, partners are very often striving for a fair exchange with an equitable input-output relation, which allows for a long-term relationship of mutual trust. The transference of exchange theory considerations and insights to economic affairs is therefore a central topic. Economic activity is always characterized by the social interaction of market participants. Thus the experience of fairness plays an important role in negotiations and in long-term business relationships. This also applies to the payment of employees in companies, and can also be applied to macroeconomic questions, for example, to the appropriate contributions made by companies toward the solution of societal tasks, or to taxation policy.

QUESTIONS FOR DISCUSSION

1. Explain exchange theory and how it relates to other economic theories such as individuals always acting in their own self-interest.
2. How might your organization maximize long-term, profitable customer relationships via the exchange theory?
3. How does complaint resolution of a firm effect the customer's perception of the value of the relationship?
4. Describe the investment model and how it can be utilized by marketers to improve the value of a given customer relationship.

Bibliography

Adams, J.S.: Inequity in social exchange. In: Berkowitz, L. (ed.). *Advances in Experimental Social Psychology*, vol. 6, New York: 1965, 267–299.

Adamson, C.: Evolving complaint procedures. *Managing Service Quality*, 1993, 1, 439–444.

Buss, D.M.: *The Evolution of Desire*, New York: 1994.

Bunk, B.: Das Geschäft mit dem Ärger. *Absatzwirtschaft*, 1993, 8, 65–69. (Dealing with anger).

Buunk, B.P.: Affiliation, zwischenmenschliche anziehung und enge beziehungen. In: Stroebe, W.; Hewstone, M. and Stephensen, G. (eds). *Sozialpsychologie*. Berlin: 1996, 363–393. (Affiliation, interpersonal attraction and narrow relations. In *Social Psychology*).

Clemmer, E.C. and Schneider, B.: Fair service. In: Swartz, T.A., Bowen, D.E. and Brown, S.W. (eds), *Advances in Services Marketing and Management*, vol. 5, Greenwich, CT: 1996, 109–126.

Critelli, J.W. and Waid, L.R.: Physical attractiveness, romantic love, and equity restoration in dating relationships. *Journal of Personality Assessment*, 1980, 44, 624–900.

Festinger, L.: *A Theory of Cognitive Dissonance*. Stanford: 1957.

Finn, R.H. and Lee, S.M.: Salary equity: Its determination analysis, and correlates. *Journal of Applied Psychology*, 1972, 56, 283–292.

Fischer, L. and Wiswede, G.: *Grundlagen der Sozialpsychologie*. München: 1997. (*Foundations of Social Psychology*).

Fisk, R.P. and Coney, K.A.: Postchoice evaluation: an equity theory analysis of consumer satisfaction/dissatisfaction with service choices. In: Hunt, H.K. and Day, R.L. (eds). *Conceptual and Empirical Contributions to Consumer Satisfaction and Complaining Behavior*. Bloomington: 1982, 9–16.

Furnham, A. and Argyle, M.: *The Psychology of Money*. London: 1998.

Hansen, U. and Jeschke, K.: Beschwerdemanagement für dienstleistungsunternehmen—beispiel des kfz-handels. In: Bruhn, M. and Stauss, B. (eds): *Dienstleistungsqualität*, Wiesbaden: 1995, 525–550. (Trouble management for service enterprises—an example of the motor vehicle trade. In *Service Quality*).

Herkner, W.: *Einführung in die Sozialpsychologie*. Bern: 1991. (*Introduction to Social Psychology*).

Homans, G.C.: Status among clerical workers. *Human Organisation*, 1953, 12, 5–10.

—— Social behavior as exchange. *American Journal of Sociology*, 1958, 63, 597–606.

—— *Social Behavior: Its Elementary Forms*. New York: 1961.

Homburg, C. and Rudolph, B.: Theoretische perspektiven zur kundenzufriedenheit. In: Simon, H. and Homburg, C. (eds). *Kundenzufriedenheit: Konzepte—Methoden—Erfahrungen*. Wiesbaden: 1998,

33–55. (Theoretical perspectives on customer satisfaction. In *Customer Satisfaction: Concepts—Method—Experience*).

Huppertz, J.W.: Measuring components of equity in the marketplace: perceptions of inputs and outcomes by satisfied and dissatisfied consumers. In: Day, R.L. and Hunt, H.K. (eds). *New Dimensions of Consumer Satisfaction and Complaining Behavior*, Bloomington: 1979, 140–143.

Jacobs, G.: Personalentscheidungen in europäischen banken—welche (kulturellen) regeln widerstehen der deregulierung. In: Fischer, L.; Kutsch, T. and Stephan, E. (eds): *Finanzpsychologie*. München: 1999, 387–406. (Personnel decisions in European banks – which (cultural) rules resist the deregulation. In *Finance Psychology*).

Jonas, E., Heine, K. and Frey, D.: Ein Modell der steuerzufriedenheit—psychologische grundlagen (un)ökonomischen Handelns. In: Fischer, L.; Kutsch, T. and Stephan, E. (eds): *Finanzpsychologie*. München: 1999, 160–187. (A model of tax satisfaction—psychological foundations of (un)economical actions. In *Finance Psychology*).

Kiell, G. and Müller-Peters, A.: Die einstellung der Europäer zum Euro. In: Fischer, L.; Kutsch, T. and Stephan, E. (eds). *Finanzpsychologie*. München: 1999, 273–297. (The attitude of Europeans to the Euro. In *Finance Psychology*).

McClinttock, Ch., Kramer, R.M. and Keil, L.J.: Equity and social exchange in human relationships. *Advances in Experimental Social Psychology*: 1984, 17, 183–228.

Mowen, J.C. and Grove, S.J.: Search behavior, price paid, and the comparison other: an equity theory analysis of post purchase satisfaction. In: Day, R.L. and Hunt, H.K. (eds). *International Fare in Consumer Satisfaction and Complaining Behavior*, Bloomington: 1983, 57–63.

Müller, G.F. and Crott, H.W.: Gerechtigkeit in sozialen Beziehungen. In: Frey, D. and Irle, M. (eds). *Theorien der Sozialpsychologie*, vol. 1: *Kognitive Theorien*. Bern: 1984, 218–241. (Justice in social relations. In *Theories of Social Psychology*, vol. 1: *Cognitive Theories*).

Oliver, R.L. and Swan, J.E.: Consumer perceptions of interpersonal equity and satisfaction in transactions: a filed survey approach. *Journal of Marketing*, 1989, 53, 21–35.

Plinke, W. and Söllner, A.: Kundenbindung und abhängigkeitsbeziehungen. In: Bruhn, M. and Homburg, C. (eds). *Handbuch Kundenbindungsmanagement*. Wiesbaden: 1998, 55–79. (Customer loyalty and dependence relations. In *Handbook on Customer Loyalty Management*).

Pritchard, R.D.: Equity-theory: A review and critique. *Organizational Behavior and Human Performance*, 1969, 4, 176–211.

Ramthun, Ch.: Bürger Bayer. *Wirtschaftswoche*, 2000, 39, 18–26. (Citizen Bayer).

Rusbult, C.E.: Commitment and satisfaction in romantic associations: a test of the investment model. *Journal of Experimental Social Psychology*, 1980, 45, 172–186.

Tax, S. and Brown, S.W.: Kundenbeschwerden: Was fairness bringt. *Harvard Business Manager*, 2000, 22, 1, 94–107. (Customer bonds: What brings fairness).

Thibaut, J.W. and Kelley, H.H.: *The Social Psychology of Groups*. New York: 1959.

—— and Walker, L.: *Procedural Justice*. New York: 1975.

Tyler, T.R., Rasinski, K.A. and Spodick, N.: Influence of voice on satisfaction with leaders: Exploring the meaning of process control, *Journal of Personality and Social Psychology*, 1985, 48, 72–81.

Walster, E., Berscheid, E. and Walster, G.W.: New directions in equity research. *Journal of Personality and Social Psychology*, 1973, 25, 151–176.

—— *Equity: Theory and Research*. Boston: 1978.

Wiswede, G.: *Einführung in die Wirtschaftpsychologie*. München: 1991. (*Introduction to Economic Psychology*).

The Layperson as Psychologist, and the Search for Insight

19 *Lay Epistemology*

Theory

With regard to social interaction, everyone is continuously engaged in explaining the behavior of others. They want to know why people display a certain behavior because they want to react appropriately to that behavior. In what way do these attempts differ from scientific explanations? Are they simpler, and therefore more useful than scientific explanations, because they are oriented toward everyday life, or are they perhaps actually incorrect and also inappropriate, perhaps merely being the expression of prejudices? Kruglanski's theory of lay epistemology (the theory of lay epistemology) takes this as its subject matter (Kruglanski, 1989 and Kruglanski, Baldwin and Towson, 1993).

According to Kruglanski, Baldwin and Towson (1993, p. 296), the layperson's search for insight can be explained via the following three classes of motives:

a) The desire for structure.
b) The desire for specific conclusions.
c) The desire for validity.

The desire for structure denotes that people are motivated to operate according to appropriate, structured knowledge. Confusion and ambiguity by contrast are avoided as much as possible. This has the consequence that, in certain areas, people are intent on working with information that is free from contradiction. Contradictions are experienced as unpleasant states of tension, together with the motivation to alleviate these unpleasant states. The parallel to the theory of cognitive dissonance is obvious. People are motivated to strive for consistency, or for freedom from contradiction. While the scientific search for insight is characterized precisely by the search for contradictions, in order to explain them, the layperson's search for insight is characterized by the avoidance of contradictions. From a scientific point of view contradictions can be identified as a kind of error that can be explained, thereby leading to the improvement of theories. Laypeople tend more to see the danger that their existing presumptions regarding reality might have to be abandoned. This may perhaps be seen as more problematic than the attempt to avoid contradictions right from the beginning, for example, through selective perception, as has already been analyzed in the context of cognitive dissonance. Those items of information that are consistent with the prevailing insights will be preferentially perceived. If inconsistencies cannot be avoided, the attempt will be made, via reinterpretation, to emphasize adaptable, and to de-emphasize inadaptable information, that is, to obtain consistency using mechanisms that we are already familiar with from the theory of cognitive dissonance. Thus, people do not necessarily seek out new, interesting, ambiguous or evocative information, but rather prefer information that obviously fits with previous information. In this way many new forms of information are missed. Kruglanski (1989, p. 85 et seq.) has additionally demonstrated connections between the theory of lay epistemology and attribution theory (dealt with in this book) and basically to all of the consistency theories we have discussed in this book: the theory of cognitive dissonance, including Irle's reformulation, and Heider's balance theory. The processes by which people explain the world, as explained in attribution theory, differ from scientific explanations—they constitute lay epistemology. The striving for consonance is also included here, in that information is irrationally reinterpreted, avoided or devalued. This entails a quite irrational, lay-oriented involvement with information.

The desire for specific conclusions also has a close connection to attribution theory as dealt with in Chapter 6, "Attribution Theories", pp. 77–85. We can think, for example, of external and internal attributions of success and failure. People are motivated to attribute success to themselves, and failures are gladly attributed to external sources, whereas the observed success of other people is gladly attributed to external factors, and observed failure is easily attributed to personal, internal factors. In this regard, people do not seek out insights systematically; instead they infer causes from observations. This occurs to a large extent according to self-worth motivation, that is, such that in the doing of it the feeling of self worth is not put in danger and where possible is increased. In the course of this, people lose sight, in their amateurishness, of the fact that they can never know all of the influencing factors. They come to conclusions according to a self-determined plausibility. They overlook, for example, that always and everywhere every behavior is equally a function of both personality and environmental variables. When observing the behavior of others around them, people in particular overlook that they are themselves a part of the environment, and therefore can themselves be a triggering factor for the given behavioral patterns of the other people in their environment.

Furthermore, out of all of the possible sets of conditions, people as a rule only seek a single cause or only a few causes. They fail to realize that most sets of conditions are triggered by many factors. But on which explanations will they settle? They will choose:

a) that explanation that best fits their own idea, which is understandable via the consistency theory;
b) the first explanation that they find that appears plausible, which among other things can be understood via the theory of social perception, whereby previous assumptions influence the subsequent perception;
c) that explanation which is shared by other people who are considered to be important. People believe themselves to be correct if their opinion is held by the majority. This is made understandable by the fact that people, as social beings, are almost always influenced in their behavior by others.

The need for structure involves a general desire for clarity and orientation with regard to a given problem; …. People need, or often desire, the maintenance of specific convictions, because these convictions are in agreement with their desires (Kruglanski, Baldwin and Towson, 1993, p. 297).

The desire for validity means that people have the easy-to-understand desire to know things, whereby they can assume that they are not in error. Very generally and roughly formulated, people want to be right as far as their assertions and assumptions are concerned. This can be explained in that people want to (and have to) react successfully and thus appropriately to their surrounding environment.

This desire for validity also explains the avoidance of inconsistency, since whenever information contains contradictions this information cannot be free from errors. The perception of inconsistency leads to uneasiness, which then inclines toward avoidance. Laypeople seek certainty for the same reasons. While the scientific endeavor constantly entails the search for fault—we constantly subject our scientific hypotheses to critical examination—the layman's search for insight is more a search for certainty, having a finalistic bent. The scientific search for insight accepts the thesis that the search for certainty does not allow for the furtherance of insight, because certainty is impossible. The layman's search for insight is oriented toward certainty: "Belief means ignorance"— that is a typical layperson's saying. Since the perception of error or contradiction leads to uneasiness, the following statement is widespread: "The exception proves the rule". Is everyone who speaks this sentence really clear about how illogical this statement is, how obviously meaningless, in fact how dangerous this sentence is? It is dangerous because it makes clinging to error easier.

The layperson's search for insight is also characterized by the use of so-called cognitive schema. Schemas are assumed knowledge structures that describe particular, but not all, characteristics of a set of conditions. On the basis of various (layman's) observations, person X might arrive at the assumption that other people can be described by the characteristics: a, b, c and d. They then perceive an actual person to have the characteristics a, b and c. The person may be quite sure that they also perceived characteristic d. That fits their person schema. What we are demonstrating here with regard to perceiving people can also apply to the perception of products, or to the perception of organizations. That should not result in uncritically applying the theory of perceiving others (see Bierhoff, 1986, 1989) to products and organizations, as has often happened in management practice in connection with the concept of corporate identity. The concept of corporate identity (see Unger and Fuchs, 1999, pp. 8–11) may in general be beneficial for the management of organizations. However, the parallel with the perception of personality that is assumed by many management professionals and even theoreticians is also simply an act of lay psychology.

Scripts are a particular form of cognitive schema. A script is a sequence of occurrences that a person has learned to perceive. In other words schemas pertain to the perception of objects, and scripts pertain to processes, or sequences. For example, a person believes to have often perceived: "When a occurs, then b follows, which is followed by c". If they have perceived a and c (and perhaps they only believe they have perceived a and c), then they will be quite sure that in between they have also perceived b.

Schemas allow for the rapid perception and belief that one has understood complex circumstances. They are therefore certainly to be understood as a necessity of human existence which presumably has arisen over the course of evolution as significant help for survival. If we have learned that a circumstance is constituted by a great deal of nuances, then it is often enough if we only perceive a part thereof, in order to be satisfied that we have perceived all of the nuances.

The problem here is that learning the content in question may already be based on faulty assumptions or on information that has not been checked by another party (indirect information).

So on the one hand, schemas are necessary in order to come to terms quickly enough with a relatively complex environment. On the other hand, they lead to perceptual errors. They significantly influence our ability to remember. We are often very sure that we have perceived certain sequences, even though we have actually only perceived a part of them. In this regard we are all the more certain, the more so a perceived aspect is part of a very intensely learned script. Since in the sequence of occurrences we tend to achieve confirmation of our learned scripts, we also tend to falsely or not at all perceive certain occurrences that do not fit into our scripts. The same goes for schemas of people. Here too we do not perceive or we falsely perceive aspects that do not fit. If we have learned person schema a, b, c and d, then the perception of a, b, c and e will either be perceived as a, b and c (with the consequence that we believe we have perceived a, b, c and d), or we perceive e to be the same as d. This is, for example, how prejudices against foreigners arise (such as xenophobia). All of this has the consequence that schema and scripts (as a special form of schemas) are relatively resistant to change. We may think here of the hypothesis theory of social perception.

Often every irrational way of relating to information that is explainable via psychology is labeled "Lay psychology", which is how Kruglanski relates to attribution theory to a large extent, and also to dissonance theory or to sequential effects. Lay psychology then merely becomes an umbrella term for many other social psychology theories.

Actual lay psychology does not apply to everything that social psychology theories explained long ago, but rather it applies to those behavioral patterns that contain unscientific behavior:

- The search for certainty, because certainty is not obtainable.
- Belief in correlations as an explanation for causes, because correlations cannot explain causes.
- Tracing effects back to one seemingly plausible cause, because it is more appropriate to always look for many causes.
- Belief in majorities, because majorities cannot deliver a contribution to the furtherance of insight.
- The belief that experts (of marketing, of personnel management) display rational behavior, while those being guided (consumers, "subordinates") display layman's behavior. Experts believe they exercise power, and that they apply social techniques in a rational manner. They overlook the fact that social psychological theories regarding the inappropriate, partly irrational way of handling information, also apply to them.

The following differentiation (points 1 through 6) between lay and scientific theories can largely be traced to Furnham (1988, p. 2 et seq.):

1. Lay theories are more implicitly and less formally formulated. By comparison scientific theories are explicit and formally expressed. Hypotheses are precisely formulated.
2. Lay theories are more contradictorily and less clearly formulated, and possible connections are not considered as much as tends to be the case in scientific proposition systems. It would certainly be an overestimation of scientific proposition systems to attribute to them fundamental clarity, freedom from contradiction and consideration of all interrelationships. A proposition like that would more likely

be identified as a subjectively distorted perception of reality from the point of view of science, explainable via bolstering of self-worth, or via reduction of cognitive dissonance. That would then be a "layperson's theory held by scientists themselves". The differentiation is a matter of degree!

3. Science seeks error; laymen seek verification. Science sees the recognition of errors as progress; laypeople see verification as progress.

4. In lay theories, cause and effect are often confused, which is a result of laypeople's belief in correlations. If in reality X and Y occur together, then laypeople assume that one of the two factors has triggered the other. If one of the factors also occurs before the other in time then the matter appears to be clear cut. In reality a third factor Z could also have triggered both of the others; perhaps X reacted more quickly to Z than Y. To naive observers however it appears that X has clearly caused Y.

5. Laypeople tend to consider existing states, whereas scientific propositions are more directed toward interest in the processes by which states come about. Scientists want to know why a certain state has come about. Laypeople attempt more to understand existing structures. But this is futile if it is not known why a particular state has come about.

6. As much as possible, scientific theories are oriented toward propositions that are universally valid, whereas laypeople are content with very specific propositions. Laypeople often contradict universally valid propositions, using the excuse: "that is completely different in our market, in our case, etc.". Laypeople are content with mini-theories that describe a particular case. And also in "scientifically oriented studies", mini-theories are often worked with: case studies are greatly emphasized. It goes unrecognized here that case studies do not have any predictive power if there is no universally valid theory backing them up. What should a student learn from a case study that describes a single case? Case studies merely have the function of illustrating theories. As our book contains case studies, we do deem them useful for illustration!

7. Furthermore, a differentiation is made between "strong" and "weak" theories (Eysenck, 1960). Strong theories are characterized by having a greater amount of systematic, and as precisely described as possible, empirical substantiation. Weak theories are not based on much, only little, or on no comprehensible data at all. As far as weak theories are concerned we are aware of one well-known example from marketing: the widespread belief in influence via subliminal perception. This assumption is supported by a report that was circulated in the 1950s by a United States advertising agency, which described how during the course of movies, statements that were inserted regarding Coca-Cola® and popcorn resulted in an increase of their consumption. The insertions only lasted for fractions of a second and so could not be perceived consciously. The belief in this effect is widespread, even though there is no serious scientific evidence for it, and despite knowing nothing of the experimental setup then used and the fact that there were scientific errors. It is just as possible and certainly probable that those assertions were deceptive.

8. To a large extent laypeople proceed inductively; they believe they can arrive at universally valid propositions from individual observations. That induction offers this possibility is logically contradicted by the critical application of reason. There is no reason why arriving at an assumption regarding one case should also apply to another case. Inductive reasoning can only serve the formulation of new hypotheses, but it

cannot gather new insight (see Popper, 1979, pp. xxx–xxxiii). Scientific propositions start with the deductive procedure, with positing (of something) and the attempt at proof, which if necessary may lead to proving the thing wrong, but it will never lead to ultimate verification.

9. Laypeople tend more to believe in objectivity in the sense of impartiality; from the scientific point of view objectivity can merely indicate impartiality.

10. In scientifically-oriented theories, tests are made against hypotheses. Whoever seeks insight scientifically formulates a hypothesis and then attempts to refute it. As long as refutation of the hypothesis meets with failure, it is tentatively considered to hold true. In the layperson's search for insight there is a tendency to confirm less definite hypotheses. This has something to do with the fact that laypeople seek certainty. The search for certainty is irrational however, because there can be no certainty. After a visit to the doctor laypeople want to know (!) that they are healthy, but scientifically one can only tell them that no evidence has been found of certain illnesses.

Lay theories are oriented within a system of culturally or societally relevant value systems or systems of norms, and are consistent with these. They are changed if these overarching value systems and systems of norms change. Scientific theories are changed if their propositions are proven false. On top of this there is a multitude of "folk sayings" that are, unproven, accepted as valid:

"Risk known is risk avoided" and "the exception proves the rule", are two such dangerous sayings. Since there is no such thing as an unbiased description of a problem, and since certain solutions are already contained in the problem description, which are just as biased as the problem description, this seeming recognition of risk will by no means automatically lead to a solution. This "wisdom" is dangerous because it hastily leads to possibly false solutions. One only has to quickly review the history or financial markets to see that simply identifying risk does not alleviate it from the equation. In the words of Galbraith (1993), "financial genius is before the fall".

The exception does not prove the rule at all; the exception is an interesting instance of the rule being contradicted. The exception is a problem in need of an explanation. This folk wisdom is dangerous because it fixates false assumptions, whereby every contradiction can be taken as confirmation.

Lay theories are often characterized by belief in authorities. We very often come across in dissertations (and in lectures) the statement: "So and so has said …" This is not the scientifically correct form of citation (against which no objection can be directed), but rather it is much more the attempt to strengthen an assertion through citing an authority. In reality there is no authority that can claim the truth. The search for authorities we can appeal to is seemingly an ancient one. "How do you know that?" We do not answer this question by telling of how we acquired this knowledge, but by the naming of authorities, which in ancient times may have been visionaries. "Visionaries" invoke powers of all kinds: spirits, holy wolves, etc. (Gear and O'Neal Gear, 1990, p. 127). Today we call upon well-known personalities; the insight exhibited is the same. If a significant personality stands behind a proposition, this has absolutely nothing to do with the amount of insight it holds. As something expressed in language (but only as such), the proposition itself is a part of reality and can trigger tremendous consequences. In the Middle Ages people sought the cause of the plague. Without any basis in reality, it was suspected that people poisoned the wells (this saying exists to this day). The suspicion became a psychological reality and still has an effect amongst the people. People latch onto authorities because they are seeking certainty. If they cannot find an explanation for something, then they will invent one, which for lack of better alternatives is taken to be an unquestionably correct proposition. The doubter will be all the more persecuted, the more unlikely a better alternative appears to be, or the more another explanation that comes close to the truth triggers cognitive dissonance; in other words the doubtful but more consistent explanation appears to be more pleasing.

Lay theories are often more superficial than scientific propositions; laypeople are too readily satisfied by a seemingly plausible explanation (Furnham, 1988, p. 31), and in particular they are more strongly oriented toward certain people than they are toward scientific propositions. In the latter case, it is overlooked that these people are/were themselves part of the set of conditions to be described, and therefore a universally valid proposition regarding the set of conditions is not admissible. Many "success stories of famous managers" may serve as a disturbing example.

Laypeople hold what they understand to be correct.

Aversion to theories is a typical characteristic of laypeople. What is being overlooked here is that every insight is nothing other than a theory. What is disregarded is that practical experience is nothing other than theory formation. Practical experience is simply less critically and less systematically examined. Practical experience has arisen in that the given person has continuously attempted to confirm his assumptions (which to him appear to be more like knowledge than like assumptions). Practice is finalistic and focused on the result of action; theory is a never-ending process of searching for insight. The distinction between the layperson's and the scientific search for insight is certainly not always clearly brought out. Furnham (1990, p. 178) cites (without listing the source) Julian Huxley: "Science is nothing but trained and organized Common Sense, differing from the latter only as a veteran may differ from a raw recruit: and its methods differ from those of Common Sense only as far as the guardsman's cut thrust differs from the manner in which a savage wields his club." If we make it clear that scientists also definitely (though maybe only partly) behave like laypeople do, then the basic tendency toward this differentiation only seems logical. The program of study in lay epistemology consists of the attempt to develop a scientific concept of human behavior, which is then equally applicable to scientists, who are also human beings (Groeben, 1990, p. 21).

The differentiation between lay and scientific thinking should by no means be understood as scientism. We (the authors) do not believe in the "fundamental superiority" of science. We do certainly think that insight can be generated and improved via the critical examination of hypotheses and solutions to problems (the latter are hypotheses in reality). That applies to science and practice equally. Comparing theory to practice, which is a way of thinking that first arose in the nineteenth century (see Luhmann, 2000, p. 473), does not hold up logically. It would be beneficial to the furtherance of insight if this superfluous and error-generating separation were done away with. The fact that in this book we set examples of application (from the field of practice) against every theory only serves as illustration, and is in no way a "contrast". Examples from practice also do not serve to "prove" a theory. They are (and this only applies provisionally due to the possibility of their being unchecked, unobserved influencing factors) to be understood as instances in which the theory has proven itself for the time being.

Applications

PERSONNEL MANAGEMENT

People conduct themselves in the way that they believe they are expected to behave. This means that personnel will behave in a way that conforms to the hypotheses of managers; in reality what is at hand is merely the well-known "self fulfilling prophecy" effect. Managers unconsciously communicate their hypotheses regarding the behavior of personnel, and in the long term this will correspond with their hypotheses.

McGregor (1960) holds this view. A consequence of this is that managers evoke behavior that corresponds with their basic attitude, which is also reflected in the behavior of managers with regard to the staff (see also Bröckermann, 1997, p. 262). McGregor has characterized a negative basic attitude on behalf of managers as theory X; a more positive basic attitude is theory Y. Theory Y and theory X are therefore lay theories held by the managers with regard to the attitudes of the staff toward work.

In the end both types of managers believe themselves to be in the right, even though from a psychological point of view the tendency is that theory Y is the one that ought to be affirmed. The respective convictions that managers have regarding people, when taken together with the tendency people have of behaving the way they are expected to behave, leads to the conclusion that the lay theory of managers does appear to make sense.

MARKETING AND COMPANY MANAGEMENT

In market communication, social technicians exercise commercial influence over the widest diversity of target groups. Social technicians are all those people who put social scientific knowledge into practice in order to achieve whatever goal. That could be for example marketing managers or specifically communications managers. They hold assumptions regarding the behavior of the people in their target groups and the possibility of influencing them. These managers are not always trained social scientists. They often have enjoyed an education with a completely different focus. But as far as trained social scientists (psychology, sociology, economic science) are concerned, it has for a long time not been said that here the respective social science techniques are realized at a scientific level. These remarks should by no means create the idea that the respective practically implemented social science techniques are in some way negatively constrained by scientific modes of proceeding. It is simply significant that both the behavior of people within the groups targeted by these measures (for example, consumers), and the behavior of those engaged in the measures meant to influence those targeted, can be the subject matter of social scientific research.

Lay epistemology can explain with what assumptions social technicians plan, realize, and subsequently evaluate their activities. It can be asked in what way the assumptions of social technicians differ from those of social scientists, or to what extent they are similar. In this regard studies conducted by Friestad and Wright (1995) show that there are many similarities as well as differences. Accordingly the assumptions of laypeople and scientists correspond with regard to:

- the necessity of internal occurrences (excitation),
- the significance the sequence of advertising impulses has in a TV advertisement,

- the significance of independent activities on behalf of those targeted by the advertising, or of those activities triggered by the advertising,
- the question of how important very specific psychological effects, certain associations, cognitions, and feelings, are for the advertising effect.

In this respect laypeople and scientists are of one mind. The biggest difference that came out was with regard to assessment of advertising's influence on purchasing. Laypeople tend to assume that occurrences triggered by advertising of feelings, strong emotions, ideas and memories, or visual advertising content, have more of an effect on purchase behavior than scientists tend to assume (Friestad and Wright, 1995, p. 69). This can possibly be explained in that professionals want to trigger purchasing behavior as a personal goal. It seems obvious that in this respect they rate the significance of their own activity more highly, perhaps overestimating it. An attempt at explanation of this sort is in keeping with consistency theory.

So, marketing managers presumably overestimate their knowledge of consumer behavior and the possibilities of influencing. In so doing this they also overestimate their own ignorance regarding communications' affective mechanisms.

Probst and Gomez (1993) have presented various specific cognitive errors that often occur in management:

- Problems are objectively there and only need to be clearly formulated. Here what is overseen is that the formulation of a problem may itself be a problematic condition in need of explanation.
- Every problem is a direct consequence of one cause. The problem already spoken of above occurs in management because decisions often have to be made under considerable time pressure. If a plausible cause is found then managers are strongly motivated to take this to be the actual and essential cause of the original problem.
- A clear picture of the actual state of things is enough in order to understand a situation. What is being overlooked here is that we cannot formulate an unbiased picture of any situation. Positive thinking in management comes into play here.
- Behavior is predictable; all that is needed is an extensive enough basis of information. In this case the level of information is simply overestimated. Other causes that are not known at the time of behavior prediction are not taken into consideration enough.
- Problem situations can be dominated; it is just a matter of effort. In this instance it is a matter of overestimating one's own influence on the environment. This may be a typical way of thinking of success oriented managers. The following is a similar idea: In practice a "doer" can make the solution to a problem happen. What is overlooked here is that human problem-solving behavior in all fields is a matter of context, that every problem appears in a very particular light. This context already contains essential assumptions regarding the given possibilities of solution, which can be seen by the decision-maker. Albert (1978, pp. 23 and 24) has made it clear that this dependence on context within problem-solving behavior plays a role in the results of many sciences, and at the same time is an important element of human practice overall. The selection of a problem is already often influenced by habits, attitudes, prejudgments, fears or so-called experiences. "Many components of such problem situations remain for the most part in the background, without being focused on,

others are made explicit during the course of trying to solve the given problem, and still others are significant right from the beginning" (Albert, 1978, p. 23).

- By implementing a solution a problem can be solved once and for all. The attitude results from the layperson's presumption of the monocausality of occurrences. If it is assumed that a problem can be traced to a single cause, there then follows the assumption that it can be alleviated by a single solution.

- People seek certainty. In general, people seem to have a problem with accepting uncertainty. This explains why for many people positive thinking is more attractive than critical rationalism. The attractiveness of hermeneutics (which does amount to relying on a "correct understanding") can be explained as striving for certainty. This motivation toward certainty appears to be one of the big problems of human existence, because certainty is not obtainable. In the practice of management, market research and corporate consultation are welcome transmitters of the illusion of certainty. To a large extent managers also believe that they must demonstrate their certainty. They often believe that the revealing of uncertainty will be perceived as weakness.

- People want to be right (as we have already discussed), and they believe they are right if others are of the same opinion. In management this is easy to achieve, since managers often surround themselves with people who think the managers are right.

- People engage in self protection; they want to defend their own feeling of self-worth and perhaps also even improve it. This motive of human behavior is applicable in general. As far as managers are concerned this is a particularly relevant factor, because they often believe they have to establish and demonstrate the quality of their management to the staff.

From all of these examples it is clear that management, in particular managers, are a special case of lay epistemology. The same goes for staff perception of the behavior of managers. The staff also pose questions regarding the motives and goals of managerial behavior, and in doing so this also sets scripts and schemas into motion. Lay hypotheses regarding the personal and professional reasons for the behavior of people in management positions are thus formed, which in turn influence the behavior of the staff. There then arises the strange situation of a mutual layperson's understanding of the behavior of all involved.

In management practice the belief in authorities is widespread to a particularly large extent. If a well-known one-time German professor makes the statement: "Quality requires time", then general agreement can be expected, even though this hypothesis has been contradicted empirically. Successful companies are simultaneously faster, better, and more cost effective than their less successful competitors (Rommel, Brück, Diederichs et al., 1993, p. 6). The often uncritical belief in the accuracy of statements made by well-known company consultants is further proof of the faith in authorities in management. The belief in ever-changing management doctrines also appears somewhat curious from an epistemological point of view. Whoever follows the publications coming out of this field quickly gets the impression that new management doctrines come and go like fashions. Kieser (1997, p. 49 et seq.) has shown that with respect to published materials, these kinds of concepts almost behave in accordance with the market life cycle: Quality circle, lean production, business process reengineering, total quality management. The sequence may proceed as follows: lean production, kaizen, total profit management. Kieser (1997, p. 57 et seq.) has shown that as a rule the management doctrine that becomes fashionable is a question of rhetoric. Management doctrines are then taken up in a very indiscriminate manner, that is, they are taken up by a great many companies without being examined. Some of them have success. Whether this is due to the management doctrine remains unproven. However, the success is touted as proof of the rightness of the given management doctrine. The ever-renewed search for healing doctrines is the irrational attempt to arrive at a concept that offers certainty. It seems difficult to accept that all human decisions and the solutions to problems that stem from them, arise from incomplete, uncertain, and with a high degree of likelihood, faulty information, and that thus these decisions are also quite likely to be faulty. "In this sense all solutions to problems in practice are, in the end, provisional and thereby are to be observed as revisable, including when they are also to a large extent socially entrenched" (Albert, 1978, pp. 26 and 27). In this respect, underlying all undertakings there is the continuous task of seeking better alternatives. This would only become unnecessary if we were in the position to establish decisions once and for all—however, that is impossible. Therefore "… the search for alternative solutions and comparative assessment of competing solutions is an important challenge with regard to the rational conception of practice, as long as the costs that arise from such an endeavor remain reasonable" (Albert, 1978, p. 26). It is becoming clear here that criticism takes on a fundamentally positive value. Whoever criticizes an existing solution to a problem also carries the responsibility of improving it. Criticism then becomes a necessary condition for every instance of progress. Managers tend, like all humans do, to want to see their assumptions confirmed, even if a critical assessment of existing information has to lead to a different view. An organization's way of thinking may in this way be based on a critical and rational way of learning (according to the currently accepted hypothesis).

CONCLUDING REMARK

The acceptance that we cannot know anything is by no means cause for pessimism. Just the opposite: everything that we attempt can be improved. The fact that we cannot know anything directly leads to the demand that greater allowance for creativity be granted. Since we cannot know anything for certain, we always need new ideas that no authority will put to a stop. We also have no reason to be afraid of pessimistic prognoses; since those who assert these prognoses also have no certainty, we can counter optimistic prognoses with just as much authority. We have the possibility to continuously develop new solutions to problems and to compare them to those that have been implemented thus far. A critical comparison of their advantages and disadvantages becomes apparent in rational practice (Albert, 1978). We also continuously need new ideas that can be examined as hypotheses, and in the case of success that can serve the evolutionary betterment of human existence in all fields (not just in management). Whoever is looking for the final, problem-free form of life, will meet with despair; we have to accept that our life consists in the solving of problems. That is our task, from which derives Popper's claim (1994, p. 326): "Optimism is a duty".

QUESTIONS FOR DISCUSSION

1. Define Lay Epistemology, specifically discuss the three classic motives for insight.
2. What are the primary differences between laymen and scientists?
3. How can the knowledge of Lay Epistemology help to structure better marketing campaigns? You may find citing the pharmaceutical industry helpful in your answer.
4. Discuss any personal experiences that you have in dealing with theory X and Y managers.

Bibliography

Albert, H.: *Traktat Über Rationale Praxis*. Tübingen: 1978. (*Treatise on Rational Practice*).

Bierhoff, H.W.: *Personenwahrnehmung—Vom ersten Eindruck zur Sozialen Interaktion*. Berlin, Heidelberg, New York, Tokyo: 1986. (*Personal Perception—Of the first impression of social interaction*).

Bierhoff, H.W.: *Person Perception and Attribution*. Berlin, Heidelberg, New York: 1989.

Bröckermann, R.: *Personalwirtschaft—Arbeitsbuch für das praxisorientierte Studium*. Köln: 1997. (*The Personal Economy—Workbook for Practice Oriented Study*).

Eysenck, H.J. (ed.): *Experiments in Personality*. London: 1960.

Eysenck, H.J.: The place of theory in psychology. In: Eysenck H.J. (ed.): *Experiments in Personality*. London: 1960.

Frey, D. and Irle, M. (eds): *Theorien der Sozialpsychologie, vol. III: Motivations- und Informationsverarbeitungstheorien*. Bern, Göttingen, Toronto, Seattle: 1993. (*Theories of Social Psychology, vol. III: Motivation Theories and Information Processing Theories*).

Friestad, M. and Wright, P.: Persuasion knowledge: Lay people's and researcher's beliefs about the psychology of advertising. *Journal of Consumer Research*, 1995, 22, 62–74.

Furnham, A.F.: *Lay theories—Everyday Understanding of Problems in the Social Sciences*. Oxford, New York, Beijing: 1988.

Furnham, A.F.: Common sense theories of personality. In: Semin, G.R. and Gergen, K.J. (eds): *Everyday understanding—Social and scientific implications*. London, Newbury Park, New Delhi: 1990, 176–203.

Galbraith, J.K.: *A Short History of Financial Euphoria*, Houghton Mifflin, Boston, 1983, 17.

Gear, W.M. and O'Neal Gear, K.: *People of the Wolf*. New York: 1990.

Groeben, N.: Subjective theories and the explanation of human action. In: Semin, G.R. and Gergen, K.J. (eds): *Everyday Understanding—Social and Scientific Implications*. London, Newbury Park, New Delhi: 1990, 19–44.

Kieser, A.: Rhetoric and myth in management fashion. *Organization*, 1997, 4, 49–74.

Kruglanski, A.W.: *Lay Epistemics and Human Knowledge*. New York, London: 1989.

——, Baldwind, M.W. and Towson, S.M.J.: Die theorie der laienepistemologie. In: Frey, D. and Irle, M. (eds): *Theorien der Sozialpsychologie, vol. III: Motivations- und Informationsverarbeitungstheorien*. Bern, Göttingen, Toronto, Seattle: 1993, 293–314. (The theory of lay epistemology. In *Theories of Social Psychology, vol. III: Motivation Theories and Information Processing Theories*).

Luhmann, N.: *Organisation und Entscheidung*. Wiesbaden: 2000. (*Organization and Decision*).

McGregor, D.: *The Human Side of Enterprise*. New York: 1960.

Popper, K.R.: *Die Beiden Grundprobleme der Erkenntnistheorie*. Tübingen: 1979. (*Two Basic Problems of Insight Theory*).

—— *Alles Leben ist Problemlösen*. München: 1994. (*All Life is Problem Free*).

Probst, G.J.B. and Gomez, P.: Die methodik des vernetzten denkens zur lösung komplexer probleme. In: Probst, G.J.B. and Gomez, P. (eds): *Vernetzes denken—Ganzheitliches Führen in der Praxis* (3rd edn). Wiesbaden: 1993, 3–20. (Networked thinking: The methods to the solution of complex problems. In *Networked Thinking—Integrated Leading in Practice*).

Probst, G.J.B. and Gomez, P. (eds): *Vernetztes Denken—Ganzheitliches Führen in der Praxis* (3rd edn). Wiesbaden: 1993. (*Networked Thinking—Integrated Leading in Practice*).

Rommel, G., Brück, F., Diederichs, R., Kempis, R.-D. and Kluge, J.: *Einfach Überlegen*. Stuttgart: 1993. (*Simply Consider*).

Semin, G.R. and Gergen, K.J. (eds): *Everyday Understanding—Social and Scientific Implications*. London, Newbury Park, New Delhi: 1990.

Unger, F. and Fuchs, W.: *Management der Marktkommunikation* (2nd edn). Heidelberg: 1999. (*Management of Market Communication*).

20 *Biological Psychology— Scientific Bases of Economical Behavior*

Concept and Relevance

Biological psychology is a branch of psychology in which the connection of biological and psychological circumstances comes to the forefront. This means that a biological viewpoint is included in the explanation of the experiences and behavior of a person. Psychic processes are examined with respect to psychological bases, and with respect to biological aspects. Biological psychology is concerned, in the broadest sense, with those physiological processes that have to do with understanding the importance of a person's experiences and behavior. It is a heterogeneous research area with various branches such as physiological psychology, neuropsychology and evolution psychology. Biological psychology is seen also as a branch of neuroscience which studies all activities having to do with neural structures and processes (Birbaumer and Schmidt, 2003, pp. 3–11; Schandry, 2003, pp. 1–2). Additionally, it has been documented that the self-concept of psychology has also become a science, as it is one of the focal points of scientific research among the sciences and social sciences (Fröhlich, 1981, p. 27; von Rosenstiel, 2003, p. 3).

Biological psychology is more broadly defined than physiological psychology. Physiological psychology concentrates on the connections between the primary nerve system (PNS) and its behavior, has a strong scientific basis and serves a less practical orientiation rather than considering the investigation of phenomena outside of the theory of development. Studies frequently move into the biological area primarily by means of electric stimulation. Other studies are conducted by the manipulation of neurochemicals or by surgical intervention. Then the variations are increased to include behavior parameters. Predominantly studies involve animal experiments. A problem exists in the scope of this analysis, as other body systems are neglected. Additionally, most peripheral organ systems are driven by the central nervous system (CNS). In biological psychology, it is even more important, because the CNS is influenced peripherally by physiological processes and also by the behavior of joint neurobiological processes (Schandry, 2003, p. 1).

In the field of neuropsychology, the influences on the processes of the brain are studied on patients with interferences in the functioning of the brain. These interferences could be in the form of illnesses, injuries or neurological interventions, all of which would influence their behavior. Behavioral interferences are then assigned to the locatable brain regions so that conclusions can be determined on the processing of this brain region in healthy patients. This direction of research is very practically oriented. The goals of the research are to improve diagnostics and to develop new methods of rehabilitation (Schandry, 2003, pp. 1–2).

In evolution psychology, the phylogenetic development of experience and behavior is investigated. The behavior of the person is compared and analyzed in light of their family history (Janke, 1993, p. 106). Thus, evolution psychology explains the frequently cited fact that in comparison to women, men possess a better spatial orientation capability, as they had to move away and orient themselves in this way in their early historical development in order to support the family from far distances, while women were concerned with other more locally-bound tasks.

The relevance of the insights of biological psychology is that it contributes to a better understanding of the physiological, biochemical and central nervous processes of human experience and behavior. This relevance is further documented in the young and interdisciplinary research area of neuroeconomics. The insights of biological psychology can be used at the same time in the framework of scientific and practical questions. This concerns, for example, the formation of brands, the effects of advertising, and the selection of personnel. Before we turn to the use of the insights of biological psychology, we will discuss briefly in the following sections some basic insights from brain research and the central investigation methods of biological psychology.

Brain Regions and Their Functions

In order to enable an understanding of the studies cited later and their practical implications, the following section explains the different areas of the brain and their functions.

The brain is usually segregated into the following areas and/or sections (see Figure 20.1).

* Medulla oblongata (extended mark).
* Pons (bridge).
* Mesencephalon (midbrain).
* Diencephalon (interbrain).
* Cerebellum (small brain).
* Telencephalon (cerebrum, large brain, end brain).

The medulla oblongata is the lowest part of the brain. Above the medulla oblongata and the spinal cord is the pons (bridge). The medulla oblongata contains important nuclei zones that receive functions concerning vegetative control. From here the respiratory and the circulatory functions are driven. Other different brain nuclei are also located here. Heavy damage to the medulla oblongata leads to interference with circulation, and eventually to death (Schandry, 2003, p. 109). The connections between the small brain hemispheres are through the bridge, and like the medulla oblongata, it also contains a row of brain nerve nuclei. The most important functions of the small brain are coordination and motor control. The small brain is connected to numerous other regions of the brain, and it is also integrated with the regulation of motor activity. The information coming from the small brain provides for the smooth sequence of movement activity. In addition the small brain plays an important role in understanding automatic action flows (Schandry, 2003, pp. 110 and 111).

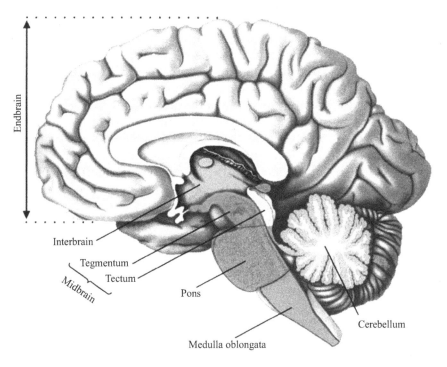

Figure 20.1 The primary sections of the brain (Schandry, 2003, p. 107)

The internal part of the brain stem comes from the medulla oblongata over the bridge to the mid-brain via a structure of networked neuron zones reached through the reticular fomation. This acts as a driving network and is connected with all important brain regions. Its most important function lies in the regulation of the general activity of the cortex. Above the cortex, the reticular formation receives information about sensory inputs, modulates the awareness processing of this information and then sends unspecific activating impulses over climbing pathways at the cerebral cortex. Over descending pathways, the reticular formation is involved in the control of the most important body functions (Schandry, 2003, pp. 111–115).

The mid-brain designates the transition area between the lower brain stem regions and the front brain, and it contains important nuclei groups of brain nerves. The interbrain (diencephalon) forms the front brain (large brain, prosencephalon) with the end brain (telencephalon) together. The most important structures of the diencephalon are the thalamus and the hypothalamus. The thalamus has a lens shape and consists of an aggregation of nerve cell bodies. It contains prior connections processed previously by almost all parts of the cerebral cortex, and is also furnished with subcortical structures that contain sensory information. The thalamus is designated as a "gate to the consciousness" because it filters all flowing sensory information (with exception of the system of smell) that are handled with awareness processing of perception contents, before it forwards the sensory information to other regions of the brain. Certain nuclei zones of the thalamus can influence motivational, emotional and cognitive processes. The hypothalamus is above all responsible for the regulation of vital functions such as respiration, circulation and body temperature. It is also of large importance for emotion accompanying physical body processes (Schandry, 2003, pp. 117–127).

The large brain makes up 85 percent of the total brain weight in humans and is further organized into the large cerebral cortex and the large brain marrow. The large cerebral cortex is subdivided into two hemispheres. The surface is made up of numerous furrows (sulci) and turns (gyri). In the large brain marrow lie the basal ganglions; these are aggregations of nerve cell bodies. They consist of final brain nuclei, which include the striatum with both substructure nucleus caudatus and putamen as well as the pallidum. The putamen and pallidum are also designated together as a lens nuclei. The basal ganglions are associated with the substantia nigra and, some researchers also believe, the amygdala. The amygdala plays an important role in the experiencing of anxiety and in the storage of emotional memory. The basal ganglions have an important role in modulating movement control, in that they drive the motor impulses of the cortex over complex interconnections in a more varied manner (Schandry, 2003, pp. 121–141).

The cortex forms the external layer of the large brain hemisphere and consists predominantly of nerve cell bodies. It contains over 10 billion neurons that are arranged in several layers. It becomes subdivided in the iso- or neocortex and in the phylogenetic of the older allocortex. The limbic system designates a summary of different structures of the cortex. Until recently, no unified rules existed about which structures were involved. Today, most researchers agree that the hippocampus, amygdala and the gyrus cinguli, are included. The limbic system is involved in the control of all behavior and thinking processes and also involves emotional processes. The hippocampus plays a decisive role in the storing and recalling of memory contents. The gyrus cinguli regulates respiration and circulation, which includes digestion and motor activity. In animal experiments, stimulation in the front region of the gyrus cinguli caused variations in emotional behavior, above all in the area of aggressive behavior. These features of the gyrus cinguli led to social interest in the topic and the possibility of reducing aggressive behaviors (Birbaumer and Schmidt, 2003, p. 466; Schandry, 2003, pp. 135–140).

The neocortex, which is the phyologenetically youngest part of the large cerebral cortex, is encased with very many nerve cells in a complex pattern. Here the most demanding intellectual processes reside, for example, the understanding of language or the pursuing of strategies. The neocortex is subdivided into four lobes (lobi) (see Figure 20.2):

- the frontal (or forehead) lobe,
- the temporal (or temple) lobe,
- the parietal (or top of the head) lobe, and
- the occipital (or rear of the head) lobe.

The frontal lobe is highly important in motor activity and also for language motor activity, while the prefrontal area is important in complex functions of working memory, action planning, motivation, and the personality. The prefrontal cortex is a phylogenetically new area. It has an abundance of functions. Patients who have damage in this zone frequently display large personality impairments. These patients often experience disturbed long-term action planning which controls motivational and emotional impulses, as well as effects on the ability to concentrate and on the motor drive. Also involved here are principles such as ethics and morality, as some patients

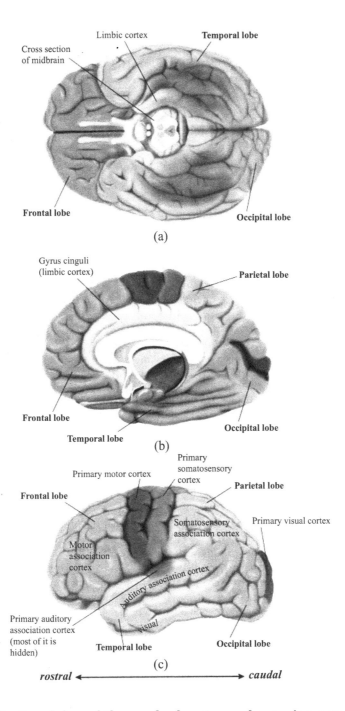

Limbic cortex

Temporal lobe

Cross section
of midbrain

Frontal lobe

Occipital lobe

(a)

Gyrus cinguli
(limbic cortex)

Parietal lobe

Frontal lobe

Occipital lobe

Temporal lobe

(b)

Primary
somatosensory
cortex

Primary motor cortex

Parietal lobe

Frontal lobe

Somatosensory
association cortex

Primary visual cortex

Motor
association
cortex

Auditory association cortex

Primary auditory
association cortex
(most of it is
hidden)

visual

Temporal lobe

Occipital lobe

(c)

rostral ← → *caudal*

**Figure 20.2 The four lobes of the cerebral cortex and some important cortex
areas, from Carlson (2004, p. 96)**

can show an indifferent or emotionally unstable behavior. In the temporal lobe lies the sensory language center and the end of the auditory system, while in the parietal lobe, mostly somatosensible cortex areas are located. The visual cortex lies in the occipital lobe (Birbaumer and Schmidt, 2003, pp. 720–727; Schandry, 2003, pp. 145–155).

Investigation Methods of Biological Psychology

The investigation methods of biological psychology can be divided into three groups (Bortz and Döring, 1995, p. 256). Each will be discussed in the sections that follow.

INVESTIGATION METHODS OF THE PERIPHERAL NERVE SYSTEM

Cardiovascular, electrodermal and muscular activity are the central indicators of the peripheral nerve system. Cardiovascular activity is assessed by the heartbeat frequency and the blood pressure. The best-known procedure for the continuous measurement of heart activity is the electrocardiogram (ECG), which continuously shows the electric excitement processes of the heart. Blood pressure is usually measured with the cufflink pressure process developed by Riva-Rocci. In this process, a pressure is exercised outside of the artery wall, whose pressure suffices to compensate the interior pressure. The outside pressure is registered over a manometer.

The most important indicator for electrodermal activity is skin conductivity. It is measured by attaching electrodes to two points on the hand area. This process also allows one to distinguish tonic skin conductivity mass, which indicates the height of the electrodermal activity ("skin conductance level"), and phases that mark reaction to external stimuli (skin conductivity reactions, "skin conductance response"). In order to measure the electrical muscle activity, Electromyography (EMG) is used. For this test, two bipolar electrodes are raised at the end and the beginning of the body surface of the muscle.

INVESTIGATION METHODS OF THE CENTRAL NERVE SYSTEM

The Electroencephalogram (EEG) is still the most commonly-used method for the detection of electric brain activity. In the last few years, imaging procedures have become much more meaningful.

Electroencephalogram (EEG)

Electro-chemical processes and resulting action potential forms the basis of neural activity. In the EEG, these electric brain processes are recorded at the surface of the skull. At the top of the skull, the synchronic potential variations of larger associations of neurons are measurable. In electric brain activity, one distinguishes between:

1. spontaneous activity, and
2. evoked activity.

Spontaneous activity appears as a tension variation registered continuously from the skull surface. Concurrently, alpha waves with a frequency of 8–13 Hz mark the relaxed waking state. Next to alpha waves, the EEG of an awake person also always shows beta waves between 14–30 Hz). Theta waves (5–7 Hz) are to be found mostly in the waking state or in the transition to sleep. Delta waves (0.5–4 Hz) are found in healthy adults only in phases of deep sleep (see Figure 20.3). Activity in the gamma volume (30–100 Hz) appears as an accompaniment to the interaction of different and spatially separated neuron groups. The evoked activity appears in connection with attractions, motor activity and action intentions. Herewith one can distinguish early and late components. The early components are influenced by the attraction characteristics, and are represented by the subject-specific processing processes during the late components (Schandry, 2003, pp. 565–573).

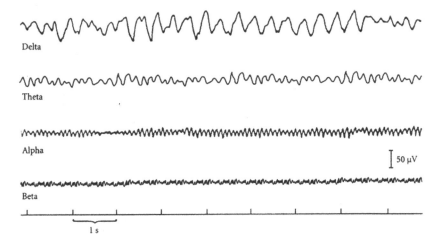

Figure 20.3 Activity rhythmic example for the four most frequent types of spontaneous EEG (Schandry, 2003, p. 567)

Imaging procedures—Neuroimaging

Today, a multitude of imaging procedures (known as Neuroimaging) are available in order to examine the structure, construction, biochemistry and function of the brain (Birbaumer and Schmidt, 2003, pp. 498–514; Schandry, 2003, pp. 577–587).

• **Cat scan (CT)**

The cat scan (CT) functions similarly to classic x-ray technology, but with a much better picture resolution. A further advantage exists as sectional images can be prepared. To this a more folded-shaped x-ray is sent sequentially out at different directions through each single layer of the body. For each single layer, the computer calculates an exact picture out of the single records of the different angles.

- **Magnet resonance tomography (MRT)**

Similar to the CT, the MRT also produces sectional images. It differs from the CT in that it does not involve radiation exposure, cuts planes in all spatial directions which can be freely selected, and the pictures produced possess a higher resolution.

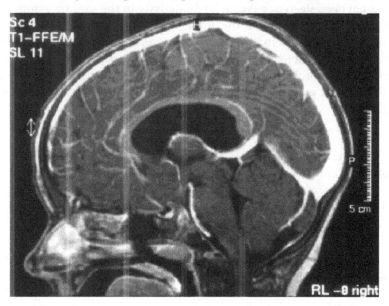

Figure 20.4 MRT picture

- **Functional magnet resonance tomography (fMRT)**

The fMRT is one of the most important imaging procedures in medicine. Using this procedure, the working brain can be represented. It can be determined, for example, which attractions excite the emotional centers of the brain, and where expression-like feelings or thought in neural activity can be located. The fMRT records two-dimensional and three-dimensional pictures of organs by means of strong magnetic fields and radio waves and forms separate images of bone and tissue structures. In contrast to x-rays of single organs which enable only on-the-spot notations, consecutive brain activities can be portrayed in the fMRT indirectly from the blood flow. The procedure focuses on those regions with increased nerve cell activity where the oxygen and glucose levels climb. Active nerve cells require high levels of oxygen that is delivered with an increased influx of blood. The blood functions at the same time as a contrast agent whereby the device identifies the oxygen particles in the blood. This method reacts with time delay and does not distinguish whether increased blood flows derive from the inhibition or activation of nerve cells.

The strength of the procedure is that it can determine which brain regions are important to certain functions. It is suited above all to the investigation of "input systems", for example, the visual system. By means of the fMRT, the areas of the brain that react respectively to faces, places or bodies can be located. The focus on an object, or just the imagination of it, can activate the specific area. A disadvantage of this procedure is that the test subjects must avoid movement in order to guarantee sufficient picture sharpness.

• **Positron emission tomography (PET)**

In the PET (see Figure 20.5), the metabolism processes in the body are examined with the help of energy emissions that appear in the form of positrons.

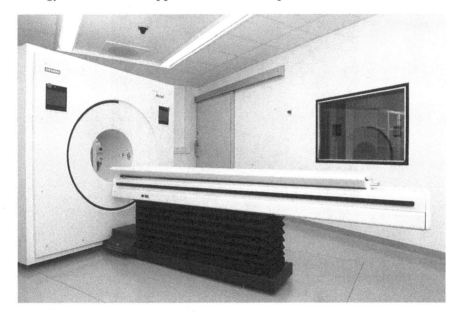

Figure 20.5 PET-Scanner

In this procedure, the test subject receives a weak radioactive contrast agent that travels via the blood into the brain and accumulates in regions of high metabolic activity. These areas of increased activity can be identified and become visually represented by means of a computer (see Figure 20.6).

• **Functional transcranial doppler sonography (fTDS)**

In fTDS, the speed of blood flow in both sides of the brain is measured via ultrasound. If the blood flow rises from certain tasks that the test subject carries out, the difference in the blood flow speed relative to the activity of the one side of the brain to the other provides insight (Birbaumer and Schmidt, 2003, pp. 498–514; Schandry, 2003, pp. 577–587).

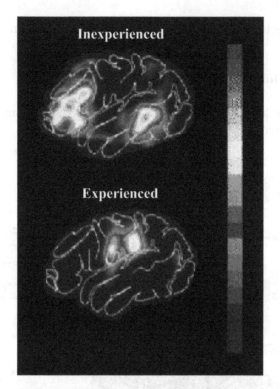

Figure 20.6 PET pictures of differing experience phases in the learning of foreign-language texts

INVESTIGATION METHODS OF ENDOCRINE SYSTEMS AND THE IMMUNE SYSTEM

Psychic factors influence the hormonal balance and the immune system. The activity of the immune system can be reversed again as the behavior drive (that is, sleep behavior and appetite), and hormonal processes play an important role in the regulation of actions, motivation and emotions. The concentration of hormones in blood, urine and saliva is determined by the Radioimmunoassay method (RIA method). In order to study the contents of saliva, cotton wool is carefully chewed for less than a minute and subsequently spun with centrifugal force. The determination of immune activity takes place via biochemical blood analyses. The concentration of immune active cells in the blood is determined with the flow cytometry method. In this approach, the cells marked with flourescent substances are counted (Bortz and Döring, 1995, pp. 266–268).

Present Examples of Biological Psychology

BRAND AWARENESS AND ADVERTISING

A successful brand can strongly influence the purchase decisions of customers. But why do people prefer a certain brand when they could buy the same product with a generic label for a fraction of the cost? Why do customers apparently behave so irrationally?

Which processes are active in the brain when observing advertising? What makes some products more likely to act as status symbol objects?

Classic economical decision theory cannot answer these questions satisfactorily because it comes from the viewpoint of the rational person, who is interested solely in maximizing their own utility. Emotional phenomena such as confidence or fairness cannot therefore be explained in this way (Akerlof and Shiller, 2009). Customers are not always driven by reason and utility maximization. Personal decisions are controlled strongly by emotional processes, and these can be studied by means of the described investigation methods of biological psychology.

With imaging methods and brain research, some marketing experts hope to gain a direct view of the customer's brain functions. Market research is connected with the most progressive analysis methods under the auspices of "neuromarketing". An advantage of neuroimaging procedures as opposed to conventional enquiries is that the unconscious processes are portrayed and thus the results cannot be falsified by socially desirable behavior answers. A further advantage lies in the fact that processes at the moment of decision can be examined and possible falsification tendencies avoided, which can occur in other enquiries due to the temporal delay between the decision event and the measuring moment.

A use of imaging procedures exists to examine why certain brands in anonymous taste tests where the subjects do not know which brand they are eating or drinking, performs more poorly than when subjects know which brands they are drinking or eating. An example of this phenomenon is the brand Coca-Cola®. In anonymous taste tests, Coca-Cola® has for decades performed more poorly than the brand Pepsi® (see Figure 20.7). If the test subjects know the brand that they are drinking, when they are drinking it, Coca-Cola® is typically preferred (McClure et al., 2004). By means of modern neuroimaging procedures it can be shown that Pepsi® in the blind attempt caused a stronger reaction in the ventromedial prefrontal cortex. If the test subjects were informed however about the brand, their preference changed and therewith the pattern of brain activity. The enjoyment of Coca-Cola® activated the medial prefrontal cortex that is responsible for higher cognitive functions. The positive performance of Coca-Cola® in a test where the subjects know which brand they are drinking is assumed here because this brain region has been activated if test subjects think about all of the positive characteristics of Coca-Cola®'s advertisements or they strongly identify with the product. More positive associations were connected with the brand Coca-Cola®, and it was linked more strongly with a positive self-image. This and the taste contribute to the value of the brand and lead to the purchase of the product.

However, other researchers did not view these brain pictures as a reference to increased, but rather to reduced, activity in the front brain, that is, as a sign of cortical relief. In easily remembered brands, the intellect "is removed" (Schnabel, 2003).

In a study in which 24 test subjects were presented various coffee brands in a random sequence, the pictures from the fMRT showed that for persons with a strong affinity for a brand, there was a diminished activity in the areas of the prefrontal cortex which is responsible for rational decisions, and an increased circulation in areas that are responsible for feelings, affective actions and perception. These activation patterns appeared in both sides of the brain. This means that there exists a measurable connection between the decision for a strong brand and neural activity. Strong brands are those which succeed in binding emotions into the decision-making process and that are addressed on both sides of the brain, not only the right side.

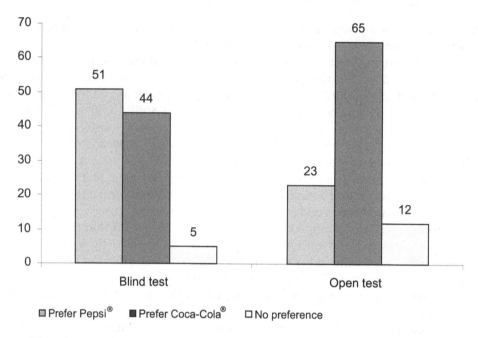

Figure 20.7 Comparison of the results of a blind taste test and an open taste test between Coca-Cola® and Pepsi® (Chernatony and McDonald, 1992, p. 9)

For each person, however, only one brand of the mentioned product category was able to cause the described effect, and emotionalize the decision process (Kenning et al., 2005; Kenning et al., 2002). Emotions are an important component of a brand. A brand that can exactly match the emotions and desires of a target group can anchor itself especially well in the minds of these people. Yet the question of at which moment emotions influence the decision-making process for or against a brand is still unexplained. Is the perception of brand information changed through the emotions or does the process run the other way around (Kenning et al., 2005)?

What are the consequences for brand management? The last study clearly made the point that a strategic realignment of advertising is necessary. Managers often rely only on the concept of the relevant set in data clustering. This includes the primary statement that constomers in a purchase decision only concentrate on a certain small number of competing products, while other products remain unconsidered. The goal of the concept of the relevant set exists therefore to arrive at this narrower choice of products. If there exists a large distance between the brand with the highest attractiveness and that in second place, and a very much larger distance between brands two and three, the goal of a brand manager should lie in landing few customers from the first place brand as there are many customers in places two and three to obtain. This goal can be probably be reached sooner through surprising, experience-oriented brand imaging, than through frequently repeated, weakly emotion-oriented advertising (Kenning et al., 2005).

The described newer methods can serve therefore as additional value for strategic decisions in brand management. Firms that ask these additional questions may find answers about the potential or the culture-spreading effect of a brand more easily (Kenning et al., 2005). Also regarding the construction and the positioning of a new brand, brain research in the sense of "limbic branding" can be helpful as the brain area of the limbic system is responsible for motivation and emotion. Moreover, it follows that from control comes knowledge of which advertising strategies and concepts strengthen a brand and which weaken the brand (Kenning et al., 2005). In a recent article in *The Wall Street Journal*, Campbell's Soup Company was highlighted for their use of "neuromarketing" techniques in order to improve the presentation of the labeling on some of its flavors of its lower selling soup brands. Steam was added coming from the soup on the label as it was expected that customers would be more emotionally engaged if the soup looked warm. Additionally, the spoon was removed and the bowl design was updated as both were seen as being dated advertising techniques. Additionally, the different varieties of soups were color-coded on the labels in order the help consumers distinguish them better (Brat, 2010, p. 6).

Modern neuroimaging procedures also open the possibility of examining the subliminal effects of advertising. To effect an awareness perception of advertising, a certain number of contacts are necessary (called the threshold effect). What happens to this threshold beneath the awareness perception? Non-stop subliminal information streams into the brain and influences the behavior, without the person perceiving anything. In order to arrive into the consciousness, an attraction must linger long enough (several hundred milliseconds) or a certain intensity threshold must be exceeded in order to synchronize a sufficient quantity of neurons. Advertising psychologists assume at the same time that unconscious information can influence purchasing behavior, because the related products are trusted and comfortably estimated earlier. Above all the sense of smell offers a way in the unconscious, as there are only two synapses of the nose to the hippocampus which leads to where memory contents are processed (May, 2003). So aromas of freshly washed linen in a t-shirt business or the smell of fresh leather in a car dealership are in a position to drive the sales figures to new heights. Pheromones that were sprayed in a large department store in London during the Christmas season, increased the time spent and the purchasing enthusiasm of the customers (Butler et al., 1999). Also the ear opens the access to the unconscious. Psychologists at the University of Leicester let a French accordian melody play every second day in a supermarket, and this led to customers purchasing much more French as opposed to German wine. In the variation with Bavarian march music, this ratio turned itself around to the German side (Luczak, 2004).

Other studies in connection with advertising investigated the question of which processes influence political advertising messages in the brain of the voter. For this purpose, subjects were examined with Magnetic Resonance Imaging (MRI) while advertisements from the 2004 campaigns by President George W. Bush and Senator John Kerry were shown. Special attention was paid to activities in the prefrontal cortex. While the medial part of the brain area plays a strong role in the self-image of a person, activity in the lower part, which is known as the ventromedial prefrontal cortex, is interpreted as emotional reaction. Increased brain activity in the upper part of this area, known as the dorsolateral prefrontal cortex, indicates the rational reactions of a person. On the pictures of the presidential candidates, the brains of the test subjects reacted first of all emotionally, therefore in the area of the ventromedial prefrontal cortex. After consideration of the message, an emotional reaction was shown only for the candidate of the preferred party, as the other candidate signaled increased activity in the dorsolateral prefrontal cortex, where rational decisions are made. In the Bush advertisement, pictures of the September 11, 2001 attacks were shown, and the amygdala (the area that plays a role in the processing of anxieties) was more strongly active for the Democratic voters. The difficulty lies in the interpretation of these results. Although the scientists saw these results as evidence in favor of the hypothesis that Democratic voters reacted in a more alarmed fashion to terrorist threats than did Republican voters, other explanations are conceivable. This is similar to when the stimulation of the amygdala cannot be determined without additional information as to whether the relevant person laughs or cries (Beak, 2004). A further problem exists where brains differ in their anatomical details. In group analyses, the pictures of all patients must be distorted so that they fit on a standardized normal brain. In this analysis, one only receives the lowest common denominator of all test subjects (Walter, 2003).

For the purposes of marketing, these results indicate that future investigations are needed. For example, it would be an important task of differentiation regarding a failed Web campaign to determine whether missing advertising pressure or another cause was responsible for the poor results. Was the advertising shown rarely to be able to control, in a sufficient number, the customers' reactions, or would a different advertising method have reached one with a better emotional anchor for the product (Kenning et al., 2005)? The methods and insights of biological psychology can form an important contribution to the clarification of this and similar questions.

CUSTOMER CONFIDENCE AND DISSATISFACTION

One question raised in the few last years concerns the interest of the business and science communities in the origin and conditions of the confidence of market participants. A high degree of confidence is seen as a central prerequisite for economic success. The sooner the members of a company tend to trust one another, the higher is the investment rate and the fewer the transaction costs concerned with time-consuming investigations about potential business partners (Zak, 2004, 2003). Game theory is an important means of studying the neurobiological bases for decision-making.

In the Ultimatum game, test subject A gets ten one-dollar bills. They can deliver to test subject B any amount from the $10. If test subject B accepts the offer, the money is so divided. If test subject B rejects the offer, neither player gets anything. Rational expectations theory would predict that test subject A would offer its partner B one dollar, as this makes test subject A the largest profit, and for test subject B, one dollar is better than nothing. Actually however, many test subjects who act as B reject this offer when playing with live partners, but accept the same offer when the game is played with a computer. Also most people who play A do not act rationally, but rather make an offer in the vicinity of a just division (about $4). The fMRT pictures show that a low offer leads to activities in the brain region (insular cortex) that are associated with annoyance and abhorrence. The larger the activity in this area is, the sooner an offer of one dollar is rejected by test subject B. Herewith a conflict ensues with the impulse to simply accept simply the dollar, and with what appears as an increased stimulation of the prefrontal cortex (Sanfey et al., 2003).

In another game, test subject A is connected via a computer to test subject B. The game lasts for 10 rounds. Subject A initially gets $10, as before. They can retain this or can invest it together with test subject B. If test subject A decides on a joint investment, the cash amount invested is tripled, but test subject B has control over the profit and thus the option to transfer some of the money back to test subject A. If A retains $5 and invests $5, test subject B can either divide the money between the players or keep it all for themself. Since the game is played over 10 rounds, test subject B will be interested in gaining the confidence of test subject A. If either player abuses the confidence of the other, an area of the gyrus cinguli becomes active. Between men and women, there are interesting differences: male brains drive down the activity after the decision-making and wait for an answer from the other test subject. Female brains show activities in at least three areas: in the ventralen striatum, a center for expected rewards, in an area of the ventromedial prefrontal cortex which is responsible for planning and organization, and in the nucleus caudatus, which is involved in the supervision and inspection of actions and plays a large role in obsessive-compulsive disorders. This can be interpreted in that women seem to dispute their decisions sooner and worry sooner about whether they made the correct decision. Interestingly, the test subjects can recognize with 85 percent accuracy whether they are playing against a man or against a woman (Adler, 2004; Montague and Berns, 2002; Montague and Quartz, 1999).

In another variant of this game, two players again must collaborate interactively in order to earn money. The first player (test subject A) must decide whether they will conclude the game immediately, and both players get 45 cents, or whether they leave this decision to the second player (test subject B). Test subject B must then decide how to divide the cash amount which has now grown to 405 cents. Player B can retain all of the funds for himself or he can return 180 cents to test subject A, and be satisfied with the remaining 225 cents. What happens if the second player gets a new opponent every round? In perfect rationality, they should always retain the 405 cents because they cannot obtain an advantage from cooperating with player A. The first player would know this also and should decide in perfect rationality against said cooperation and immediately retain the 45 cents. If players partner for multiple rounds, both test subjects should theoretically be interested in a collaboration. The typical test subject was willing to cooperate even if they encountered a new partner in every round. A perfectly rational choice arose only when the test subject suggested that they would play against a computer. Always, if the test subjects decided on cooperation, a certain region in the prefrontal cortex became more active as when they played rationally against the computer (McCabe et al., 2001).

Socially cooperative behaviour goes along with the continuous activation of brain regions associated with reward processing, for example the nucleus caudatus, the ventromedial frontal and the orbitofrontal cortex, and the rostrale front singular cortex. The activation of this neural network reinforces reciprocal altruistic behavior, motivates test subjects to resist selfish behavior temptations, and to accept cooperative behavior. Rilling and colleagues appraised this as a sign that both unselfish and cooperative behavior possess a neurological base in humans (Rilling et al., 2002). If a test subject abuses the confidence of another player, the aggrieved player wishes to punish the other, and this is seen in especially stronger activation in the dorsal striatum, an area which is involved in the processing of rewards that result out of purposeful actions. This points out that that persons receive an intrinsic satisfaction out of punishing others for breaching the rules (de Quervain et al., 2004).

Trust has become more meaningful in many areas of economic practice, especially given the current economic conditions in the United States and in Western Europe, and the strong prevalence of unscrupulous behavior by investment gurus. Until recently, no integration of this construct was included in purchase behavior theory and the empirical evidence of this phenomenon is still insufficient. Winning the confidence of customers is one of the most important goals of businesses. It is even more important to react proactively to dips in customer confidence, in order to achieve the desired level of confidence again. Two firms where this is understood and who control the highest degree of customer confidence in Germany are, according to a study of Roland Berger Strategy Consulstants (2004), IKEA and H&M. The customer confidence of a trade enterprise is influenced through two central determinants: through personal confidence and through a noted related system confidence, which can be won only by the consistent construction of a business brand (Kenning, et al., 2002). The knowledge of the neurobiological bases of these confidence components could help firms in the systematic construction of customer confidence.

The newer methods of neuroimaging can also be used to answer questions about customer dissatisfaction. In a study of the effect of different types of salesroom situations, the brain activities of women were analyzed relative to the behavior of salesmen and of advertised gifts as well as discounts, by means of PET. The women involved in the study experienced three different sales situations in a car dealership. One customer experience was characterized by obtrusive salesmen and dirty salesrooms, the second situation was described as having helpful salesmen and nicely-established salesrooms, and in a third situation, gifts were advertised and discounts offered. The women preferred the second sales situation. This result is certainly not surprising. It is decisive and relevant that the pictures of the PET showed that in unpleasant sales situations other brain activity was an active cortex prefrontal in the right dorsolateral, which signals withdrawal. In comfortable sales situations, the secondary visual cortex was stimulated. Stimulation in this area of the brain is connected with lively and positive memories (Schenker, 1999).

PERSONNEL DECISIONS

Behavior of humans has phylogenetical roots, with which evolution psycholgy concerns itself. Personnel decisions can also be analyzed by biological psychology. Above all, physical attractiveness plays a large role, as the appearance can influence the career decisively. In a recent study, 93 percent of 1,300 American and British personnel managers were convinced that attractive people get jobs more quickly (May, 2003). Additionally, almost 80,000 Germans annually undergo cosmetic surgery for career reasons, of which 80 percent are male (Kirsten, 2001).

A long-term study started by Bischoff in 1986 has regularly questioned management as to how largely they estimate the influence of outward appearance on the career. In this study, an increase in the attractiveness factor over the years was seen as highly significant. While in 1986 appearance was estimated as highly important to only five percent of those questioned, by 1991 it was already at 14 percent, and by 1998 it had increased to 22 percent. Since that time, the value has probably risen even higher (Bischoff, 1986, 1991, 1999).

So, how is attractiveness defined? Following evolional psychological extensions, there are culturally-based attractiveness standards that have an evolution biological construction (Henss, 1992). Attractive persons are typically perceived with similar characteristics, such as feature combinations that focus on youth, health and vitality, and, for example, smooth skin and symmetrical features. With men, a ratio of waist to hip size of 0.9 to 1.0 counts as especially attractive because it refers to a high testosterone level and to sexual power. Men typically prefer women whose waist amounts to a waist-to-hip ratio of 0.7. This desired form points out high reproductive capability. Full lips and a narrow chin signal a high estrogen level and therefore fertility (Singh, 1994; Singh, 1995; Singh, 2002).

The results of this study pertain to German attractiveness standards, and there would be slight differences in the ratios for other cultures. What is important from a cultural perspective is that the descriptive factors which determine attractiveness are fairly standard.

According to social psychology extensions, the "beauty bonus" can be explained above all by the effect of stereotypes. Also if they are sometimes connected with vanity and egoism, above-average attractive persons are viewed as more intelligent, more open and self-confident. In attributes such as scrupulousness, balance and compatibility, they perform no better than those of average attractiveness (Henss, 1998; May, 2003). Attractiveness based on the "what is beautiful, is also good" stereotype provides for better starting conditions, for example, through more attention and better schooling in childhood. This increases self-confidence and leads to persuasive power. In the area of personal relationships, the attractiveness effect is magnified further because intelligent persons with highly prestigious occupations can find more attractive partners and can provide genetic features for their children, which controls yet more favorable starting chances (May, 2003; Kirsten, 2001).

In a recent study, managers were asked to judge equivalent résumés from the financial sector for male applicants to a trainee program. The attractive men had the best chances to be included in the program. Also these individuals rose more quickly in the company than their less-attractive colleagues. Managers with more experience in personnel judgment let the attractiveness of the applicant less strongly influence them (Kirsten, 2001). The influence of the attractiveness on the selection of colleagues also appears in other studies. In experiments with visible photos in application portfolios, applicants with partly or completely bald heads received rare invitations to be interviewed. In addition, they were considered less career-oriented and less creative. Although the judge saw only their faces, the applicants with more hair appeared four years younger and were more highly valued (Henss, 2001; May, 2003).

Height also has an influence on personnel selection and compensation (Schultz, 2002; Steckel, 1995). An above average height is associated above all with men with authority, ability and success. Size is a product of the genes, and it reflects partially however also their nourishment and health behaviors. Persons from lower social classes are typically smaller than those from higher social classes (Boström and Diderichsen, 1997). German students are on average three centimeters taller than their contemporaries in skilled-labor education (May, 2003). In a study in Norway, a strong positive relationship between the average height and socioeconomic factors was determined. The average size differences between the highest and lowest development level group and between the highest and lowest income group were about three to four centimeters (Meyer and Selmer, 1999). Of course, height is only one factor of many that influence socioeconomic status.

Below average-sized men must accept less salary than with the comparatively higher salary that above average sized women and men can experience (Hamermesh and Biddle, 1994). Men, who are larger than 1.82 m, bring 6 percent more salary home than their more average colleagues (May, 2003). For every inch of additional size, there is 205 percent more salary (Miter, 2001) concerning women and men in the same professional positions.

In connection with the described effects, it is also interesting that businesses obtain higher revenues and profits with strong-looking leadership, and show higher growth rates than comparable firms with less attractive leadership personnel. The effect on the profits of the business is larger than that of the salary of the management. This shows that attractiveness creates firm specific advantages, for example, better relations with colleagues, whereby the profits of not only the relevant leadership persons are affected, but also the business will experience success overall (Bosman et al., 1997). It is still unexplained, however, to what extent the stereotypical effect of the "beauty bonus" leads back to actual productivity differences. For example, the question remains whether customers seeking beauty can discriminate or whether an attractive person can pull more money out of the customer's pockets (Hamermesh and Parker, 2003). It can be said that the described effects do not fit very well into our rational expectations and social understanding about how things like personnel decisions are or should be approached. At the same time, the question about which processes underlie these phenomena remains unexplained. If one assumes that the salary differences are themselves above all the consequence of these stereotypes and from that result self-fulfilling prophecies, those involved in personnel selection will try to act more responsibly and not be blinded by the external packaging, and instead concentrate on the actual qualification profile of the potential candidates. The acceptance of this premise should also mean that if size and attractiveness differences hold together with actual productivity differences, this could be explained either genetically or by the stereotype effect, and that these factors should be considered in the personnel selection process.

Summary

Throughout the preceding discussion it has become clear that the investigation methods and insights of biological psychology are also relevant for economic questions in business. They enable a better understanding of the behavior of customers, suppliers, management and colleagues. This understanding can be used for example in developing more effective and more efficient advertising concepts and brand strategies. The utilization of the investigation methods and insights should be restricted not only to businesses, but also should be used in the areas of consumer relationships and consumer protection. Based on the rapid development in this research area, it is likely to be further advanced with deepening insight in the future.

In this discussion of biological psychology, we want to remind the practioner that having too strong or a one-sided focus does not appear well founded in this area of research. Just as it is incorrect to deny the biological bases of human behavior, it is just as incorrect to assume that this is the central cause (that is, biological development which denies upbringing) of human behavior. Neuro-economics as an interdisciplinary extension of economic science, psychology and neuroscience must be included in the analysis if economic and marketing theorists wish to claim that the theories of economic science comprehensively describe human behavior.

QUESTIONS FOR DISCUSSION

1. Elaborate on the practical benefits of biological psychology research for marketers.
2. What implications might an increasingly digitized world have on biological psychology research in the future?
3. How might educators benefit from knowledge of biological psychology in regard to learning and intercultural communication?
4. As you read through the case studies that follow, consider how biological psychology can aid the search for insight in a global marketing context.

Bibliography

Adler, J.: Mind reading. *Newsweek*, 5 July 2004, 43–48.

Akerlof, G.A., and Shiller, R.J.: *Animal Spirits: How Human Psychology Drives the Economy and Why it Matters for Global Capitalism*, Princeton University Press, 264, 2009.

Anderson, M.C., Ochsner, K.N., Kuhl, B., Cooper, J., Robertson, E., Garieli, S.W., Glover, G. H. and Gabrieli, J.D.E.: Neural systems underlying the suppression of unwanted memories. *Science*, 2004, 303, 232–235.

Averett, S. and Korenmann, S.: The economic reality of the beauty myth. *Journal of Human Resources*, 1996, 31, 304–330.

Biddle, J. and Hamermesh, D.S.: *Beauty, Productivity and Discrimination: Lawyers' Looks and Lucre*. Austin: 1998.

Birbaumer, N. and Schmidt, R.F.: *Biologische Psychologie* (5th edn). Berlin: 2003. (*Biological Psychology*.

Bischoff, S.: *Frauen und Männer in Führungspositionen—Ergebnisse einer schriftlichen Befragung*. Köln, Hamburg: 1986. (*Women and Men in Leading Positions—Results of a Written Inquiry*).

——— *Frauen und Männer in Führungspositionen der Wirtschaft der BRD—1991 im Vergleich zu 1986*. Köln, Hamburg: 1991. (*Women and Men in Leading Positions of the Economy in Germany—1991 in Comparison with 1986*).

——— *Frauen und Männer in Führungspositionen der Wirtschaft in Deutschland—Neuer Blick auf einen alten Streit. Schriftenreihe der Deutschen Gesellschaft für Personalführung*. Köln: 1999. (*Women and Men in Leading Positions of the Economy in Germany—New View of an Old Dispute. Writing series of the German Company for Personnel Leadership*).

Bosman, C.M., Pfann, G.A., Biddle, J. and Hamermesh, D.S.: *Business Success and Businesses' Beauty Capital*. Austin: 1997.

Boström, G. and Diderichsen, F.: Socioeconomic differentials in misclassification of height, weight and body mass index based on questionnaire data. *International Journal of Epidemiology*, 1997, 26, 860–866.

Brat, I.: The emotional quotient of soup shopping: Campbell taps 'neuromarketing' techniques to find why shelf displays left some customers cold, *The Wall Street Journal*, 17 February 2010, p. B6.

Breiter, H.C., Aharon, I., Kahneman, D., Anders, D. and Shizgal, P.: Functional imaging of neural responses to expectancy and experience of monetary gains and losses. *Neuron*, 2001, 30, 619–639.

Butler, D., Gibson, H., Noble, K. and Salz-Trautman, P.: Attention to all shoppers. *Time*, 2 August 1999, 34–39.

Cawley, J.: *Body Weight and Women's Labor Market Outcomes*. Austin: 2000.

de Quervain, D.J.-F., Fischbacher, U., Treyer, V., Schellhammer, M., Schnyder, U., Buck, A. and Fehr, E.: The neural basis of altruistic punishment. *Science*, 2004, 305, 1254–1260.

Fröhlich, W.: *Wörterbuch zur Pyschologie*. München: 1981. (*Dictionary of Psychology*).

Glimcher, P.W.: *Decisions, Uncertainty, and the Brain: The Science of Neuroeconomics*. Princeton: 2003.

Glimcher, P.W. and Rustichini, A.: Neuroeconomics: The concilience of brain and decision. *Science*, 2004, 306, 447–452.

Hamermesh, D.S. and Biddle, J.: *Beauty and the Labor Market*. Austin: 1993.

—— and Parker, A.M.: *Beauty in the Classroom: Professor's Pulchritude and Putative Pedagogical Productivity*. Austin: 2003.

Haskins, K.M. and Ransford, H.E.: The relationship between weight and career payoffs among women. *Sociological Forum*, 1999, 14, 295–318.

Hassebrauck, M.: Physische attraktivität—eine evolutionstheoretische Perspektive. In: Fritsch-Rößler, W. (eds): *Frauenblicke, Männerblicke, Frauenzimmer. Studien zu Blick, Geschlecht und Raum*. St. Ingbert: 2002, 37–50. (Physical attractiveness—an evolutionary theoretical perspective. In *Where Women Look, Where Men Look, Wenches. Studies on Looks, Gender and Space*).

—— and Küpper, B.: *Warum wir Aufeinander Fliegen—Die Gesetze der Partnerwahl*. Reinbek: 2002. (*Why we Fly Together—the Laws of Partner Choice*).

——. and Niketta, R. (eds): *Physische Attraktivität*. Göttingen: 1993. (*Physical Attractiveness*).

Henss, R.: "*Spieglein, Spieglein an der Wand... ": Geschlecht, Alter und physische Attraktivität*. Weinheim: 1992. (*"Mirror, Mirror on the Wall...": Sex, Age and Physical Attractiveness*).

—— *Gesicht und Persönlichkeitsausdruck*. Göttingen: 1998. (*Face and Personality Expression*).

—— Social perception of male pattern baldness. *Dermatology and Psychosomatics*, 2001, 2, 63–71.

Janke, W.: Biopsychologie. In: Schorr, A. (ed.): *Handwörterbuch der Angewandten Psychologie*. Bonn: 1993, 99–109. (Biopsychology. In *Handbook of Applied Psychology*).

Kenning, P. and Ahlert, D.: Marke und hirnforschung: Status-quo. *Marketing Journal*, 2004, 44–46. (Brand and brain research: Status quo).

——, Plassmann, H., Deppe, M., Kugel, H. and Schwindt, W.: *Die Entdeckung der kortikalen Entlastung*. Münster: 2002. (*The Discovery of Cortical Relief*).

——, Plassmann, H., Deppe, M. and Schwindt, W.: Wie eine starke marke wirkt. *Harvard Business Manager*, 2005, 53–57. (How a strong brand works).

Kirsten, N.: Schöne bevorzugt. *Wirtschaftswoche*, 2001, 28, 100–107. (Beautiful preference).

Luczak, H.: Das unbewusste. *Geo*, 2004, 12/2004, 142–172. (The unconscious).

Mai, J.: Schön und gut. *Wirtschaftswoche*, 2003, 105–111. (Beauty and goods).

McCabe, K., Houser, D., Ryan, L., Smith, V. and Trouard, T.: A functional imaging study of cooperation in two-person reciprocal exchange. *Proceedings of the National Academy of Science USA*, 2001, 98, 11823–11835.

McClure, S.M., Li, J., Tomlin, D., Cypert, K.S., Montague, L.M. and Montage, P.R.: Neural correlates of behavioural preferences for culturally familiar drinks. *Neuron*, 2004, 44, 379–387.

Meyer, H.E. and Selmer, R.: Income, educational level and body height. *Annals of Human Biology*, 1999, 26, 219–279.

Mitra, A.: Effects of physical attributes on the wages of males and females. *Applied Economic Letters*, 2001, 8, 731–735.

Montague, P.R. and Berns, G.S.: Neural economics and the biological substrates of valuation. *Neuron*, 2002, 36, 265–284.

Montague, P.R. and Quartz, S.R.: Computational approaches to neural reward and development. *Mental Retardation and Developmental Disabilities Research Reviews*: Special Issue on Early Experience and Intervention, 1999, 5, 1–14.

Perrig, W.J.: Implizites lernen. In: Hoffman, J. and Kintsch, W. (eds): *Enzyklopädie der Psychologie, Serie Kognition* (Bd. Lernen). Göttingen: 1996. (Implicit learning. In *Encyclopedia of Psychology*, Cognition series).

Perrig, W.J., Wippich, W. and Perrig, P.: *Unbewußte Informationsverarbeitung*. Bern, 1993. (*Unconscious Information Processing*).

Rilling, J.K., Gutman, D.A., Zeh, T.R., Pagnoni, G., Berns, G.S. and Kilts, C D.: A neural basis for social cooperation, *Neuron*, 2002, 35, 395–405.

Sanfey, A.G., Rilling, J.K., Aronson, J.A., Nystrom, L.E. and Cohen, J.D.: The neural bases of economic decision-making in the ultimatum game. *Science*, 2003, 300, 1755–1760.

Schandry, R.: *Biologische Psychologie*. Weinheim: 2003. (*Biological Psychology*).

Schenker, J.L.: Reading the mind of the market. *Time*, 1999, 2 August, 39.

Schnabel, U.: Der markt der neuronen, *Die Zeit*, 2003, 13 November, 35. (The market of the neurons).

Schubert, S.: Dem kunden ins gehirn geschaut. *Psychologie Heute*, 2004, November, 38–41. (Looking into the customer's brain).

Schultz, P.T.: Wage gains associated with height as a form of health human capital. *AEA Papers and Proceedings*, 2002, 92, 349–353.

Sczesny, S. and Stahlberg, D.: Geschlechtsstereotype wahrnehmung von führungskräften. *Wirtschaftspsychologie*, 2002, 1, 36–41. (Gender stereotype perceptions of management).

Singh, D.: Ideal female body shape: Role of body weight and waist-to-hip ratio: *International Journal of Eating Disorder*, 1994, 16, 283–288.

—— Female judgement of male attractiveness and desirability for relationships: Role of waist-to-hip ratio and financial status. *Journal of Personality and Social Psychology*, 1995, 69, 1089–1101.

—— Female mate value at a glance: Relationship of waist-to-hip ratio to health, fecundity, and attractiveness. *Neuroendocrinology Letters*: Special Issue, 2002, 23, 81–91.

Steckel, R.H.: Stature and the standard of living. *Journal of Economic Literature*, 1995, 33, 1903–1940.

von Rennenkampf, A.: *Aktivierung und Auswirkung geschlechtsstereotypischer Wahrnehmung von Führungskompetenz*. Mannheim: 2004. (*Activation and Effect of Gender Stereotypes on Perception of Leadership Competence*).

von Rosenstiel, L.: *Grundlagen der Organisationspsychologie*, 5th edn. Stuttgart: 2003. (*Foundations of Organization Psychology*).

Walter, H.: Können hirnforscher gedanken lesen? *Psychologie Heute*, 2003, December, 64–69. (Can brain researchers read thought?).

Zak, P.J.: Trust. CAPCO Institute *The Journal of Financial Transformation*, 2003, 7, 13–21.

—— Neuroeconomics. *Philosophical Transactions of the Royal Society* B, 2004, 359, 1737–1748.

PART VI

Case Studies in Market Psychology

VI Case Studies in
Market Psychology

Case Study 1
The Global Housing Boom: Local Dimensions

G. JASON GODDARD

The phone was ringing off of the hook. Larry Welch, senior mortgage loan underwriting officer at La Vista Community Bank was having a busy day. Having just come back from a senior leadership meeting in downtown Phoenix, he had a multitude of voicemails and emails to return. La Vista Community Bank was beginning a new low rate mortgage program aimed at attracting new customers to the floundering community bank.

La Vista Community Bank was one of the oldest community banks serving the Phoenix market, but had been late to the game in gaining market share and shareholder returns due to the fantastic housing boom in the Phoenix area. La Vista was known as a boutique financial institution for the area's wealthy clients, and had built up a solid portfolio of loans and other financial assets from serving this niche in the Phoenix financial market. Over the last five years, La Vista's market share had eroded owing to the entrance of newer, more aggressive community banks, and due to the expansion into the Phoenix market of larger banks from California. La Vista's financial performance for fiscal year 2006 showed a continuing decline in both market share and overall firm profitability, a trend that started in 2002. A bright spot in the firm's financial performance was the almost non-existent provision for loan losses. Given La Vista's history of solid underwriting, the firm had little need for creating a significant provision for loan losses. Over the last five years, La Vista's financial performance could be summarized as follows:

La Vista Community Bank	2002	2003	2004	2005	2006
Growth in revenue	4.50%	2.20%	2.00%	1.10%	-0.50%
Change in market share	3.50%	2.75%	2.50%	-3.20%	-3.75%
Net income as % of revenue	9.82%	8.35%	6.43%	6.75%	4.85%
Provision for loan losses	0.15%	0.32%	0.63%	0.24%	0.31%

The situation at La Vista was problematic. The entry of newer, more aggressive lenders in the area meant that there was much more liquidity in the local lending markets than in years past. Based on the tone of the day's meeting in downtown Phoenix, Larry felt that the means of success for the company in the past might need to be altered given today's heretofore unseen optimism in financial markets. Based on his notes at the day's meeting, the US Economy had seen housing prices rise by 124 percent between 1997 and 2006 (*The Economist*, 2007). The Phoenix market had been one of the strongest housing markets in the United States over this same period, with the Paradise Valley area leading the charge with a median house price of $1.6 million (ASU, 2007). Given the poor performance of La Vista over the last few years, many executives in the company wondered aloud at the meeting whether the company was forsaking growth and profitability in order to maintain a pristine balance sheet for their loan portfolio.

Many of Larry's salespeople, who were primarily compensated on a commission basis, felt that the time was right for a change in strategy at La Vista. Hank Jansen, head of mortgage sales for La Vista, had complained to Larry for the last two years that the terms and underwriting criteria that La Vista employed were simply not competitive in the marketplace. Hank cited the example of Loan First Phoenix, an upstart community bank which seemed to always undercut La Vista in competitive mortgage situations. Loan First Phoenix was able to offer higher loan to value ratios, lower pricing, and more favorable fees than did La Vista. If the company was going to turn things around, the lending criteria had to be liberalized. When Larry Welch questioned Hank and his sales staff during client mortgage origination discussions, the sales staff pointed to the strong current housing market in Phoenix, as well as the overall success of the housing market in the United States over the preceding ten years. These types of discussions were common in many other banks during the time period, but this was of no concern to Larry (*The Economist*, 2008b). What he needed was a way to stop his existing customer base from leaving La Vista, a way to return the company to profitability, and a way to appease an increasingly unsettled sales staff at La Vista.

"Come and Get It!"

The June 2007 meeting in downtown Phoenix was seemingly upper management's official recognition of the need for a strategic change of direction. Larry, Hank, and others in the mortgage line of business listened attentively to leadership meetings during the half-day meeting. La Vista's upper management felt that the current incentive structure for the employees should be modified. Rather than providing incentives to the sales officers and loan underwriters based on the overall profitability of the mortgage business at La Vista, the time was right for a movement to a growth based initiative. Effective immediately, the underwriting process at La Vista would be streamlined, with the intended effect to increase the bank's success rate in winning mortgage loan origination business in the Greater Phoenix market. Given the unprecedented success of the local and national housing market, these few changes in bank lending policy would help ensure success for La Vista in the new era of safe and sound financial markets.

The first criterion to be changed in the new regime was the loan to value requirements. Many of La Vista's competitors approved up to 100 percent of purchase price, using a variety of new and improved financial products such as junior mortgages, bridge notes, government guarantee programs, and streamlined appraisal evaluations. La Vista had traditionally sought to offer their customers conservative, fixed rate loans, but given the low rate environment, the movement to adjustable rate mortgages seemed prescient.

Another lending criterion to be changed was the verification of borrower income and employment status. Much of La Vista's competition had all but done away with loan underwriting due diligence, as the final appraised value of the property in conjunction with the final sales price negotiation between buyer and seller was proof enough of a property's value. A third criterion of change was to increase the scope of customers that could be approved for mortgages. La Vista had traditionally only loaned to customers with clean credit reports, which was typically defined as not having any prior bankruptcy, collection accounts, judgments or tax liens, and not having a pattern of slow payment on their existing trade accounts. The upper management of La Vista felt that by increasing the breadth of focus of their target consumer, that the result would be increased firm profitability. While the upper management believed that there would be an increase in the level of problem accounts, the recent history of financial institutions in the United States revealed that the increase in firm profitability more than offset any increase in loan loss provisions. In order to help increase the scope of the bank's potential universe of applicants, the sales force would be encouraged to seek loan opportunities from both local and out of market brokers, rather than simply sourcing the opportunities themselves. As long as the property was located within the Greater Phoenix area, the sales force at La Vista was encouraged to put their best foot forward in an effort to win each and every deal. A final change in La Vista's strategy concerned loan pricing authority. Since the mortgage sales officers were closer to current market intelligence on the pricing necessary to win mortgage loan business, the sales staff would henceforth be provided with the authority to price loans *in order to win them.*

In keeping with the firm's market expansion plans, the advertising slogan "Come and Get It!" was chosen to exhibit to the market that La Vista was open for business. The slogan was equipped with a picture of a Caucasian male wearing a cowboy hat, dressed in full western regalia, ringing the cow bell, an image ingrained in the minds of many inhabitants of the western part of the US as meaning that it was time for dinner, or at least something just as pleasant.

Initiating the Plan of Action

The "Come and Get It!" campaign was an instant success. Upon returning from the meeting, Larry found that he had over 20 voicemails and emails from La Vista's sales staff discussing possible avenues for growth utilizing the new strategy. Hank Jansen, long a proponent of increased pricing authority for his sales force, informed Larry that he had "lost his last loan to Loan First Phoenix" over pricing. Beavis Cooper, a mortgage sales officer in El Mirage, had already contacted area brokers to obtain any business for residential mortgages in the area. The new campaign was off to a great start!

In order to win mortgage origination business from the competition, La Vista began offering Adjustable Rate Mortgages (ARMs) for all new applications beginning the Monday after the Friday meeting announcing the campaign. These are variable rate loans that are tied to a specific index (such as Prime, ten-year treasuries, etc.) that were outside of the control of both the customer and the bank. Larry felt that fixed rate mortgages were safer for the bank and for the customer as the payments were certain over the life of the loan, and were not subject to adjustments as is the case with variable rate loans. Larry spoke with Hank about this concern, and both agreed to offer both fixed and variable rate loan terms for all applications. Unfortunately, part of the "Come and Get It!" campaign consisted of offering very low variable rates for the first 12–24 months of the loan, as this was what the competition was currently offering. Given the presence of these teaser rates, few customers chose the fixed rate pricing option. Since Larry no longer possessed pricing authority for the loans that he underwrote, he had no control over which customers chose the variable rate options. Since many of the new customers were attracted to buying homes given the currently low payments associated with ARMs, many of the new customers desired the variable rate loan option.

Another improvement in the success rate of winning mortgage business was increasing the loan to value ratios at La Vista. La Vista had historically approved residential mortgages up to 80 percent of the appraised value of the property, but this was no longer competitive in the market. La Vista now consistently offered mortgages with loan to values up to 90 percent of the appraised value, sometimes even higher when competitive pressure dictated terms. These loans were insured by government sponsored enterprises such as the Federal National Mortgage Association (known as Freddie Mac) and the Federal Home Loan Mortgage Corporation (known as Fannie Mae). Given the government guarantee, lenders such as La Vista were protected in the unlikely event that the borrower would have trouble making the loan payments. In the event that the borrower could no longer make the loan payments, the vast price appreciation of housing in the Greater Phoenix area, when coupled with the government guarantee programs, ensured a soft landing for mortgage lenders. To quote Hank Jansen, "was it really likely that the US Housing market would experience a sustained decline in home prices? Individual properties might experience a decline in value, but we have never seen a systemic reduction in home values in this country."

The market was so hot that even current homeowners wished to capitalize on the strong returns in home value appreciation. Many of the new borrowers that La Vista courted over the next few months were novice investors who felt the time was right to purchase a second or third home as an investment. Many of these homes were in areas of Phoenix that had not yet experienced the high levels of price appreciation, but with some modernization and good marketing efforts, those investments could be quickly sold at a profit. La Vista's competitors offered interest only loans for the purchase of "fixer-upper" investment homes, providing customers with loan mortgage rates for the first 12 months. This would allow for plenty of time to purchase the home, make the necessary repairs, and then sell the home at a profit, before the mortgage amortization of principal began in the 13th month. "House Flipping" became common, and many investors were able to make quick profits given their shrewd investment decisions and "do-it-yourself" sweat equity techniques.

Changing Underwriting Environment

Now that La Vista was implementing a growth in market share philosophy for its mortgage underwriting business, Larry's daily job duties changed slightly. Rather than spending time verifying a borrower's income, employment, or reference information, Larry spent his time in the office feverishly approving borrowers for home loan applications. As long as the appraiser could validate the negotiated sales price via a final appraised value, new loan requests had a strong chance of approval at La Vista. Larry was now judged on his overall loan approval percentages, as well as the speed with which he made his loan decisions. Last year, before La Vista's change in strategy, Larry was judged on the overall profitability of the loans that closed in his portfolio. Now, Larry was viewed by upper management based on the volume of business closed, and the percentage of approvals for loans that crossed his desk.

As the months went by, La Vista's new strategy appeared to be successful. His relationship with Hank Jansen and the sales staff improved immeasurably, and Larry even was able to accompany the sales team on a company-sponsored trip to Acapulco, Mexico after a successful 2007 financial campaign. During this four-day trip, Larry and Hank discussed how other banks were further profiting from the volume of business in residential markets by packaging groups of mortgage assets and selling them in the conduit market. It seemed that investors were willing to pay a premium for mortgage backed securities, and La Vista had a great advantage here relative to its competition. Since La Vista had a large book of conservatively underwritten (pre-2007) loans on their balance sheet, including some of these assets in a conduit offering would help decrease the default risk for the group of assets being sold. Hank and Larry sipped their mango margaritas and looked back fondly on a successful 2007. As their conversation went on, they were also excited about the prospects for continued success in 2008. Things were definitely looking up!

QUESTIONS FOR DISCUSSION

1. Describe the state of the Phoenix housing market during the time of the case. What inherent assumptions of market psychology led to the firm's changing of their underwriting strategy for mortgage loan originations?
2. What was the primary difference between the existing portfolio of loans on the company's balance sheet prior to mid-2007, and the majority of those made subsequently afterwards?
3. How effective was the "Come and Get It!" marketing campaign in its efforts to gain increased market penetration in the Greater Phoenix market? What did the increased penetration imply about company profitability?
4. Explain the role of organizational structure in changing the strategic direction of the firm.
5. How typical does this case seem for sub-prime lenders? Discuss some underlying flaws in the new strategic direction at La Vista Community Bank.
6. Discuss how the theories of Cognitive Dissonance and Psychological Reactance were at play in this case.

The Global Housing Boom: Aftermath of a Global Financial Crisis

Mortgage lenders like Larry Welch, and financial institutions such as La Vista Community Bank certainly had company in the creating of the Sub-Prime mortgage crisis in the United States. In fact, when our small example is multiplied one thousand times over, it goes a long way in describing the psychological reasons behind the crisis. As we now understand, the crisis was certainly not limited to just the United States. Global markets are too interconnected for the contagion of over-valuation in the US Housing Market to not spread throughout the world. The Bank of China, long a primary holder of US dollars given its large trade surplus with the United States, announced that they held almost $10 billion worth of sub-prime debt (Shaw, 2007). Additionally, Northern Rock, a British financial institution, collapsed in late 2007, and was subject to the first bank run in England in over one hundred years (*The Economist*, 2008a). The bank, which was eventually nationalized after tax payers were still due $27 billion at the end of 2007, saw the source of its trouble in the same issue that plagued La Vista Community Bank: over-lending on residential mortgages to less than credit-worthy borrowers under the faulty assumption that what goes up will keep going up.

This speculative fervor spread into other areas of the world economy as well. In the case of Northern Rock, as well as the US financial institution Indy Mac, the percentage of problem assets in the bank portfolio caused customers to feel that the bank could not honor their deposit balances, as banks typically only hold a small portion of their deposits in reserve. The thought of the bank not being able to produce a given customer's deposits caused many of them to seek their deposits in their hands. Thus, customers sought to recoup their deposits from troubled financial institutions at precisely the wrong time. As was alluded to at the end of the La Vista Community Bank case, many financial institutions packaged their residential mortgage loans and then sold them to investors in the form of collateralized debt obligations, or mortgage backed securities. Ratings agencies were unaccustomed to the best techniques to rate the financial strength of many of these new investments, as they consisted of a mixture of both credit and derivatives exposure. The new assets were also delineated into various tranches, depending on the quality of the assets comprising the tranche. Ratings agencies tended to rate the overall security higher given the prevalence of a higher percentage of lower risk assets (*The Economist*, 2008b). When the value of the sub-prime mortgages began to fall, a similar panic was created in the investment banking arena, which in part led to the collapse of Bear Stearns in March 2008 (Guerrera and Sender, 2008). Once the sub-prime crisis affected a renowned investment bank, other commercial banks followed suit by writing off billions of dollars of sub-prime debt, in an effort to mark to market their portfolios. The sub-prime collapse served as catalyst for further weakening of the US economy in 2008, something that immediately began to surface in other economies throughout the world as US consumers and businesses alike began to curtail their expenditures. The collapse of confidence of the US consumer held such strong implications for the rest of the world, as given the large trade imbalance in the United States over the last decade, US consumers were regularly purchasing goods imported from abroad. A slowdown in import purchases would certainly impact export oriented economies such as Germany, Japan, and China. The slowdown in commercial real estate, especially in the office sector, would affect the performance of service oriented economies such as India.

By September of 2008, the daily news broadcasts revealed just how quickly the status quo in the financial industry can be undone. Lehman Brothers, a 158-year-old Wall Street investment banking firm, declared Chapter 11 bankruptcy in early September. Barclay's purchased the North American operations of Lehman Brothers a few days later, while other portions of the failed and once storied investment bank were purchased by Nomura (Story and White, 2008). During the same time, Merrill Lynch was purchased by Bank of America, and Goldman Sachs and Morgan Stanley converted their storied franchises from investment banks to bank holding companies. In a span of a week the leading investment banks on Wall Street were either obliterated or forever changed.

But the investment banks were only part of the problem. On 17 September 2008, Lloyd's TSB Group agreed to purchase Halifax Bank of Scotland for $22 billion (Menon, 2008). On this same day, seven central banks (US Fed, Bank of Canada, Bank of Japan, Bank of England, ECB, Swiss National Bank, and Bank of China) injected a combined

$180 billion into global markets, only the fourth time this had been done on a coordinated basis. This was then followed with the initial rejection and then passing of a $700 billion bailout plan by the US Congress to purchase toxic mortgages from troubled financial institutions (Herszenhorn, 2008). On 25 September 2008, the US Government's Office of Thrift Supervision announced the closing of Washington Mutual, at the time the largest Savings and Loan institution, and to that point the largest bank failure in the history of the United States. The 119-year-old company was later sold to JP Morgan for a mere $1.9 billion (*The Economist*, 2008c). By the end of September, it was announced that Wachovia Corporation, the fourth largest commercial bank in the United States, was subjected to two silent runs on its deposits, and was to be bought in part by Citi Group for $1 per share. A subsequent offer, seven times higher, by Wells Fargo led to a legal battle for control of the once proud financial institution, eventually won by Wells Fargo (Guerrera and Chung, 2008).

The financial crisis then spread to insurance companies, as the US Government announced the bailout of AIG, the largest insurer in the world, who received $85 billion from the Federal Reserve in exchange for ownership of 79.9 percent. By essentially nationalizing this insurance giant, the government guaranteed that insurance claims of financial institutions worldwide would be redeemed. The bailout helped save the insurance giant, and also allowed their executives to conduct a post-bailout meeting at a posh California resort at a cost of $400,000 (Whorisky, 2008).

By October of 2008, the financial crisis began severely impacting financial institutions and sovereign nations in Europe. On 4 October, Hypo Real Estate was the subject of a second German government rescue plan for $48 billion. The German lender had purchased Depfa Bank, which specialized in public works projects, as they could no longer finance their operations after the Lehman Brothers bankruptcy (Dougherty, 2008). On 13 October , Spain set aside $134 billion to guarantee inter-bank loans, while on that same day Great Britain announced a plan to inject $64 billion into their national banks. The Swiss government agreed to provide a $9 billion lifeline to UBS, and the US Government agreed to take an ownership interest in each of the country's top nine banks. The tiny nation of Iceland, a relatively new player in global markets with a stock market that began in only 1985, had seen aggressive lending balloon bank debts to over nine times as large as its gross domestic product. The slowdown in global financial markets coupled with lower consumer spending both at home and abroad led the country to seize two of its largest commercial banks, and declare that the entire country was near bankruptcy. Iceland sought a loan from Russia for $5.5 billion to help keep the economy afloat. The country also was forced to fix the national currency, the Krona, to a basket of currencies including the Euro (Pfanner and Werdigier, 2008). During this same time, the British government announced an $87 billion bailout plan of their own in an effort to provide much needed liquidity into an anemic financial system. In an effort to spur bank lending once again, the Bank of Australia dropped their key rate by 100 basis points, and this was followed by coordinated action by the majority of the seven central banks mentioned earlier, plus Sweden and the United Arab Emirates, in dropping their key lending rates by 50 basis points (Crooks and Cohen, 2008). The desire to expand the US housing market in an unsustainable way has indeed had terrible consequences for world financial markets.

On 19 October, the French bank Caisse De'Epargne reported losses of $800 million, while the Dutch government was forced to provide a rescue package of $30 billion to ING. Toward the end of October, the Federal Reserve Bank of the United States lowered their federal funds rate by 50 basis points (to 1.00 percent). In early December, the Fed lowered the federal funds rate to 0.25 percent, showing just how dire the financial crisis had become.

The international monetary fund (IMF) opened access to new funds specifically for the crisis. The caveat was that recipient countries must have shown stable policies before. In an apparent break from that ideal, the IMF loaned $2.1 billion to Iceland near the end of November 2008.

Offering further proof of the global dimensions of the credit crisis, China announced a $586 billion stimulus plan, which consisted of government spending, industry-specific subsidies, tax cuts, and a loosening of credit policies. China's response was primarily due to the decline of the Shanghai Composite Index, which had fallen by 67 percent by November. The lifelines and bailouts continued, as the US Government extended a $20 billion lifeline to Citigroup (who a few months earlier had attempted to acquire Wachovia Corporation). This lifeline was later increased to a $300 billion government guarantee of Citigroup assets. The US Congress then fiercely debated the calls for a bailout of the "Big 3" automobile manufacturers in the United States (Ford, General Motors, and Chrysler), when their CEO's appealed for aid in order to save their storied franchises from bankruptcy. During this same period of time, the EU Commission proposed a €200 billion stimulus package to help aid the crisis, although there were some disagreements in how the funds should be utilized. The proposed stimulus package by itself represented 1.5 percent of EU GDP. The crisis had certainly become global.

A further point of discussion concerns how periods of speculation seem to plague world financial markets. In the recent past, prior to the Sub-Prime crisis, we experienced the Asian Financial Crisis during the late 1990s. The root cause of that crisis was again financial institutional lending gone wild. Speculative loans were made during economic boom years, with the same belief that everything would turn out just fine (Ajami, et al., 2006). Vast office buildings were constructed on a speculative basis, which means that these investment properties were built before any tenants agreed to lease the space. The "if you build it, they will come" mentality certainly owes allegiance to the assumption "what goes up will keep going up". The further back in financial market history we look, we see continuing cases of manic behavior by otherwise rational professionals. In the 1980s, we witnessed the Savings and Loan scandal in the United States, which looks surprisingly like our current situation, only today the numbers are larger. Earlier in the 1980s, the world experienced a financial crisis in Latin America, which was again fueled by speculative lending as wealthy oil producing states provided "Petrodollars" for investment in the emerging economies of Latin America. The influx of cash was loaned out in haphazard fashion, or at least in ways that favored the riskiest of projects for their potential rewards, with limited analysis of the downside risks.

In the words of economist John Kenneth Galbraith, "financial genius is before the fall"(Galbraith, 1994). The questions that many participants in world financial markets were wondering during the aftermath of the Sub-Prime mortgage crisis were why did markets fall periodically, and why must financial genius continue to be tested at so high a price?

QUESTIONS FOR DISCUSSION

1. Explain the underlying psychological components of a bank run.
2. How does the theory of social comparisons help to explain the continuing peaks and valleys of world financial markets?
3. How might the psychological concept of control help to explain why the ratings agencies rated the mortgage backed securities that contained Sub-Prime debt so highly?
4. What does the interconnectedness of world markets in the Sub-Prime crisis say about the cultural implications of market psychology?

References

Ajami, R.A., Cool, K., Goddard, G.J. and Khambata, D.: *International Business: Theory and Practice*, 2nd edn, London: 2006, pp. 86–87.

Arizona State University: Greater Phoenix Resale Market Strengthens in March, 10 April 2007, ASU website, http://www.poly.asu.edu/news/2007/04/10/, accessed 1 September 2008.

The Economist: CSI: Credit Crunch, 18 October 2007, web edition, http://www.economist.com/specialreports/displaystory.cfm?story_id=9972489, accessed 1 September 2008.

—— What lies beneath, 3 April 2008a.

—— Confessions of a risk manager: A personal view of the crisis, 9 August 2008b, 72–73.

—— From Whoo Hoo to Boo Hoo: Regulations Seize Washington Mutual and Sell Most of it to JP Morgan Chase, 26 September 2008c.

Crooks, E. and Cohen, N.: Central banks launch rate cut, *Financial Times* website, http://www.ft.com/cms/s/0/5fce75b2-949f-11dd-953e-000077b07658.html, accessed 8 October 2008.

Dougherty, C.: Germany moves to shore up confidence in its economy, *New York Times*, 6 October 2008.

Galbraith, J.K.: *A Short History of Financial Euphoria*. New York: 1994.

Guerrera, F. and Chung, J.: Recriminations fly in scuffle for Wachovia. *Financial Times* website, http://www.ft.com/cms/s/0/3e7eed00-94d2-11dd-953e-000077b07658.html?nclick_check=1, accessed 8 October 2008.

Guerrera, F. and Sender, H.: JP Morgan to buy Bear Stearns for $236 billion. *Financial Times* website, http://www.ft.com/cms/s/0/e2206ed2-f380-11dc-b6bc-0000779fd2ac.html, accessed 4 September 2008.

Herszenhorn, D.: Bailout plan wins approval; Democrats vow tighter rules. *New York Times*, 3 October 2008.

Menon, J.: Lloyd's TSB progresses with plan to buy HBOS. Bloomberg website, http://www.bloomberg.com/apps/news?pid=20601102&sid=axWpAJVxx6w8, accessed 8 October 2008.

Pfanner, E. and Werdigier, J.: Iceland, in a precarious position, takes drastic steps to right itself. *New York Times*, 8 October 2008.

Story, L. and White, B.: The road to Lehman's failure was littered with lost chances. *New York Times*, 5 October 2008.

Shaw, R.: Sub-prime effects worldwide. 24 August 2007. Straight Stocks website, http://www.straightstocks.com/foreign-markets/subprime-effects-felt-worldwide/, accessed 4 September 2008.

Whorisky, P.: After bailout, AIG executives head to resort. *Washington Post*, 8 October 2008.

Case Study 2
Gadgetry and the Elusive Search for Self

G. JASON GODDARD

The early morning sun was very bright as Victor Tong got in his car heading toward his early morning tennis match. Victor always played tennis very early on Saturday mornings to make sure that he and his partner got the best court, and in order to beat the heat of the hot summer days in Atlanta, Georgia. As the clock turned to eight in the morning, Victor listened to the news in his car. Victor had recently purchased satellite radio for his car, as he really enjoyed listening to the news back home in his native China. He was previously only able to catch up with the happenings back home via the internet, and based on his membership in the local Chinese American club in Atlanta. As he listened to the news, Victor noticed that there were very few people on the roads so early in the morning. As he drove his car down Piedmont Road, he passed the Tech Now store, which sold home electronics and other appliances. "Wow!" thought Victor as he passed by the immense retail location. "Just look at all of those people lined up outside of the store". Victor remembered from a recent trip that the store did not open until nine in the morning on Saturdays. He wondered why people would be lining up a full hour before the store opened, and on a Saturday morning of all days.

First Impressions

After his tennis match was over, Victor remembered that he wanted to purchase a few items from Tech Now. After saying goodbye to his tennis partner, and having a quick shower at the club, Victor was off to Tech Now. As the time was now close to ten in the morning, the store was open, and the lines outside had dissipated. The sense of urgency that was seen outside the store prior to its opening had been simply moved inside. "What a madhouse!" Victor thought, as he entered the store. Everywhere he looked, he saw people eagerly taking items from the shelves: VCR/DVD combination units, high definition flat screened TVs, video games galore, and MP3 players. He noticed mothers shopping with their children, with shopping carts filled with video games, DVDs of popular children's films, and electronic learning devices, to help the youngest in the family learn their ABCs. Victor also noticed men of all ages, filling their shopping baskets with the latest in computer accessories, with large memory flash drives, and with sports video games. In one corner of the store, where cell phone accessories were maintained, Victor noticed what appeared to be teenage boys and girls purchasing personalized covers for their cell phones, ring tones, and other customized products. Victor, recently a naturalized citizen of the United States having come to the country to receive his undergraduate education, was still not completely comfortable with the scene in front of him. Under the bright lights of the store, customers from all walks of life quickly piled expensive retail items in their carts, and there Victor stood, dazzled by it all.

The Pitch

"May I help you?" Victor turned as he was addressed by Steve, an employee of the store. Victor noticed that Steve appeared to be in his late teenage years, and had five gold stars on his name tag. "Yes", said Victor, "I am looking for the *Commanding Heights* series VHS cassette tape. I have enjoyed watching this series since it came out, but the third tape in the series recently broke, and I would like to replace it." "Well", stuttered Steve, "typically we do not carry VHS tapes anymore as they have been replaced with DVD and Blu-Ray disks. Come with me over to the video area of our store and we can see if it is in stock." Victor followed Steve and they found that the only VHS tapes available for sale were cheaply priced popular films, and they were being offered for sale sporadically displayed in a metal bin at the end of the aisle, the place that discount items are usually offered. "Have you considered upgrading to Blu-Ray?" Steve asked. "Not really", said Victor, "I am really a laggard when it comes to technology, plus I don't really want to repurchase all of my existing VHS tapes as it costs too much money." Steve mentioned to Victor that he had heard this before, and that most people only repurchase the videos that they watch over and over, or when tapes break, as in Victor's case.

"Blu-Ray disks have much better quality than anything out before. Unlike your three tape video series, the Blu-Ray disks are easy to store, and you can skip to your favorite parts of the film, rather than rewinding them. Do you watch a lot of movies?" Victor replied that he wasn't a big movie watcher, but did like educational videos and documentaries. "Well", Steve exclaimed, "Blu-Ray would be perfect for you. It's kind of like the difference between an audio tape and a compact disk. You are probably old enough to remember having to rewind tapes if there was a particular song that you really enjoyed, now this problem is a distant memory." "That's true", replied Victor, "it might be really beneficial to be able to fast forward conveniently to the part of the film that I am most interested in."

"Let me show you the difference." With that, Steve led Victor to the video area of the store, to show him the new High Definition DVD and Blu-Ray disk players. "In order for you to get the best quality, you really should get a new flat screen television. What kind of set do you have now?" Victor said that he couldn't remember what type of television that he had, but that it was an older set. "A lot of people are buying these HD televisions right now, and I have only heard great things about them. Take a look at the picture on this set, isn't that amazing?" Victor had to admit that the picture was of very high quality. Steve continued, "What do you do for a living, sir?" "I recently graduated with a business degree and I now work for a local bank", replied Victor. "So you work hard, and probably look forward to coming home after a long day's work and relaxing, correct?" enquired Steve. "That's for sure. We have been really busy in the branch lately, and I have been putting in a lot of extra hours. Home is always a welcome place at the end of a long day", Victor replied.

Steve continued, "A lot of people come in our store, and they are just like you. They work hard all day, and find a lot of pleasure in spending time with their families and friends at home, watching television or movies. You should really consider getting an upgrade to your home entertainment system." "I don't know", replied Victor, "I really just came in for the one VHS cassette." "Unfortunately, that technology is outdated. I would bet anything that you will not regret it if you upgraded your system. You should reward yourself for beginning your new career in banking, making the change is something you will never regret!" said Steve. Victor said that he would think about it. "Now is the best time to buy in months", replied Steve. "We are having our Fourth of July sale this weekend, and the prices have never been better. If you have any interest at all in upgrading your system, now is the time to go for it! I know you said you were only interested in buying the VHS tape, but you came in at the perfect time with our sale going on today." So this is why all the people were standing in-line outside the store this morning, Victor thought. They must really be offering some good prices today, to have that kind of impact. "Which model do you recommend, Steve?" Victor asked.

Great Decisions

Steve showed Victor his top selling high definition television as well as DVD Blu-Ray disk player. While Steve was giving Victor a demonstration, other shoppers gathered around to watch. One of them included a middle-aged man wearing a jagged t-shirt and flip flops. "Those are some pretty good players", he uttered. "I bought one of those televisions last month, and I really love it", he continued. "I am thinking about getting one of those Blu-Ray players. I saw it in this week's circular. At this price, it's a pretty good deal." This was all that Victor needed to hear. After Steve finished with his brief demo, Victor decided to purchase both the HD TV and the DVD Blu-Ray disk player.

As he was putting the disk player in his shopping cart, Victor noticed something that caught his attention. The satellite radio company that he uses in his car had an aisle of the store devoted to their products and accessories. Victor wheeled his shopping cart toward that aisle, and Steve followed along. "Do you like satellite radio?" asked Steve. "Yes, I do. I listen to it in my car all the time", replied Victor. "You might consider a home installation kit as well. This allows you to listen to your favorite channels at home or in the car", Steve described. "This would certainly be a great addition to your home entertainment system, and if you were to purchase a surround sound system for your home, you would be able to listen to your favorite music channels, and watch your favorite shows and films while experiencing theatre-like sound quality", Steve explained. That would be great, thought Victor. He could listen to his satellite radio stations while he was at home, which would keep him fully integrated to the news back home, while at the same time, he could experience all of the conveniences of having a home entertainment system with surround sound. He remembered listening to his new co-workers at the bank discussing their home entertainment systems. He had not seen the convenience and luxury of these items before now. It sure would be nice to have a complete, new home entertainment center, Victor thought. As Victor placed the satellite radio home installation kit and surround sound speakers into his shopping cart, he felt the breeze of a young lady quickly running by him. She was running frantically to the computer accessories aisle, and Victor noticed that she was in need of yellow, red, and white cable wires. She was obviously in the midst of a home installation, and realized that she needed longer cables. Victor pictured his living room, and decided that it was best that he purchase the same thing, just in case. It would save him an extra trip to the store. Victor mentioned this to Steve, and Steve surprisingly told him not to worry about it. "You are purchasing equipment that already comes with sufficient cables for 80 percent of home installation projects. If it turns out that you really need the longer cables, you can always come back. I wouldn't worry about that now."

The Checkout Process

Victor thanked Steve for all of his help, and decided that it was time to purchase his new home entertainment system. As he proceeded to the check-out area, Victor reminisced about his days growing up in China. He felt a little guilty about all of the wonderful opportunities that were available to him in Atlanta. How many of his friends back home could play tennis at such a fine club, and could have the opportunity of purchasing such fine technological equipment for their new homes? At the same time, he felt very proud of his recent completion of his college degree as well as his successful, while at times stressful, new beginning of his banking career. Steve was right. Given all his hard work, he deserved a new home entertainment system. Victor thought of all of the fun that he would have with his new purchases. He could invite some of his new co-workers to his apartment to watch football games on Saturdays, and he could watch theatre-quality movies in the comfort of his own home. "Next!" Victor was startled as he realized that his time had come at the checkout counter. "Did you find everything that you wanted today, sir?" said the cashier. Victor noticed that the cashier's name was Shelby, but that she did not have any gold stars on her name badge. "Yes, I found everything just fine thank you", Victor responded. "Would you like to pay with your Tech Now credit card today and save ten percent?" inquired Shelby. Victor informed her that he did not yet have a Tech Now credit card, but would like to save on his purchase. "All you have to do is fill out an application form for our card. It is very easy and only takes a few minutes."

Victor stepped aside and let other customers purchase their items, as he filled out the company credit card application. Victor was surprised at the small amount of information required in the application. The application asked Victor for his age, date of birth, home mailing address, cell phone number, email address, name of his employer, and other such information. Once Victor completed the demographic section of the application, the remainder of the form concerned what Victor had purchased that day and how likely he was to purchase other home electronics and appliances in the next 12 months. As he completed the application, Victor noticed that the line of customers waiting in the check-out counter had not diminished since he first entered the store. This is a fine business, he thought. They are really providing a great service, helping people to find enjoyment in their homes after their long hours of toil each day.

Victor stepped back in line, and was immediately served by Shelby. Since he had already waited in line, he only had to finish his application, and she completed his purchase. Victor was stunned by the final purchase price. "That will be twenty-seven fifty-three, seventy-three please" said Shelby. Confused at the way the final price was stated, he looked at the screen. Wow! That's $2,753.73! Well, at least it is after saving ten percent, and it is on credit, so I can pay it over the next few months without too much trouble, he thought. Victor remembered from his personal finance class at college that when purchasing a large item on revolving credit, you should treat it as a term loan, and decide from the start how many months it will take to pay back the loan.

"Thank you Mr Tong, please come again", uttered Shelby, as she quickly turned to greet the next customer in line. Victor made his way from the checkout counter, and was greeted by another store employee. Otto was an older gentleman, whose job it was to make sure that people were leaving the store with only the items that they purchased. Otto crouched over and looked into Victor's shopping cart. "Good day sir. May I see your receipt for purchase?" Victor handed Otto his receipt, and Otto spent a minute reading over the receipt and carefully verifying that the cart only contained the items listed on the receipt. "I don't see that water bottle on the receipt, sir" he said. Victor informed Otto that he had just come from a tennis match, and had brought the bottle in with him. "I just wanted to make sure, as we sell that same brand near the checkout aisle." Otto retorted. "Based on the looks of it, you have had it for a good while. Good day sir." With that Victor took the receipt and walked with his shopping cart out into the parking lot.

Victor walked out to his car, and had to remember exactly where his car was located within the sea of cars, trucks and sports utility vehicles in the parking lot. He then remembered that he had parked his car under the lone tree in the parking lot. Victor remembered thinking to himself that the tree reminded him of the Charlie Brown Christmas tree, a small lifeless bush, littered with water bottles and other throwaways, sitting in the middle of the vast parking lot.

As Victor got in his car, he realized that it was almost time for lunch. He was excited about his new purchases, and couldn't wait to get home to install them. As Victor drove back down Piedmont Road, he thought of all of the new possibilities that life offered, and thought about how his new home entertainment center would look in his new apartment. He wondered if the shiny new equipment would make his worn furniture look all the more in need of replacement. As he drove down the road, he passed a billboard for a local furniture store offering "no interest for 12 months" with "guaranteed credit approval". Victor's head was spinning as he thought about all the new things that he needed; everything it seems, except the *Commanding Heights* video series on VHS cassette.

QUESTIONS FOR DISCUSSION

1. How was the purchasing decision changed during Victor's visit to the store, and by whom was it changed?
2. Why would Steve, who was an advocate for Victor's continued buying, show caution when it came to the purchase of the extra-long cable wire?
3. How did culture play a role in Victor's initial trepidation of the store, as well as in his eventual acceptance of upgrading his entire home entertainment system?
4. Discuss how the theories of motivation, emotion, and perception were at play in this case.
5. How does sensation seeking contribute to the "elusive search for self" as shown in this case study?
6. How did the arrangement of the store aid Victor in his purchasing decisions?

Case Study 3
Niche Markets for Organic Agricultural Products: Pars and the EU

MASOUD KAVOOSSI
Howard University, USA

Capacity building is an increasingly used phrase in the jargon of international development. This phrase is normally used in terms of building capacity at the macro level of a country towards economic development. Capacity is here used in terms of the private sector building market capabilities. There are a number of international organizations such as the United Nations Conference on Trade and Development (UNCTAD) and country specific agriculture and food agencies that have been looking into private sector capacity building and the benefits of organically produced products. There is also the niche global marketing aspect of organic produce.

Over the last decade, the demand for organically produced food products in both the European Union and the United States has increased substantially. Specialty grocery store outlets have been established which cater specifically for organically grown products, and the shoppers of these stores have not diminished their purchases even as the difference between the cost of organically produced items and traditional products has increased. In fact, the weekly grocery bill at an organic grocery store can be significantly more expensive than at a traditional grocer, but the performance of these specialty grocers has not materially diminished even in the troubling economic environment of 2008 and 2009. The desire to acquire or maintain a healthy diet would appear to be more important to many middle and upper income consumers in the West than savings at the checkout counter.

The desire to consume organically grown products does not end simply at the produce counter. Shoppers of organic grocery stores cringe at the thought of artificial sweeteners added to their sodas and pre-packaged foods, and the organic farming community has provided those consumers with organically grown, albeit more expensive, substitutes such as agave nectar and stevia. These natural sweeteners, which were long forgotten in a world dominated with sugar-based products, have risen to prominence on the shelves of the organic grocers. Marketing campaigns in the West have opined on the possibility that various health problems experienced by the public at large had more to do with non-organically produced products than with the fact that many office workers live stressful and sedentary lifestyles. Organic grocery outlets have now begun to sell magazines, clothing, and other items that allow consumers to broaden their usage of organically produced products, whether for general consumption or longer-term usage.

Such organic markets represent significant opportunities for small and medium enterprises in the Middle East of which Pars Mahsoulat, here after referred to as Pars, can take full advantage by presenting its organic products. Pars is a Doha based agribusiness family farm with operations and farm land in the Lebanon and across the Persian Gulf in

Iran. It grows organic leafy produce as well as fresh cut flowers. It has a relatively low yield per hectare as it is an organic producer and does not use chemical fertilizers.

Organic agriculture in The Middle East North Africa area (MENA) helps maintain and improve soil fertility over long periods of time, which translates into sustainability. In such cases organic agriculture can increase productivity in the long run, improve and protect the environment, protect human health, and ensure sustainable growth and development.

Marketing of organic products is a major problem for MENA farmers. There is no critical mass of producers in many sectors to enable economies of scale for processing, servicing, research and market development.

In order to take advantage of the market, Pars needs to overcome a number of internal and external constraints to make its products acceptable in the EU. It requires certification, a sound and executable marketing strategy and luck. Mr Ali Khani is the energetic agricultural engineer who is the owner of Pars.

Challenges Confronting Pars in Penetrating the EU Market

Mr Khani is operating in three distinctly different sets of environmental circumstances now. He has farmland in the dry desert environment of Qatar, in the mild climate of Southern Lebanon and in the lush farmlands of Northern Iran on the Caspian coast. These experiences have given Mr Khani an understanding of regulations. Primary areas of concern in regulations surround export barriers. A primary question is how Pars can seek the help of local governments and businesses to address export barriers.

In Iran, Pars can receive some of their support directly from non-governmental organizations (NGOs), cooperative agencies, some university projects, and philanthropists. In Doha, Pars cannot receive subsidies as it violates WTO trade rules. In Southern Lebanon, certain financial resources are available, in particular through international aid agencies, NGOs, the Ministry of Foreign Trade and the Ministry of Agriculture and Livestock. Although not currently aimed at organic producers, other governmental trusts can eventually be used. National banks in Iran and Lebanon are starting to show some interest in organic agriculture, but the interest rates and requirements they apply to organic agricultural producers remain the same as those for conventional agricultural producers.

Another important question in order to penetrate the EU market is how Pars can receive aid and assistance from international organizations. Many international organizations have been active in their support of organic producers from developing countries. The UNCTAD, in their July 2001 meeting held in Geneva Switzerland, agreed to enhance the capabilities of developing countries in taking advantage of niche markets. Additionally, in November of 2002, The Conference on *International Harmonization and Equivalence in Organic Agriculture* was organized by the International Federation for Organic Agricultural Movement (IFOAM), the Food and Agriculture Organization (FAO), and by UNCTAD. In that same year, the Policy Dialogue on Promoting Production and Trading Opportunities for Organic Agricultural Products under UNCTAD was held in Brussels. Companies like Pars can benefit from these agreements, but even with financial and other assistance by these organizations, there are still key strategic marketing issues that Mr Khani needs to be made aware.

Market Opportunities in the European Union

Demand for agricultural products is increasing by approximately 10 to 20 percent per year in several European countries. The overall increase averages out at around 12 percent per year in the EU. Much of the current demand for agricultural products in the EU is either satisfied at home or via prior colonial linkages in Africa and the Caribbean.

The current market share for organic agricultural products is not more than 1 to 2 percent of the total demand for food products. Thus, demand is still relatively small. In the European Union, markets in Germany and in the Nordic countries rank the highest in terms of organic product demand. The market for organic products in the European Union is estimated to amount to approximately $12 billion, slightly higher than the United States.

The estimated value of the Japanese market is much smaller, with a value of US $0.3 billion since the introduction of Japanese Organic Standards. The demand for organic products is on the increase given the higher disposable income for the consumers in these markets, as well as the desire to improve or maintain a healthy diet and lifestyle.

In MENA countries, certified organic agricultural production is still very limited. However, significant shares of agricultural land are under traditional production methods, with little or no use of agrochemicals. Such areas could be converted to certified organic agriculture, provided that markets are available and certification costs can be kept low and the process is efficient.

European consumers perceive the Middle East and North Africa as agrarian societies. They are also perceived as being culturally distinct from much of Europe and technologically behind in terms of agro industrial complexes. These perceptions may be helpful when positioning the region's agricultural products as organic, more down-to-earth alternatives, and grounded in production of methodologies which were perfected before today's volume-oriented genetically modified approaches to production.

Major questions concern whether the EU countries can take account of the special conditions and needs of Pars operating out of the MENA area in their national organic standards and regulations, and if they can facilitate imports of organic products from small agro business firms in MENA countries without any new or revised treaty agreements.

Constraints

In order for Pars to take advantage of niche markets in the European Union for organic agricultural products, they need to overcome a number of production and export constraints. Some of these are common to any exporter.

Pars also needs to compete in markets with stringent quality requirements, which increase pressure for subsidies, uncertain price premiums and preferences for locally-produced food. One constraint for MENA producers with a relatively large potential is the small share of the market taken by countries in and around the Middle East and North Africa in the organic market of the EU.

PRODUCTION CONSTRAINTS

Lack of technical know-how on organic production practices is a constraint. Government agricultural extension services do not include organic farming. Another problem area is lack of organic production inputs. Pars Mahsoulat has reported difficulties in acquiring the necessary organic composting materials, bio-pesticides, and bio fertilizers.

Obtaining high quality seeds and planting materials also has been cited as a problem. With the exception of Iran, there has been little research and development in the MENA countries on varieties and production known to be best suited to organic agriculture. In some cases, securing the additional skilled farm labor required for organic agriculture also has created difficulties. In addition, Pars does not have the financial strength and the economy of scale of larger South East Asian and Latin producers.

The main institutional and policy constraints may be summarized as follows:

- Absence of effective government policies on promotion of organic products or financial or other support available to entrepreneurs and farmers.
- Lack of a national body to support organic agriculture exports through national coordination and international negotiations.

EXPORT CONSTRAINTS

Constraints to increasing exports of organic products from MENA countries include: high costs of production including water; lack of market information and marketing strategies; insufficient export experts on organic products, difficult procedures in importing EU countries, and tariff and non-tariff protection in EU import markets. Furthermore, organically grown agriculture that has been practiced for centuries often does not get appropriate recognition in European country markets. Clearly there are two market segments in the EU: one for organic and the other for non-organic agricultural products.

Standards and Import Regulations

There is concern that the multiplicity of national and EU-wide standards and import procedures in European countries create obstacles to imports of organic products originating in MENA countries. The transaction costs resulting from the existence of multiple standards are significant. In addition, obtaining import permits is time-consuming and costly as it requires resources. In MENA, where Pars relies on many small suppliers who are poor and run small businesses, inspection and quality control is excessively expensive.

Organic Labels

Current rules concerning the use of official organic labels are sometimes discriminatory. For example, the use of official organic labels in the European Union is not open to non-EU producers. It is to be noted that such labels are not widely used even by EU producers. The use of organic labeling is more prevalent in the United States, as customers look for them as a sign of safety and quality.

Entering European Markets: Risks for Pars

Certification is a necessary, but not sufficient condition for entering EU markets for organic products. For example, the effects of increases in organic production in European countries (to a considerable extent induced by ambitious Government plans and subsidies) on imports are uncertain. Some have expressed concern that if markets fail to expand at the same rate as production, there will be downward pressure on prices and greater incentives to keep out foreign produced organic imports.

Limited market information and poor marketing channels can hamper exports of organic products from MENA producers. There is a better likelihood for selling products produced in MENA countries as conventional products.

EU Council regulations on organic production and labeling entered into force on 22 July 1991. The Regulation covers production, processing, labeling and inspection of agricultural products and foodstuffs from organic agricultural production. The regulations opened the market for organic food markets to "third country" (non-EU) members. Israel is the only one in the Middle East out of a total of seven countries that is granted access to the EU.

Organic products from countries which are not on the "third-country" list can be marketed in the EU provided the importer submits documentation to confirm that the products are produced and certified according to rules equivalent to those of the EU.

An EU Member State may assess an inspection body in a third country and ask the Commission to approve it. The Commission can then add it to the "third-country" list. Some 90 developing countries export to the European Union under this framework. In order to be able to import under the provisions of the framework, an importer must provide the member state with sufficient evidence to show that:

- The imported product was produced according to organic rules equivalent to EU standards;
- The imported product was subject to inspection measures equivalent to EU inspection requirements;
- The inspection measures are permanently and effectively implemented;
- The inspection body operates in compliance with the International Organization for Standardization (ISO).

Each importer must obtain a separate authorization for each consignment. Some other factors may adversely affect demand for products from MENA countries. First, consumers of organic food are increasingly placing emphasis on locally supplied food. Second, the eastward enlargement of the European Union will affect the organic food market in Western Europe. Several countries with economies in transition in Central and Eastern Europe are in a similar position as MENA countries in the sense that an important number of farmers use little or no agro-chemicals. For example, a substantial share of agricultural output in Poland is effectively produced by organic methods. With these countries joining the European Union, their organic producers would be in a strong competitive position vis-à-vis producers from MENA countries because of being relatively close to the main consumer markets and being inside the EU market.

This might imply that MENA countries would run a marketing risk if they chose to substantially increase the output of temperate organic products to serve the EU market. It follows that the commercial risks of embarking on large-scale promotion programs for organic agriculture require careful attention, as meeting standards that are credible in EU countries is expensive.

AGRICULTURAL POLICIES

Several EU countries provide subsidies to assist farmers in the conversion process to organic agriculture. Compensation is also extended to established organic farmers for their services to the environment. In some countries where these last subsidies were not available (such as in the UK), pressures were applied to increase post-conversion subsidies. The granting of subsidies in some European countries may result in competitiveness concerns in other EU countries, for example in the form of research and development. MENA countries do not provide subsidies to organic farm producers, particularly in the upstream part of the value chain that starts with the seeds.

Farm subsidies in general can lead to inefficient use of resources in organic agriculture as in conventional agriculture. In other words, subsidies in one country, by affecting the price level and the quantity of production (number of farmers who can stay in business), affect farmers in other countries. This can distort the true picture of efficiency in resource use between organic farmers in different countries. The issue that may require attention is whether increased pressure for subsidies to promote organic agriculture could eventually adversely affect the competitiveness of products from developing countries particularly those of the Middle East and North Africa.

QUESTIONS FOR DISCUSSION

1. In the three countries, what are the major constraints to production and exports of organic produce?
2. What policies have been adopted by national governments and Pars toward organic agriculture?
3. What are the major experiences with regard to exports to the EU or United States (countries may be examined separately), in particular with regard to:
   a) How is certification obtained?
   b) What difficulties, if any, to comply with import requirements?
   c) How might cultural differences play a role in this case?
4. How should national governments and Pars address their production and export constraints?
5. In your view, how can European countries facilitate imports of organic products from MENA countries?
6. How can bilateral and multilateral aid agencies assist MENA countries in promoting production and exports of organic agricultural products?
7. What are the key marketing issues in the area of organic products?
8. Are organic products healthier than non-organic products? If not, what might this imply about the psychological impact of organic product advertising?

References

Global Monitoring Report 2006: *Millennium Development Goals*. Washington, DC.

Ishac, D. et al.: *Economic Development and Cooperation in the Middle East and North Africa (MENA)*. Washington, DC: 1993.

Kaufmann, D.: *The Governance Gap in the Arab Countries: What Does the Data Say?* Washington, DC: 2006.

Mustapha, K.N. et al.: *Reforms and Growth in MENA Countries: New Empirical Evidence*. Washington, DC: 2004.

Mustapha, N.: *Explaining Growth: Some Experiences from the MENA Region*, Washington, DC: 2008.

Sutherland, P. et al.: *The Future of the WTO: Addressing Institutional Challenges in the New Millennium* (Geneva: 2004). Available at http://www.wto.org/english/thewto_e/10anniv_e/future_wto_e.pdf accessed 23 June 2008.

Case Study 4
Marketing Microfinance in Ghana

G. JASON GODDARD

By all accounts it was a tranquil affair. The third fight between boxing legends Azumah Nelson, 49 years old, and Jeff Fenech, 44 years old, was held in June 2008 in Melbourne, Australia. After ten rounds of lackluster action, Fenech won a close decision in a fight that most observers saw as meaningless. The pair first met in 1991, for Nelson's World Boxing Council Super Featherweight championship. The bout was hotly contested and was controversially scored a draw. Many observers felt that Fenech had held the day. The second fight was contested in 1992, in Fenech's native Australia. Nelson dominated the second fight, knocking Fenech down numerous times and finally out in the eighth round. Azumah Nelson was known as "the terrible warrior" in his early fighting days, and known as "the professor" in the latter days of his career, as he would literally teach his opponents new tricks while beating them in the ring. Azumah Nelson is arguably the greatest professional boxer that the continent of Africa has ever produced. What many of the observers of the third fight failed to realize was that there was a purpose to the contest between two aged fighters clearly past their fighting primes. Back home in his native Ghana, the Azumah Nelson Foundation was launched so that the national hero of Ghana could give back to the people who so adored him during his pugilistic career. The primary aim of the foundation is to provide social services to the poor and needy in Ghana through the use of sports and education (*Modern Ghana News*, 2008). The following case discusses issues surrounding the hypothetical expansion of the Azumah Nelson Foundation (AZNEF, 2007) to include the creation of a microfinance institute under the direction of the foundation.

Brief History of Ghana

Ghana is a western African state which borders Cote d'Ivoire on the west, Burkina Faso to the north, Togo to the east, and the Gulf of Guinea to the south. "Ghana" was the title of the kings that ruled the ancient empire known as Wagadugu from the fourth to the thirteenth centuries. Portuguese explorers came to Ghana in the fifteenth century and found large gold deposits, hence the name of the country until modern times. The Portuguese built a castle with the aim to trade in gold, ivory and slaves (Ghana web, 2008). After being under Portuguese and Dutch rule, Ghana was controlled by Denmark from 1658 until 1850. The Danes set up two trading posts, which were originally for the slave trade, and then subsequently attempted to start a plantation economy. After these efforts were unsuccessful, Denmark sold all claims in Ghana to the British in 1850. The cash crop for Ghana has been cocoa, with the first export to Britain occurring in 1885.

Ghana was known as the Gold Coast prior to March 1957 when it obtained independence from Great Britain.

While Ghana has remained a primarily agricultural based economy with the cocoa crop at the center of importance, there have been many efforts at diversifying the economy since independence in 1957. Based on a recent study, it was determined that Ghana was still very dependent on the gains from exports in the agricultural sector, primarily in cocoa, timber, gold and other minerals (Buatsi, 2002). Ghana's national vision for the future is evidenced in their "Vision 2020" plan which spells out pathways to lead Ghana to a middle income country by the year 2020. In order for this to become a reality, the small African nation will need to expand their export base into non-traditional areas such as horticulture, seafood, prepared food and beverages, handicrafts, and other light manufacturing items. In 2000, the Ghanaian government created the Export Development and Investment Fund in order to aid small entrepreneurs in funding and developing the export sector. The initial performance has not been as successful as hoped, as imports have continued to exceed national exports for each of the last ten years (World Bank, 2008). Figures compiled by the African Development Bank, the OECD, and the Ghana Statistical Service reveal the following trends in Ghana's current account (AfDB/OECD, 2007).

Ghana current account as percentage of GDP							
	1998	2003	2004	2005	2006	2007	2008
Exports	28.0%	32.4%	31.4%	25.6%	25.9%	25.1%	24.5%
Imports	39.0%	42.7%	48.5%	49.0%	51.6%	50.2%	50.4%

As you can see from the table above, even as the price of cocoa has risen in recent years, Ghana has still produced a negative result in the national current account. Experts have surmised that the reason for this has been lack of knowledge of Ghana's Export and Development Fund, lack of organization among exporters, and a lack of access to primary credit sources (Buatsi, 2002; Kalavakonda, 2008). It has been estimated that only ten percent of Ghanaians have adequate access to credit services, and only six percent have adequate access to insurance (Kalavakonda, 2008). When traditional banks are involved in helping to finance entrepreneurial activities, they often are missing the mark by requiring liquid collateral, or offering loans at very high interest rates given the associated risk (Buatsi, 2002). In order for Ghana to improve from an export viewpoint, banks must be willing to offer more flexible lending requirements, borrowers must be better informed concerning the federal funding programs, and there must be increased education regarding the use of insurance programs to pool risk and regarding improving local knowledge of international markets. In the long run, the establishment of an export bank for Ghana should be considered, especially with a focus on non-traditional exports. The need for more flexible lending requirements and insurance implies that microfinance would be a good place to start.

In recent years, a myriad of development and finance experts have come to Ghana to discuss the possibility of significant economic improvement via microfinance initiatives (Public Agenda, 2007, 2008a, 2008b; Ghanaian Chronicle, 2007a, 2007b).

The Politics of Development

While Ghana has been trying to diversity their economic base, the government has been trying to both decentralize as well as increase revenue. Both a presidential and parliamentarian structure began in the country in 1988. A three-tier structure was adopted to include a regional coordination council (with ten regions), a district assembly (with 110 districts), and various town and area councils (Boko, 2002). In an effort to decentralize governmental controls, the district assemblies were changed where two-thirds of the officials were elected, with the rest being appointed. The central government still appoints the district assembly chief, so in essence the government appears to be only partially decentralized. Eighty percent of the district assembly's budgets are funded via the parliament, and the central government provides funding based on the need of the district, and not necessarily based on the purpose of the funds (Boko, 2002). Article 254 of the constitution states that the central government should steward decentralization, and not control the districts. If this is the case, then it would appear that moving to a completely elected official status is very important in Ghana's three-tiered government.

Unfortunately, the decentralization process has come with increased taxation. The central government taxes income as well as Ghana's primary export products such as cocoa, coffee, cotton, and shea nuts. District assemblies are able to have a poll tax, property tax, and a tax on corporate assets. Districts can further levy taxes against crops other than those previously mentioned, and can also obtain revenue via licensing (Boko, 2002).

It would appear that the government's aim for increased revenue through taxation is having a deleterious effect on Ghanaian business expansion efforts. On the one hand, the government has set aggressive economic expansion goals to reach the "Vision 2020" plan, while at the same time has allowed the various levels of government to tax the growth of enterprise. These trends are moving forward while at the same time the citizens of Ghana are not getting access to bank funding without having strong financial backing. Thus, those borrowers who have been successful in the past are more likely to obtain credit than those that have not, or that are new to a specific industry. Ghana's situation is currently thus: a nation in desperate need of additional microfinance organizations that can increase the access to credit for Ghana's citizens.

Microfinance Industry in Ghana

Microfinance, or what used to be called micro-credit, has gotten much press in the last few years. Whether the publicity was from the United Nations calling 2005 "the year of micro-credit", or whether it was from Grameen Bank founder Muhammad Yunus winning the Nobel Peace Prize for his work in Microfinance in 2006, the world of economic development has taken notice of the amelioration of poverty that occurs in many cases from obtaining small loans for productive purposes. There have been numerous books and articles on the subject of microfinance, which is defined as lending small amounts of money for productive purposes, and often on an unsecured basis, to the poorest of the poor. Muhammad Yunus has said that his Grameen Bank, which is replicated in many countries throughout the world, lends to people based on their survival skills (Yunus, 2003 and 2007). The Grameen Bank does have a presence in Ghana, as it partners with Sinapi

Aba Trust (SAT), which means literally "mustard seed", implying the ground-up nature of the loans being provided (Getu and Mensah, 2003). There have also been successful partnerships between SAT and Opportunity International, one of the world's leading microfinance charities (New African, 2006a). Additionally, there have been partnerships between traditional banks such as Barclays, with the susu collectors in Ghana (New African, 2006b). Susu collectors have been in operation in Ghana for three centuries. They are the informal money lenders with whom microfinance efforts typically compete. Susu collectors gather the income of their clients and return it for a small fee. In lieu of traditional savings accounts in rural areas, this provides greater security for their clients' money than would be the case had they kept the funds themselves.

While there has been a modicum of success previously in microfinance in Ghana, the Azumah Nelson Foundation would not find itself competing in a saturated microfinance marketplace in Ghana; at least from a profitability standpoint. In fact, a recent study of microfinance in Ghana has shown that there have been several problems in the governance of microfinance institutions in Ghana (Kyereboah-Coleman and Osei, 2008). One problem has been the lack of clarity in terms of whether the purpose of the organization is reach (that is, serving the highest number of people), or whether it is profitability (that is, successful repayment typically not from the poorest of the poor). The study also found a link between misguided organizational objectives and the structure of the board of directors in the organization. Problems ensue when the same individual assumes the roles of both the CEO and the chairman of the board of directors. Additional problems materialize when the percentage of board members that are also employees of the organization increases. As an independent board of directors serves as a check on management to protect shareholder interests, the more independent the board of a microfinance organization is, the less probability of mission drift. This has high relevance for our case here, given the notoriety of Azumah Nelson. While he is beloved in his home country, the foundation must ensure that "the professor" does not take too large a role in the new microfinance organization, at least based on prior results in the existing literature (Kyereboah-Coleman and Osei, 2008). The authors of the study also mention that transparency is very important, as the availability of financial information on the Ghanaian microfinance institutes is poor, despite attempts to consolidate the industry under the auspices of the Ghana Microfinance Institute Network, which comprises 70 microfinance organizations serving 26,000 customers.

There are over 130 rural and community and 200 credit unions in Ghana (Kalavakonda 2008). In 2004, the Ghanaian government started the Microfinance and Small Loans Centers (MASLOC) which are now available throughout Ghana to help entrepreneurs gain access to affordable credit (Ghana Government, 2008). When this is combined with the availability of susu collectors, and other informal savings organizations, there would appear to be multiple organizations serving the same clients. If access to credit is as poor as previously indicated, it certainly implies an overlap in micro-lending clientele. A leading microfinance textbook cites that having multiple microfinance organizations lending to the same clients creates repayment problems (Armendiaz and Morduch, 2007). If the purpose of the microfinance institution is to make loans to the poorest of the poor, the fact that there are competing institutions erodes the significance of the loan. If one individual is having trouble paying back an existing micro-loan, that individual may seek a loan from a competing institution, in a microfinance version of a pyramid scheme.

A recent study of repayment records of microfinance initiatives in Ghana revealed that performance ranged from less than 70 percent repayment to over 95 percent repayment. Interest rates charged for each surveyed enterprise was 20 percent per annum, while the higher repayment initiatives were from organizations that loaned primarily to females; replicating the Grameen Bank's modus operandi (Asiama and Osei, 2007). Loans made by these institutions were for purposes such as housing, small trade, and start-up loans for farmers to buy inputs for farming which includes rice, fertilizers, and agricultural tools. Some of the loans were for non-agriculture purposes such as basket making, woodworking, cloth trading, and pottery manufacture. Most of the loans were made to individuals, although there were some cases where loans were made to groups of people, for collective enterprises such as irrigation pumps, power looms, and the construction of sanitary latrines. The Bank of Ghana study on microfinance concluded that since young people aged 15–24 years old account for one-third of Ghana's population and over half of its unemployed, true success would be achieved only by a special targeting of entrepreneurial development of the youth of Ghana (Asiama and Osei, 2007).

Psychology of the Start-up Enterprise

Now that we have discussed the strengths and weaknesses of Ghana's microfinance and economic development efforts, the next step is to discuss what sort of microfinance institution should be created by the Azumah Nelson Foundation. With the plethora of microfinance institutions already present in Ghana, AZNEF would certainly have name recognition, with it being associated with one of the most famous athletes the country has ever produced. Given our discussion about ensuing problems associated with one strong leader in microfinance institutions, assuring proper governance will be a key to success.

Another key to success of the AZNEF microfinance organization will be in establishing the proper methodology needed to attract the best borrowers. As prior evidence has revealed, there has been largely divergent repayment performance achieved in Ghana's existing microfinance institutes. Might it make sense for the new organization to follow a Grameen Bank replication strategy and offer loans primarily to women, and primarily in groups of five? The Grameen Bank has been successful by making small unsecured loans primarily to women in small groups. Typically, groups are allowed to self-select into five member teams. Since the Grameen Bank traditionally lends in small rural communities, self-selection by the members typically ensures that similar risk profile borrowers form in small groups (Armendariz and Morduch, 2007). A key to success of the five member team is the implicit guarantee of the other four members that if one member cannot repay their loan, the others will step up and secure repayment. Otherwise, none of the other members will receive future loans. Another key to success of the Grameen Bank replication model is that five member teams are placed in larger "centers" of 40 individuals (eight five-team groups). If there is a problem of repayment for any of the groups, this fact will become obvious to all in the "center" during the weekly public repayment meetings. Grameen Bank lending officers have been known to stay in rural villages for long periods of time to ensure that their books are balanced.

Some microfinance organizations have achieved successful loan repayment by making larger, collateralized loans to individuals. Rather than opting for the group lending platform made famous by the Grameen Bank, lenders such as Bank Rakyat Indonesia have chosen to trade "reach" for profit by lending to borrowers with sufficient collateral to secure the loan (Armendariz and Morduch, 2007). In Ghana, this would limit the number of borrowers, but this does not have to limit them to as great an extent as it would appear. Traditional banks often lend for commercial purposes, but do not take collateral that is truly equal to the amount of money being extended. An example of this would be business assets: while the market value for the assets of the company may theoretically equal the amount of loaned funds, the value of those assets in a foreclosure situation would be far less than the amount of indebtedness. Should AZNEF decide upon the "profit" format, loans could be collateralized with whatever the funds are being used to acquire. Borrowers will thus understand that if they do not repay their bank obligations, they have something to lose which is of considerable value to them.

Whichever organizational model is chosen, AZNEF must ensure that they do not fall into traps set by their predecessors. AZNEF must seek to balance the competing ambitions of all microfinance institutions: impact, outreach, and financial sustainability (Zeller, 2003). Outreach strategy will be decided based upon the "reach" and "profit" orientation as discussed previously. Impact is typically measured based on the amount of poverty amelioration experienced in the area served. Financial sustainability speaks to the ability of the microfinance organization to survive without government subsidies. Given the high transaction costs for microfinance institutions in getting to know the creditworthiness of their clients, there is a trade-off between outreach and impact with financial sustainability.

Another trap to be avoided is a lack of adequate start-up capital for the new microfinance organization. AZNEF would probably have some of the funds from the foundation available in order to begin operations. Given the Ghanaian government's interest in promoting their MASLOC program, AZNEF foundation directors would most certainly seek seed money from the government, at least during the first few years of operation. Other funding sources available to AZNEF would be via donations from friends and supporters of Azumah Nelson, as well as various non-governmental organizations (NGOs). A key to successful accumulation of funds would be the successful market positioning strategy of AZNEF, which would utilize the fame of its founder to spread the word about the good work that they plan to accomplish.

Loan repayments must be tied to when the income is received, thus repayment should be quicker during the high season for agricultural borrowers. Additionally, AZNEF must represent an honest broker in the Ghanaian financial services industry. The selection of loan officers at AZNEF will materially impact the public's thoughts concerning the quality of the organization. Since loan officers are typically the primary source of market information for a microfinance organization, making sure that the loan officers are well suited to the task is critical for the overall success of AZNEF (Grant, 1999). Should the lending officers of AZNEF appear to be motivated by their own personal financial incentives rather than by honoring the vision of AZNEF to "improve the lot of the disadvantaged but talented in Ghana", all of the advantages of the celebrity status of the organization's founder will be for naught.

Reaching the Target Market

As previously discussed, experts predict that the best avenue for improvement in Ghana would be in pursuing a youth oriented strategy. One area of concern with this approach is the implied lack of business experience and acumen of the targeted customer base. As of 2000, only 65 percent of females and 76 percent of males aged 15 to 24 were literate in Ghana (World Bank, 2008). This is better than the literacy rate for all people in Ghana of 58 percent for the same year, but the lack of universal literacy and basic education will make marketing efforts very difficult, especially in the sea of competition already in place.

AZNEF's leadership team must consider the options currently available. One successful strategy employed by others was the use of dramas and plays, which taught lessons on the importance of saving and self-sufficiency. Other options employed in other countries include the creation of comic books that help the target audience understand the basics of saving, business accounting, and money management. The Federal Reserve of New York has a successful comic book series aimed at high school aged students, but this requires basic reading skills. AZNEF's publications will need to range from high school level reading to picture-only formats, depending on the literacy of the consumer.

Another method of differentiation for AZNEF in the microfinance arena will be skills training sessions for prospective borrowers. If the first AZNEF microfinance branch was based in Bokum, a seaside town which is an hour's drive from Ghana's capital of Accra (and the childhood home of Azumah Nelson), it is expected that many of the borrowers would come to AZNEF seeking finance for products associated with the fisheries industry or exporting in general. Thus, the first branch location will dictate the types of basic business skills training that will be required. For example, beyond offering clinics helping prospective borrowers make the transition from the susu collectors to AZNEF from a savings standpoint, there would be a need for skills enhancement in basic refrigeration and packaging of products for export. The AZNEF branch would work in conjunction with the Bank of Ghana to promote existing government sponsored borrowing programs, and with the susu collectors to determine which borrowers locally have a head start in savings experience. Thus, the susu collectors and their most experienced customers will serve a valuable role in helping to bring the mission of AZNEF to life: "establishing youth leadership training centers that will offer educational, vocational, professional and sports skills development opportunities" (AZNEF, 2008).

Once AZNEF approves its first series of loans, the next step in the marketing process of the new organization will be in successfully promoting the products of their borrowers to the general public. Since a weakness outlined earlier was the lack of collective strength for small businesses in Ghana, AZNEF should work to ensure that best practices for the marketing of the various product lines for their borrowers will be communicated to all borrowers. AZNEF should also seek to create a local "AZNEF market" where their borrowers can sell their wares to the general public in a "one stop" shopping experience. The market would also serve to further publicize the benefits of becoming a microfinance entrepreneur to other potential borrowers. AZNEF would advertise the new organization via television, radio, and print media, and may also sponsor local sporting events. It is envisioned that banners with the likeness of Azumah Nelson will be strategically placed in town centers and marketplaces in order to help promote the brand identity of the new organization.

Profile of the Prospective Borrower

Whether AZNEF chooses the group lending format or pursues lending to individuals, a key to success will be in attracting the types of borrowers that will lead to successful repayment records. This will entail that AZNEF have a good idea about the desired profile of their target consumer. Since Ghana has both existing microfinance organizations as well as room for growth, AZNEF should not have a problem attracting borrowers; the problem is getting credit-worthy borrowers. As mentioned previously, Ghana has seen successful microfinance initiatives in the past when the borrower base has consisted mainly of women. Lending strictly to females would be contrary to the mission of AZNEF, so the organization would likely plan on lending to the youth market regardless of gender. While prior loan repayment experience is always preferred, AZNEF would like to avoid borrowers that have relationships with other microfinance organizations. The foundation directors of AZNEF should mandate that all borrowers agree to only borrow with AZNEF, and not to entertain competing offers at other financial institutions during the term of their loan with AZNEF. Since AZNEF would be investing a significant amount of time and money in training their borrowers on required skill enhancements, AZNEF will want to ensure that their borrowers remain loyal to the organization, at least while their loan is still being repaid. Borrowers at AZNEF should also be required to maintain their savings account balances with AZNEF, which over time will help free the organization from subsidies from the national government.

AZNEF should develop a prospective borrower questionnaire that can be completed either orally or in writing depending on the literacy of the client. The survey should contain questions about the prospective applicant's familial background, prior lending experience, review of marketable "survival skills" exhibited in the past, itemization of any personally owned assets for collateral, and details on their educational background. These characteristics will be very helpful determining the first borrowers at the new prospective organization.

Conclusion

This hypothetical case study has presented factual data concerning Ghana's present economic development situation, with a particular emphasis on the microfinance industry. While the Azumah Nelson Foundation does in fact exist, the discussion about the creation of a microfinance organization sponsored by the foundation was speculation on the part of the author. This case lays evidence to the strong ties between market psychology and microfinance, and provides a roadmap for taking the necessary steps to make a crucial difference in Ghana's future.

QUESTIONS FOR DISCUSSION

1. How best can the celebrity of Azumah Nelson in Ghana be used to ensure a successful start-up of the new microfinance organization? How limited should be his involvement in the daily operations of the microfinance organization?
2. Describe how market psychology is at play in the group lending phenomenon of microfinance. How might group psychology achieve better security for a small loan than actual tangible collateral? When might it be worse?
3. Should AZNEF pursue a "reach" strategy in order to increase the amount of clients served, or would a "profit" strategy make the most sense during the start-up phase of the new microfinance organization?
4. What problems do you envision with the plans to start-up the microfinance organization? How might these problems be avoided?
5. Elaborate on the various elements of Developmental Psychology at play in this case.
6. Explain how the theory of social comparisons is utilized in this case, especially as it pertains to the group lending concept.
7. Assess the strengths and weaknesses of the following elements of AZNEF's proposed marketing program: market analysis, competitive analysis, customer behavior analysis, strategic planning and positioning, product analysis and product differentiation, promotion and outreach communications, organizational structure.

References

African Development Bank (AfDB) in conjunction with the Organization for Economic Cooperation and Development (OECD): *African Economic Outlook: Ghana*, AfDB website, http://www.afdb.org/pls/portal/docs/PAGE/ADB_ADMIN_PG/DOCUMENTS/ECONOMICSANDRESEARCH/GHANA2007.PDF, accessed 24 December 2008.

Armendiaz, B. and Morduch, J.: *The Economics of Microfinance*. Cambridge, MA: 2007.

Asiama, J.P. and Osei, V.: *Microfinance in Ghana: An Overview*, Bank of Ghana study, Economics web institute, http://www.economicswebinstitute.org/essays/microfinanceghana.htm, accessed 29 December 2008.

Azumah Nelson Foundation (AZNEF) websites http://azumahnelsonfoundation.com/, and http://www.azumahnelson.org, accessed 16 December 2008.

Boko, S.: *Decentralization and Reform in Africa*. Springer Publishers: 2002.

Buatsi, S.N.: Financing non-traditional exports in Ghana. *Journal of Business & Industrial Marketing*, 2002, 17, 6, 501–522.

Getu, M., and Mensah, K.A.: CMED, kingdom building and the local church: The case of Sinapi Aba trust in Ghana, *Transformation*, July 2003, 20, 3, 178–184.

Ghana Government: *CEO Advises MASLOC Loan Beneficiaries*, website, http://www.ghana.gov.gh/ghana/ceo_advises_masloc_loan_beneficiaries_.jsp, accessed 29 December 2008.

Ghanaian Chronicle, Ghana: Providing financial services to the poor is compatible with financial sustainability, 31 January 2007a.

—— Ghana: Ajumako market women educated on micro-financing, 12 December 2007b.

Ghana Web, internet site: *History of Ghana*, http://www.ghanaweb.com/GhanaHomePage/history/, accessed on 24 December 2008.

Grant, W.: Marketing in microfinance institutions: The state of the practice, (1999) study funded by USAID, Bureau of Global Programs, Center for Economic Growth and Agricultural Development, Office of Micro-enterprise Development, through funding to the Microenterprise Best Practices Project, website, www.microfinancegateway.org/files/1716_file_01716.pdf, accessed 29 December 2008.

Kalavakonda, V.: Making finance work for Ghana: Entry point for micro-insurance, Washington, DC: 2008. The World Bank, Power Point Presentation.

Kyereboah-Coleman, A., and Osei, K.: Outreach and profitability of microfinance institutions: The role of governance. *Journal of Economic Studies*, 2008, 35, 3, 236–248.

Modern Ghana News: Azumah Nelson foundation launched, 28 September 2008, http://www. modernghana.com/sports/184181/2/azumah-nelson-foundation-launched.html, accessed 16 December 2008.

New African: What £32 can do in Ghana. January 2006a, 17.

—— Ghana Susu collectors connect with formal banking, August/September 2006b, 74.

Public Agenda, Ghana: Central region benefits from education on micro-finance, 14 December 2007.

—— Ghana: Microfinance identified as a tool to achieve MDGs (Millennium Development Goals), 15 January 2008a.

—— Ghana: Financial experts storm Accra, 16 June 2008b.

World Bank, internet site: Country Reports- Ghana, http://web.worldbank.org/WBSITE/EXTERNAL/ COUNTRIES/AFRICAEXT/GHANAEXTN/0,menuPK:351958~pagePK:141159~piPK:141110~ theSitePK:351952,00.html, accessed 24 December 2008.

Yunus, M.: *Banker to the Poor: Micro-Lending and the Battle against World Poverty*, New York: 2003.

—— *Creating a world without poverty.* New York: 2007.

Zeller, M.: *The Triangle of Microfinance: Financial Sustainability, Outreach, and Impact.* International Food Policy Research Institute, Baltimore: 2003.

Case Study 5
Bon Appetit Café and Deli

G. JASON GODDARD

Bon Appetit Café and Deli is a restaurant located in downtown Winston-Salem, North Carolina, USA. The restaurant provides lunchtime food service to various diverse clienteles in downtown Winston-Salem. Winston-Salem has undergone much revitalization over the last five years, spurred by funding provided by the city government for small businesses, as well as local and regional real estate developers seeking to convert old underutilized warehouse space into luxury condominiums for occupants seeking an upscale urban setting. The restaurant is located on the corner of Fourth Street and Liberty Street, an area of downtown that has not as of yet experienced economic revitalization. There are various lower end businesses along the Liberty Street Corridor, including a pawn shop, small neighborhood grocer, tattoo parlor, and newspaper retailer, with the restaurant being located on the corner, next to a vacant former Woolworth's location. Given my proximity to this restaurant from where I work, I have frequented this restaurant for much of the last few years. The following case study represents the travails of a small enterprise competing in a highly differentiated market, as one part of the downtown Winston-Salem area is thriving with high end restaurants, theater, and jazz clubs, while the area that surrounds Bon Appetit Café and Deli has yet to experience that kind of success. Location being an important consideration for the success of any venture, Jimmy (the owner) has had the opportunity to experiment with his clientele in an effort both to increase restaurant profitability, while at the same time fulfill his vision of being the only restaurant with an Arab flavor in a conservative town in the Southeastern United States.

Eclectic Origins, Diverse Menu

Jimmy Al-Najjar is Jordanian, and was educated as a chemist, with a degree from Sofia University in Bulgaria. After a job as a water treatment plant engineer, as well as owning a grocery store in Louisiana, and running a grocery-restaurant in the Washington, DC area, Jimmy decided to open the restaurant in Winston-Salem during the summer of 2005. Jimmy's wife is from Honduras, and she, as well as the couple's son and daughter, works in the restaurant from time to time between classes at local area universities. In a review in the local paper of the restaurant when it first opened, the menu was called "the United Nations" with everything from Italian subs and pastas, to Greek gyros and souvlaki, to Mediterranean hummus and baba ghanouj (pureed eggplant), to traditional hamburgers and hot dogs on offer. I might never have tried the restaurant, had they not advertised their Mediterranean menu in the window.

Upon entering the restaurant, you can tell that it is a family run establishment. Rectangular wooden tables, black metal chairs with cushions, and "Do-It-Yourself" interior painting and tapestries makes this clear. Two television sets hang from opposite ends of the restaurant. If you come to eat around noon, you will be able to watch the local news network that specializes in providing us all with other things to worry about such as whether the local school buses are safe, and whether the water that we drink is healthy. If you prefer dining after one in the afternoon you will either be able to watch a soap opera like *Days of Our Lives*, or possibly a wonderfully entertaining episode of the *Tyra Banks Show*. Customers in the restaurant range from financial industry professionals such as myself and co-workers, to random jury pools from the court house nearby, to employees of Reynolds America (especially a particularly devoted Indian contingent who enjoys the Mediterranean menu options), as well as passersby from the city bus terminal at the corner of Liberty Street and Fifth Street.

The initial problem that Jimmy had was how to serve such a diverse population of customers, especially given that they all tend to show up within a narrow band of time between 11.30 a.m. and 1.30 p.m. Quickly realizing that success depended on getting adequate serving staff, Jimmy added an elderly Hispanic man called Cesar to do much of the cooking for the first year. After Cesar left to start his own ill-fated business in downtown Winston-Salem, Jimmy added Yolanda and Susan to his cooking and service staff. Regular customers in the restaurant were subjected to many "short-timer" employees before Yolanda and Susan were added. For a period of months, Jimmy hired a series of service employees, some overly friendly, others highly introverted. The common thread of these employees was that they did not stay employed for very long. During the periods of transition between the cast of characters there was high absenteeism. This caused the family much stress, as Jimmy at once became cook, cashier, and server, all while customers waited in line for their lunches.

For the first few years of operation, Bon Appetit provided "all-you-can-eat" pizza, something that Jimmy eventually decided to discontinue. The "all-you-can-eat" concept tends to attract undesirable customers, as Jimmy spent many days patrolling whether customers had actually paid for the consumption of pizza or were simply "sharing". Additionally, the pizza program attracted a few very large people who ate more than their share of pizza each day. Inevitably, "all-you-can-eat" pizza became a thing of the past.

The Arab Tavern

Living in the south-eastern United States has many advantages. Namely the weather is pleasant, the cost of living is reasonable when compared to the North-eastern US and West Coast US, and people are generally very polite. Something that Jimmy considered to be a disadvantage was a distinct lack of Arab restaurants in the area. Over the last 20 years, Winston-Salem has grown in terms of population, as people from points north, south and west came to the area. During that time, the number of restaurants has also grown, as large national franchises have come to dominate the restaurant scene in town. There are some very successful local restaurants, but many of them cater for specialties such as Chinese, Japanese, and Italian cuisine. There is also a preponderance of Greek-owned restaurants, thus many restaurants in the area have traditional Greek menu items such as gyros and souvlaki along with standard lunchtime choices. Jimmy felt that the time was right for a locally owned restaurant which offered a more Arab flavor. Since the restaurant menu already contained Mediterranean food selections, Jimmy decided to make them more prominently displayed by creating a whiteboard of the Mediterranean menu on the wall near the cash register. Based on these changes, the percentage of lunch orders from the Mediterranean menu increased. Jimmy was also able to obtain catering business, as customers soon realized the health benefits associated with a Mediterranean diet. Since many of the business professionals are concerned with maintaining a healthy lifestyle, the Mediterranean diet fits in nicely with their daily routine. Soon after placing the whiteboard in a prominent location in the restaurant, calls for lunchtime catering services increased. Jimmy's restaurant offered a lower priced alternative to many of the restaurants located in the downtown area which thrived via on-premises lunch meetings. Jimmy was able to keep his costs low by making leasehold improvements at the restaurant himself, by purchasing vegetables from local area Hispanic farmers, and by having the majority of the labor hours in the restaurant taken up by his family members.

Over the next few months, as sales were increasing, Jimmy decided to work on the appearance of the restaurant in order to more directly promote his desired cultural niche. Consistent with his vision for the restaurant, Jimmy hung pictures of Petra, Jordan, and of traditional Middle Eastern men smoking hookah pipes. The hookah uses charcoal bricks to burn tobacco. Users can draw wrapped hoses, pulling the smoke through the water base. Depending on the number of hoses, up to six people can smoke from the same pipe. The use of the hookah pipe is a social activity in the Arab community, and the pictures on the restaurant wall helped to introduce this activity to the lunchtime customers.

The next step in the transformation of the restaurant from a traditional family restaurant into a Middle Eastern niche restaurant was with regard to the televisions hanging on opposite sides of the restaurant. Rather than showing customers local television programming, Jimmy began running Arabic music videos during lunchtime. The videos were broadcast from a satellite and the music ranged from western sounding with an Arab flare to music that was entirely Middle Eastern in origin and style. Over the next few weeks, Jimmy hung tapestries on the ceilings, which, along with the pictures on the wall and the music in the restaurant, completely changed the look and feel of the dining experience. Jimmy had changed the paint on the walls from drab white to a light pink, which when coupled with the tapestries, had a distinctly Arab feel. Since Jimmy made all of the improvements himself, toiling long hours in the evenings and on weekends, there was not a change in the pricing or staffing of the restaurant. The menu remained the same, the prices remained the same, and Jimmy maintained the same employees as before the change. What had changed was the implementation of the cultural vision of the Arab tavern.

This was a unique period in the history of the restaurant. Each day I would go to lunch unsure of what the next change would be, and how it would be perceived by the clients of the restaurant. After having a morning of investment real estate loan underwriting and negotiation, I would walk a few steps down the street and literally step into a different world. As the changes were being implemented, one thing was clear: business was down from before the more direct changes were made. Based on observation during lunchtime, the change with the television was most obvious. When the music videos consisted of Arab popular dance music, the reaction of the patrons was not apparent. When the music selection was centered on less western-sounding music, some of the clientele in the restaurant appeared a bit uncomfortable. In one particular case, a customer who had ordered from the Mediterranean menu complained about the music selection. This would seem to be a case of too much cultural dissonance in too short a period of time. Wanting to experiment with a foreign cuisine is one thing, wanting to experiment with the cuisine while hearing music from that same culture seemed to be a bridge too far to cross for that one particular customer.

The music videos did not last very long. As is the case with most businesses, most customers who were disenchanted with the restaurant due to the music did not complain, they simply stopped coming. I am not sure if Jimmy realized the link between the music videos and lower customer traffic, but in any event, the restaurant patrons were soon reminded of the benefits of watching the local news, infomercials, and mindless afternoon television programs. When asked about the television programming change, Jimmy mentioned that he was planning on installing satellite television, but this never transpired.

The Next Big Thing

After the initial setback with the music videos, in the spring of 2007, Jimmy decided that the next step was to focus his efforts on the social benefits of the communal smoking of the hookah pipe. Soon after the music videos vanished, patrons could see numerous hookah pipes in the restaurant. Jimmy's plan was to offer a place for customers to smoke the hookah in the late afternoon to evening hours. Coupled with the new extended hours was an expanded dinner menu, with belly dancers coming in the nighttime hours on weekends. In order to promote the hookah business, Jimmy purchased two large couches, which now sat at opposite ends of the restaurant, under the televisions. In order to turn the restaurant location into a more party-friendly atmosphere, Jimmy purchased large speakers and hired a DJ for Friday and Saturday nights. On first impressions, the extended hour idea was very risky, as there was no such thing as a hookah bar in Winston-Salem, nor had there ever been one. The likelihood of this service being successful in a conservative southern town seemed remote, especially given the less than excited response to the music videos offered during lunchtime. Jimmy's response to the failed lunchtime Arab restaurant was to create a nighttime Arab tavern.

And Jimmy's hookah bar thrived. Initially, the restaurant was filled in the evenings by private parties. These parties were usually focused on Middle Eastern clients from neighboring Greensboro, where there is a larger Arab population. When venturing into the restaurant on Mondays for lunch, Jimmy would show clips taken on his cell phone of the party that had ensued over the weekend. The tables and chairs that were necessary for the lunchtime business were extraneous at night. The tables were pushed to the side, as Jimmy's nighttime crowd danced the night away. The crowd was almost without exception of college age, and the patrons were willing to drive over half an hour to come to the hookah bar.

The question now was concerning the sustainability of the hookah bar. Now that the idea was gaining momentum, Jimmy's Arab tavern was publicized at local campuses. The word of mouth advertising was done by the initial nighttime customers, by Jimmy's children at their universities, and by small leaflets left in residence halls and cafeterias at the various area colleges and universities. Jimmy was interviewed by the local newspaper, and the report on the activities appeared in college newspapers and websites.

Jimmy's hookah bar became a hit with the local undergraduate community. While a hookah bar was not specifically lacking in the downtown revitalization effort in Winston-Salem, what was lacking was a meeting place for young people that allowed them to smoke. The evidence of the early success of the hookah bar was apparent on the walls of the restaurant. The pictures that Jimmy had placed on the walls of the restaurant of Middle Eastern men smoking the hookah pipe were replaced with photos of young area college students doing the same thing.

Spread Your Wings

Jimmy's first expansion effort was the purchase of an existing mid-priced Italian restaurant in Greensboro, NC in mid-2006. The purchase of this restaurant was during the "music video period" of the Winston-Salem restaurant. Jimmy spent much of his time traveling between the two stores, and this restaurant was sold within six months of purchase in late 2006. Emboldened by the success of his hookah bar, Jimmy felt that the time was right to attempt another expansion. Jimmy felt that if there was a market for hookah bars in Winston-Salem, that there might be other cities in the southeastern US where this was a possibility. It appears that the key to success was having a college aged market where there were not a lot of nighttime alternatives for entertainment.

Jimmy began negotiations for a lease of an empty retail space very close to the campuses of Guilford College and the University of North Carolina at Greensboro, in Greensboro, North Carolina. The location would have been perfect given its proximity to students. The lease fell through when the owner asked for a five-year commitment, something Jimmy was unwilling to do given the lack of a proven track record with the hookah concept.

Given that a large portion of his customer base was willing to drive over a half an hour to his current location, Jimmy decided, in late winter of 2008, to sign a lease in an old retail building in Greensboro which was not as convenient to his customers as he would have liked. The building had been converted into various uses over the years, but was currently empty. Jimmy's idea was to offer only hookah and coffee at this location, passing on the idea of opening a second restaurant in the city. While the building was in poor condition, the immediate area was undergoing development, with a large planned apartment complex underway directly across the street from the new location. Unfortunately, the progress of this complex was behind schedule, given the credit crisis in the United States which was unfolding at the same time the lease was executed. This credit crisis stopped many projects in mid-construction, and this was the case here as well. Thus, Jimmy's second foray into a Greensboro expansion was painfully slow. It was well into the summer of 2008 before the new location saw its first clients.

The winter and spring of 2008 were not particularly strong for the hookah business in Winston-Salem. Since the early successes, things had slowed down considerably. Jimmy thought that the weather played a part, and hoped that things would turn around as the weather turned warmer.

Given the initial early success of the Winston-Salem hookah bar, Jimmy entertained many ideas for other ways to exploit this competitive advantage. Jimmy considered franchising the hookah bar concept throughout the Southeastern United States, and also considered opening a second restaurant in Winston-Salem. In the spring of 2008, Jimmy signed a lease for his second store opening in Winston-Salem. This time, the location of the restaurant was away from the downtown area, in a small retail building located outside of a Food Lion anchored retail shopping center. Given the thoughts of franchising, and given the start-up costs necessary for the new restaurants in Greensboro and Winston-Salem, Jimmy made the decision to sell his downtown Winston-Salem restaurant in the fall of 2008.

Final Analysis

The story of Jimmy's small enterprise is an unusual tale given the cultural nuances, but the search for a sustainable competitive advantage is certainly familiar. Given the plethora of higher priced restaurants in the downtown area, and given the success of other ethnic-based restaurants locally, Jimmy felt that he could fill a niche in the Winston-Salem restaurant market by bringing certain cultural elements to the public. This case provides a detailed roadmap to the trial and error process that is often necessary for small entrepreneurs who compete in saturated markets. While all of Jimmy's efforts were not successful, it does prove an interesting tale of the psychology of marketing.

QUESTIONS FOR DISCUSSION

1. Elaborate on some of the good marketing ideas attempted in this small business as well as others that were not as successful.
2. What were some specific marketing efforts aimed at promoting Arab culture in this case? Discuss how those efforts were received by the public and how any cultural dissonance may have been avoided.
3. How much culture is too much in a restaurant setting? Are customers of ethic restaurants generally seeking a cultural experience in addition to good food?
4. Describe how variety seeking was at play in this case, both from the owner as well as the customer perspective.
5. Elaborate on how the various mechanisms of the psychology of perception affected both the real and imagined performance of this small enterprise.

Case Study 6
Lappset: How to Market an Innovative Product in a Highly Competitive Arena

WENCKE GWOZDZ, KAI HOCKERTS AND LUCIA A. REISCH
Copenhagen Business School, Denmark

At the beginning of 2006 everything was quite new and pretty confusing to Anna. She had recently started work as a marketing manager for the playground producer Lappset, which is based in Lapland (Finland). Here, she now faced the biggest challenge in her professional life so far. After being employed for several weeks at Lappset, she became more familiar with the company's structure and the product she was supposed to market: an interactive, technology-based playground mainly targeted to older children. Day after day she worried over the problem of how to sell a product—playgrounds—that usually attracts younger rather than older children.

Lappset: Producer of Playgrounds

Lappset is a Finnish manufacturer of playgrounds, established in the 1970s. It started as a small family run business founded by Antero Ikäheimo. Due to its unique concept of building wooden playgrounds for children that combined play with learning, the company grew fast. In 2006, it employed almost 300 people. Lappset considered itself a pioneer in the playground industry as well as an innovative expert in play. The company sold not only the manufactured playgrounds, but emphasized also the importance of high quality in providing services that were especially needed when implementing computer technology in playgrounds. Lappset—still a family owned business—has expanded from a one-man company to an international group with subsidiaries in five different countries. Distributing its playgrounds in over 40 countries, more than 70 percent of the group's turnover came from overseas exports resulting in a turnover of 39.4 M€ in the fiscal year 2006 (Lappset, 2008a). Lappset always stressed the need to take a long term perspective in its business philosophy. Being the third largest playground producer in Europe and market leader in Finland, Lappset is well aware of the keen competition within the playground market. To gain competitive advantages, in 2002, Lappset decided to develop a new kind of playground that would not only attract young children, but also teenagers. To attract the latter seemed to be the hardest task as teenagers were more interested in computer games and other technical gadgets. The company came up with the idea of combining playground and information technology—a real product innovation.

After conducting three research and development projects on pedagogy, technology and product design including research partners such as the University of Lapland and the

Rovaniemi University of Applied Sciences, Lappset installed in 2004 a so-called "bubble team". This team was completely free to develop a product. Lappset's management was convinced that in order to achieve the intended radical new design an exceptional space of autonomy was needed. The team started out with three people from different disciplines and ended up with eight persons involved: two educational experts and one information technology expert, an interface designer and a software engineer as well as an industrial researcher and two industrial designers. The pressure on this team was very high: the management expected remarkable results and took a big risk in allowing the team such a great latitude. However, in 2006, these efforts yielded fruit: the "SmartUs playground" was born which accounted as a radical innovation merging playground and information technology that successfully combines play and education.

SmartUs Playground: The Product

SmartUs is the product Anna was supposed to market now, but before she could devise a strategy, she needed more information about the product itself. She picked up the receiver and phoned Mikka, the information technology expert who had been the leader of the bubble team. Having been involved in the product development process from the start, Mikka had valuable information off pat: the SmartUs playgrounds are very flexible; its many components can be installed either indoors or outdoors. She did not really understand everything Mikka talked about: among the components are, for example, things called iGrid, iPosts, iCards, iStation etc. Anna, a bit confused, asked Mikka what these features look like, what children can do with them, and what makes this playground special compared to traditional ones. Mikka, completely delighted to be able to share his technological knowledge, started his flood of words in technical jargon. Anna succeeded in extracting that the components have different functions: the iPosts are more or less normal gaming posts marking the field, the iGrid turns out to be a jump mat and the iCard is the personal identification of a player. All components are connected to the iStation which administers all incoming information and is thus, the "brain" of the playground guiding the games with audio and images as well as entering results into the players' registers (Lappset, 2008b). Feeling a slight dizziness in her head, Anna decided that she did not need more technical details but rather information on the opportunities offered by the playground.

Back into her office and pretty exhausted, she thought about who could be a good source of the needed information. Suddenly, it became very clear in her mind: one of the educational experts. Not wasting any time, she went straight into the office of Sakke and spoke with him for a few minutes to gain some information. Here, she learned that the most important thing is that SmartUs creates an environment where children and teenagers are encouraged to play interactively, to be physically active while still leaving them the modern technology of which they are so fond. The whole product provides stimulating play environments, widens the usage of standard playgrounds by the implemented computer elements, incorporates technology to connect users with other users, parents, teachers and playground owners who can all access information from the playgrounds. All this did not mean that SmartUs playgrounds provide a substitute for traditional learning methods, but they could support them by exploiting children's natural desire to move and play. As their market researcher had shown, one of the most important advantages over traditional playgrounds seemed to be the fact that this playground attracted children up to the age of 14 years.

Tweens as Consumers

To market playgrounds to younger children was well explored, but how does it work with this older age group? Several new questions arose: What differentiates them from the younger ones? Anna asked herself who these youngsters are and how one can attract them. What do they find appealing? How can you persuade children aged between 11 and 14 to play on SmartUs playgrounds? Pondering these questions, it occurred to Anna that the youngsters do not usually buy the playgrounds themselves, but rather that they would be purchased by institutional buyers. This means there was a more complex relationship where one had to account for the end-users, but also for the buyers. The latter were the buyers that actually purchase the playgrounds and offer them to the relevant age group. Taking one step at a time, Anna did some research to define the target group of end-users in appropriate scientific journals. In the end she came up with the following:

THE END USERS

"Tweens", repeated Anna, was the term for the specific age group that was supposed to be opened up and it stood for "in-be-tween", that is, between childhood and adolescence (Tufte, 2007). She also read that the consideration of these tweens as consumers was not new. Tweens do not behave like children anymore—nowadays an 11-year-old does not want to play on playgrounds with the younger children; they rather try to imitate the behavior and habits of the "real" young people (Tufte, 2007). This is a specific stage of consumer socialization in which they acquire knowledge about the consumption process on their own. The prominent concept of consumer socialization—originally developed by Scott Ward in 1974—describes the developmental process that passes through various stages and where tweens are considered to be in the last, the so called "reflective stage" (Roedder John, 1999). It is basically the transformation process from childhood into adolescence. Piaget's theory of cognitive development classifies tweens within the so called "stage of formal operational thinking" (Effertz, 2008). Anna wondered what these concepts mean for the "real life" and whether this textbook knowledge would help her better to understand her targets. Thus, she looked for real life practices and behavior.

Tweens are recognized as an interesting target group since they have fairly significant means to spend on their own. Moreover, they exert strong influence on some of their parents' purchasing decisions. The perception of tweens has changed over the last 30 years from the picture of young consumers as vulnerable creatures to tweens as active and competent actors in the market place and public. Tweens do experience a variety of challenges in their life such as the transition from the elementary school to the secondary school, entering puberty and increasing responsibilities.

As regards their leisure activities, tweens spend their leisure time with friends and the family, but are also interested in television, video games, internet, internet communities, (online) games, magazines and books. However, to date, researchers do not really agree on tweens' level of physical activity: some argue that levels of physical activity steadily decreased over the last decades, others find constant levels. The same holds true for television viewing hours of tweens (Diehl, 2005). A fact is that tweens in the US and Europe watch, for example, more than two and a half hours television daily (Diehl, 2005; Holt et al., 2007).Moreover, the availability and use of audio-visual media such as televisions, computer and video games has strongly increased over the last decades. Spending time with these technical gadgets decreases time available for other activities.

Peers play an important role in tweens' lives. Additionally, they adapt faster than grown-ups to new technological developments. Gender differences seem to exist in how leisure time is spent: boys have generally fewer activities, and spend more time on computer games or playstations; girls prefer spending time with their family, friends and/or pets (Tufte, 2007). However, both sexes are considered as hard to get inspired about anything. "Could the curiosity of tweens about new technology motivate them to use the SmartUs playgrounds?" Anna wondered.

THE BUYERS

After having done some reading, Anna had a good idea about who the tweens are. This knowledge helped a lot to understand who was going to buy the playgrounds: institutions and organization where tweens spend their time. At this point, she needed more information about the potential group of customers. To start with, Anna went back into the past and looked at the history of Lappset and its main group of buyers. All she needed to do was to go to the archives that were placed in a dark and dusty cellar room. She ran down the stairs and opened the rusty door, switched on the glimmering light bulbs and started to dig into the records.

Schools were always, next to other public institutions such as kindergartens, the most important purchasers of playgrounds. Lappset was aware of one important feature of this group of buyers: the slow process on financial decision making and the limited disposable budget of public schools in most European countries. As a general rule, it took about two years from first contact until the execution of a contract, due to the long administrative and decision processes that schools have to follow. This would not become any better with SmartUs considering its higher price compared to traditional playgrounds. However, schools were the main group of buyers for SmartUs.

Anna thought that it must be possible to find other buyers as well—but whom? Looking out of her office windows she enjoyed the terrific view of the public park. Suddenly she knew that public organizations that operate public areas such as parks or exercise areas could be other potential buyers. Thinking further along this line, she came up with other places where SmartUs playgrounds could be of interest: child-care or after-school clubs of corporations, amusement parks, sports centers, museums and shopping malls. All these commercial organizations could be potentially interested in these playgrounds. Possibilities had to be explored further.

Having an idea about who tweens and potential clients are, Anna faced the next challenge: how to convince institutions with tight budgets to invest in SmartUs playgrounds?

Arguments to Buy SmartUs

Having piled up lots of information, Anna was still lacking a brilliant idea for an argument to market the SmartUs playgrounds. Let's summarize shortly: SmartUs combines information technology with traditional playgrounds, tweens benefit most from this type of playground and the buyers could be public institutions or commercial organizations.

In order to convince buyers to buy SmartUs, Anna came up with three arguments:

1. **Its value lies in creative play and social interaction.**
   Science-based internal market research had shown that these kinds of playgrounds positively affect children's physical development and creativity. The development of the playgrounds was done in cooperation with several research institutions, some of them experts in education. The result had to please and convince educational experts. Not only do tweens play with each other, but the quality of family time could also be improved because tweens and their parents could enjoy the playgrounds together.

2. **Another competitive advantage of SmartUs playground is its flexibility.**
   It can be adjusted to different age groups. Thus, not only conventional buyers such as schools could benefit from the product, but also commercial organizations. It is not only the flexibility with regard to age groups, but also the flexibility in the size of the playground and the possibility to install them indoors or outdoors. Where children and tweens might get bored rather fast, a SmartUs playground might keep them engaged and enthusiastic.

3. **Physical activity and the matter of overweight and obesity.**
   It could be a good idea to use the health argument to activate and motivate adolescents aged between 11 and 14 years. Lappset aimed to open the market to include youngsters who seemed to lack physical activity and preferred playing computer or internet games. Today's lifestyles are said to be sedentary, that is, they lack physical exercise and are characterized by sitting, reading, watching television and using the computer for many hours, with little or no vigorous exercise. One consequence of the change in lifestyles that we experience today is the rise of overweight and obesity in all age groups. Anna could not believe what she read: in Europe, the prevalence of obesity among young people was between 6 and 14 percent and between 14 to 34 percent for overweight—an increase of between 10 to 40 percent—depending on the country, in the last ten years (Ofcom, 2004). While the reasons for becoming obese seemed to be very complex to Anna, she knew that to prevent overweight and obesity is an important issue in which two aspects play a crucial role: nutrition and physical activity. Thus, to succeed in motivating and activating tweens to move more could contribute to the fight against the rise of obesity. To intervene and prevent overweight and obesity in childhood and adolescence, many initiatives already existed. Schools and communities all over Europe had entered in a variety of programs to curb childhood obesity—and there appeared to be a need for more. There was the sales pitch! The topic of overweight and obesity as well as its health consequences in later age was a highly sensitive but important topic. So why not follow this path and

introduce the playgrounds to schools and communities as something that helps to activate and motivate this otherwise difficult-to-approach-group?

Possible Marketing Strategies

Anna collected a lot of information about the company, the product, the end users and the clients. She also looked into promising sales pitches. Returning to her marketing lectures, she recalled the "4 Ps" needed to market products, all together called the "marketing mix". She tried to transfer her fading university knowledge to her current challenge:

1. **Place/distribution channels**
   Due to the specific characteristics of playgrounds, the buyers were not the same as the end-users. The buyers were institutions and organizations that provided playgrounds to end-users—children and tweens. Thus, a sound strategy was the traditional way of selling playgrounds directly to buyers or via wholesalers. Moreover, Lappset could make use of already existing channels such as partners and associates that built the playground and would in return benefit from the good publicity. A third option was to sell SmartUs as a source of income for business clients. Playgrounds were known as recreational goods and thus, are usually free of charge. Only the iCard, that each individual on the playground requires, allows profit potential and hence, expanding the group of usual buyers of playgrounds. These iCards could be sold in kiosks, cafés or shops nearby a playground.

2. **Promotion**
   A direct contact to potential buyers was essential for the success of SmartUs. Lappset always fostered contact to its clients and the strategy was to follow on this path and even increase efforts. This was not only to attract new clients via word-of-mouth advertisement, but also to improve feedback. Still deep in thought, she opened another record in the archives and could not believe what she read: the answer to her question! Lappset used to organize about 200–250 clients' visits to the headquarters every year. The visitors came in groups of 15–20 and stayed for about four days. The advantages of arranging activities like this were palpable: Lappset received direct feedback from the clients about SmartUs and its other products; it could customize the relationship towards clients; it got further ideas for future needs and the visits could become a good advertisement for Lappset. This could also give an ideal opportunity to convince these clients of the health benefit for tweens and to present SmartUs as an alternative to other overweight and obesity prevention programs. Although the arrangement of clients' visits required a lot of effort, the pros outweighed the cons.

3. **Price**
   The price of SmartUs playgrounds was probably its main disadvantage. It was more than four times that of Lappset's classic playgrounds. There were not many opportunities to go for the pricing strategy. The only argument that could sell was that commercial buyers can compensate some of the investments by selling the iCard and using the indirect income sources from SmartUs—such as a larger number of shoppers in a shopping mall. However, the high price had to be outweighed by

convincing arguments for the playground. Anna did not like to conceal disadvantages of marketing the playground to the management when talking about the possibilities to market SmartUs playgrounds.

4. **Product**
   With regard to a potential social benefit of the SmartUs playground, the timing could not have been any better for Lappset: tweens were leading passive, sedentary lifestyles while, simultaneously, the overweight and obesity problem rose within this age group. SmartUs offered an alternative, complementary solution to fight overweight and obesity in young age. Here, tweens could spend their leisure time with their friends in a more active way without taking away their beloved technological toys.

The next morning, Anna was simmering with excitement. This was her big day: she had to present her findings and proposals to the management which would then decide on the strategy to be followed. This was not only about a good strategy to sell the SmartUs playgrounds but also about Anna's future prospects at Lappset. However, she was well prepared and so it was no surprise that her presentation was a success.

A Story of Success?

Lappset adopted most of Anna's proposals. It sold SmartUs playgrounds by arguing for the health of tweens and the potential to activate and motivate them. This, as an alternative to get tweens away from their gaming paddles and televisions, convinced buyers to invest in the playgrounds. Thus, the great financial success of Lappset came as no surprise: in the fiscal year 2007, the company again increased its turnover, this time by 16 percent to 45.7 M€ with SmartUs having made a significant/major contribution to this growth. The atmosphere at Lappset was good and the future looked promising.

Anna was glad that the effort paid off. Nevertheless, she did not rest on her laurels, but already started thinking ahead: When marketing playgrounds, the producer itself usually had no direct contact with the end users. In the special case of SmartUs that relied on the purchase of iCards, would it not be smart to have this direct contact via viral marketing? Viral marketing was a relatively new tool that means to place a "virus" among tweens and worked equally to word-of-mouth or peer-to-peer marketing. This sounded like a promising idea for the future. Maybe it was also possible to increase feedback rates from end users via this direct marketing. "My Mum always says that it's always good to have another iron in the fire and I think she's right" was Anna's last thought before falling asleep exhausted but pleased with herself.

QUESTIONS FOR DISCUSSION

1. Describe the characteristics of children, tweens and teenagers as consumers.
2. What are the differences between the consumer socialization theory and Piaget's theory of cognitive development?
3. Marketing products to children and tweens leave marketers in a special situation. They do not only have to sell a product to these end-users, but also to several other social agents. These social agents, such as schools, are potential buyers. Think of other buyers that purchase products for children and tweens and explain your examples. Describe the features of these more complex relationships.
4. Where do you see the opportunities of this new product? Which of the three arguments that were presented in "arguments to buy SmartUs" is the most promising one?
5. Where do you see drawbacks? Is the high price of SmartUs playgrounds a real competitive disadvantage or do the advantages really outweigh it?
6. Discuss the advantages and disadvantages of being the innovator in a new market.

References

Diehl, J.M.: Macht werbung dick? Einfluss der lebensmittelwerbung auf kinder und jugendlich, *Ernährungs-Umschau*, 2005, 52, 40–46. (Does advertising make you fat? Food advertising's influence on children and adolescents.)

Effertz, T.: *Kindermarketing: Analyse und Rechtliche Empfehlungen*. Frankfurt: 2008. (*Marketing to Children: Analysis and Legal Recommendations*).

Halme, M. and Kajosaari, J.: Lappset—SmartUs: Interactive playing for everyone. Helsinki: 2008, Unpublished case study.

Holt, D.J., Ippolito, P.M., Desrochers, D.M. and Kelley, C.R.: Children's exposure to TV advertising in 1977 and 2004—Information for the obesity debate. Washington: 2007, 133. Bureau of Economics Staff Report, ed. Federal Trade Commission.

Lappset 2008a: Economic Review 2007 [cited 04 April 2009]. Available from http://www.lappset.com/includes/loader.aspx?id=7930309a-3a12-4b81-9cca-93d35dba4713

Lappset 2008b: SmartUs handbook http://www.lappset.com/loader.aspx?id=94686205-0add-4878-b7f7-3607e5e72837

Ofcom: *Childhood Obesity—Food Advertising in Context*. London: 2004.

Roedder John, D.: Consumer socialization of children: A retrospective look at twenty-five years of research. *Journal of Consumer Research*, 1999, 26, 3, 183–213.

Tufte, B.: Tweens as consumers: with focus on girls' and boys' internet use, In: Eckström, K.M. and Tufte, B. (eds): *Children, Media and Consumption: On the Front Edge*. Gothenburg: 2007. (Yearbook 2007).

Case Study 7
O' Fortuna

RONALD K. PALMGREN[1]

It had been a tough day at the office. After dinner, I sat down to watch the news, which was depressing. I turned it off in the middle of some mind-numbing drivel about Trooper gate. I turned on my favorite classical music channel and took up where I had left off in the latest Dale Brown novel. As I sipped an ice cold Corona and lime on this warm Indian summer evening, I was abruptly distracted by the opening chorus of Carl Orff's *Carmina Burana*. I had sung that piece many times and had listened to its many variations over the years. To me it always revealed surprises and evoked many memories. As I took another sip I was transported to a hot sultry afternoon in San Luis where I first saw a beer bottle actually being made.

I was a young banker at the time having been recently assigned to the Latin America desk at a small regional bank in the midst of the large money center behemoths such as First National City Bank, Chemical Bank, Manny Hanny (Manufacturers Hanover Trust) and of course JP Morgan. In Connecticut, we had many of the Fortune 500 companies including General Electric, GTE, Xerox, United Technologies, Stanley Works to just name a few. At that time there were over one hundred "national" and "international" companies that had operations in our state. This list included IBM, Lego, Ingersol Rand and Perkin Elmer. My assignment was to tap into that reservoir of names and develop international business for the bank and this required extensive travel to Latin America.

One of the main aspects of the job was to compile and present a Country Report which summarized the bank's exposure in a given country with a breakdown according to the various types of risks, tenor of the facilities, and committed versus outstanding exposure. The Country Report also included an extensive narrative section which provided analysis of the economic state of the country, the assessment of the political climate and a discussion about the strength of the financial sector including comments on the current lending activity of both foreign and domestic banks. Much of this information was gathered prior to the trip but the interviews and discussion during the trip put the data into a clearer perspective. Also, much of the published information was months, if not years, behind. Some of the information was not available at all from third party sources so that data had to be gathered on site.

As part of the discussion of the state of the economy there was an analysis about a given country's reserve position, factors affecting the trade balance, a discussion of changes in GNP and GDP including the nature and composition of services in the "invisibles" account, and of course, the current year's outlook for each of these components. The data

1   Ronald Palmgren has had over 30 years experience in the banking industry as a lending officer with significant experience in the international arena. He was formerly the head of the Latin America desk at former Connecticut Bank and Trust Co. and is currently a Business Banking Risk Manager for Connecticut at Wachovia, a Wells Fargo Company.

was gleaned from a number of sources including publications from the IMF; monthly publications provided by the major government and private banks; and for the most recent news, "unofficial" data from local financial journals.

The discussion regarding the current political climate usually contained a synopsis of political structure and the basic tenets of the major political parties. This was usually followed by a discussion of any upcoming elections and how the most likely outcome of those elections would affect US/Mexican relations. The sources for this type of information were from the various Mexican and foreign bankers I met during my trip, American and Mexican corporate executives, and the local national newspapers. The weekly local English newspapers and the *Miami Herald* which was delivered daily were particularly important.

Information on the strength of the financial sector and availability and cost of credit was almost exclusively obtained from discussions with the local bankers and professionals. However, the IMF's monthly publication, Polk's yearly review, and Lloyds Bank's periodic Bolsa Review were particularly helpful.

All of this information was carefully compiled into the yearly Country Review. At this time the current economic political and baking climates were discussed and overall country limits were determined. The post-trip country updates were also incorporated. These updates were useful in finalizing recommendations for the dreaded credit committee meeting where invariably the morning's headlines in the *NYT* would take precedence over the analysis and provided the committee members with an instant analysis of the country's situation. To partially combat this issue, I would open my discussions with the credit committee with a very un-American sounding "Buenos Dias" followed by some comment that included several persons, places or things that were heavily filled with rolled R's and other effects, to give them the impression that I knew what I was talking about. Internal marketing is just as import as external marketing!

I had scheduled a trip to Mexico and Central America and had spent a month reviewing the financial statements of companies and banks that I would be visiting. I had also set up meetings with correspondent bank officers of the local banks, US Bank representatives, and treasurers of those companies that had business or potential business with our customers in the US. Prior to my trip I also talked to my counterparts at the other local regional banks such as HNB, IBR, and the money center banks such as Manny Hanny, Irving, and Chemical to get a feel for their insights into the business climate that I would be visiting. With the help of my secretary, I assembled an extensive trip book which detailed the purpose of each call, time, place, facilities offered, previous pricing and any anecdotal comments regarding my customers or prospects. I remembered that Gus liked Cuban cigars and Johnny Walker Black Label® Scotch, Heliodoro always had Poire on hand, Luis Manuel liked to read the latest *Fortune* magazine. Gus was in the finance business and ran a leasing and factoring company; Heliodoro owned and operated a joint venture company with a multinational chemical company. I remember him especially since he was the first to demonstrate the effectiveness of antioxidants. He used to take them straight from the barrel and pop them in his mouth like taking a vitamin pill. Luis Manuel was born in Mexico but spent much of his youth in the US and had graduated from MIT. He owned and operated a company that produced T-shirts for a major US underwear retailer. And then there was Frank, a middle-aged traveling salesman for one of the major manufactures of bottle making machinery. I recall Frank vividly. He was always full of enthusiasm, extremely friendly, and knew his products well. Frank was in the business of equipping bottle making manufacturers throughout the region. The owners of these companies were some of the most well established and wealthy families in Latin America.

Making bottles is a highly technical art which involves getting the right mixture of raw materials including recycled glass, heating the mixture in lehrs to the point of producing a lava-like flow, then dropping the molten material onto molds in which the gobs are either pressed or blown into shape. At Envases San Luis they produced bottles for the local Corona® and Dos Equis® plants.

I remember Frank taking me on that tour. The Treasurer of his company had arranged for Frank to take me to Envases San Luis. Frank introduced himself to me in the lobby of the Sheraton in Mexico City where we had a typical business breakfast. Although he was rough around the edges he was a Midwesterner at heart and had traveled throughout Latin America for over 15 years. Remarkably his Spanish was almost non existent. Since I had grown up in Latin America my Spanish was fluent and maybe because of the language difference we had a certain connection. He knew the territory and I knew the language.

After trading oral resumes we took off in his rented jalopy and headed north for the Pan Am highway and San Luis Potosi. It proved to be an exhilarating and fascinating four-hour drive. I was amazed at the shantytowns of north Mexico City, the isolated dwellings cropping up in the middle of the desert, and the seemingly endless number of people walking to and fro.

We finally arrived at the Hacienda de los Hermanos in San Luis where we were warmly greeted by Don Manuel Esquivel who promptly brought us into the spacious and extremely well appointed living room. We exchanged business cards and sat down and had a cold cerveza with a few taco chips, empanadas and an assortment of veggies. We talked about the Mexican economy and how inflation was affecting the Mexican peso vis-à-vis the US dollar. Of course we also talked about the Mexican political scene, as this is great sport in Mexico. At this point Don Manuel's wife Dona Maria came in and invited us into the dining room. The table was set with the finest Mexican silver, crystal, and china. The kitchen staff had prepared a sumptuous meal of chicken mole with fried yucca and local vegetables. We were completely entertained with Don Manuel's and Dona Maria's tales of their travels throughout the world and the antics of their three children who were now all married with children. The history of the la Hacienda de los Hermanos spanned six generations and innumerable stories of intrigue and mayhem. The two hours at the dinner table passed as if it had been 15 minutes.

Finally, after dinner, Don Manuel asked if we would like to see his factory. We arrived a few minutes later and the plant was humming with activity. With great pride he showed me around *his* place. Without condescension, he explained how glass was made and the intricacies of the close tolerances needed to make a bottle of beer versus a crystal goblet.

After the plant tour, we went into his office where he described his expansion plans. He wanted to add another "color" line because some to his clients were interested in "green" bottles. The new line would cost about US$500,000. He asked if I would be interested in the financing. Armed with a full list of possible financing alternatives I eagerly discussed the various options including Eximbank financing, FCIA financing, straight term financing guaranteed by a local bank, or one of several local government programs offered by NAFINSA We agreed that a straightforward term financing with FCIA coverage was the most appropriate for this size transaction. Without commitment, I gave him an indication of rate and other conditions and said I would follow up with a proposal as soon as I returned to the US in two weeks. Before leaving I was introduced to his controller who supplied me with the requisite financial statements that had been prepared by one of the well-known CPAs in Mexico City. We took our leave and headed back.

On the way back to the hotel, Frank and I discussed the various suppliers that were to be involved and whether or not his company was going to be the sole US supplier and installer. We also discussed the timing of the shipments and their installation. Frank was also concerned that MBRO (Maul Brothers, his competitor in New Jersey) might be making a similar financing proposal. Having seen the operation, taken a quick look at the financial statements, and having discussed the importance of this piece of business to his company, I told Frank that I was very much in support of this project and would give it my priority. We arrived back in Mexico City later that night.

Upon our arrival Frank and I had a sandwich and a beer at the hotel bar. At the bar Frank asked me where I was going next. I showed him my itinerary which showed a couple of more days in Mexico City, then it was on to Guatemala, Costa Rica and Panama. Frank asked if I had time to stop in on Envases Balboa in Panama. He was working on a new plant for the owner of the company that supplied bottles to the largest rum bottler in the region. Frank asked if I ever had the chance to go Chile or Argentina, where some of the world's best wines were located. Prior to turning in for the evening, we discussed similar issues and swapped stories of our experiences in Latin America.

QUESTIONS FOR DISCUSSION

1. In order to be competitive in Latin America, it helps to have certain competitive advantages. How did knowing the language and being familiar with local customs help in this case?
2. How did cultural differences express themselves in this case? Were any mistakes made and if so, by whom?
3. Discuss the strengths and weaknesses of the following characteristics of an international banking operation:
   - Local (home) office vs. corporate office,
   - Family setting for company vs. traditional office setting,
   - Integration of business and pleasure vs. the defined workday.
4. What specific techniques can a small regional bank use to compete with a large money center bank? Are the advantages expressed in this case still valid today? How might a foreign investor research the United States today?
5. Research how international banking is conducted today. How have best practices changed regarding the following traditional business development plan?
   - Preparation.
   - Identification of specific objectives.
   - Use of existing resources.
   - Follow-up with client.
   - Use of Referrals for success.
   - Consultative sales techniques.
   - Product knowledge.

Index